The Problem of Perception and the Experience of God

The Problem of Perception and the Experience of God

Toward a Theological Empiricism

Sameer Yadav

Fortress Press
Minneapolis

THE PROBLEM OF PERCEPTION AND THE EXPERIENCE OF GOD

Toward a Theological Empiricism

Cover design: Alisha Lofgren

Library of Congress Cataloging-in-Publication Data

Paperback ISBN: 978-1-4514-8885-2

Hardcover ISBN: 978-1-4514-9973-5

eBook ISBN: 978-1-4514-9671-0

The paper used in this publication meets the minimum requirements of American National Standard for Information Sciences — Permanence of Paper for Printed Library Materials, ANSI Z329.48-1984.

Manufactured in the U.S.A.

This book was produced using PressBooks.com, and PDF rendering was done by PrinceXML.

To Whitney

Contents

Acknowledgements

Like any major commitment that one enters into—religious confession, marriage, raising children—I had no idea what I was getting myself into when I committed to writing this book, whether in its first incarnation as a doctoral dissertation or its second coming as the volume you now hold in your hands. As with all those other meaningful events in life, I have experienced it both as something I decided to do and something beyond my control, something to be passively suffered. What I've done leaves me with both a certain sense of pride and acute tinges of regret at the many failures surely to be discovered in it. My gratitude, on the other hand, is entirely free of such ambivalence. For the many debts I owe to the people who contributed to the shape of this project and helped it on its long road to completion, I am simply, profoundly and deeply thankful.

When I arrived at Duke Divinity School to begin the newly minted Th.D. program in the Fall of 2007, I had planned to continue pursuing some interests in theological ethics and political theory that I had developed while at Yale Divinity School. I wanted to work with Stanley Hauerwas in the Divinity School and Romand Coles in the Political Science department. But after a single semester my plans changed drastically when Rom told me he was leaving Duke. Stanley knew that at the core of my research agenda was a question about how Christian perceptions of God's ongoing and public availability to the Church enable and constrain our civic and political participation. On one side of that agenda was the political question of the nature and scope of practical demands placed on us by our claimed experiences of divine presence and agency in our midst. On the other side was a philosophical and theological question of just what is involved in claiming such experiences as a source of information and rational justification for our beliefs and practices. What Stanley suggested was that I develop my thinking about this latter question, leveraging my background in the philosophy of religion and interests in theological method. As a potential advisor he directed me to a newly appointed faculty member who was coming to us just as Rom was leaving—Paul J. Griffiths. I am so thankful that he did.

Paul proved to be an invaluable advisor and friend. Just about every main idea and argument I offer in this book has benefited from the great many hours I spent in his office discussing them. Talking with Paul always pushed me into greater clarity. Quite often we disagreed. But the sharpening of arguments and mutual appreciation forged by our disagreement made our conversations some of the most enjoyable and rewarding I have ever had. This is in part because of the wide-ranging interests and competencies he brings to theological problems, displaying a promiscuity of mind that I strive to emulate. This would make him an intimidating figure, were it not for his warmth. The birth of my first child (Noah) revealed to me Paul's kind affection for children and my final two years in residence at Duke included as many conversations about the pains and joys of family life as they did about the nature of perceptual experience and the God-world relation. In addition to working closely with Paul on this project, I am enormously grateful for the wise counsel and encouragement I received from Willie Jennings. When, Lord willing, I return to consider the social and political pedagogies of the body that have come to form and deform our spiritual senses in the West, it will be Willie's work on belonging and place that sets my trajectory.

I am thankful as well for my other committee members in helping me to navigate all of the disparate literatures represented in this book. Stanley Hauerwas had always read something enormously helpful and relevant that I was unaware of before he brought it to my attention. I consider much of the substance of my argument in this book to be an exposition of a dictum I heard him repeat many times when I was a preceptor in the very last Christian Ethics course he taught before retiring: "You can only act or refrain from acting according to what you can *see*, and you can only see what you've been taught to *say*." Like much of what Stanley says, there are many possible interpretations on which it seems patently false. Still, it would not be wrong to take my book as an attempt to interpret Stanley's dictum so that it comes out true. Gregory of Nyssa came to be a key figure in the history of theology whom I have taken to be important for specifying how what we can do is dependent on what we "see" of God and further how what we are capable of seeing is dependent on a form of bodily and linguistic *training*. Indeed, I originally conceived of this book as a full-blown rational reconstruction of Gregory on the spiritual senses. Its current shape reflects my realization about how much philosophical and theological ground-clearing was required to properly situate such a reconstruction.   By far the greatest influence and help I received in my reading of Gregory was given me by J. Warren Smith, both in his *Passion and Paradise* and from our many conversations over tea and then by phone. Warren's patience and grace with me was exemplary, especially given all the historical and exegetical fumbling one might expect from a contemporary theologian. His consultation in my translations or exegesis at various points were a great gift. Finally, I want to thank Sarah Coakley for her patient reading and penetrating questions about my argument, especially in my reconstruction of Gregory, which differs in many ways from her own. I could not have asked for better readers of my work, and in case it needs to be said, any faults that remain are of course entirely my own.

I am thankful to have had various forums in which to float arguments and offer criticisms related to the question of the metaphysics and epistemology of God's perceptibility. These have included a panel discussion in which I was able to present some early criticisms of Kevin Hector's *Theology without Metaphysics*. I profited immensely from my brief engagements with Kevin, whose dissertation prompted a good deal of my thinking on these issues. Fuller Seminary was gracious enough to invite me to present some of the material from this book in a Graduate Theology Colloquium, and I am particularly grateful to Oliver Crisp and Tommy Givens for their friendship and support. Tommy deserves special mention: our intellectual and spiritual journey together began in a coffee shop in Valencia, CA reading Yoder together, and subsequently took us both to Duke where we were constant companions. His friendship has impacted my thinking and my work in more ways than I can (or care to) calculate.

When I left Duke in 2012 to take a postdoctoral teaching fellowship at the John Wesley Honors College of Indiana Wesleyan University, I took this project with me. My colleagues there have been an unflagging source of moral support, and I thank Charles Bressler, Rusty Hawkins, David Riggs, Lisa Toland and Sara Scheunemann for their friendship and encouragement. Students also provided a great source of help in preparing various parts of the manuscript. The exposition of Gregory's theology contained herein grows out of an honors research tutorial I taught in the Fall of

2013, and I'm grateful to the students of that course for their work. Kelsey Evey was a wonderful help in assisting me with some early copyediting, and I thank G.B. McClanahan for his careful and meticulous work in preparing the index.

The pressures of completing a doctoral program and starting an academic career often project a rather narrow and cramped space within which to live a normal and healthy personal life. I am keenly aware of how much I have needed to lean upon my family. Shambhu and Pushpa, my parents, regularly exuded an unmerited confidence in me; Rashmi and Varun, my sister and brother-in-law, often cheered me on. Sharad, my identical twin brother, was always a willing and eager sounding board. This project was nourished by their love, as well as by the prayers of my small group at Blacknall Presbyterian Church in Durham, NC and the members of Gethsemane Episcopal Church in Marion, IN, especially, Josh Molnar. Of all the prayers for which I am thankful, possibly the most earnest and effectual came from Sue, my mother-in-law, whose love and loyalty to her daughter's husband regularly astonishes me.

But it is to Whitney, my wife, that I dedicate this book. That is not to say that she will read it. I hope she doesn't – it is aimed primarily at theologians and philosophers of religion who puzzle over how to theorize God's availability to us in experience, and she is certainly not among them (their number is blessedly few). I therefore did not have her at the forefront of my mind in all my moments hunched over a book or straining at my desk to produce a few lines of clearly formulated text. Whitney has instead been the lamp in whose light reading became possible and the open laptop that has made my writing possible. Her constancy of love and her unwillingness to flee from me when my academic vocation exacted demands upon her, upon me, upon our family that she had every right to refuse–in that faithful self-giving love I have most clearly tasted and seen that the Lord is good. And that experience will continue to prompt my deepest gratitude, even if the theoretical account of all such experiences in the pages that follow turns out to be mistaken.

Sameer Yadav
Lent, 2015

1

Introduction

A fundamental problem in Christian theology has been that of determining whether God is available to us in experience, and, if so, how to account for the nature of that availability and the role putative perceptions of God have in informing and justifying our theological claims. In addressing this matter, it has become widely assumed among Christian philosophers and theologians that this problem of Christian religious experience cannot be adequately addressed without also confronting more basic philosophical problems about the nature of perceptual experience per se. Broadly construed, perceptual experiences are just states or episodes in which some mind-independent reality (a) impresses itself on us, (b) enables our intentional directedness upon it in thought, word, or deed, and (c) is capable of determining whether or not the intentions grounded by such impressions are correct.[1]

---

1. This rough construal will be refined later. For now, note that here, as throughout, what distinguishes "perceiving" or "perceptually experiencing" from merely "experiencing" is the directedness of a perceptual experience upon reality. Insofar as reality-directedness is not constituent in an experience or in the way it seems to us, I exclude it from consideration.

So how do our ordinary perceptual experiences manage to make mind-independent realities available to our mental lives, such that our mental acts—what we think, say and intend to do—can somehow "reach out" to reality, can be "about" it? Conversely, how do realities outside the mind manage to "reach in" to impress themselves on us in our experiences, such that our experiences manage to be "of" them? In what way does the bearing of reality on us in experience determine whether what we think, say, or do is correct? What limits or constraints does the nature of reality itself impose upon the sorts of impressions reality can make on us? How is the nature or content of such impressions shaped by our own bodily or mental constitution? Are the impressions of perceptual experiences mental states, episodes, or acts of some sort, or are they fundamentally nonmentalistic in character?

All of these questions could just as well be asked about the putative perceptions of bumblebees and bellhops as they could about our perceptions of God. Moreover, whatever the purported object, each question above is usually regarded as philosophically controversial—it names a puzzle that we need to solve or a mystery demanding an explanation in order to determine just what sort of acquaintance with reality is capable of being brokered by perceptual experience. These various philosophical controversies cluster around a more fundamental puzzle: how are our perceptual capacities capable of

---

Moreover, as I use it, "perception" is a success-term, indicating the veridicality of a perceptual experience. When I wish to speak of experiences that seem to direct us on some reality without any presumption of whether or not they succeed in so directing us, I will usually affix some qualifier such as "putative." I sometimes mark the distinction between perceptual experiences and putative perceptual experiences by a (confessedly contrived) distinction between "perceptions" and "experiences." Because perceptual experiences are the focus of this study, and for stylistic reasons, I sometimes drop the adjective "perceptual" and speak simply of "experiences." But context should make it sufficiently clear whether I mean to refer to a veridical perceptual experience, a putatively veridical one that *seems* veridical without judging whether it is or isn't, or a falsidical putative perceptual experience in which such a seeming is illusory or hallucinatory.

enabling reality itself to inform and justify what we think, say, and do? This is what I call "the problem of perception," and it will receive plenty of attention in what follows. At present the point is that—however we spell out the philosophical worry—we seemingly cannot address the theological problem of *God's* availability to us in experience without also confronting the more general problem of perception. Accordingly, contemporary Christian philosophers and theologians have invariably appropriated various theories addressed to the problem of perception in the course of trying to say both (1) how God's self-presentations to us might serve as a source of theological knowledge and a standard of correctness for what we say about God and (2) how theological talk grounded in such presentations manages to be directed on or "about" God. Both questions are interpreted and answered by deploying one's preferred theory of perceptual experience. That preferred theory is then incorporated into one of two kinds of theological stories.

On one sort of story (the "cataphatic" sort), the structure of our perceptual relation to God is fundamentally the same as our perceptual relation to ordinary objects in the world. On another sort of story (the "apophatic" sort), we must say that because God is fundamentally different than any creaturely object of experience, the structure of our perceptual relation to God fundamentally consists in some disruption or overturing of the ordinary situation. But the crucial point is that on either sort of theological theory, the analysis of "experience" the theologian deploys (either for God to instantiate it or overthrow it) does not serve merely theological interests. It also aims at resolving the more general philosophical problem of perception, even if that aim is merely implicit. Therefore, most often a very heavily ramified conception of "perceptual experience" is brought to bear on the question of whether Christian beliefs and practices might be informed or justified empirically, whether cataphatically or apophatically. Accordingly, contemporary philosophical theologians have tended to give various accounts of the Christian experience of God that differ from one another primarily in taking up opposing sides of controversies belonging to the philosophical problem of perception.

My purpose in this book is not primarily to wade into these controversies and take up my own position on the field, defending my own general theory of perception and then advocating for my own story about the sense in which God is and is not empirically available to us, cataphatically or apophatically. Instead, I aim to intervene on this entire way of proceeding. More specifically, I contest the idea that our theological interest in an empirical basis for Christian belief and practice must confront a general philosophical problem of perception in the first place. I claim not only that an entanglement of the theological problem with the philosophical one is avoidable but that the failure to avoid it proves disastrous for a Christian theology of religious experience. My aim, then, is to disentangle our theological interest in our perceptual relation to God from the philosophical interests motivating the problem of perception.

Prima facie, that claim seems utterly counterintuitive. If there are conceptual difficulties that attend the concept of perceptual experience itself, then any question about what it is to perceive God must confront those difficulties. But while I grant the truth of the conditional, I deny the antecedent. Contrary to the way things appear to Christian philosophers and theologians working in the epistemology of religious experience, the alleged conceptual difficulties about the nature of empirical content thought to lay behind the questions listed above are illusory. Such questions do not warrant the competing explanatory theories about the empirical grounds of our beliefs and practices to which they have given rise. No

4

doubt there have been philosophical *anxieties* about how experience can supply us with a kind of representational conduit or content that could serve to inform and rationally guide our thinking, and these anxieties have issued in a lot of spilled ink attempting to cast them as philosophical problems along with proposed solutions.

But despite an illusory surface clarity, in the final analysis none of these attempts has proven successful at presenting us with an intelligible difficulty that stands in need of a philosophical resolution. And without any coherent statement of a so-called problem of perception, there is nothing about the conjunction of (a), (b), and (c) above that requires a philosophical explanation. No account we might offer gives us any more fundamental insight than can be had by articulating our ordinary intuitions about the nature of experience.[2] Further, insofar as extant formulations of the "problem" of perception turn out to be *pseudoproblems*, the various sorts of philosophical theorizing aimed at answering such problems simply inherit the form of incoherence internal to the formulation of the question. This is precisely what creates trouble for contemporary theories about the nature and modes of God's self-revelation. The most influential philosophical theologians working on those theories have been motivated by the problem of perception, and, as such, their theological accounts are inflected by underlying theories of empirical content addressed to that problem. As a result, theology too inherits the incoherence that infects that pseudophilosophical project.

The basic idea, then, is that we cannot formulate an intelligible Christian theology of religious experience unless we sever it from the problem of perception to which it has been wedded. But many

---

2. That is not to say, however, that the ordinary conception is not susceptible to any clarifying philosophical analysis, but while such an analysis might further elucidate our ordinary presumption that experience can make our mental lives rationally accountable to reality itself, it does not purport to furnish us with any further information about *why*, or *how*, or *how it is possible* that this is so.

question the value of maintaining a theological interest in "religious experience" in the first place. To those of a generally "postmodern" cast of mind, it is not merely the philosophical *problematizing* of our mental receptivity and accountability to the impressions of a mind-independent reality that is ill-conceived, but the very notion of any rational receptivity and accountability to a mind-independent reality. From this perspective, that "reality" is a domain independent of what we happen to make of it, is somehow conveyed to us in experience, and imposes its own rational demands on our thinking about it can only be seen as an objectionable "modernist" hangover.

Rather than radically rejecting the problem of perception as a pseudo-problem, this sensibility simply accepts the terms it sets forward—the requirement of a satisfactory philosophical explanation for how experience mediates between mind and world—and then concedes that the requirement cannot be met. For some, that concession gives way to a somber charge to keep a stiff upper lip and soldier on without the idea of "experience" embodied by the conjunction of (a), (b), and (c) above. For others, the concession signals the removal of an oppressive burden—freedom from the idea of experience as the imposition of a rational constraint on our intentions by the way things are external to our socially ratified conventions.

So whereas one theological attitude toward the problem of perception is to attempt to resolve it via a philosophical explanation of empirical content and then to deploy that preferred theory in one's theological account, another is to regard the problem as genuine but intractable, and therefore to give up the very idea of "experience" as an epistemological ground of rational accountability to reality. But if the problem of perception is a pseudoproblem, then refusing to engage it by way of a radical concession is no less problematic than engaging it with the hopes of a resolution. In both cases, one's picture of God's self-disclosure in experience is ultimately determined by an incoherent notion of "experience."

If we are to have any hope of making sense of the idea of experiences that directly acquaint us with God's presence and agency in the world, then we must first disentangle that idea from the pseudophilosophical problem of perception with which it has been unfortunately alloyed. Still, while effecting that disentanglement might be a *necessary* step in showing that Christian beliefs and practices that purport to direct us on God can be grounded in experience, freeing theology from the problem of perception would not be *sufficient*. Being unable to problematize the notion of "perceptual experience" summarized above does not show that it is unproblematic. Clearly, there is a difference between being unable to show that position X is problematic and showing that X is unproblematic. But even if we were to grant that the notion of "experience" with which we began is prima facie unproblematic, whether a *theological* empiricism is coherent remains an open question.

On the conception of "perceptual experience" with which we began, a minimal theological empiricism would hold that it is in virtue of God's impressing Godself upon us in experience that at least some of what Christians think, say, and do succeeds in directing us upon God, and those impressions serve to determine the correctness or incorrectness of what Christians think, say, and do.[3] But suppose that the notion of "experience" involved in this claim in fact courts no genuine philosophical controversy in what we take it to affirm. Still, there might be something about a Christian concept of "God"

---

3. Note that, as I am characterizing it, such a theological empiricism is minimal in that it only requires that *some* Christian belief and practice is fundamentally informed and justified on the basis of experience. It is also possible to hold a maximal theological empiricism according to which *all* Christian belief and practice must be fundamentally informed and justified on the basis of experience, but I do not wish to commit myself to maximalism in what follows.

or a Christian conception of human cognitive capacities that makes it incoherent to suppose that God could be an object of perception. This would be an obstacle to theological empiricism distinct from the one raised by the problem of perception. Whereas the problem of perception imposes an explanatory burden on the notion of "experience" required by a theological empiricism, the sort of obstacle just mentioned is free from any such burden. Instead, the explanatory burden would rest on the question of whether Christian theological commitments can comport with that unproblematic and uncontroversially held empiricism.

We can therefore characterize the explanatory burden for the advocate of a minimal theological empiricism in one of two ways. On one reading, any problems we might encounter working out the theological bit of a theological empiricism logically depends on prior and more fundamental worries concerning the empiricism bit. On the other reading, the empiricism bit is unproblematic, and the explanatory burden of theological empiricism lies primarily in working out the theological bit. All of the most significant literature problematizing God's availability to us in experience since the scientific revolution has been predicated on the first reading. In this book, I argue that that widely presumed reading is not merely false but also incoherent, and I explore the prospects for a Christian theology of religious experience instead predicated on the second reading.

My argument is divided into three parts. Part I identifies the problem of perception in Christian theology and exposes its incoherence. Accordingly, in chapter 2 I show how the problem of perception has historically and conceptually come to shape our understanding of the problem of religious experience in Christian theology. In chapter 3, with my reading of the *status quaestionis* in hand, I introduce a "therapeutic" approach to freeing theology from the problem of perception. To do away with an alleged philosophical difficulty therapeutically is, first, to deconstruct that problem, exposing it as an incoherent pseudoproblem, and, second, to offer an "exculpatory explanation"—an explanation for why this particular bit of disguised nonsense should have appeared so compelling to us.

The purpose of chapter 3 is to unmask the problem of perception as ill-conceived and to expose the incoherence of the theories aimed at resolving it. Here I look to John McDowell's recent deconstruction of the problem, and I elaborate his strategy for doing away with it. McDowell argues that the problem of perception is ill-conceived insofar as its various formulations require a solution of one of two sorts, which he calls "Givenist" and "Coherentist." Givenism names the world's giving or impressing of a mental content on the norms of our thinking that is itself independent of those norms, while Coherentism claims no need to acknowledge standards of correctness inhering in the world itself and presented to us as mental content independent of our established norms. Instead, the rational answerability of our thinking to the world in experience can be accounted for in terms of our irreducibly norm-governed dispositions to respond both to it and to one another.

But neither Givenism nor Coherentism can possibly succeed in characterizing "experience" as making us rationally answerable to the world, McDowell argues, because Givenism necessarily requires that our answerability fails to be a properly *rational* one, while Coherentism necessarily requires that our rational responses fail to be properly *answerable* to the world rather than merely to our own responsive dispositions. Since each view has what the other lacks in order to minimally make sense of "experience" as a kind of rational answerability to the world, they have been locked in a vicious and "interminable oscillation." To hold together both Givenism's conception of answerability and Coherentism's conception of the irreducibly rational constitution of that answerability in the most minimally consistent way, however, does not yield a new philosophical theory of "experience" so much as simply return us to our naively held view that in experience our thinking is capable of directly taking in or being presented with the way the world is anyway, the way it would be even if no humans were equipped to recognize it as such.

Having singled out the problem and entitled ourselves to ignore it as failing to surface any genuine philosophical worry, the task in part 2 is to show that contemporary approaches to the problem of God's perceptual availability to us in experience are in fact essentially wedded to the pseudoproblem and, as such, are inheritors of its incoherence. In chapters 4 and 5, I therefore deploy the McDowellian strategy to critique some recent and influential accounts of our perceptual relation to God, both cataphatic and apophatic. I argue that Jean-Luc Marion ought to be regarded as offering us a theological Givenism of an apophatic sort, while William P. Alston relies on a theological Givenism of a cataphatic sort. Victor Preller and Kevin Hector, on the other hand, present us with theological Coherentisms of an apophatic and cataphatic sort, respectively.

Whereas the moves made in the first and second parts of the book are primarily critical and ground clearing, I turn in the third part toward constructively staking out the prospects for a minimal theological empiricism. My first step is to clarify the philosophically unproblematic notion of "experience" on which such a theological empiricism depends. In chapter 6, I therefore elaborate and extend McDowell's retrieval of our ordinary naive realist conception of perceptual experience in terms of what he characterizes as a "naturalized platonism." A naturalized platonism, McDowell claims, does not constitute a philosophical theory of perception but the fundamental conceptual grammar according to which the very notion of "experience" is intelligible—that which we must minimally affirm in order to avoid the vicious oscillation between Givenism and Coherentism.

This idea—that a naive or common-sense understanding of "experience" is not only philosophically unobjectionable but unavoidable on pain of falling into incoherence—is precisely what calls out for an exculpatory explanation. It raises the question of how we were ever tempted away from the naive conception and toward our compulsion to worry about the problem of perception. In chapter 7, I therefore offer a broad sociological explanation of our bewitchment by the problem of perception as the product of a very wide cultural phenomenon involving not only philosophers and theologians, but diverse registers of society in modern Western, secular social orders. McDowell, for his part, gestures toward a Weberian genealogy of the problem of perception as a particularly modern prejudice that arises from a disenchanted conception of nature emerging in and around the birth of the modern sciences. That genealogy however, is inadequate to account for the nature and scope of the problem of perception as a *religious* problem. I therefore look to Charles Taylor to show how his narrative of disenchantment offered in *A Secular Age* can correct and buttress McDowell's genealogy. Integrating McDowell's story with Taylor's has a mutually chastening effect that helps us distinguish between a genuine freedom from the characteristically modern problem of perception in our theological reflection and the nostalgic fantasy of returning to the "innocence" of a premodern conception of nature.

Finally, we must show how freeing theology from the problem of perception, which was the task of the foregoing chapters, actually reorients us toward the central question that the problem of perception has served to obfuscate: the theological question of how to properly characterize our perceptual relation to God. Chapter 8 offers a critical retrieval of Gregory of Nyssa's theology of the "spiritual senses" as a performative display of how we might theologically account for our perceptual relation to God free from the problem of perception. In Gregory I find a viable contemporary theological empiricism—an account that characterizes both tasks of theological contemplation and spiritual formation in terms of a receptivity and responsiveness to the perceptible presence and agency of God in the world. The constructive account I appropriate from Nyssen requires further elaboration, but my aim in articulating it is not so much to demonstrate its correctness as to show how it manages to surmount a minimal obstacle that the most influential accounts do not manage to clear—that of consistency with a minimal empiricism.

PART I

Theology and the
Problem of Perception

2

The Problem of Perception and the
Perception of God

In Christian discourse, our talk about God is replete with the language of ordinary experience. When I behold profound acts of kindness or self-sacrifice, I am inclined to think (or say) that I "see the love of God," or in receiving such acts from the hand of others I might take myself to have "tasted the goodness of God." In quiet moments of contemplation or in prayer I might regard myself as having "touched God" or as having been "touched by God." In hearing Scripture read or preached I might "hear God speaking," addressing me in particular.[1] In taking these experiences to manifest

---

1. The use of the language of ordinary experience to describe the self-presentation of God to God's people can be traced directly to the language of Christian Scripture, as, for example, when Moses is given a visual presentation of the divine glory in Exod. 33:22-23, or when the prophets hear the voice of the Lord as in Isa. 6:8, or when we are encouraged to taste and see that the Lord is good" in Ps. 34:8. Similarly, we are told that in seeing and touching the person of Jesus, we behold and handle the Word who is God (1 John 1:1; cf. John 1). For a biblical theology ordered entirely by the notion of theophany, or divine appearing, manifest within the history and context of ordinary human life and sacralized by the cultus, see Samuel

15

God's presence and agency, I ordinarily take them to supply me with reasons to form beliefs about God. To take the first of these examples, I take myself to see God's love in the benevolent act of another, and on the basis of that experience I find myself forming the belief that God's loving presence has been manifested in this act of benevolence, or perhaps simply that God is loving. Although I need not, I might verbally express my belief that God is loving with an observation report such as "this act of kindness reveals God's love," or some such.

When Christians talk this way, such talk proceeds from a rather common-sense assumption about their relation to the world in which God appears to them—they assume that they are *open* to God in the sort of lived experiences described above. By our assumption that we are "open to God" I mean to single out two assumptions, one quite general and the other particularly theological. First, I have in mind a sort of "naive" or "common-sense" realism; our prereflective "default" understanding about the *directness* with which ordinary perceptual experience puts us in touch with a world not of our own making.[2] Second, I have in mind the idea that this default understanding forms the backdrop against which to understand the sorts of observation reports mentioned above that Christians routinely make about their experiences of God.[3]

Terrien's remarkable *The Elusive Presence: Toward a New Biblical Theology* (New York: Harper and Row, 1978). See also Marianne Sawicki, *Seeing the Lord: Resurrection and Early Christian Practices* (Minneapolis: Fortress Press, 1994).

2. What marks an experience as *perceptual* in the sense that I shall be assuming throughout this study is that it involves the *qualitative and passive presentation* of something, typically of some feature of our environment. So while we may be able to identify a passive or qualitative dimension of, e.g., memory or abstract reasoning sufficient for them to count as experiential, they are not perceptual experiences insofar as their (purported) directedness on the objects of memory or abstract reasoning do not or need not involve the presence of that object to the subject of the experience. I expand and elaborate considerably on this intuitive way of carving out my topic in what follows.

3. The phrase "openness to the world" as a gloss on our implicit assumption that in experience we directly "take in" the world has come to prominence primarily through its usage by John McDowell in *Mind and World* (Cambridge, MA: Harvard University Press, 1996), on which, more later. But the fundamental idea captured by that phrase—that the world is not reducible to

2.1 Naive Realism and Our Openness to God

Taking both assumptions together, we might say that implicit in our observation reports about God are some of the very same naive realist assumptions we ordinarily make in our observation reports about everyday features of the world. Central among those assumptions is the notion that there is such a thing as the way the world is, irrespective of our thoughts or opinions about it (except, of course, when the things in question themselves involve our thoughts and opinions). Take, for example, an observation report such as, "My computer screen is cracked." When I look at my computer screen and see that it is cracked, I take it that it would have been cracked even if I had not noticed it, and indeed even if no one had noticed it. If it could be sent back in time before any humans existed, before any cultural, linguistic, or social conventions even existed for identifying it *as* cracked, then it would still *be* cracked.

The more sophisticated among us might point out that what we really mean to say here is that it would still be what we now mean when we use the word *cracked*. Smart alecks notwithstanding, we ordinarily take it that however dependent our *recognition* of the way things are might be on our social or cultural formation, *that* they are the way they are does not depend on any recognition on our part.[4]

or dependent upon human minds and that such a world can nevertheless be perceptually present to the mind—is a standard gloss given by philosophers for the prephilosophical intuition about experience that forms the starting point for philosophical reflection.

4. The point is sometimes put by saying that—unless we think ourselves victims of illusions—we ordinarily regard our experiences as *factive*: as simply presenting us with the way things are, and not merely with the "raw materials" out of which we *construct* or *interpret* the way things are. As Heidegger memorably puts it in "The Origin of the Work of Art," in *Poetry, Language, Thought*, trans. Albert Hofstadter (New York: Harper Collins, 1972), "Everything that might interpose itself between the thing and us in apprehending and talking about it must first be set aside. [In perception] . . . we yield ourselves to the undisguised presence of the thing. . . . We never really first perceive a throng of sensations, e.g., tones and noises, in the appearance of things. . . . [W]e hear the three-motored plane, we hear the Mercedes in immediate distinction from the Volkswagen. Much closer to us than all sensations are the things themselves. We hear the door shut in the house and never hear the acoustical sensations or even mere sounds. In order to hear

Thus, for example, it might be that in hearing a homily preached at our local worship gathering you perceive that God is addressing our congregation. I, on the other hand, did not recognize God as addressing us, or I did not recognize God addressing us in the way you are now reporting. Of course, that does not prevent me from believing that God in fact did address us—it might be that among my various background beliefs is the belief that God can or does address us through the homily in worship, and from this I might *infer* that because I have just heard a homily, whatever has been said in the homily must have included God's address to us.[5] But whereas you take your experience to have made the fact of God's address directly present to you, I had to reason it out from the background belief. Whereas for my observation of the situation, my reasoning from the background belief does all the work, your belief arises from God's actual *manifestation* to you in this particular homily.[6] From the standpoint of hearing the homily, your

a bare sound we have to listen away from things, divert our ear from them, i.e., listen abstractly" (25–26). As McDowell has it in *Mind and World*, "when we see that such-and-such is the case, we, and our seeing, do not stop anywhere short of the fact. What we see is: that such-and-such is the case" (29).

5. See, for example, John Hick's distinction with respect to how we "become conscious of the existence of other objects in the universe"—that is, "either by experiencing them for ourselves or by inferring their existence from evidence within our experience." "The ordinary religious believer," he goes on to say, "is one of the former kind. He professes, not to have inferred that there is a God, but that God as a living being has entered into his own experience." *Faith and Knowledge* (Ithaca: Cornell University Press, 1966), 95.

6. When God is present with us or acts on us by way of creaturely objects and events, is the divine manifestation direct or indirect? Phenomenologically, at least, we might imagine the addressee of God's speech-acts taking things either way. If, for example, properties belonging properly to God are in any sense present in the address, then in directly taking in that address she directly takes in those properties, and, as such, directly takes in divine properties. Presumably, the direct perceptual intake of divine properties is sufficient for a direct perceptual relation to God. If, on the other hand, what is perceptibly present in her experience is only an intermediary that manifests divine properties extrinsically as a kind of proxy for God, then her direct perceptual intake will not count as a direct perception of God, but an indirect one. At this point, I do not wish to stake a claim in either direction, since the phenomenology I sketch is consistent with both sorts of analyses. If, therefore, I go on to describe a "naive realist" phenomenology as supposing one rather than the other, this should not be seen as a necessary analysis of how one takes oneself to encounter God, but only a phenomenologically possible one. If direct

sensitivity or receptivity to God produced in you an observational belief about God's address, whereas for my part nothing actually struck me as being any different from an observational standpoint than it might have struck the unbeliever who did not share the relevant background beliefs about God.

Part of what it would mean for me to take seriously your claim to have observationally registered God's address in the homily is to acknowledge the possibility that I was unreceptive to something that was nevertheless *there*—something you genuinely perceived and I missed. Even with our shared background belief in place, the belief that God does indeed address us in the homily of Sunday worship, it remains possible for me to acknowledge my failure to have *discerned* God's address—my "deafness" or lack of sensitivity to it. Moreover, to acknowledge that this happened is also to recognize that in claiming to have heard God's address you did not simply hear what you wanted to hear, or what your training or your formation alone had determined you would hear. Certainly, you might recognize that apart from what your mother taught you or your Sunday School class drilled into your head, you might not have been adequately *disposed* to hear God. But what you think you heard in such an instance is God, not your mother or your Sunday School teacher, and what you take to have triggered that belief is not a mere inclination but the perceptible presence of God.

In this way, we ordinarily assume that the way the world actually stands (and not merely what we happen to think about it) can exert a direct impact on what we think. In looking at my computer screen when the screen is in fact cracked, I take that fact to be crucial in accounting for my visual experience of it *as* cracked. In other words,

---

perception of God turns out not to be metaphysically possible, then the phenomenology of directness is illusory. I will not stake a metaphysical claim on the matter, however, until the final chapter.

my thought that the screen is cracked reaches "all the way out" to the reality of its being cracked, and its being cracked reaches "all the way in" to determine my thought. There is no distance between the qualitative character of my experience and an objective state of the world in the sense described above.

By fixing on the qualitative character of my experience, I mean to highlight that to have perceived something involves more than that the way the world is can itself determine our thinking about it. It is also to make a claim about *how* the world determines our thinking about it, the *mode* of its determination of my thinking. In experience we take it that some feature of the way the world is has become immediately present to us in our thinking about it. The distinctive phenomenal character of visually beholding my cracked screen (for instance, the appearance of a dark two-inch line zigzagging up the bottom left-hand side of my screen) names the particular *way* in which some state of the world is present to me (in this case, a small bit of the world—my computer screen—has presented itself to me *visually*). In taking my experience to be a disclosure of some feature of the way the world actually is under some perceptual mode of presentation (visual, auditory, and so on), and in taking my observational belief to be "based on" that presentation, I therefore take my belief to be directly informed by the world itself.[7]

7. To identify the qualitative or phenomenal character of experience with the way in which reality presents itself to thought—as a mode of object-presentation—will strike some as an unjustified preference for one theory of "qualia" (the subjective element in experience), and a controversial one at that. But at this stage I am not attempting any theoretical account, but only trying to describe our ordinary assumptions. Nevertheless, there are theoretical accounts of qualia predicated precisely on the attempt to capture our ordinary assumptions. Thus, e.g., it is this ordinary notion of a belief's dependence on the world that Timothy Williams is attempting to capture in *Knowledge and Its Limits* (New York: Oxford University Press, 2000), when he says that we "conceive mind and external world as dependent variables" such that "belief as attributed in ordinary language is a genuine mental state constitutively dependent on the external world" (5–6). Likewise, the intuition that when I see that x is blue, its looking blue to me is determined by its *being* blue guides Gareth Evans in offering his controversial reading of Frege on "object-dependent senses" in *The Varieties of Reference*, ed. John McDowell (New

Similarly, when hearing God address me in particular, in hearing a homily, what I take to be the most fundamental explanation for what I heard is the fact that God is now speaking to me. The distinctive phenomenal character of this impression, such as the auditory experience of my pastor's delivery of a sermon, names the way in which God's address has become present to me—"what it is like" for the world itself to be present to me in that way. My observational belief that God is addressing us in the homily is therefore "based on" my experience of hearing God's address in the homily. In virtue of hearing the homily, I take myself to have heard God's address in the same way that in virtue of seeing the zigzagged line, I take myself to have seen that the screen is cracked.[8] To recall a point I made earlier, this is not to say that I made any *inference* from the way things appear to me in experience to an observational judgment about the way things are. On the contrary, our beliefs and practices can be noninferentially grounded in perceptual experience. Precisely in perceptually experiencing some object X as having the property F, I can find myself immediately saddled with the belief that X is F. In such cases, my perceptual belief is rationally "based on" the

York: Oxford University Press, 1982). He argues that a Fregean analysis of thoughts is best rendered by the notion of a sense (*Sinn*) constituted by its referent (*Bedeutung*).

8. That is, in experience some feature of the world has been made directly present to my thinking, and that presentation of the world provides me the reason to form the belief in question—I thus form the belief *because of* the way in which my experience takes in the world, in virtue of it. But the world's saddling me with a reason to believe that-p does not imply that going on to believe that-p requires any additional move from passively registering the reason to actively reasoning my way to the belief. It is equally possible that the world's impartation of itself to me, e.g., my seeing that p, itself occasions my belief that-p—seeing the cup on the table might therefore itself "wring from me" the belief that the cup is on the table. In such cases, however, it remains true that the experience provides the reason for my belief. Suppose that you call out to me while stooped over a box looking for this particular cup and ask where it is, and I reply, "It is on the table." If you don't remember leaving it on the table, you might doubt or even outright reject my claim, and reply, "No, I didn't leave it there—how do you know that's where it is?" I might well reply, "Because *I see it sitting there on the table*." It is natural to suppose that this reply indeed gives an accurate picture of *why* I found myself passively saddled with the belief that the cup is on the table—my reason for holding that belief—even before needing to draw upon it in an active exercise of reasoning to counter your challenge.

experience in that the very formation of the belief is constituted by the experience as a form of rational responsiveness to my environment.

In our perceptual experiences, the direct impact of the world on us can thus function as a rational "tribunal" for what we think, say, and do.[9] When all goes well and we are not misled, we rely on our experiences as one way to hold our thinking and acting accountable to the way things actually stand in the world. Our perceptual experience of the world serves not simply to refer us to the world, but also to "check" the world in order to align our thinking with the way things are, to ensure that our thinking is justified by how things really are. When I went to bed last night, I wiped off my computer screen carefully and did not see any cracks, but this morning I do see one. I ordinarily take it that, provided I am not being misled, my cracked computer screen has corrected my prior belief or disposition to believe that my screen is perfectly intact. What does the correcting is not fundamentally my "interpretation" of the world but the world itself. Our ordinary presumption is that the way the world is affords me the ability to adjust my thinking to fit the facts by forming a belief (for example, "my screen is cracked").

The support that the world lends to the adjustment of my beliefs or bodily responses is thus "rational" support, in the minimal sense of supplying me with *reasons* to make up my mind or act in some ways and not others. Similarly, if God is in fact addressing us in the homily

---

9. As Williams puts it, "If the content of a mental state can depend on the external world, so can the attitude to that content" (*Knowledge and Its Limits*, 6). In the case of perceptual experiences, it is not just that the content of our observational beliefs can be imparted directly by the world itself but also that stance or attitude that we take up to that content—believing, knowing, doubting, commanding, exclaiming, etc.—can also be imparted to us by the world itself. The image of the world as a "tribunal" comes from W. V. O. Quine, "Two Dogmas of Empiricism," *Philosophical Review* 60, no. 1 (1951): 20–43. When Quine says that "our statements about the external world face the tribunal of sense experience" (38), he means simply that we must take the impact of the world registered by our senses to function as a norm, a standard of correctness that either vindicates or indicts our judgments about the world.

and that address is manifestly presented to me, impressing itself upon me in experience, then God's presence and agency in the world itself determines the reasons I have for forming beliefs about God's address to us in the homily. A Christian conception of "revelation" in its most general sense seems to include God's making the divine presence and agency available to us in experience, as well as our becoming appropriately sensitive or receptive to the relevant mode of God's availability so as to be successfully presented with God's presence and agency as a "tribunal" or standard of correctness against which to adjust our thinking.

The idea I have been elaborating is that we are perceptually open to God's presence and agency in the world in much the same way as we are perceptually open to the world itself. That is, God's presence or action in the world can make an immediate rational impact on our observational thinking, such observational thinking can represent the ways in which God is actually present and active in our immediate environment, and our ability to detect God's perceptible relation to the world can therefore furnish us with rational support for our dispositions to form beliefs about God or to respond bodily to God in some ways and not others. Our experiences of the world allow us to take in facts about the way the world is, including facts about God's manifestation in it.[10] This "naive" or "common-sense" conception of our perceptual relation to God has important implications for the overall shape of our moral-practical reasoning about God.

From what has been said thus far, it is clear that, rather than seeing ourselves as purely imposing our will to believe upon reality, we most often take it that reality itself "tells" us what we ought to think, in the sense of rationally guiding our beliefs.[11] The same can be said

---

10. McDowell draws frequently on the image of "taking in the world" as a paradigmatic description of our ordinary conception of experience. See *Mind and World*.

11. That is not to say, of course, that our discernments or judgments about such matters are always correct, only that ordinarily they seem to us to be fitting responses to the way the world is. In

not only for our dispositions to form beliefs about the world but also—and perhaps even more fundamentally—for our dispositions to act. The way things are can call us not merely to think, but also to speak and more generally to act as we should, and it can impose its own demands on our practical reason no less than our discursive reason. For example, when I see a jaywalker darting into the road in front of my car, I might find myself forming a belief such as "I am going to hit him if I don't slow down!" Or, perhaps in addition to or instead of forming that belief I simply find myself stomping on the brake in order to avoid hitting him. In such cases, I take it that there are a number of relevant facts—features of the way the world is—that appear to me via my visual apprehension of the jaywalker before me. Among the facts thus presented to me by my observation of the pedestrian are that he stands in danger of being hit, that I must avoid hitting him, and that applying the brake is my best bet for achieving that outcome. Such facts, we ordinarily think, are plainly before me—they become manifest to me in these circumstances, not because I have puzzled them out but because they directly present themselves to me as features of the way the world is that are disclosed in my passive experience of the jaywalker. In this case, the relevant facts are conveyed to me visually.[12]

those cases in which it turns out that we have thought or acted improperly, we regard what previously seemed to us fitting responses to the way the world is as mere seemings, while taking some set of revised responses as in fact fitting responses to the way the world really is.

12. There is a question here about the sense in which "seeing" the facts in this example is metaphorical. Clearly, we cannot see moral-practical facts in the same way that we see concrete particulars such as tables and chairs. We will have occasion to revisit this issue at a later point. At the moment, one brief observation will suffice to make explicit our prephilosophical views. Recall (e.g., from note 3 above) that we ordinarily do not take ourselves to experience "bare particulars" but everyday objects as they figure into facts: when I see a cup on the table, what I visually take in is not a mass of atomized features ("Look! A solid, cylindrical, hollow, liquid-containing thing—from which I may abstract out 'this-cup,' contiguously positioned on top of another solid, horizontally extended thing from which I can abstract out 'this-table.' Therefore, the cup is on the table!") No, if anything, the abstraction goes the other way—we have to take a philosophy class in order to learn how to abstract from our ordinary experience to parse out an analysis. Instead, what we immediately observe phenomenologically is that a cup is on the

As such, we ordinarily presume in such circumstances that what I observed, not solely my dispositions as an observer, made my stomping on the brakes the right thing to do. The jaywalker's darting in front of me *called upon me* to form something like the above-mentioned belief or intention to act. Had I been deaf or improperly disposed to recognize what the situation itself required of me, we would understand this failure of my practical rationality as a failure to pick up on some reasons to apply my brakes that my immediate environment made readily available to me. Another way of putting this is to say that, in our everyday navigation of the world, our naive realist presumptions about what features of the world are available to perception includes a kind of realism about properties of value.[13] Visually perceiving a crack in my computer screen as providing me with an objective reason to form certain beliefs and action-intentions bears an important parallel with visually perceiving a jaywalker as

---

table, a fact that in various circumstances furnishes us with correspondingly various reasons to think or do something (e.g., if it appears to be mine, reasons to pick it up or take a drink; in a coffee shop, reasons to wonder if someone else is sitting at this table, etc.). But how is taking in facts about cups and tables that we ordinarily see as giving us reasons to think and act in some ways and not others different in kind from taking in facts about jaywalkers as giving us reasons to think and act in some ways and not others? It is not.

13. Akeel Bilgrami contrasts the third-person perspective on ourselves as objects characteristic of scientific understanding with the first-person perspective of ourselves as agents characteristic of the evaluative stance. See "The Wider Significance of Naturalism: A Genealogical Essay," in *Naturalism and Normativity*, ed. Mario de Caro and David MacArthur (New York: Columbia University Press, 2010), 23–54. Bilgrami asks: "What must the world be like . . . such that it moves us to such practical engagement [of the agent-perspective] over and above detached observation and study?" The "obvious answer," he says, is that "over and above containing the facts that natural science studies it contains a special kind of fact, evaluative facts and properties . . . *values*, and when we perceive them, they put normative demands to us and activate our practical engagement" (26). Such a view, he emphasizes, is not particularly philosophical, but "commensensical" (27). Just as, when asked "Is it raining?" we do not attempt to examine our interiority to find the answer, but instead *look outside*, so when asked "Do you desire x?" we are prompted not to scan our own minds but to look at the world to determine whether x is in fact *desirable*. (28). If only a third-person point of view directed at our own minds could explain why x is desirable, then, since agency is a first-person phenomenon, we would have to deny not just that the world contains values, but the very fact of our agency. But precisely because we ordinarily regard ourselves as agents, we also regard the world as capable of calling upon our agency.

providing me an objective reason to form certain beliefs and action-intentions.

Ordinarily, we would say that the defect of practical reason on such an occasion is not that I failed to invent or *construct* the relevant reasons but that I failed to *recognize* them, in one of two senses. Either I failed to take in or *detect* the relevant reasons that were there anyway, or I failed to properly *acknowledge* those reasons I detected that were in fact salient to me in my experience of the situation. In the latter case, I failed to be properly motivated by the reasons I detected and hence failed to act in accordance with what the situation itself required of me. While this example draws particularly on our naive realism with respect to moral properties (broadly understood as features of the world that place rational demands on our conduct), something similar could be said about aesthetic properties.[14]

In much the same way, I might think that, for example, in silent prayer God has presented the divine presence to me as majestic in a way that calls for me to act by moving my body into a kneeling posture of humility. I could have responded instead by jumping on one leg and rotating at successive ninety-degree angles until I fell down, but I would not have considered that a *practically rational* response given what I was presented with. Kneeling, though, and not jumping on one leg, was what I observed God's particular way of impressing Godself on me to have required of me on that occasion. If it is possible for my observation of God to have figured into my practical reasoning in that way, then my failure to kneel on that occasion could rightly be analyzed either as a failure to pick up on the relevant reasons for kneeling made available to me by my perception

---

14. Though I think the matter is a bit more complicated here: whereas the action-guiding focus on agency is a fairly clear indicator for what we have in mind by "values," it is not so clear what sort of "calling from the world" we have in mind by notions such as beauty.

of God's presence or as a failure to comply with the rational demands imposed on me by those observational reasons.

Of course, just as we can imagine many different sorts of rational responses afforded by the situation of the jaywalker (such as swerving rather than braking, and so on), so too we might also recognize many other actions as suitable responses to the way in which God appeared to me, such as bowing my head or even remaining still. In such cases, it is perhaps better to say that my kneeling in response to a presentation of God's majesty was rationally *permitted* by that experience rather than rationally *required* by it. But we might equally well imagine a scenario in which only kneeling would do or in which it figures among many possible actions, at least one of which is required of me. Whatever the case, however, Christians can take the mode of God's presentation to us as evoking in us some disposition to exercise our agency precisely because the action in question is what we observe reality itself to demand of us.[15]

In this sense, the bodily act of kneeling is as much a rational response to reality as presented to me in my experience as my forming some perceptual belief such as "God is majestic" or "here is a manifestation of divine majesty" would have been. But this is not to say that I had to form some such belief before acting on it or that in the act of kneeling in response to perceiving God as majestic I thought much about what I did. What afforded me a

15. While the suitability of our ordinary understanding of perceptual experience vis-à-vis value properties would surely be disputed, the corresponding notion of "reality's demands" leaves it an open question how we should as Christians construe God's calling or demand on our practical reasoning. It is thus consistent with all theological metaethical proposals insofar as they espouse a "realist" understanding of value properties as genuine objects of intention. See, e.g., Herbert McCabe's Wittgensteinian-Thomist conception of natural law in *Law, Love and Language* (New York: Bloomsbury, 2003), Robert Adams's version of divine command theory in *Finite and Infinite Goods* (New York: Oxford University Press, 2002), Linda Zagzebski's motivation-based virtue theory in *Divine Motivation Theory* (New York: Cambridge University Press, 2004), and John Hare's Kantian "prescriptive-realism" in *The Moral Gap* (New York: Oxford University Press, 1997).

reason to act in that instance was not any explicit formation of the belief that God is majestic, but a perceptual experience of God as majestic. Sometimes we recognize the need to deliberatively reflect on what reasons our experiences have actually afforded us in order to determine what exercises of our agency the relevant realities demand of us. For instance, while praying I may be strongly impressed with the idea that God is urging me to yield my will, but I may not be certain what exactly he is calling me to do.

But much (perhaps most) of the time, the reasons afforded us by God's presence and agency impinging in our experiences inform and justify our actions without our ever needing to actively reflect on them. Consider the batter who exhibits a practical rationality in knowing how to adjust his stance and his swing according to the way he perceives the pitch coming at him. Without needing to make any conscious decisions or assessments about what to do with his body, he attempts to determine what the situation requires of him and responds accordingly. If asked why he rotated his hips at angle X instead of angle Y, he might well respond, "I don't know, I just did." But if asked why he did whatever he did when swinging the bat, he confirms that his bodily actions were rationally motivated when he responds, "I was just trying to hit the ball." He saw the pitch coming at him, recognized what he saw as imposing on him a requirement that he attempt to hit it, and by calling upon his agency to hit the ball, eliciting his evaluative dispositions, desire, background knowledge, and prior training, moved his body appropriately in response.

Certainly, he did all of this unreflectively, but we nevertheless understand his action as rational, as a form of practical responsiveness to reason, as exhibiting a performative (rather than contemplative or discursive) understanding of what ought to be done. In this case, we take it that the reason in question was that a ball was rapidly approaching him and that he should try to hit it. And it was his *seeing* the ball, his openness to it entering his visual field, that we take to have afforded him that reason, to have provided him the rational basis on which to appropriately adjust his stance and swing the bat. My kneeling in response to God's presentation to me was of this sort—a perceptual experience of God which afforded me a reason to act that in turn elicited the act itself, without any reflective or deliberative delay acting as intermediary between observing and acting, between God's majesty being made present to me in some way and the calling forth of my disposition to kneel.

2.2 Perceptual Knowledge versus Perceptual Intentionality

Thus far, I have been arguing that it is, in at least some sense, natural for Christians to think of themselves as capable of a perceptual "openness" to God's presence and agency in the world and as involved in various forms of moral-practical reasoning that presume our openness to God. Moreover, the sort of perceptual openness to God's presence and agency in the world I have been describing is intelligible in terms of the very same sort of perceptual openness we naively presume in our ordinary experience of worldly objects, properties, relations, and events. Importantly, however, to be *open* to some feature of reality in perceptual experience is not the same as having a perceptual *knowledge* of that feature of reality.

Rather, the notion of perceptual or observational openness to God is in a sense more fundamental than—logically prior to—the notion of perceptual knowledge of God. For me to know God, or to know something about God, is for my way of thinking about God to possess the epistemic credentials relevant for that way of thinking to constitute knowledge. But whatever credentials those might be, in order for my thinking about God to have them, such thinking must indeed be *about* God in the first place. The question of whether a judgment about God is true or false cannot even arise if that judgment has not succeeded in being about God at all, if it fails to actually involve or have to do with God. This "aboutness" is what gives a judgment its content, whatever its epistemic credentials.

Our openness to something is our capacity to be directed on it, to have some aspect of that thing "in mind" such that our thinking, speaking, and acting are properly understood as world-involving. Being open to God is thus having our experiences *direct us upon* God such that our thinking comes to involve God, so that the beliefs and practices that include such thinking accordingly have to do with God. To be open to God is thus to presume that God (and not merely our socially and institutionally ratified way of using the word or concept "God") rationally bears on our thinking and that our thinking reaches out to God. If what I imagine to be my experiences "of God" are in fact not in any sense directed on God but instead pick out or direct me on some other sort of thing (for instance, my participation in a religious community's symbols of ultimate concern or my unresolved anxieties about death), then the beliefs that I form on the basis of such thinking cannot say anything truly *or* falsely about God because they are not in the first instance about God at all. As such, purportedly theological thinking would not succeed in being theological; it would not actually have anything to do with God, at least not as Christians have usually understood the intentional referent of their beliefs and practices.

To claim that we are open to God is therefore to claim that what we think, say, and do genuinely has God as its content, whether our thinking, speaking, and acting get things right with respect to God or not. For our thought, language, and performances to be God-involving, therefore, is a necessary but not a sufficient condition for our knowledge of God. If what I think, say, or do is capable of reaching out to how things actually are with God, then it is possible for how things are with God to form the standard of correctness for our beliefs and practices about God, and it is thus possible to have responded rightly or wrongly to what God's presence or agency demands of us. To claim that we are open to God by way of *perception* is to claim that God can enter into our experiences and thus that our observational thinking and reporting can have God as their empirical content. Our perceptual knowledge of God, on the other hand, presupposes that we are open to God in this way, and it is constituted by the correctness of our rational responsiveness to the demands impressed on us by our openness to God's presence or agency.

So a Christian's common-sense or naive presumption that she is open to God does not necessarily imply that she gets things right in her judgments about how God has presented Godself to her in experience or how she has responded to God's self-presentations, but rather that, given the proper circumstances, she *can* get things right in these respects. Our implicit assumption when we take ourselves to have a perceptual knowledge of God is that we have gotten things right, that our experience discloses that our judgments about God are correct or that our practical responses to God are what were called for (that is, because they are either required or permitted by whatever feature of the world our experience is an experience of).

Marking off the foregoing distinction by a bit of terminology, we can say that openness has to do with the *intentionality* of our experiences—their two-way directedness in which reality's bearing on our thinking affords us the rational resources to adjust and revise our beliefs and practices with its demands. The notion of our perceptual knowledge, on the other hand, has to do with the *epistemology* of our experiences, our ways of evaluating the credentials of the beliefs and dispositions to act that are based on experience, our attempts to identify or establish their correctness and the conditions under which our directedness on reality counts as knowledge.

Our naive or common-sense idea that we are perceptually "open" to God is thus equally well stated by saying that, when not misled, we perceive things to be a certain way with respect to God precisely because that is the way things in fact are with God. The epistemological question is just what constitutes things having gone well or badly, what is required for our experiences of God to afford us reasons for belief or action that, when based on those experiences, can be thought to furnish us with knowledge of God, whether reflective or practical.

If our ordinary and common-sense view of theological intentionality is that Christians are open to God in a way that possibly affords us a perceptual knowledge of God, this is only because we take ourselves to be similarly open to the world as the arena of God's manifestations to us. When I take it that in the benevolent act of another I have seen the love of God, I can only regard my experience as directing me on God in that act if I am also perceptually open to that human act of benevolence. Similarly, I can only take the perceptual judgments about divine love that I have based on my experience of human benevolence to amount to a perceptual knowledge of God to the extent that I regard myself as having a perceptual knowledge of the human act of benevolence in which God's love was made manifest to me. Or, openness to the perceptible presence of God in the Eucharist depends on our openness to the perceptible presence of the elements themselves.

If God is to impinge on my thinking in my experiences of the world by reaching out to me in it, then the world must likewise impress itself on me with reasons for forming my beliefs about it and responding practically to it. There is thus an internal relationship between our prephilosophical assumption that the world lies open to us, making possible our perceptual knowledge of it, and our assumption that God's presence and agency lies open to us as a feature of the world, making possible our perceptual knowledge of God. All of this is another way of saying that Christians customarily engage in observational talk about God and that such talk seems to work much like our ordinary observations of the world around us—it evinces the same kind of naive realism that underlies our perceptual talk about everyday objects, properties, and events in the world.

If I want to know if it is raining outside, I simply "consult the world" by looking out the window or by holding the door open and sticking my hand out to see if I feel any droplets. If I want to know whether my chutney needs salt, I can taste it to find out. In this way, my perceptual experience of the world affords me the ability to change what I think and do to fit what the demands of my immediate environment, whether in forming the belief that it is raining or that my chutney is bland, or in being appropriately disposed to exercise my agency by, say, looking for my umbrella or fetching the salt. In the same way, when I wish to know how God is addressing me in this morning's homily or how God is reaching out to me in my silent contemplation or whether the Lord is good to me, Christians have thought—and many still do think—that I can in the same way consult God's presence and agency in the world: I can listen for God's address, I can receive God's touch, I can taste and see that the Lord is good. God's presence or agency can then itself impress itself on me and rationally shape my dispositions to believe or to act in whatever way such realities might require of me.

2.3 Ordinary Perception and the Perception of God in Premodern Theology

So this thought—that when everything goes as it should and I am not misled, mistaken, or deceived, my experience both puts me immediately in touch with the world and renders my thinking vulnerable to correction by the world—is basic for us.[16] It enjoys a kind of "default" status. We did not invent it to solve any prior theoretical problems, and we do not come to believe it on the basis of any explicit arguments.[17] Rather, it thematizes a basic intuition the relinquishing of which would require some forceful and compelling reasons.[18] While there is no universal agreement about the constituents of reality to which we are or can be open in experience, the idea that we are perhaps not open to reality at all is a suspicion only a philosopher would dream of entertaining.[19] Moreover, until fairly recently, most philosophers entertained no such suspicions. Ancient and medieval philosophers for the most part simply presumed as a given that we are perceptually open to the world, even while they offered different accounts of that fact.[20] Similarly,

16. Here I mean "basic" in something like Plantinga's sense of "not being believed on the evidential basis of other propositions" and in that sense fundamental to our "noetic structure." See *Warranted Christian Belief* (New York: Oxford University Press, 2000), 83. But it also has something else in common with the sorts of beliefs (testimonial, memory, etc.) that Plantinga uses for his examples. Namely, it is largely implicit, tacit, or assumed and need not be consciously held at all, until perhaps it is challenged.

17. And for precisely that reason even the label "naive realism" seems inappropriate, insofar as it projects the notion of a metaphysical doctrine. But holding a metaphysical position is a bit too high-flown a way of characterizing our ordinary assumption.

18. As P. F. Strawson rightly notes, the notion of our openness to the world or "the immediate consciousness of the existence of things outside us" is the commonsense point of departure for any subsequent thinking about the philosophical problems of perception. See Strawson's description of "common-sense realism" in "Perception and Its Objects," in *Vision and Mind: Selected Readings in the Philosophy of Perception*, ed. Alva Noë and Evan Thompson (Cambridge, MA: MIT Press, 2002), 91–110, reprinted from *Perception and Identity: Essays Presented to A. J. Ayer*, ed. G. MacDonald (London: MacMillan, 1979), 41–60.

19. Of course we might—and often do—disagree about the constituents of reality upon which our experiences direct us. We may even disagree about the way in which those constituents make themselves available to perception (e.g., I think particles in a collider are "observable," you think that, strictly speaking, they are not). But those are disputes about the way the world is and the way it bears on our thinking, not disputes about whether it does in fact bear on our thinking as described above.

20. There was, for the most part, a shared assumption about the object-dependency of thought, which implies, first, that the extramental world is intrinsically meaningful and, second, that in perception its meaning is impressed upon the perceiver. Debates were primarily ordered by the question of whether to think of that imposition in Aristotelian terms of the "form" or "intelligible species" belonging to the extramental object or in some other representationalist terms. See Julia E. Annas, *Hellenistic Philosophy of Mind* (Berkeley: University of California

most ancient and medieval Christian philosophers and theologians presumed that we are open to God's presence and agency in the world. Insofar as God was taken to be present in and to the world and dynamically active within it, it was taken for granted that we are open to God in and through the world no less than we are to the world itself. The disagreements that arose were about how to best account for that fact.

In other words, the controversial theological question was not whether we are open to God in the common-sense way described above, but how—what such an openness consists in when it has God as its object. What do Christians regard as the modes of God's presentation to us, and what sorts of rational and moral-practical demands does this make available for us to perceive and respond to? The challenges of specifying the Christian's perceptual relation to God therefore lay primarily in marking out the dogmatic constraints that configure God's availability to perception and championing the philosophical stories thought to best accommodate those constraints, not in resolving any pressing challenge confronting the idea that reality can directly inform and justify perceptual beliefs per se.[21] The aim was instead to distinguish correct ways of analyzing our de facto openness to God from mistaken ones.[22]

Press, 1994); Dominik Perler, ed., *Ancient and Medieval Theories of Intentionality* (Leiden: Brill, 2001); Simo Knuuttila and Pekka Kärkkäinen, eds., *Theories of Perception in Medieval and Early Modern Philosophy* (New York: Springer, 2008); H. Lagerlund, ed., *Representation and Objects of Thought in Medieval Philosophy* (Aldershot: Ashgate, 2007); and Robert Pasnau, *Theories of Cognition in the Later Middle Ages* (Cambridge: Cambridge University Press, 1997).

21. See, for example, Aquinas under the heading of "How God Is Known by Us" in *ST* 1a, q.12.

22. While there were always debates about the *mode* of God's perceptible self-presentation in Israel's theophanies and in the person of Jesus, no Christian theologian qua theologian disputed that God was indeed *somehow* perceptibly present—in some sense manifest or revealed. The question was just how so. As Paul Gavrilyuk and Sarah Coakley put it in their introduction to *The Spiritual Senses: Perceiving God in Western Christianity* (Cambridge: Cambridge University Press, 2012), "Theories of divine self-communication tend to focus on the properties of divine action, rather than on the features of human knowers that make the reception of revelation and religious experience possible. Nevertheless, numerous thinkers throughout Christian history have attempted to probe the conditions of divine-human encounter further. In the process these

Platonic, Aristotelian, and Stoic philosophical traditions contributed most substantially to working out a theological understanding of our openness to God from late antiquity to the early modern period.[23] Theologians appropriated and innovated on the basis of these philosophical traditions to elaborate the nature of perceptible reality entailed by a properly theological conception of God's relation to the world.[24] In the same way, the various philosophical anthropologies by which these philosophical schools accounted for our openness to the world also heavily informed premodern theological analyses of the structure of the human person by virtue of which we are capable of being sensitized to and directed upon divine or spiritual realities.[25] Finally, their various conceptions of the virtues contributed centrally to competing frameworks of moral knowledge and of the form of responsiveness to reality involved in the spiritual transformation of the self.[26] But again, while such philosophical disagreements no less than dogmatic ones led to (sometimes radically) different theological construals of the *mode* of the Christian's openness to God in the patristic and medieval periods, a fundamentally naive realist conception of openness itself was never problematized in any serious or pressing way in premodern

thinkers have come up with various approaches, some of which could be subsumed under the general idea of spiritual perception" (2).

23. See A. N. Williams, *The Divine Sense: The Intellect in Patristic Theology* (New York: Cambridge University Press: 2007); and Pierre Hadot, *What Is Ancient Philosophy?*, trans. Michael Chase (Cambridge, MA: Harvard University Press, 2002), 237–52.

24. For example, the nature of the created world's participation in God could receive different analyses depending on the philosophical commitments through which they are inflected.

25. As the contributors to the Gavrilyuk and Coakley volume *The Spiritual Senses* demonstrate, much of the debate about human capacities of spiritual sensation or perception has to do with the proper way to relate the intellectual apprehension of God to the five bodily senses, and the question of whether our perception of God involves any necessary distinction between faculties of "inner" and "outer" sense. See Gavrilyuk and Coakley, *Spiritual Senses*, 12–19.

26. See Hadot, *What Is Ancient Philosophy*, 237–52; Hadot and Michael Chase, *Philosophy as a Way of Life* (Oxford: Wiley-Blackwell, 2002); and cf. Stanley Hauerwas and Charles Pinches, *Christians among the Virtues: Theological Conversations with Ancient and Modern Ethics* (Notre Dame, IN: University of Notre Dame Press, 1997).

philosophy and theology.[27] Rather than being rooted in any philosophical disagreements about naive realism, the differences and disputes about how to properly construe the mode of our perceptual openness to God during this period were rooted in three difficult problem areas of theological description.

First, there are difficulties in describing God's side of the perceptual relation, in saying what we take ourselves to be aware of when we are aware of God. A central question is how to properly characterize God's immanence to us in the created order given our conception of God as transcendent. This is a question about what features of God can actually present themselves to us or phenomenally appear to creatures constituted like we are. An ontological gap between God and creatures was often thought to generate puzzles about what of God is actually manifest to us in the various ways that God reaches out to us in Christ by the Spirit, puzzles related to what God-talk is properly about.[28] Christians take it that God's ways of reaching out to us in Christ by the Spirit have been extended to us from beyond the created order.[29] While taking for granted that, when all goes well, the phenomenal content of God's manifestations to us does in fact refer us to God, we can wonder whether God's ways of being manifest to us could ever include the manifestation of divine transcendence to us. How can God, who alone exists uncreated and in absolute transcendence of everything created, ever appear to us under that

27. This is only to say that the competing theories of intentionality for the most part presumed that we are open to the world—there could have been some who challenged that view, but there was no widely shared or pressing reason to put the "default" view on the defensive.

28. That is, what are the features of God that can become manifest to human creatures? This question lies behind theological debates about the eschatological vision of God and its continuity or discontinuity of God's availability to perception now as compared with the eschaton. See Vladimir Lossky, *The Vision of God* (Crestwood, NY: St. Vladimir's Seminary Press, 1983); A. N. Williams, *The Ground of Union* (New York: Oxford University Press, 1997).

29. For a useful conceptual analysis of the uniqueness of Christianity as consisting in its particular unpacking of God's bearing on the world as that of the uncreated upon creation, see Robert Sokolowski, *The God of Faith and Reason* (Washington, DC: Catholic University of America Press, 1995).

particular mode of presentation, given that we belong essentially to the created order? If we can only be perceptually directed on God in ways that fail to disclose divine transcendence of creation, then in what sense do we take it that God's transcendence has been (or can be or will be) disclosed or revealed to us?

The question of what properties of divine presence and action we can and cannot possibly perceive of God and the further question of whether and how the phenomenal content that we *can* perceive succeeds in disclosing to us the fact of God's transcendence are heavily thematized problems among writers of the so-called Christian mystical tradition.[30] But this problem was never conceived as an inducement to give up the implicit assumption that God in God's immanence (however construed) is perceptibly present to Christians and that we in turn are open to God's immanence in the naive realist sense specified above. Rather, the problem was conceived to be whether, in addition to or by way of our presumed openness to God's immanence to the created order, we are also in any sense open to God's transcendence of it. So the problem was not so much whether we ought to regard God as in some sense transcending creation (God does) or in some sense immanent to it and therefore to us (God is), but whether and how we can properly affirm the perceptual availability of God's transcendence *in* immanence.[31]

---

30. There is a debate here about whether to construe the Christian mystical tradition as properly oriented toward the cultivation of any particular sort of perceptual experiences, and consequently whether it is properly seen in terms of the structure of any such experiences. In *The Darkness of God: Negativity in Christian Mysticism* (Cambridge: Cambridge University Press, 1995), Denys Turner argues that "in so far as the word 'mysticism' has a contemporary meaning; and that in so far as that contemporary meaning links 'mysticism' to the cultivation of certain kinds of experience . . . then the mediaeval 'mystic' offers an *anti-mysticism*" (4). Bernard McGinn, on the other hand, claims in *The Foundations of Mysticism* (New York: Crossroad, 1999) that mysticism involves "the immediate consciousness of the presence of God" and the attempt to express its inner structure (xix). But this is not a debate about whether the tradition in question is constituted by the question of the availability of God's transcendence within immanence, it is only a debate about whether "mystics" have offered a negative reply (Turner) or an affirmative one (McGinn).

A second and related problem area addresses a difficulty of theological intentionality from a different angle, from our side of the perceptual relation rather than God's. This is to raise a question not about the content of our perception but its mode: what it would be like for whatever we take God to be to become perceptible by physical creatures configured as we are. In the first place, we ordinarily recognize that my seeing my computer screen and my "seeing" God are different because the former involves a distinctively sensory way of being directed on a material object,[32] whereas we take it that God is not a material object and as such does not have intrinsically sensible qualities in anything like the same way if at all. What phenomenal character, then, belongs distinctively to the manifestation of God to us? Further, what sorts of perceptual capacities can we be thought to possess that are receptive to those modes of presentation? Clearly, this question cannot be answered independently of the first matter above—different conceptions of the God-world relation will place different demands on our theological anthropology.

For example, in the illustrations at the head of this chapter about observation reports we make about our perception of God, we often take ourselves to perceive God as present or active *in* material features of the world that we take to be perceptible in an ordinary sensory

---

31. That is, given the ontological "gap" between God and creatures—the *diastema*, as Gregory of Nyssa calls it in his controversy with Eunomius—how can any creaturely form of thinking take in those features of God in virtue of which God transcends creation? As Scot Douglass summarizes Gregory's version of the question in "A Critical Analysis of Gregory's Philosophy of Language" in *Gregory of Nyssa, Homilies on the Beatitudes: An English Version with Commentary and Supporting Studies*, ed. Hubertus R. Drobner and Alberto Viciano (Leiden: Brill, 2000) "More simply put, on what 'ground' can a creature speak from within a *diastemic episteme* about a transcendent creator?" (449). This is arguably the same question that the Pseudo-Denys was attempting to answer in his corpus.

32. It is important to recognize, however, the wider sense of the "material" prior to the physical sciences. Most notably, "material" was taken to be entirely compatible with its being intrinsically formed or informative. The question was only whether to think of matter's form in holistic or aggregative terms. See Annas, *Hellenistic Philosophy of Mind*, 202–11.

way. I hear God's address *in* the auditory experience of hearing my pastor give a homily. Whatever sense we manage to make of material creation's being able to bear divine presence and action will place corresponding limits on the role that human sense perception plays in our experiences of God.[33] Origen of Alexandria is well-known in part for having held a strict metaphysical dualism of spirit and matter and thus a sharp division between our spiritual capacities to perceive God and our bodily sensory capacities as analogously parallel faculties of intentionality belonging to our natural constitution.[34] This began an entire trajectory of reflection extending outward from the second century in theological anthropology focused on the notion of the "spiritual senses."[35]

Finally, a third worry characteristic of patristic and medieval accounts of the Christian's perceptual relation to God concerns nature and grace. The central problematic in relating nature to grace is that of specifying what role our natural constitution as part of the created order plays in making possible the movement toward God involved in our redemption in Christ and our final beatitude. In what respects, if any, are we intrinsically or "naturally" ordered to receiving those gifts and moving toward our final beatitude? In what respect, if any, must God act on the perceptual capacities belonging to our created natures in order for us to become either potentially or actually directed upon God in the manner requisite to our redemption?[36]

33. See Mariette Canévet, "Sens Spirituel," *Dictionnaire de spiritualité ascétique et mystique doctrine et histoire*, vol. 15, ed. Marcel Viller, assisted by F. Cavallera, J. de Guibert, et al. (Paris: Beauchesne, 1993): 14–41, 15 (598–617).

34. As Canévet puts it, "Origène penche pour une discontinuité entre les deux modes" (ibid., 604). It remains debated whether this reception history of Origen's philosophical anthropology is just. For a nuanced treatment, see Mark McInroy, "Origen of Alexandria," in Gavrilyuk and Coakley, *Spiritual Senses*, 20–35.

35. See Karl Rahner's influential article "Le debut d'une doctrine des cinq sens spirituels chez Origene," *Revue d'ascetique et de mystique* 13 (1932): 112–45.

36. For example, is it necessary for us to acquire, *ad extra*, a capacity to contemplate God by way of a union with God's essence that imparts the "light of glory" to see God in terms of the divine self-understanding, as St. Thomas seems to have thought (as expressed in, e.g., *ST* 1a,

Included in these questions about how our natural constitution as perceivers is related to God's enabling grace is the question of the extent to which the desiring dispositions of our agency and the believing dispositions of our intellects are "naturally" inclined toward God. Does God's reaching out to us in Christ serve primarily to remove the problem of sin as an impediment to our intrinsic and natural directedness on God, or does it create in us, *ad extra* and *de novo*, a supernatural capacity to perceptually receive and respond to God over and above anything our natural constitution could possibly make available to us, even when bracketing the problem of sin?[37]

Obviously, these three matters were and continue to be theologically adjudicated in various ways. But in trying to figure out how to properly construe the structure of theological intentionality—the form of perception by which Christians become directed on and responsive to God in the world—one can observe in the tradition an overarching strategy of analyzing our experiences of God on the presumption of a naive realist construal of ordinary intentionality. That is, the unchallenged presumption underlying all three issues as characterized above is that the way the world is lies (potentially, at least) open to our view—it is by nature the home of meaning, and our capacities of perception name the subjective configuration in virtue of which its meaning immediately and transparently impresses itself on our thinking. One courted

q. 12.4)? Or, does our contemplation on God in the beatific vision simply perfect our mutable and creaturely understanding of God by its infinite "stretching out" toward God, as Gregory of Nyssa seems to have thought (as expressed in, e.g., "On Perfection")?

37. Henri de Lubac champions the former sort of view in his *Surnaturel: Etudes Historiques* (Paris: Aubier, 1946) against what he takes to be the modern encroachment of the latter through Cajetan's reading of St. Thomas on "natural desire" in the sixteenth century. Controversy over the question still rages, as most recently evidenced in John Milbank's vitriolic engagement with Lawrence Feingold in *Nova et Vetera* 6 (2008) over Feingold's defense of Cajetan's views in *The Natural Desire to See God according to St. Thomas Aquinas and His Interpreters* (Rome: Apollinare Studi, 2001). For a good overview of the issues, see Nicholas Healey, "Henri de Lubac on Nature and Grace: A Note on Some Recent Contributions to the Debate," *Communio* 35 (Winter 2008): 535–64.

philosophical controversy only in specifying what sort of meaning resides in it and what about us enables our receptivity to it in perceptual experience. A Christian commitment to revelation courts philosophical controversy not because of a commitment to our perceptual openness to the world as the home of objective rational demands with which we can be properly configured to resonate, but because of the particularly theological specification of those demands and the sorts of human capacities required to detect and respond to them.

2.4 The Problem of Perception

But the three theological problematics just canvassed underwent a fundamental shift in orientation by the time of the early modern period.[38] A distinctive form of skepticism emerged as a direct challenge to the naive realism implicit in the idea of perceptual openness sketched above. The very idea that the world can rationally impress its meaning on us and serve as a tribunal for the correctness of what we say and do came to seem implausible. Certainly, ancient and medieval theologians and philosophers raised the question of intentionality and addressed themselves to difficulties presented by the possibility of being misled (such as by illusion or hallucination).[39]

---

38. The shift in question had its roots in the later medieval period, but it is not easy to locate. The nature of that shift will be investigated in chapter 7. An often-suggested candidate is the rise of Scotist and Ockhamist nominalism that presaged the development of a modern scientific outlook. See, for example, Brad Gregory's *The Unintended Reformation: How a Religious Revolution Secularized Society* (Cambridge, MA: Harvard University Press, 2012), especially ch. 1. But another possible candidate is the rise of a particular way of distinguishing between the vehicle and content in mental representation that we see in Henry of Ghent (1217–1293), which made it possible to conceive of the way things appear as accidents of the mind, rather than as necessarily dependent upon their objects. See Lambertus M. de Rijk, *Giraldus Odonis O.F.M.: Opera Philosophica, vol. 2: De intentionibus* (Leiden: Brill, 2005), 81–84.

39. In other words, in most ancient and medieval theories of perception, "the distinction between illusions or misperceptions" on the one hand and veridical perceptions on the other "was not meant to imply a basic gap between appearance and reality, although it led to discussions

However, they were relatively innocent of the idea that the world might not be a natural home for the kind of meaning we take to inform our ordinary experiences of it, an idea that had taken center stage in philosophy by the seventeenth century.[40] There were, to be sure, global forms of epistemological skepticism to the effect that we could not *know* anything about the world and should therefore refrain from believing anything about it (for instance, Pyrrhonian skepticism).[41] But the alleged difficulties for knowledge and belief were not on the whole taken to stem from any deeper problems about intentionality, any denial that our thoughts reached out to reality and thus succeeded in being about the world. By contrast, philosophical anxieties about whether we are entitled to think of ourselves as directly in touch with reality have become a pressing worry for moderns in a manner that was virtually nonexistent in late antiquity.[42]

A commonly cited source of these worries is the rise of the natural sciences, and with it a newly minted conception of the natural world as intelligible purely in terms of law-like principles indifferent to the meanings or values characteristic of human needs or interests.[43] Put crassly, once it appeared that the world is not most fundamentally constituted with an idea-like normative structure suited to our

of perceptual skepticism." Simon Knuuttila, "Aristotle's Theory of Perception and Medieval Aristotelianism," in Knuuttila and Kärkkäinen, *Theories of Perception*, 17.

40. Canonically, with Descartes. See René Descartes's *Meditations on First Philosophy*, ed. John Cottingham with intro. by Bernard Williams (Cambridge: Cambridge University Press, 1996).

41. See Richard Bett's introduction in *The Cambridge Companion to Ancient Skepticism*, ed. Richard Bett (Cambridge: Cambridge University Press, 2010), 1–10.

42. See Michael Williams, "Descartes' Transformation of the Sceptical Tradition," in Bett, *Cambridge Companion to Ancient Scepticism*, 288–313. This is not to say, however, that the anxieties about the mind/world relation that arose with Descartes were properly understood as stemming more deeply from questions about intentionality—quite often, the focus was instead on the epistemological consequences of those anxieties.

43. The threat of disenchantment was a straightforward corollary to the so-called mechanical philosophy that arose during the seventeenth century. See R. S. Westfall, *The Construction of Modern Science* (Cambridge: Cambridge University Press, 1977).

thinking but rather was brutely thing-like in nature, we confronted the difficulty of how our minds could accommodate the alien character of the world.[44] Given that alien character revealed by natural scientific understanding, how is openness in the naïve sense possible? The advancements of the sciences thus reinforced an emerging distinction between explaining the world of our everyday experience in terms of the purposive and value-rich frameworks of meaning characteristic of religion and explaining that world in terms of exceptionless and value-neutral laws adduced within carefully controlled experimental frameworks.

Max Weber famously described the modern colonization and cannibalization of the former sorts of explanation by the latter as having brought about a "disenchantment of the world."[45] The scientific rendering of the world as an intrinsically nonnormative domain of objects, events, and relations makes the world more susceptible of human calculation and mastery but also seemed to alienate human subjectivity from it, since our "minded" way of taking in the world seems to consist precisely in *projecting* normative properties onto the world's inert objects, events, and relations. In addition to the complex social and institutional impact wrought in the wake of that disenchantment, it served as the impetus for a peculiarly philosophical problematic that has come to set the agenda for the philosophy of mind at least since Descartes.[46]

---

44. See Akeel Bilgrami, "The Wider Significance of Naturalism: A Genealogical Essay," in *Naturalism and Normativity*, ed. Mario De Caro and David MacArthur (New York: Columbia University Press, 2010), 23–54.

45. Max Weber, "Science as a Vocation," in *From Max Weber: Essays in Sociology*, ed. and trans. H. H. Gerth and C. Wright Mills (London: Routledge, 1970), 128–58.

46. Thus, for example, Descartes's form of dualism was motivated by the need to "find a place for irreducible mental properties in a world that seems largely to be explainable as a mechanical system reducible to parts which themselves are exhaustively characterized in terms of their primary qualities." Kirk Ludwig, "The Mind-Body Problem: An Overview," in *The Blackwell Guide to Philosophy of Mind*, ed. S. Stich (Oxford: Wiley-Blackwell, 2003), 14.

The problem confronting philosophers after the scientific revolution, then, was how to reconcile a disenchanted conception of perceptual objects—no longer thought to be intrinsically meaningful constituents belonging to a coherent purposive and rational order—with the apparently normative and evaluative character of our subjective experiences that purport to be about the world. The content of the latter seems essentially to involve properties of meaning and value constituted by a normative framework of rational relations that informs what we think and do. But in what possible sense can normative features such as these be objective constituents of the world itself? If the world in itself is inert of the normative character essential to our empirical or observational thinking, how can such thinking be taken to be *informed* by the world or to *represent* it in any sense? How is "empirical content" possible, understood in the sense of reasons delivered to us by the world itself? And if we thus confront a problem of intentionality—if we cannot see how our mental lives give us any traction on the objective layout of the world—then we must also confront a corresponding epistemological problem: how could anything constitutive of our mental lives furnish us with content whose credentials secure knowledge of the world outside the mind?[47]

47. This is the problem of the mind as a "phenomenological box," which Descartes famously posed in the First Meditation with the thought experiment of an "evil demon" who so deceives our senses that what appears before the mind has no correspondence with the external world. See *Mediations*, 15ff. Whereas Descartes emphasizes the phenomenological box as a "knowledge" problem—one whose upshot was that we cannot have any certainty that the appearances we enjoy truly represent reality, contemporary philosophers recognize that this is more fundamentally a problem about intentionality—whether what we think is so much as "about" the extramental world at all, whatever the epistemic credentials of such thinking. See Putnam's reimagining of the Cartesian demon scenario as the possibility that we are simply brains in a vat of amino acids, kept alive by an evil scientist who stimulates our tissues in just the proper way to make it seem to us as if we were fully embodied persons inhabiting the world in the ordinary way. In such a case, it is not just that my belief that this sandwich is tasty is not true, it is that my experience is not "of" a sandwich at all. See Hilary Putnam's "Brains in a Vat," in *Reason, Truth and History* (Cambridge: Cambridge University Press, 1981), 1–21. In order to secure the intentional relation between mind and world, Putnam emphasized, the

This problem—reconciling a world not intrinsically constituted of normative properties and rational relations to the properties and activities of the mind that precisely *are* constituted by norms and rational relations—sets the agenda for the modern philosophy of mind. To resolve that problem would be to specify how perception enables the normative properties and relations of the mind to be constrained or guided by the norm-independent layout of reality. But the constitution of reality as alien from the rational character constituting thought makes it difficult to see how to bring about such a resolution. What seems to be needed is some account of how our perceptual capacities function as the site at which a nonnormatively constituted world and our norm-governed mental lives touch. To resolve the modern problem of perception is to give a philosophical explanation of how realities independent of the standards of correctness we deploy in our thought and language can figure as the content of our thought and language[48]—the nonnormative objects, properties, and relations to which our norms apply. Conversely, it is to explain how our thought and language can be properly understood as rational responses to the bearing of nonnormatively constituted realities on us.

Broadly speaking, philosophers have proposed two sorts of explanations to meet this challenge. Although both proposals will be analyzed in more detail later, we can get a sense for what they involve by imagining our minds as enclosed by a boundary. On the inside, our mental lives are the normative context of thought and

content of our thinking has to break out of the phenomenological box—we have to conclude that "meaning just ain't in the head." See "The Meaning of 'Meaning,'" in *Mind, Language and Reality* (Cambridge: Cambridge University Press, 1975), 215–71, 226.

48. The question of whether or how to distinguish the content of thought from the content of language is of course controversial. I do not take them together as an implicit identity claim about the relation of mental content to semantic content. Rather, I take them together insofar as both equally exemplify forms of mindedness whose content we want to construe as in some sense fixed by the way things are.

language in which our beliefs (and other propositional attitudes) are rationally connected with one another and purport to intend reality (that is, to direct us on it in various ways). Outside the boundary is the extramental reality that is not rationally ordered according to the normative character of our mindedness but stands independent of any such ordering. The challenge posed by the problem of perception is, on this image, the challenge of showing how the objects, properties, and relations that figure outside the boundary bear on those that figure inside it.

On one sort of explanation, the world is capable of affecting the mind at the site of the boundary that marks off mind from world. Reality makes itself available to perception insofar as we are capable of mentally *registering* those effects as mental objects or events. The concept of an "experience" is, on this approach, simply the concept of an impression that reality makes on the mind. We can recognize such impressions as mediating across the boundary precisely because of their hybrid character. On the one hand, such impressions are fundamentally constituted by the brute character of reality itself insofar as they give us a kind of mental content independent of the normative character of thought. On the other hand, this nonconceptual content that such impressions impose on us is a feature of our mental lives, and, as such it can ground our rational and normative framework of beliefs. Impressions thus form the boundary between our norm-governed mind and the non-normatively structured world.

We can therefore appeal to these boundary impressions as fundamental sources of information that tether us to the world. The idea of a mentalistic object or event that grounds perception implies a foundationalism about intentionality in which our observational beliefs can be thought to have empirical content (that is, to direct us on the world) just to the extent that they can be traced back to a boundary impression. This foundationalism about intentionality, moreover, gives rise to a corresponding foundationalism about empirical knowledge. If any of our observational beliefs are informed by a boundary impression in the right way (however that is to be properly understood), then that belief has the credentials to count as an instance of empirical knowledge. While the appeal to boundary impressions is the classically empiricist way to resolve the problem of perception, such as we find in Locke and Hume, there are also contemporary versions.[49]

But one need not appeal to any hybrid mentalistic entities such as boundary impressions as the way in which the normative framework internal to the mind mediates external realty to us. A second and more recently developed proposal is that the layout of reality can determine the content of our beliefs apart from any such mentalistic objects or events. In other words, we cannot have any mental access to anything other than our normative framework of beliefs itself and the social-practical contexts in which they occur. Characteristically human ways of perceiving and responding to reality do not require anything other than the normative forms of meaning-making erected by our social practices of belief formation and embodied habituation. The whole idea that the world external to the boundary furnishes us with basic warrants for what we think and do imposed on us from outside our established conventions is a myth.

---

49. Classically, the notion is worked in terms of "sense data" or some mental image that stands between perceiver and perceived, as found in, e.g., John Locke, *An Essay Concerning Human Understanding*, ed. Peter Nidditch (1689; Oxford: Clarendon, 1975); or David Hume, *A Treatise of Human Nature*, ed. L. A. Selby-Bigge, 2nd ed. rev. P. H. Nidditch (1739; Oxford: Clarendon, 1975). For a contemporary version of a sense-datum theory, see José Luis Bermúdez, "Naturalized Sense Data," *Philosophy and Phenomenological Research* 61 (2000): 353–74. But there are also direct realist versions, in which the boundary event does not consist in the creation of a mental object as a *tertium* that represents mind-independent reality, but rather consists in the immediate presentation of reality itself as having various sensible qualities in principle independent of our frameworks of belief. See, for example, Fred Dretske's *Seeing and Knowing* (Chicago: University of Chicago Press, 1969).

Rather, as long as our beliefs and practices are *caused* in the right way by extramental realities, those realities needn't impose any kind of special mental content upon us. The context of social practices in which we form observational beliefs only makes sense on the presumption that such practices are in some sense responses to reality external to the boundary. But while such responses may be causally determined by a reality external to our established concepts, we can never "get outside of our own skin" to observe that determination independently of the normative contexts in which they are embedded. Our only way of being informed by the influence of extramental reality is by way of its effects on us and our responses to those effects, i.e., the social practices themselves. The epistemological implication is that any credentials our perceptual beliefs can have will depend on their capacity to satisfy the intersubjective standards of correctness given by our social practices.

One influential way in which each of these strategies has found contemporary expression has been via a longstanding debate about how best to understand Kant's distinction between "noumena" and "phenomena." What is often characterized as a debate between a "one-world" and a "two-world" reading of the relationship Kant posits between the noumenal and the phenomenal realms can be seen as a debate between reading Kant in terms of a "boundary-impression" theory and reading him in terms of a "social-practical" theory of empirical content.[50] To see how such a characterization would go, take the noumenal realm to be roughly equivalent to the way the world is prior to or independently of what we make of it by way of our normative conceptual thinking. Take the phenomenal realm to be roughly equivalent to the way that the noumenal world appears after it has been subjected to or subsumed under our

---

50. K. Ameriks, "Recent Work on Kant's Theoretical Philosophy," *American Philosophical Quarterly* 19 (1982): 1–24.

normative concepts—its presentation to our sensory capacities as a fundamentally intelligible order. On a one-world reading, the noumenal and phenomenal realms are connected by our capacity to mentally represent or internalize the impact of the noumenal world on us by way of our perceptual capacities. The bearing of the noumenal world on our sensibility as an undivided flood or "manifold" of sensation undergoes a "synthesis" with the "pure concepts of the understanding" such that it always appears to us under the normative structure imposed by our conceptual frameworks.[51] So on a one-world view, empirical content just *is* noumenal reality under a phenomenal mode of presentation.

On a two-world reading, the phenomenal and noumenal are not two ways of thinking about the same world as it figures into empirical content—as nonconceptualized (presyntehsized) rather than conceptualized (postsynthesized) content. Rather, the noumenal and the phenomenal name two fundamentally different and radically divided *domains*—two distinct worlds sharing no objects, properties, or relations with one another. The familiar world of objects, properties, and relations that constitutes the whole of our experience of reality is the phenomenal world. But while the only objects, properties, and relations available to us are phenomenal objects, properties, and relations, we cannot make sense of our perception of phenomena without positing their dependence on another domain—a noumenal world whose contents are never present to us or represented to us in experience. The phenomenal thus cannot be merely one mode of presenting us with the noumenal (that is, the one determined by a particularly human form of sensibility ordered by normative concepts). Rather, the noumenal realm forms the condition for the possibility of the synthesis of phenomenal content

51. See Immanuel Kant, *Critique of Pure Reason*, trans. Norman Kemp Smith with intro. by Howard Caygill (New York: Palgrave-MacMillan, 2003), A491/B519–A494/B522.

from sensory content and our normative concepts. The unspecified and essentially *unspecifiable* noumenal world thus bears a purely *transcendental* relation to the phenomenal realm, and as such it never comes into view for us *as* a phenomenon.

One way to construe a one-world reading is to regard the nonconceptual manifold and its synthesis with the pure concepts of understanding as specifying the relationship between a preconceptualized boundary impression and its foundational role in informing our beliefs.[52] Similarly, one way of construing a two-world reading is to identify the synthesizing of the manifold with the transcendental relation between the phenomenal and noumenal domains. If the bearing of the manifold on sensibility represents the transcendental condition for the possibility of the synthesis that gives rise to the phenomenal world, then the act of applying concepts to the manifold can never be represented within consciousness. All that ever shows up in the phenomenal domain of our beliefs is the phenomenal synthesis, the union of sensibility with the normative categories of understanding. The synthesis by which an essentially unspecifiable manifold is subsumed under the categories of the understanding thus names a process which is not itself phenomenal but noumenal, not any kind of mental content available for our introspection but a transcendental condition for the possibility of having phenomenal experiences in the first place. A nonconceptual, brute or uinterpreted "sensation" can thus only be a theoretical posit.

52. On this reading, the reception of an impression has different epistemological implications than that of classical empiricism, insofar as one can never appeal directly to the representations given in the manifold itself to justify a perceptual belief, but only to the way in which some bit of the manifold has been synthesized in a normative concept. Still, what is given in one's reception of a manifold is a nonconceptually cognized representation of reailty. We find a version of this one-world picture in Husserl's notion of "hyletic data" as the content of thought that directs us on reality when it is "adequated" by a corresponding concept. See Edmund Husserl, *Logical Investigations*, trans. J. N. Findlay (New York: Humanities, 1970); and Walter Hopp, "Husserl on Sensation, Perception, and Interpretation," *Canadian Journal of Philosophy* 38, no. 2 (2008): 219–46.

It follows from the assumption that the bearing of extramental (noumenal) reality on us is always already embedded in what actually shows up in our mental lives, which is never bare perceptual (phenomenal) content but only our perceptual (phenomenal) beliefs and practices.[53]

2.5 Theologies of Religious Experience: Cataphatic and Apophatic

Whereas Christian philosophers and theologians prior to the modern era could problematize the perceptual relation to God on the presumption of our openness to the world, the problem of perception confronts us with a new obstacle. The three particular problems of theological description canvassed above thus seem to confront us with a logically prior and perfectly general problem. For clearly, any difficulty about the very possibility of perceptually taking in the way things are as a normative affair is logically prior to difficulties about the particular norms that govern how we perceptually take in some specific aspect of the way things are. We therefore take ourselves nowadays to be obligated to specify some resolution to the problem of perception and then to appropriate it in our analysis of the content of revelation and the capacities operative in our reception of it.

---

53. For a close reading of Kant along these lines, see Wilfrid Sellars, *Science and Metaphysics: Variations on Kantian Themes* (New York: Humanities, 1968); and Sellars, *Kant's Transcendental Metaphysics: Sellars' Cassirer Lecture Notes and Other Essays*, ed. Jeffrey F. Sicha (Atascadero, CA: Ridgeview , 2002). There are also deep affinities between Sellars's version of the two-world picture and the pictures of intentionality we find in W. V. O. Quine in, e.g., "On What There Is," *Review of Metaphysics* 2 (1948): 21–38; and Donald Davidson in, e.g., "Mental Events," in *Experience and Theory*, ed. Lawrence Foster and J. W. Swanson (London: Duckworth, 1970), 79–102. They have in common a conception of the content of perception as furnished by the world in a nonmentalistic way, external to the perceiver's direct conscious awareness. Quine appeared to waver on whether the world's presentation to us in experience could be thought of as delivering any sort of cognitive content, but Davidson was probably right to see Quine's talk of "stimulus meaning" as a lapse in his otherwise externalist inclinations. See Davidson, "Quine's Externalism," *Grazer Philosophische Studien* 66, no. 1 (2003): 281–97.

More particularly, we seem obligated to modulate our theological account of what "of" God is made available to us in perception according to either a "boundary-impression" or a "social-practical" conception of what it is for anything at all to be available to perception. If, for example, the content of an experience is a nonconceptual "impression" whose qualitative character registers the impact of God on our thinking independent of our established normative frameworks, then we must specify how something like "God," as Christians understand the divine, is capable of making an impact of that sort. If, on the other hand, the content of an experience is embedded in the normative contexts of our social practices, then we must specify how the content of revelation is fixed within the normative context of Christian belief and practice. Whatever particular theological constraints we might entertain about what "of" God is manifest in the world, our capacities to become directed on God will have to be inflected according to a prior theoretical commitment aimed at resolving the problem of perception.

A theological approach of this kind may appear to imply that we regard the perception of God as merely one particular instantiation of the more general structure of "ordinary perception" established by our preferred philosophical theory. On this reading, the structure of our perceptual relation to God is given by straightforwardly slotting God (under some suitable theological construal) into the object pole of the intentional relation of subject to object specified by that theory. So however much we acknowledge that God is not an ordinary object of perception, we must nevertheless account for our perceptual directedness upon an extraordinary God in the ordinary way—that is, in a manner that complies fully with our general theory of the intentionality of perceptual experience.

But acknowledging that a theology of revelation or religious experience supervenes on the problem of perception does not require that we assume the experience of God is always a straightforward instance of ordinary perception as given by our preferred theory.[54] It might also (or instead) be possible to regard the structure of intentionality involved in our ordinary perception of everyday objects as insufficient to account for our experiences of God (and perhaps insufficient as well for some particular features of the world). If so, we could reason from the theological claim that a Christian conception of God is not that of an ordinary object of perception to the claim that experiences of God require positing a fundamentally different mode of intentionality, an extraordinary form of perception. The structure of intentionality in the properly theological case could thus be construed as differing from every other form of perception qua ordinary perception insofar as it is uniquely suited to the extraordinary character of God (however construed).

Still, on accounts of this sort, how shall we mark the difference between the intentionality belonging to ordinary perception and the extraordinary intentionality belonging to the perception of God? The difference will be marked precisely by the way in which God's self-presentation to us allegedly *disrupts* ordinary intentionality as we theorize it, in some sense reconfiguring its structure. In that sense, some prior theoretical commitment about the intentionality of ordinary perception remains fundamental to the analysis whether one accounts theologically for our perceptual relation to God as a straightforward instantiation of a boundary-impression or social-practical theory of ordinary perception or as some sort of radical difference between, for instance, an ordinary boundary impression and a divine boundary impression.[55]

---

54. The idea that God could be an object of perception in the same way that created beings form objects of our perception is the hallmark of ontotheology, which, its detractors suggest, is tantamount to reducing God to the level of a creature. See Merold Westphal, *Overcoming Ontotheology: Toward a Postmodern Christian Faith* (New York: Fordham University Press, 2001).

These observations allow us to abstract two basic elements that figure into both standard perception and nonstandard perception accounts of the Christian experience of God: such accounts are comprised of, first, a constructive philosophical account addressed to the problem of perception and, second, the deployment of that philosophical account within a set of theological problems about the intentionality of our experiences of God and God's relation to the world. This accordingly gives us two axes along which to classify a theological account of our perceptual relation to God. The first axis involves the question of which kind of philosophical theory best addresses modern problems about intentionality: those that bottom out in some conception of the boundary impression or those that deny any such conception and bottom out instead in some conception of social practice? The second axis involves the question of which kind of theological appropriation of such theories is best suited to a theological account of our perceptual relation to God: a standard-perception account in which the structure of our ordinary experience can accommodate our experience of God, or a nonstandard-perception account in which God somehow uniquely disrupts that structure?

The difference between the two accounts gives us broad constraints in theorizing the perceptual availability of anything, including God, to anyone, including Christians. The difference between standard and nonstandard appropriations of those theories gives us, respectively, a more cataphatic or a more apophatic account of God's availability to Christians. Some illustrations in the recent literature will prove helpful to elucidate the currently available options.

---

55. And, mutatis mutandis, on the assumption of a social-practical account of ordinary experience: it would be a matter of stressing some radical discontinuity between the way our "ordinary" social-practical norms embed our extramental relation to the world and the way our "theological" norms embed our extramental relation to God in the world.

Along the cataphatic/apophatic axis, I take William P. Alston's magisterial *Perceiving God* and Kevin Hector's more recent *Theology without Metaphysics* to exemplify the former pole.[56] Both regard our perceptual relation to God as capable of being accommodated by the same structure of intentionality exhibited in ordinary experience. While God is very different from a doorknob or a dandelion, all exhibit the same basic structure of intentionality. Whatever is minimally required for a dandelion to appear to us and whatever is minimally required for our experience to be properly about that dandelion are also minimally required for God to appear to us and for that experience to direct us on God.[57] In taking this line, Alston and Hector are both highly critical of a central feature of what I have characterized as apophatic theology—namely, that our experience of God's presence or agency requires us to radically disrupt or negate our ordinary observational thinking, to fundamentally reconfigure our analysis of the structure of intentionality to see how God's presentation to us makes possible a directedness on God in thought, word, and deed. Thus, Alston and Hector accordingly think that ordinary experience can accommodate God without in any way requiring a special or sui generis understanding of "experience" per se or the form of God-talk that arises from it.[58]

---

56. William P. Alston, *Perceiving God: The Epistemology of Religious Experience* (Ithaca: Cornell University Press, 1991); Kevin Hector, *Theology without Metaphysics: God, Language and the Spirit of Recognition* (Cambridge: Cambridge University Press, 2011).

57. Denys Turner characterizes cataphatic theology as "the Christian mind deploying all the resources of language in the effort to express something about God" (*Darkness of God*, 20). I am suggesting that logically prior to the deployment of our linguistic competences to speak about God is our receptivity to the content that our language succeeds in being "about."

58. Thus, for example, Alston rejects Garrigou-Lagrange's arguments that the transcendent characteristics of the divine essence coupled with the doctrine of divine simplicity (i.e., that God's existence is identical with the divine essence) implies any special conceptual difficulty for our capacities for the direct perceptual experience of God (see *Perceiving God*, 59–63). He further denies that we need a special theory of God-talk in order to accommodate the meaningfulness of theological language over against ordinary discourse. See, e.g., Alston, "Aquinas on Theological Predication: A Look Backward and a Look Forward," in *Reasoned Faith*, ed. Eleonore Stump (Ithaca, NY: Cornell University Press, 1993), 145–78. A primary aim

However, the accounts offered by Alston and Hector differ fundamentally from one another in how we are to understand the structure of intentionality involved in ordinary experience and its proper relation to thought, language, and action. They offer correspondingly different philosophical frameworks specifying *why* the nonstandard-perception accounts of apophatic theologians are inadequate or unnecessary to account for our perceptual relation to God. On Alston's "Theory of Appearing," God's presence or agency must be represented as a nonconceptual mental impression that is in principle independent of the normative context of our "doxastic" (that is, belief-forming) practices.[59] Hector, on the other hand, denies this and argues that presences are not to be construed as mental impressions but as embedded in social practices. On his view, our perceptual experiences of God are to be analyzed in terms of the norms governing our observations and intersubjective practices of holding one another accountable. Such normative practices are tethered to reality not by means of mental impressions but by being reliably indexed to our differential patterns of environmental stimulus and response.[60]

of Hector's *Theology without Metaphysics* is to avoid the ontotheological impulse to "cut God down to size" by way of creaturely concepts, but without resorting to the mode of resistance taken up in "apophatic anti-metaphysics." If, he says, "we understand God on the basis of God's being-with-us, the semantics of ordinary language on the basis of recognitive practices, and the Spirit of Christ as entering into, and mediated through, these same practices, we can arrive at an account according to which one's disavowal of metaphysics does not entail that God stands at a distance from one's language about God" (45).

59. This is not to say that Alston denies that such impressions must be "concept-laden" in order to play the informative and justificatory roles involved in our intentionality; rather, the content that does the informing and justifying is the nonconceptual element in its conceptualized form. "Normal perceptual experience is shot through with 'interpretation.' Nevertheless, what makes this a matter of perceiving [e.g.,] the house, rather than just thinking about it, is the fact of *presentation, givenness*, the fact that something is presented to consciousness of which I am *directly aware*. And this is something that is distinguishable from any elements of conceptualization, judgment, belief, or other 'interpretation,' however rarely the former may be found without the latter in adult experience" (*Perceiving God*, 27).

60. Hector describes the embedding of the world's direct impact on us within our normative practices in terms of our differential patterns of stimulus and response. When such patterns

Turning to nonstandard accounts, we might consider the apophatic approaches of Jean-Luc Marion (particularly well summarized in *In Excess*) and Victor Preller (in *Divine Science and the Science of God*). Each develops a (quite different) theory of the structure of intentionality involved in our ordinary experiences and argues that that structure breaks down in the paradigmatic form of our encounter with God. Unlike Alston and Hector, Marion and Preller both think that our directedness on God requires a sui generis approach in which the perception of God overturns the structure of ordinary perception.[61] But Marion and Preller specify the nature of the breakdown of ordinary perception characteristic of our perception of God according to categorically different understandings of "ordinary perception." Since Marion construes

are aimed at the satisfaction of desire and responsive not only to the environment but also to one's own desire-satisfaction along with others, it can result in the recognition of reliabilities among stimulus-response patterns, and out of that recognition comes the institution of norms. See Hector, *Theology without Metaphysics*, 70–72, 186–89.

61. That is, because of a Christian conception of divine transcendence, both Marion and Preller see the very possibility of being perceptually directed on God as posing a special difficulty. Marion describes the difficulty in terms of Anselm's dictum that God is "that greater than which nothing can be conceived." See *In Excess: Studies of Saturated Phenomena*, trans. Robyn Horner and Vincent Berraud (New York: Fordham University Press, 2004), 150–52. By incorporating inconceivability into a formal definition of God, this dictum entails a criterion of ignorance, i.e., that "our definitive ignorance of God is the condition for God remaining God" (155). As a formal definition, it serves a regulative function that operates on any and every substantive thought we might have about God. For any substantive conception of "God" we entertain, a God greater than that conception is always conceivable, thereby disqualifying that conception from truly being about God. But any appropriate revision will simply result in another conception for which a still greater conception of God is conceivable, and so on, ad infinitum. Each and every conceptualization we attempt will thus always and necessarily name something lesser than, and therefore other than, God.Preller similarly takes us to face a "referential problem" with respect to the capacity of our thinking to be "about" God. "To have a significant concept of an object," Preller says, "is to possess an *intention* of that object. When a significant concept is used to *refer*, the user is said to *intend* the object to which the concept refers. In order to refer to God, it would seem that we must be able to intend him—to have him 'in mind.' To have something 'in mind' however, is to have some notion of *what it is*. God, says Aquinas, is that 'being' concerning which we cannot know what he is or how he exists. It is not clear, then, that we can intend him or (intelligibly) intend to refer to him." Victor Preller, *Divine Science and the Science of God: A Reformulation of Thomas Aquinas* (Princeton, NJ: Princeton University Press, 1967), 5.

ordinary perception in a kind of one-world Kantianism,[62] its disruption by our experiences of God (which he calls a "counterexperience") has to be understood as a particular way of overturning that one-world picture. Preller, on the other hand, analyzes ordinary perception according to a kind of two-world Kantianism pioneered by Wilfrid Sellars in order to identify the sense in which the ordinary structure of perceptual intentionality fails to accommodate an analysis of our perceptual relation to God. While Marion and Preller both understand the perception of God as a distinctive failure of ordinary perception, their differences about what counts as the right sort of failure are traceable to prior differences about what counts as success.

On Marion's view, the intentional act of synthesizing the manifold of intuition succeeds when the phenomenal content (that is, the content of phenomena considered prior to or apart from the application of concepts to it) is "adequated" by a concept. The ordinary process of "phenomenalizing" an intuition, such that it shows up to consciousness, involves laying down the conceptual conditions, criteria, or rules according to which it can appear to us. But this process can break down in certain forms of experience in which concepts are unable to "master" the onrush of intuition and are instead submerged in its tide. Experiences of God, he thinks, are instances in which such an excess of phenomenal impressions

62. A "phenomenon," Marion says, "ceases to refer, like a symptom, only to its subject . . . and instead gives access to a thing placed facing it (possibly an object), because some intuition in general (sensible or not, the question remains open), one actually given, finds itself assumed, framed and controlled by a concept, playing the role of a category. On these two conditions, the representation is modeled after its objective . . . such that the representation becomes the direct presentation of its objective, its appearance passes through to this object and becomes its apparition. Intuition can then become objectively intentional (like an apparition, no longer a mere appearance) in and through the concept that actively fixes it." Jean-Luc Marion, "The Banality of Saturation," in *Counter-Experiences*, ed. Kevin Hart (Notre Dame, IN: University of Notre Dame Press, 2007), 384. The idea is that while intuition, as the content of experience, is external to our concepts, it remains internal to our minds as a "representational" entity, just one which we cannot bring to conscious awareness *as an object* apart from our concepts.

are at a maximum.[63] For Preller, however, perceptual experiences are not receptive to extramental reality in any mentalistic way, but in terms of a particular sort of causal relationship between reality and the normative context of our concept and language use. But, in the present life, we lack the causal relationship to God to provide the stimulus-response patterns in which our theological thought and language would need to be embedded in order to have content.[64] So instead of coming about in the ordinary way, we have our theological concepts by the "infusion of faith," by God supplying us with a conceptual framework *apart* from its stimulus-response relationship to God as its content.

These differences in theory choice with respect to the structure of ordinary perception result in correspondingly different accounts of its disruption as well as its reconfiguration of our directedness on God and the sort of "negativity" implied for the semantics of our God-talk. For Marion, God escapes capture by any normative framework of concepts because of our reception of mental content that exceeds concepts. For Preller, God escapes capture because we possess divine concepts without the properly habituated mind-external relation to their content, such that what we lack is not mental phenomena but a proper nonmentalistic causal ordering of reality.[65]

---

63. If our concepts function as a kind of delimiting valve on the mental content furnished by reality, and if those delimiters are, on the Kantian schema, according to quality, quantity, relation and modality, then "Revelation" consists in the full exposure of our subjectivity to Reality or Being, which is God. Such an exposure not only fulfills those conceptual containers but floods them. Our inability to conceptually master that which is given to us, due to its exhausting and exceeding every possible conceptual interpretation, constitutes us as witnesses to Revelation. See Marion, *In Excess*, 112–13.

64. Preller, *Divine Science*, 192–93.

65. "In sheer response to the stimuli of our social environment—like little behavioristic machines—we learn to make the sound of 'red' at certain times and to avoid it at others . . . but we *do not* know what 'red' means until we understand the rules which govern the use of 'red' and learn consciously to obey those rules. . . . We are able to reflect upon the material moves of the intellect when we have assimilated enough of the matter of language . . . to take over and conceive immaenntly in our intentional being the rules of the game we blindly played for so long. At that moment . . . a light dawns and we *know* what we were saying and why. . . .

2.6 Conclusion

The idea that God can be manifest to us in experience plays an important role in the way many Christians think of the "revelatory" grounds for their beliefs and practices, and that idea also undergirds the moral-practical reasoning that continues to guide the everyday spiritual lives of many Christians. In both cases, such Christians think that because we have enjoyed perceptual experiences of God, what we think, say, or do manages to direct us upon God, ensuring that our thinking, speaking, and acting is genuinely "about" God. Conversely, Christians think that God's perceptible manifestation to us furnishes us (or has furnished us) with sufficient reasons to comport ourselves toward God and the world in some ways and not others in belief and practice.

In this chapter, I have claimed there are two distinct but interrelated sorts of problems that arise in making sense of our intentional relation to God as a *perceptual* relation—one in which we are capable of being informed (or misinformed), rationally guided (or misguided) by direct acquaintance with God in experience. The first, a distinctively theological problem, is how to properly construe, coordinate, and defend the three central features jointly constitutive of a Christian theological understanding of our perceptual relation to God: first, an account of the forms of divine manifestation in the world implied by a proper theology of immanence and transcendence in the God/world relation; second, an account of the sorts of divine appearing implied by a proper theological anthropology of human capacities operative in our receptivity to the relevant form of divine

---

We are now learning, Aquinas would have it, the 'material moves' of the language of God. Our mode of participation here and now . . . is the making of motions in a language we do not understand." (ibid., 266–68). In other words, we have a system of concepts, but without any more of a knowing relationship to their content than a child who does not know what "red" means, but is reliably disposed to utter the word when in the presence of red objects.

manifestation; and, finally, an account of the ground of our capacities to perceive God implied by a proper theology of nature and grace.

Our understanding of the God/world relation furnishes us with the constraints on divine manifestation that determine the putative *content* of our perceptual relation to God (what it is "of" God that is available to perception), while our understanding of the relevant capacities operative in our experiences of God determines the putative *modes of perceiving* that content (the ways in which God's self-manifestation can appear to creatures with the relevant receptive capacities). Finally, our understanding of nature and grace furnishes us with the explanatory constraints on our capacities to perceive God as determined by properties intrinsic to our created nature and properties extrinsically conferred on us by God.

But being able to specify the theological content, modes, and grounds of perception can only amount to an account of our perceptual relation to God if we know in general what we mean by a "perceptual content" and its relation to "modes of perception." Even if perceiving God presents us with a sui generis exception to the ordinary modes of perception that direct us on creaturely objects, properties, and relations, our ability to specify that sui generis character depends on the background notion from which it represents a break.[66] We often assume a kind of naive realism about our perceptual relation to the everyday objects, properties, and relations in our external environment. Similarly, premodern theologians most often simply made explicit a construal of naive realism as a backdrop to the theological problem they faced.

But philosophical thickets have grown up around the very idea that the objects, properties, and relations constitutive of reality as a

---

66. Obviously, the same point would apply equally well if we were to reverse the polarity of the apophatic account and construe revelatory experience as the "ordinary" case, the point of departure from which our everyday experience of creaturely objects represents the relevant break. I will have more to say about this in chapter 4.

whole form an intrinsically intelligible framework, one structured by rational and moral-practical norms that exist whether or not we recognize them but can directly and immediately impose their rational demands on us in experience. We therefore confront the second and distinctively philosophical sort of problem—what I have called "the problem of perception." Once we call naive realism into question, we are faced with a pressing need for an alternative construal of the perceptual relation as the proper background against which to interpret the theological problem. Two such alternatives are available: boundary-impression views and social-practical views. Since these are mutually incompatible ways of understanding the perceptual relation, they place incompatible constraints on the theological problem.

The problem of perception does not merely present us with incompatible strategies for resolving the theological problem. It also compels us toward one of two incompatible ways of interpreting the theological problem itself. That is, specifying incompatible conceptions of the perceptual relation places constraints on what counts as a resolution to the theological problem. The incompatibility of the two sorts of theories addressed to it implies incompatible understandings of the necessary and sufficient conditions for anything to be a perceptible property and accordingly generates incompatible accounts of which sorts of capacities are operative in perception and how they operate. Whatever theological construal of divine manifestation and anthropological construal of receptivity to God must therefore be interpreted against the backdrop of one's preferred theory of perception, be it a boundary-impression or social-practical theory. Thus, while apophatic and cataphatic theologies of religious experience represent two different ways of embedding the theology within the background concept, what *counts* as an apophatic or cataphatic account is more fundamentally determined by which sort of philosophical approach to the problem of perception one appropriates to specify that background concept. With this two-level account of the problem of specifying our perceptual relation to God in place, we can then ask: what sort of approach to that problem best positions us to articulate a Christian theology of religious experience?

The modern problematizing of naive realism has thus introduced an apparently novel way in which our theological account might go wrong: even if we grant that we have correctly spelled out the transcendence/immanence relations, anthropological considerations, and nature/grace distinction in our putative perception of God, we might nevertheless mistakenly integrate these theological loci into a mistaken philosophy of perceptual intentionality. Having gotten the theological subject matter right, we might get the philosophical form of the perceptual relation wrong.

3

Freeing Theology from the Problem of Perception

Given the shape of the problem I have spelled out, a theological picture appears to be rendered less vulnerable to attack and more positively persuasive to the extent that it coherently incorporates a resolution to the problem of perception. It would therefore seem that my first order of business in marshaling my own theological story is to defend the philosophical story about "experience" on which it depends—at any rate, that is what a critical readership familiar with the relevant literature is perhaps most attuned to expect (and poised to critique).[1] But on this score I aim precisely to disappoint. Rather than

---

1. The most fundamental challenges and critiques put forward in the secondary literature about Christian theorists of religious experience are not those that address the theological norms at stake, but rather those that find conceptual difficulties with the underlying ability of the philosophical theories that guide the theological norms. In other words, the primary sorts of complaint that one courts when trying to articulate an account of our perceptual relation to God are (a) that one's underlying theory of perception is inadequate to the difficulties posed by the problem of perception or (b) that one's theory is ill-suited to accommodate some given theological norms. In the former case, the fundamental problem area is not theological in the relevant sense, but philosophical. In the latter case, the complaint is quite often not intrinsically

taking as my point of departure any implicit or explicit resolution to the problem of perception, the primary aim of this book is to challenge the idea that a theology of religious experience stands in any need of such a resolution in the first place.

More particularly, I wish to defend the thesis that theologies of religious experience need not be subject to any of the philosophical norms adduced in either of the two major views already canvassed, whether "boundary-impression" or "social-practical" theories. Instead of seeing ourselves as confronted by the problem of perception as a pressing worry upon which our theologies of revelation depend, we are entitled to see ourselves as confronting no such problem, and our theological articulations can accordingly be free from any theoretical constraints it threatens to impose on us. In other words, the contestable norms in need of determination for an analysis of our perceptual relation to God involve no genuine puzzles about how it is possible for reality to be represented in experience per se. The only contestable norms at issue are the particular theological ones—norms about how to best construe the (natural and/or graced) operation of our spiritual capacities to take in the relevant features of God's presence and agency on a Christian conception of God's relation to the world. Moreover, insofar as our recognition of the problem of perception is an index of the characteristically "modern" shape of contemporary thinking about revelation, a refusal to recognize that problem makes possible the retrieval of a naive realist approach to the question of Christian religious experience, an approach that is—in a sense to be clarified in chapter 6—characteristically premodern.

Staging this particular sort of theological emancipation from a philosophical worry about perception therefore involves both the analysis and refutation of the claim that the problem of perception

theological, but only a matter of pointing out a failure to properly fit theology to a philosophical theory aimed at the problem of perception.

supervenes on the problem of the perception of God. Accordingly, in the chapters that follow I (1) analyze the way in which the three loci constitutive of the theological problem of perceiving God have become entangled with the boundary-impression and social-practical theories addressed to the philosophical problem of perception and (2) argue that the theological question can be disentangled from the philosophical question, such that the former can be intelligibly asked and answered without any reference to the latter.

How, then, do I propose that we meet these two requirements and thereby wrest the theological problem from the philosophical one? One possibility might be to establish the mutual logical independence of the two questions, perhaps by showing that we need not touch on the philosophical problem to satisfactorily address the theological one. Having thus disentangled the two questions, I could then simply leave the philosophical question open. The prospects for such an approach are rather grim, I think. If there is indeed a genuine philosophical problem about how experience manages to put our normative intentions directly in touch with reality and how it affords us reasons for what we think, say, and do, then any attempt to explicate a perceptual relation that (putatively) puts our theological intentions in touch with *God* and affords us *theological* reasons will unavoidably confront that problem. As long as we consider the problem of perception a genuine difficulty, we will have to acknowledge its supervenience on the theological problem of the perception of God.

The approach I recommend, instead, is to deny that there *is* any genuine problem of perception. Rather than resolving the problem of perception in our theologizing, we ought to dissolve it—to expose what merely *appears* to be a genuine philosophical puzzle as a pseudoproblem. By failing to make the alleged philosophical worry intelligible, both forms of philosophical theorizing addressed to the so-called problem of perception also fail to be intelligible elucidations or resolutions of any genuine philosophical worry. So unlike the (hopeless) strategy of asserting theology's independence while continuing to preserve the legitimacy of the philosophical question, disentangling the theological loci from the "problem" of perception by way of a dissolution of the latter implies not merely that we *can* sidestep the so-called problem of perception in our theologizing but that we *must*. Insofar as we take that "problem" to supervene on the problem of perceiving God, our theologizing necessarily inherits the unintelligibility of the philosophical pseudoproblem.

In order to do away with the problem of perception, I look to the recent antiphilosophical arguments about the nature of perceptual experience developed by John McDowell principally in his Woodbridge lectures, subsequently published as *Mind and World*.[2] There McDowell subjects philosophical worries about the nature of empirical content to a particularly Wittgensteinian form of philosophical therapy. Such therapy is an invitation to abandon the search for a philosophical explanation, not out of any sense of desperation or coercion but because it is possible to achieve a frame of mind in which we recognize that the apparent need for a philosophical explanation is in fact illusory.[3] Once we have diagnosed the factors responsible for creating the illusion, it loses its grip on us.[4]

---

2. The arguments in question were offered in John McDowell's controversial *Mind and World* (Cambridge, MA: Harvard University Press, 1996), but he has gone about the task of sharpening and revising the theses presented there in subsequent essays.

3. Ibid., 27–37.

4. See Ludwig Wittgenstein, *Notebooks 1914–1916*, ed. trans. G. H. von Wright and G. E. M. Anscombe (Oxford: Basil Blackwell, 1979): "[W]e must uncover the source of error: otherwise hearing what is true won't help us. It cannot penetrate when something is taking its place. To convince someone of what is true, it is not enough to state it, we must find the *road* from error to truth" (1). Cf. *Philosophical Investigations*, German text, with English translations by G. E. M. Anscombe, P. M. S. Hacker, and Joachim Schulte, 4th ed. (Oxford: Wiley-Blackwell, 2009), §255: "The philosopher treats a question; like an illness."

3.1 A Therapeutic Approach to the Problem of Perception

McDowell's therapeutic diagnosis and dissolution of the problem of perception involves the conjunction of two components. The first and most significant element in his therapy is a *deconstruction* of the problem of perception—an analysis of its inner logic that exposes it as a pseudoproblem. While that analysis is sufficient to entitle a rational refusal of the "problem" as failing to present us with any genuine difficulty, it is insufficient as *therapy* unless the deconstruction can eliminate the temptation to depart from the naive realism to which it returns us; alleviating that temptation is the second component of the dissolution. Having deconstructed the pseudoproblem and retrieved our ordinary pretheoretical conception, that deconstruction and retrieval can be reinforced by what Maximilian de Gaynesford calls an "exculpatory explanation"—an explanation of why a pseudoproblem *seemed* to present us with a genuine and pressing philosophical puzzle that appeared to stand in need of some theory for its resolution in the first place.[5]

McDowell's therapeutic dissolution of the problem of perception implies that the supervenience claim commonly assumed in modern and contemporary theologies of religious experience is false—the theological problem of accounting for our perceptual relation to God does not presuppose any genuine philosophical problem about perceptual intentionality per se. McDowell, for his part, has no interest whatever in the theological consequences or implications of

---

5. Maximilian de Gaynesford, *John McDowell* (Malden, MA: Polity, 2004), 14. This second element of his therapy is therefore to provide a plausible story about the illusory character of the so-called problem of perception and why we have understandably, even if mistakenly, fallen prey to the temptation to entertain it. McDowell's exculpatory explanation is *genealogical*. The illusion of a problem is a wide-ranging social achievement that was constructed during the modern period. Once a logical deconstruction of the problem has demonstrated that there *is* no such problem, and once we have subsequently seen how the relevant social and historical circumstances gave rise to the *appearance* of a problem, that appearance can stand revealed for what it is, a *mere* appearance.

his proposed dissolution, and I therefore take up the task of showing how his diagnosis and therapy can be extended to diagnose and cure some maladies that currently afflict our theologies of religious experience. My primary aim in this chapter is to elaborate and extend the deconstructive element of McDowell's therapy. In part 2, I then wield it against the recent and influential accounts of our perceptual relation to God mentioned above: those of Marion, Alston, Preller, and Hector.

In *Syntactic Structures*, Chomsky uses the sentence "Colorless green ideas sleep furiously"[6] to illustrate our capacity to recognize an intelligible syntactic structure even in the absence of our ability to make any sense out of the semantics of the sentence as a whole or its constituent terms. Understood literally, it makes no sense for ideas to be colored, and it is straightforwardly contradictory for a colorless idea to be green, and it is at best incongruous to attribute fury to a mode of sleep. Nevertheless, the sentence makes "syntactic" or "grammatical" sense in a way that, for example, "Furiously sleep ideas green colorless" manifestly does not. We can see that "Colorless green ideas" constitutes a well-formed subject phrase and "sleep furiously" a well-formed verb phrase, and the two are properly conjoined as regards subject-verb agreement.

By way of analogy, McDowell's arguments make available an inverse critique of the current situation in the philosophy and theology of religious experience. Like "Furiously sleep ideas green colorless," the most recent and influential theologies of religious experience are "syntactically" or "grammatically" unintelligible, irrespective of the theological semantics of the God/world relation, human spiritual capacities, and nature and grace as their constituent terms. Whether or not they get the theology right, the structure

---

6. Noam Chomsky, *Syntactic Structures* (Berlin: Walter de Gruyter, 1957), 15.

of the perceptual relation in which it is embedded is nonsensical. My aim in offering a constructive theological proposal is thus not necessarily to defend the proposal but merely to offer it as an illustration of what a properly "grammatical" theology of religious experience might look like, an account free from the problem of perception. The failure of any alternative proposal to similarly disentangle the problem of perceiving God from the problem of perception, I argue, sabotages our theologizing by embedding it in an incoherent grammar of perception. Finding our freedom from such pseudophilosophical entanglement, on the other hand, opens a much more interesting and productive way forward in our theologies of revelation and, more generally, on our understanding of the nature of theology itself as a genuinely empirical discipline.

3.2. The Limits of Therapy

Appealing to Wittgenstein to therapeutically dissolve troublesome notions that appear to confront theological claims is not a particularly new tactic. However, frequently theologians have not been the best therapists in the Wittgensteinian sense. For often what goes under the name of a Wittgensteinian approach to therapy fails at the very point it is meant to be therapeutic. It is meant to identify something you thought to be a problem and reveal it as a baseless anxiety, to unmask it or strip it of the rational impetus it appeared to have for troubling you. One way of characterizing the anxiety presently under consideration is as an anxiety about the notion of objective purport: how is it possible for our perceptual experiences to direct us upon the way things are in the world, to have the world itself as their content? The telltale sign of a poor Wittgensteinian therapist is when she ceases to diagnose your anxieties and instead begins issuing commands, beating your intuitions into submission under the force of an argument rather than revealing and undermining the underlying root source of those intuitions. But this is not therapeutic in Wittgenstein's sense at all.

On particularly obvious way to tell whether one has evaded the therapeutic task Wittgenstein envisions, succumbing instead to the temptation to "philosophize" in the sense that Wittgenstein denounces, is when that person begins striking ordinary everyday words from our vocabulary or introducing usages whose sole function is to further the game of philosophy.[7] Simply playing up the crucial significance of social practices and the notion that the intentionality of our language is cultural and linguistic "all the way down" in theology has tended to produce both misdiagnoses and the blacklisting of terms and concepts of our ordinary vocabularies.[8] In

---

7. As has often been pointed out, there are times when Wittgenstein himself falls into this, but when he does, I take him to fail by his own lights. That is, he is not always successful at showing us the "road." For example, insofar as Wittgenstein takes himself to be dissolving puzzles about the nature of intentionality in the *Philosophical Investigations* by remarking, e.g. in §445, that "it is in language that an expectation and its fulfillment make contact," he does not succeed in allaying modern anxieties about how it is possible for our thought to "reach out" to reality, he only exacerbates them.

8. For some prominent examples of this see D. Z. Phillips, *Wittgenstein and Religion* (New York: Palgrave Macmillan, 1994); George Lindbeck, *The Nature of Doctrine: Religion and Theology in a Postliberal Age* (Louisville, KY: John Knox, 2009); and Stanley Hauerwas, "The Church as God's New Language," in *The Hauerwas Reader*, ed. John Berkman and Michael Cartwright (Durham, NC: Duke University Press, 2001), 142–64. All alike read Wittgenstein in such a way as to produce a problem of how one's experiences succeed in reaching beyond a self-contained game, whether parsed in terms of "religion" as the only language-game in which "belief in 'God' has any meaning" (Phillips), or the idea of a "cultural-linguistic" system as that which gives content to our beliefs (Lindbeck), or the idea that the person shaped by Christian virtue literally inhabits a "different world" than those who do not (Hauerwas). These appropriations of Wittgenstein make it puzzling how our observational language and reporting succeeds in being "about" the world and not merely about our *talk* that purports to be about the world (or our talk about our talk that purports to be about the world). Cf. Coakley's reference to what van Beeck calls "theologology" in Sarah Coakley, "Shaping the Field: A Transatlantic Perspective," in *Fields of Faith*, ed. David F. Ford, Ben Quash, and Janet Martin Soskice (New York: Cambridge University Press, 2005), 45, and the curious parallel between Robert Brandom and Stanley Hauerwas in banning ordinary words such as "experience." Each has often remarked that "experience" is "not one of my words." See Andrew Moore's discussion of D. Z. Phillips in *Realism and Christian Faith: God, Grammar and Meaning* (Cambridge: Cambridge University Press, 2003), 73–107; and John Allen Knight, *Liberalism versus Postliberalism* (New York: Oxford University Press, 2013), ch. 9.

so doing, it has therefore tended to exacerbate the anxiety to which it is allegedly addressed rather than alleviating it. What is required instead is to deconstruct our anxiety and actually expose it as baseless, and then to show how any residue of desire for a notion of objective theological purport that cannot be so exposed can instead be *satisfied* by the underlying grammar of perception presumed in our ordinary discourse.[9]

A final, important methodological note about the therapeutic approach McDowell recommends is that Wittgensteinian commitments of this sort should be regarded as local and not global. To ask about the role of philosophical theorizing about the structure of our perceptual capacities to put us in touch with reality for our theological thinking about the way in which Christians are or can be in touch with God in Christ by the Spirit need not in and of itself commit us to a "metaphysical" or "antimetaphysical" approach to philosophy or theology generally.[10] That is, even if I can convince you that appropriating constructive philosophical explanations of empirical content in a theology of religious experience or spiritual perception is a blind alley and that theological reflection on that topic ought to proceed without such explanations, I might yet find

---

9. That is, intuitions are not suppressed under the brute force of argument—they are instead renarrated so as to make their undesirability plain and the relinquishment voluntary, or else it is shown how they can be explicitly and unproblematically accommodated. See John McDowell, "Experiencing the World," in *The Engaged Intellect* (Cambridge, MA: Harvard University Press, 2009), 248.

10. While, e.g., Marion and Hector alike construe "metaphysics" in terms of a narrowly defined sort of project dependent on a particular sort of picture of the mind/world relation, they nevertheless somewhat misleadingly see the respective systems of philosophical machinery driving their theological claims as set against (Western) "metaphysics" as a whole. Compare Jean-Luc Marion, *In Excess: Studies of Saturated Phenomena*, trans. Robyn Horner and Vincent Berraud (New York: Fordham University Press, 2004), 13–23, 128–34, with Kevin W. Hector, *Theology without Metaphysics: God, Language and the Spirit of Recognition* (New York: Cambridge University Press, 2011), 2–14. Regardless of any subsequent attempts at qualification, this way of talking courts all manner of equivocations, usually in such a way as to encourage the premature dismissal of more particularistic views about this or that metaphysical issue.

constructive philosophical work on other topics to be helpful or even necessary for theological reflection.

This is even true in the case of the philosophy of perception and questions about the nature of intentionality. While I hope to show that a particular sort of alleged philosophical explanation about the structure of intentionality must be abandoned, I do not presume that this leaves the whole topic emptied of all genuine philosophical difficulties. Whether any putative difficulty calls out for resolution by means of a characteristically philosophical mode of theorizing (however that is to be understood) depends on the particular shape of the problem being proposed. If the recent arguments developed by McDowell are correct,[11] then the putative problem of how it is possible for the way things are in themselves to present themselves to us in experience and constrain our normative thinking about them is not, all things considered, a genuine problem. But it does not follow from this that there are no contestable matters of any substance that need ironing out on that front.[12]

What I seek to show in the chapters that follow is correspondingly narrow: many of the most recent and influential accounts of our perceptual relation to God have depended on this particular problem of perception and some or other philosophical solution to it, so if this localized Wittgensteinian critique goes through, some important consequences follow for theology. Most importantly, it follows that these aforementioned accounts (and those sufficiently like them) cannot be right because their principal theological claims turn out to be inextricably wedded to some incoherent nonsense disguised

---

11. As will become apparent, the relevant arguments have been revised, extended, and developed by others such as Jennifer Hornsby, Akeel Bilgrami, and Susanna Schellenberg.

12. Indeed, as will become clearer in the chapters that follow, part of my aim in doing away with the problem of perception is to mark out the pressing philosophical difficulties we confront in spelling out the norms of Christian religious experience that have been mistakenly obscured by that overriding worry.

as genuine philosophical insight. Far from advancing theological understanding about our receptivity to God, taking up the problem of perception into our theologizing has in fact barred the way to genuine theological understanding.

Therefore, while I take the far-reaching implications of my claim to stem from its being in an important sense antiphilosophical, that claim should not be mistaken as having any particularly significant consequences for how we construe the relation of philosophy to theology as a whole, in general or as such. My argument does not amount to a skepticism about metaphysics or a metaphilosophical commitment to deflationary views of philosophical explanation per se. In fact, I make no global metaphilosophical claims whatever. Nor, I should add, does my argument bear any useful implications for the task of carving up territory to determine which questions "properly belong" to theology and which to philosophy as distinct or discrete disciplinary domains.[13] Although I do not have much occasion to argue the point one way or the other, most attempts to articulate a principled way of distinguishing theological inquiry from philosophical inquiry strike me as wrongheaded.[14] Rather, from

---

13. Thomists in particular are often inclined to marking out which issues "properly" belong to theologians and which to philosophers. See Fergus Kerr, *After Aquinas: Versions of Thomism* (Malden, MA: Blackwell, 2002).

14. Briefly put, I think that the first principles that motivate the distinction between philosophy and theology should at best be seen as involving a purely stipulative distinction between reason and revelation as distinct sources of knowledge. Attempts to sustain a nonstipulative or "real" distinction have confronted at least two difficulties. When the terms of the distinction are read as marking a difference in epistemic instrumentality, the distinction appears wholly implausible. That is, when we take "reason" and "revelation" to distinguish modes of knowing (i.e., *how* S knows that p), then their strict separation implies that, for any object of knowledge p (i.e., irrespective of what is revealed), a revelatory mode of knowing that p fails to actualize any human rational capacities. This is surely an absurd view, since revelatory episodes clearly seem to be at least partially constituted by the actualizing of distinctively human rational capacities (e.g., those of judging, perceiving, feeling, etc.). So perhaps instead the idea is that some substantive contents of knowledge (*what* S knows when S knows that p) are only made available by a revelatory mode of knowing—that is to say, such contents are not knowable by actualizing rational capacities alone. But if the distinction thus marks out a distinct body of truths for which human rational capacities are insufficient (even if necessary), then—given

the McDowellian vantage point I have sketched above, I wish to bring contemporary philosophical theology into view as bewitched not by philosophy in general but by the very particular sort of pseudoproblem that I have been calling "the problem of perception."

3.3 Givenism, Coherentism, and the "Problem" of Perception

In the previous chapter I argued that Christian philosophers and theologians wishing to analyze the structure of our perceptual relation to God have come to feel obligated to subject debates about the theological norms governing our analysis to a wider debate over the philosophical norms addressed to the problem of perception.[15] Our resolution of that problem seems to supervene on the theological sense we can make of the manifestation of God's transcendence and immanence in the world and the ordering of human perceptual capacities to it—whether construed in cataphatic or apophatic terms.

I have characterized the putative problem at issue here as having to do with the "intentionality" of experience—that is, how the world external to our thinking is able to bear on our thinking in such a way that what we think, say, and do is "about" the world. There I summarized two possible sorts of answers to this question: the

the existence of revelatory knowledge—this implies that the sufficiency condition is met by our actualizing of nonhuman (or superhuman) capacities. A sharp distinction between reason and revelation therefore entails a prior and correspondingly sharp distinction between nature and grace as knowledge-capacitating realities. There are, I think, very good reasons to reject such a sharp distinction between nature and grace, some of which I take up in the final chapter. Nevertheless, while the positive account I sketch involves a rejection of a nature/grace dualism, I will not explicitly take up the contentious development of that distinction in the Thomist tradition, nor will I there attempt to argue for the merits of opposing a sharply divided conception of the distinction in that tradition.

15. This is not to say that earlier approaches did not seek to harmonize theological norms with philosophical precommitments. It is only to say that such a task was not motivated by the problem of perception, the urgent threat to the idea that our thinking is informed by reality at all. Just *why* the problem of perception looms so large over theology is something I will explore in chapter 7.

boundary-impression approach and the social-practical approach. On the former view, the world informs our perceptual thinking by furnishing us with concept-free mental content to which we apply concepts, whether fittingly or ill-fittingly. In virtue of this picture of concept application our observational concepts have their meanings and referents, and our observational judgments their truth-values. McDowell identifies the notion of "the Given" with this idea of a concept-free impression that inserts itself into our awareness as the mental content of an experience, and we can therefore identify what I have called a boundary impression view as "Givenism."[16] Givenism turns on the idea that the world makes itself available to thought by *giving* something of itself to thought. Crucially, though, what it gives is not constituted by our norm-governed conceptual or discursive frameworks but by nonconceptual content that can be incorporated into those frameworks, thereby giving them content.

On the latter, social-practical view, our relation to the mind-independent world in perceptual experience is not best seen in terms of mental access to any concept-free mental content supplied by the world to which we apply our concepts. We cannot identify the bearing of the mind-independent world on our empirical concepts and judgments apart from the socially acquired norms governing those concepts and judgments. Instead, the world's bearing on us is always already embedded within the social formation and use of concepts we exhibit in the practical contexts of our everyday lives. Because the structure of the world is irreducibly evinced within the structure of our conceptual thinking and language use, the world's bearing on thought must be understood in terms of relationships that hold between our concepts. McDowell's name for theories of this sort is "Coherentism," because they turn on specifying the sense in which

---

16. McDowell, *Mind and World*, 4.

the world's availability to empirical thought is implicit in the way our concepts hang together or cohere.[17]

One way to characterize McDowell's deconstructive critique of the problem of perception is to see Givenism and Coherentism as premises in a reductio ad absurdum. The argument runs as follows. The problem of perception is after an explanation of how the world is available to thought in terms of some relation that holds between two logically distinct elements:

P1: a normative framework of concepts constitutively interconnected in their mutual rational relations (relations that specify, as McDowell puts it, "what is a reason for what").

P2: the world as it is constituted independently of that framework, by objects precisely *not* intrinsically structured by the rational relations constitutive of concepts.

An explanation of this sort permits only two ways in which reality construed along the lines of P2 can be made available to the domain of conceptual thought construed along the lines of P1. Either our conceptual thinking somehow internalizes the nonconceptual world (that is, the Givenism of the boundary-impression view) or it somehow registers or tracks with the nonconceptual world without any such internalization, by way of some nonmentalistic embeddedness within our conceptual thinking (that is, the Coherentism of the social-practical view).

The trouble is that we cannot make good sense of either option. Each purports to explain how a nonconceptually constituted world can become available to our conceptual thinking, but each logically entails that a nonconceptually constituted world cannot become available to our conceptual thinking. In requiring a solution elaborated either in Givenist or Coherentist terms, the problem of

17. Ibid., 14.

perception thus implies a contradiction: it expresses a desire to explain how the world is available to thought in terms of the impossibility of the world's availability to thought. Such a desire is ill-conceived, and to be motivated by it in one's theorizing is therefore literally nonsensical.

My three-year-old son often undertakes projects that are similarly ill-conceived. He has, for example, often enlisted my help in trying to squeeze stuffed animals into containers smaller than could possibly accommodate them, or to make lids and containers hopelessly mismatched in size fit snugly to one another. There are various ways he has expressed the reasons that confronted us with the challenge of putting four stuffed bears the size of an average couch pillow into a twelve-ounce mason jar ("Because it's their house and they need to go home!"), or why he should think me obligated to help him fit a round Tupperware lid five inches in diameter to an oval bowl six and a half inches in diameter ("Because they belong together."). Such explanations give us something of the rationale that has led him to believe that we confronted such challenging feats.

Now clearly, from a normative point of view, we can see that his rationale is mistaken, and that we confront no rational obligation to achieve the feats he has set before us; they are not merely challenging, but impossible. That is, he is in fact wrong to think that the bears should fit in the jar or the lids should fit the mismatched containers, wrong to think he could or should make them fit, and wrong as well to think that I could be of any help in accomplishing either task.[18]

---

18. Of course, it may well be a good sign from the standpoint of childhood development for him to attempt impossible tasks such as these, and given that vantage point on the situation I might be obligated to humor him and thereby *pretend* to undertake the project he has set before me. Perhaps. I am not a child psychologist so I have no idea. But we can clearly see that—from a rational evaluation of the task in question—to undertake it with full seriousness is wrongheaded. While we recognize this to be so, however, my son does not. Indeed, when I humor him, pretending to undertake these impossible feats and inevitably failing, he takes me to fail in a distinctly different sort of way than I have in fact failed. He simply thinks I have not tried hard enough.

Alas, no amount of industry on anyone's part would get the job done. What we can see clearly (and he cannot) is that I "fail" only because he has not succeeded in presenting me with anything to do that could be intelligibly met with success. He does not see that he has mistaken the impossible for the merely difficult. But rather than giving up the project itself as ill-conceived, he prefers that we brainstorm ideas for achieving aims the parameters of which are misshapen *as* aims: "Try putting the little bear in *first*, daddy!" or "Turn the jar *this* way, and try it *now*!" Troubleshooting the bear/jar problem in this way is something like suggesting that we experiment in drawing triangles with sides of varying lengths in the hopes that eventually we will arrive at one the sum of whose interior angles is greater (or less) than 180 degrees within a Euclidean space. That would be to play a game in a manner that flouts the very rules that constitute it.

My son's formulations of the problem (the problem of determining which order to insert the bears into the jar in order to get them all to fit) and his constructive theories about how to address it (that the proper procedure must begin from the smallest bear and work up from there) are nonsensical in just the way that the triangle game is. They are not unreasonable in the sense of being merely inadequate ways of identifying and solving a reasonable problem. If that were so, we might perhaps eventually land on a better formulation of the bear/jar problem or a constructive theory that improves our prospects for solving it. Instead, his identification of the problem as well as any suggested means of solving it are "irrational" precisely in the sense that there is no coherent way of stating the bear/jar problem as possibly soluble and therefore no constructive theories that could possibly improve our prospects for solving it.

To be motivated by the problem of perception in one's theorizing, McDowell argues, is to be engaged in an intellectual project formally parallel to my son's illusory bear/jar problem. In the case of the so-called bear/jar problem, we easily recognize that what appeared to my son to be a genuine problem (a desire to put bears into a jar too small to contain them) is in fact a pseudoproblem, and, further, we see that whatever he might imagine to be a "possible solution" (for instance, putting them in one at a time, in various different orders, simultaneously, and so on) in fact presupposed the impossibility of what it was meant to accomplish. What boundary-impression "Givenists" and social-practical "Coherentists" fail to recognize, however, is that they too have addressed themselves to a pseudoproblem, and, as such, their theorizing implies the impossibility of what it seeks to explain.[19]

3.4 Givenism and the Problem of Fit

Consider the first proposed solution, the idea that the world's bearing on us furnishes us with an "impression," a mental object or event that, in being bestowed directly by the world's impact on the mind, is constituted independently of any of the conceptual norms that characterize our everyday frameworks of belief.[20] Such conceptual thinking is governed by rational relations that form the evaluative context of our concept use.[21] Whatever the world contributes to our thinking via an "impression," however, does not come to us with

19. See McDowell, "Experiencing the World," 246: "The deeper misconception is to mistake an impossible conceptual bind for a tractable intellectual problem—something one might set out to solve without shifting one's background assumptions. The predicament is beautifully captured by a remark in Wittgenstein's *Nachlass*: 'You are under the impression that the problem is *difficult*, when it's *impossible*. I want you to realize that you are under a spell.'"

20. The notion of directness or immediacy is a necessary feature of "boundary-impression" explanations of the mind/world relation. But a commitment to the directness or immediacy of an impression still leaves entirely open the question of whether such direct impacts give rise to mental events in which what appears to us is just some particular constituent of the world itself or, rather, whether those direct impacts instead yield mental objects that mediate between us and the world. I will return to this matter of theory choice later, but the present point is that an "impression" is whatever the world directly contributes to thought.

the normative character that belongs to the evaluative context of our conceptual thinking. The world's intrinsic structure is as it is independently of the human context of concept formation and use. To be given an impression in experience is thus to be impressed with that nonconceptual structure and not in the first instance to be given anything with the normatively "charged" character belonging to our framework of concepts. But while nonconceptual, the impressions received in experience are nevertheless supposed to be cognitive, in the limited sense that they are manifest in our conscious awareness.

In virtue of their dependence on the world on the one hand and their mentalistic character on the other, impressions are capable of directly anchoring our thinking to reality, where "reality" can be understood to name a domain "outside the space of reasons"—that is, outside the normative context of rational relations constitutive of our concept use. Crucially, the anchoring function of the impression penetrates into our awareness—to receive an impression is to have "in mind" an object or event that owes its nonconceptual structure to the layout of reality and makes that structure directly available to us. On this picture, our sensory capacities (of sight, hearing, and so on) are the modes of receptivity by which we take in the nonconceptual content given by impressions. The operation of such capacities forms the permeable outer boundary between thought and the world as modes of "receptivity" to reality, sensitivities to the nonconceptual impingements of the world beyond the boundary that mediate it to our conceptual thinking.

This availability of mentalistic and nonconceptual "impressions" allows us to regard our conceptual thinking as informed and grounded by reality. The formation of an empirical concept is

---

21. These include the logical patterns of thinking, "relations such as implication or probabilification," as McDowell puts it, but also more broadly those normative relations that determine "what counts as a reason for what." See McDowell, *Mind and World*, 7.

therefore just the incorporation of a nonconceptual impression into our conceptual thinking. A nonconceptual impression of any constituent of reality as having some property (for instance, a nonconceptual visual impression of my black table) thus in some sense occasions or makes available the formation of an empirical concept ("this black table"), and that concept in turn can occasion or make available the formation of an empirical judgment ("this table is black"). The class of nonconceptual impressions thus grounds an entire class of observational concepts that are "based" on them. Those concepts can serve to tether our normative observational judgments to reality, and this explains how our claims about the way things are should arise from the way things are in fact. So, on this picture, because what we think or say can be traced out to the level of such impressions, we are justified in believing that thought or language based on such impressions are genuinely world-involving. In referring us to whatever is impressed on us, our thinking or language can therefore be "about" the world—our thoughts or words can have empirical reality as the mental or semantic "content" of our intentions.[22]

From this picture of how the world enters into thought or speech, we can fairly straightforwardly derive a picture of how genuinely world-directed thinking or speaking gets epistemically justified. Namely, when what we think or say is based on impressions, they

---

22. I am here using the term *content* in the broadest possible sense, as recommended by Susanna Siegel in "The Contents of Perception," in *The Stanford Encyclopedia of Philosophy*, Spring 2015, ed. Edward N. Zalta, http://plato.stanford.edu/entries/perception-contents. The content of a perceptual experience is just whatever is conveyed to the subject by that perceptual experience. For a helpful disambiguation of the narrower usages of content as a piece of philosophical jargon, see Tim Crane, "The Given," in *Mind, Reason and Being-in-the-World: The McDowell-Dreyfus Debate* (New York: Routledge, 2013), ch. 10. Where content is more narrowly defined in terms of the representation of an object (see the previous note), there will be those who deny that experience involves the conveyance of content at all. But this would only be to deny a representationalist account of the way in which the world is conveyed to the subject in experience and to affirm instead some nonrepresentationlist relation to the world, i.e., a nonrepresentational theory of content in Siegel's wider sense.

are genuinely world-directed, but when they are based on such impressions *in just the right sort of way*, then our intentional thinking succeeds not only in directing us on the world but in directing us on it *truly*. The proper sort of "basing" relation between our concepts and the world's impressions establishes our intending as *knowing*.[23] Our perceptual or observational beliefs about the world, then, are the ones that lie nearest to the world's experiential impact on our minds, nearest to the boundary of our thinking where our thinking "touches" the world. Such beliefs are just our rational responses to its nonconceptual bearing on us.[24]

This claim that experiences consist in worldly impressions whose function is to mediate the boundary between the conceptual structure of our thinking and the nonconceptual layout of reality is what McDowell identifies as the idea of "the Given":

> The idea is that when we have exhausted all the available moves within the space of concepts, all the available moves from one conceptually organized item to another, there is still one more step we can make: namely, pointing to something that is simply received in experience. [This is] the idea of the Given. . . . Empirical judgments in general—whether or not they reflect knowledge, and even whether or not they are justified at all, perhaps less substantially than knowledge

23. Just what constitutes the structure of an "impression" and just what constitutes a perception's being based on it "in the right sort of way" are of course controversial questions. These contested matters set the agenda for various different versions of the "boundary impression" view. See Christopher Peakcocke, "Phenomenology and Non-Conceptual Content," *Philosophy and Phenomenological Research* 62, no. 3 (May 2001): 609–15. That agenda at bottom consists in two questions: first, what is an "impression"? Second, how do impressions fix the content of conceptual thinking? To extend the account into an epistemological one would be to add a third question, i.e., what credentials must such an impression have in order to be knowledge-constituting? See also John McDowell, *Perception as a Capacity for Knowledge* (Milwaukee, WI: Marquette University Press, 2011).

24. More exactly, our observational beliefs can be thought of as rational responses to the nonconceptual impacts of the world on our capacities of "sensibility," however such capacities are to be properly conceived. Just as there have been various ways of construing what is given to us by those impacts, there are many corresponding ways of characterizing the nature of our sensitivities to whatever is given in virtue of which we are receptive to it. See Tim Crane, "The Given," in *The Myth of the Mental*, ed. Joseph Schear (London: Routledge, forthcoming).

requires—had better have content of a sort that admits of empirical justification.[25]

The idea of a Given, McDowell emphasizes, is not in the first instance an idea about how we gain empirical knowledge of the world, but more fundamentally the idea of how the world is conveyed to thought in the first place—how the world furnishes us with the empirical content that is singled out by our use of concepts. The Given is therefore a theory of how any of our concepts can come to have "empirical substance" at all,[26] whether or not our use of those concepts in assertions or judgments succeeds in meeting the criteria for knowledge. By imposing "Givens" on us in experience, the world "infuses" our concepts with empirical content, and the aforementioned idea of an empirically contentful concept (an "observational concept") is thus just the idea of a normative "container" for the Given.[27] We develop observational concepts by incorporating the Given into the rational relations of our conceptual framework and thereby grounding that framework in the immediate bearing that reality imposes on our thinking, whether such grounding is epistemically warranted or not.[28] Thus, on a "Givenist"

---

25. McDowell, *Mind and World*, 6.

26. That is, "content" in Siegel's sense in note 22 above.

27. McDowell, *Mind and World*, 7. M. J. Reddy identified the "conduit" metaphor as central to our thinking about concepts as containers of mental content. See "The Conduit Metaphor: A Case of Frame Conflict in Our Language about Language," in *Metaphor and Thought*, ed. A. Ortony (Cambridge: Cambridge University Press, 1979), 284–310. Kevin Hector takes that metaphor to undergird what he calls "essentialist-correspondentist" conceptions of the mind/ world relation. See Hector, *Theology without Metaphysics*, 48. Another prominent metaphor for the relationship between the objective purport given via impressions and its incorporation into our conceptual norms is that of sculpture. Impressions provide the mind with the raw "material" of thought that is "shaped" or "formed" by conceptual thinking.

28. If an empirically grounded observational concept figures in a belief or a judgment, we can raise the further question of whether the resulting observational belief is *warranted* or not. The answer to that question, however, depends entirely on what counts as a "proper" grounding relation from the epistemic point of view. Whereas our intentional relation to a Given furnishes us with candidates for knowledge, our epistemic relation to a Given specifies which conditions must be met in order for that intentional relation to count as instances of knowledge.

perspective, "empirical substance is transmitted from the ground level to empirical concepts that are further removed from immediate experience, with the transmission running along channels constituted by the inferential linkages that hold a system of concepts together."[29] What makes this such an attractive picture, McDowell thinks, is its attempt to preserve the idea that the observational claims we regularly entertain (the "judgments of experience") are "grounded in a way that relates them to a reality external to thought."[30]

Without such grounding, it would be hard to see how to make sense of "experience" as a source of knowledge about mind-independent reality at all. If our observational concepts could not register any outside impingements, then the judgments in which those concepts figure could not be "about" the world. At best, such thinking could succeed only in directing us upon ourselves—upon the modifications of our mental states cut entirely free of anything external to those states. So, while we ordinarily take our experiences to be experiences "of," for instance, tables and chairs, cabbages and kings, puppies and pomegranates, if we do not posit some conception of a Given to explain how our concepts "chair," "cabbage," "puppy," and so on can reach out to the things they purport to designate, then it ceases to be possible to see our concepts as vehicles for directing us on those things at all. We seem instead forced to say that our concepts are dead ends, or at best cul-de-sacs, directing us only on ourselves and not the environment we inhabit or the distal objects, properties, and relations constitutive of that environment.[31] But the idea that the conceptual frameworks that we learn, adopt, and regularly revise

---

29. McDowell, *Mind and World*, 7.
30. Ibid.
31. Notice that this is not simply the benign, perhaps banal, point that the world we inhabit is always one that we ourselves construe in normative terms. That idea itself presupposes that our construal is a construal "of" something other than our own construals. To the extent that such construals do not terminate in whatever it is they seek to construe, we seem unable to motivate the idea that thought is "about" anything other than thought.

float entirely free of the mind-external and nonconceptual layout of reality that those frameworks purport to represent or schematize seems patently absurd. We can avoid that absurdity, the Givenist story goes, only if we countenance the idea that the nonconceptual layout of reality delivers itself to thought via our taking in bits of the Given. Insofar as our practical and theoretical reasoning functions as a conduit for what is Given, such reasoning succeeds in directing us on reality.

McDowell's characterization of Givenism leaves open the question of how best to construe precisely what is "Given" in the sense spelled out above. Just what sort of nonconceptual content, afforded to us in experience, is capable of being singled out by our concepts? The most fundamental dispute among Givenists is whether to analyze the nonconceptual impressions imparted in experience as direct presentations of the layout of reality itself or whether to analyze them as representations that indirectly mediate between the layout of reality and our thinking about it. That is, Givenist philosophers have tended to construe "the Given" in either "direct realist" or "indirect realist" ("representative realist") terms.

Direct realist Givenism pictures us as taking in the nonconceptually constituted layout of reality immediately, such that the objects, properties, and relations that we have "in mind" in virtue of the world's bearing on us directly represent the objects, properties, and relations exhibited by the world itself, which exist independently of our mental relation to them.[32] The direct version thus admits of our representing the world (representation) without any mental objects that stand in for what is represented (that is, without representations). An indirect realist Givenism, on the other hand, pictures the nonconceptually constituted layout of reality furnishing us not with

---

32. For a recent defense of direct realism, e.g., A. D. Smith, *The Problem of Perception* (Cambridge, MA: Harvard University Press, 2002).

any direct re-presentation of mind-external objects, properties, and relations, but instead with mental proxies for them—"representations" of them. The Givens of direct realism are the subjective or phenomenal manifestations that accompany our immediate confrontation with the denizens of reality themselves—the nonconceptual layout of the world is given in our representing of it. The Givens of indirect realism, on the other hand, are not subjective modes of confrontation with the mind-external realities themselves, but mediational *tertia* standing between perceiving subjects and objective reality.[33] Still, as Givens, the representations imposed on us by reality do not owe their structure or content to our conceptual frameworks, but rather to the layout of reality.[34]

In addition to direct and indirect realism, there is a third form of Givenism, which we might call "idealism" (or, as it is also been called, "phenomenalism"). On this view, we cannot make any good sense of "reality" as a domain of objects, properties, or relations constituted independently of human awareness.[35] Accordingly, the

33. Perhaps the best-known (and most-maligned) forms of indirect realism are the sense-data theories of the classical empiricist tradition, according to which our direct perceptual awareness in experience is a qualitative awareness of mind-dependent sensory objects. When such objects have been properly generated in the mind by the mind-independent external objects in the world, then our awareness of the sense data can count as an indirect awareness of their causal sources. For two of the most influential formulations in the classical tradition, see David Hume, *An Enquiry Concerning Human Understanding*, in *Enquiries Concerning Human Understanding and Concerning the Principles of Morals*, ed. L. A. Selby-Bigge, 3rd. rev. ed. P. H. Nidditch (1758; Oxford: Clarendon, 1975); and John Locke, *An Essay Concerning Human Understanding*, ed. Peter Nidditch (1689; Oxford: Clarendon, 1975). For a more recent approach, see, e.g., Jerry Fodor, *Representations: Philosophical Essays on the Foundations of Cognitive Science* (Cambridge: MIT Press, 1981).

34. Of course, on a representationalist view, the way things are can impart us with a misrepresentation. How to analyze misperception and illusion on either sort of view under discussion is a hotly contested matter, but irrelevant for present purposes.

35. There are, of course, many ways in which one might find the idea of mind-independent reality problematic. The Continental phenomenological tradition beginning with Husserl should be read as a philosophical trajectory centered precisely on problematizing any "transcendence" of the Given, albeit one that admits of wide internal differentiation both in identifying what is or can be "Given" to consciousness and in locating and addressing the putative philosophical disaster alleged to ensue when we acknowledge any objects, properties, or relations that transcend whatever is actually or possibly Given to consciousness. See Robert Sokolowski,

nonconceptually constituted contents of perception neither *present* us with a supposed "mind-independent reality" nor *represent* it to us. Rather, the totality of nonconceptualized contents that we in fact passively receive in thought just *is* "reality," and the question is only whether our concepts are or are not rightly related to those contents.[36] Whereas direct and indirect realism trade on a strong distinction between appearance and reality, according to which "reality" entails something like "mind-independence," idealism reconstructs an appearance/reality distinction from *within* the domain of mind-dependent phenomena, or "appearances." *Mere* appearances (observational concepts that misrepresent or in some relevant sense are inadequately related to the preconceptual Given) are thus distinguished from *veridical* appearances (observational concepts adequately related to the preconceptual Given). Since "veridicality" in this context is analyzable entirely in terms of the fittingness, suitability, or adequacy of a conceptual "form" to accommodate whatever subjective manifestation of nonconceptual content one receives, phenomenalism can claim to account for "reality" entirely in terms of the totality of possible relations of veridicality, without any appeal to notions of mind-independence.[37]

Introduction to Phenomenology (New York: Cambridge University Press, 1999); and Dermot Moran, *Edmund Husserl: Founder of Phenomenology* (Cambridge: Polity, 2005). But there are also philosophers not traditionally located within that trajectory who count as phenomenalist on my conception, such as, e.g., Bishop George Berkeley, *Principles of Human Knowledge* (1710; New York: Penguin, 1988); and C. I. Lewis, *Mind and the World Order: Outline of a Theory of Knowledge* (1929; Toronto: Dover, 1956).

36. While I've characterized idealism as a logically distinct form of Givenism alongside direct and indirect realism, it is arguably just one variety of direct realism. Namely, it is just that form of direct realist Givenism for which there is a strict identity between "the Given" (i.e., the nonconceptual content of an "impression") and "the layout of reality." Of course, construed in this way, the notion of an impression is infelicitous insofar as there is no "whence" of the imposition of nonconceptual content that could be intelligibly characterized independently of that content itself.

37. Following Marion, I've articulated this formulation to leave room for the various conceptions of veridicality relations that have emerged from within the phenomenological tradition, some of which acknowledge only two such relations—fittingness of concept to content or ill-

Whether taken in a direct realist, indirect realist, or phenomenalist/idealist direction, Givenism derives its philosophical impetus from the idea that we need to be able to mark the distinction between reality and appearance internal to the forms of mental awareness afforded by our perceptual relation to the world. If we are not recipients of a nonconceptual Given as a standard against which our observational concepts can be judged, then we cannot sensibly regard such concepts as world-directed and world-involving. What we think and say and do directs us on the world only insofar as whatever is conveyed in thought and language "bottoms out" in (or "opens onto") our awareness of the Given, which is itself intrinsically independent of any such conceptual structure.[38] This understanding of empirical content as "nonconceptual," it is important to note, is perfectly consistent with a weak form of "conceptualism" about perceptual intentionality that I have marked out as "one-world Kantianism."[39]

That is, we can hold that the nonconceptual bearing of the world on receptivity (on "sensibility") yields nonconceptual mental content of which we are consciously aware, yet insist that the Givenness of sensation needs to be subject to the categories of understanding before it can inform the "spontaneity" of our intentional stances toward the world. Sensory content, therefore, is a mode of (re)presentation by which the world itself—the "noumenal"—actually "shows up" in thought as a "brute" nonconceptual appearing.

fittingness—mappable to truth and falsity, respectively, and others of which include two forms of "ill-fittingness" between concept and content: one in which the content is insufficiently suited to the concept and another in which the concept is insufficiently suited to the content. See Jean-Luc Marion, *Reduction and Givenness: Investigations of Husserl, Heidegger and Phenomenology*, trans. Thomas A. Carlson (Chicago: Northwestern University Press, 1998).

38. The possible exception here, of course, is when the object of our thinking and talking belongs to the normative domain of our thinking and talking themselves. In such cases, though, the relevant distinction is between a normative reality and a further normative claim about it, wherein the former is to be construed as constituted independently of the latter.

39. See above.

Noumenal appearing, however, has to be domesticated by the structure of our thought and language if it is to inform and justify what we intentionally think, say, and do. Nonconceptual sensation must pass through the concepts that structure our "spontaneity" in order to constitute the "phenomena" that inform our free exercises of that spontaneity as an intermediate stage between the world's bearing upon us and our intentional responses to that bearing. This synthesis between concept and content—the imposing of categorical form on the indistinct and inchoate sensory substratum that delimits it and gives it the intelligibility needed to respond rationally to it—takes place as an involuntary mental event within consciousness. As such, it is analyzable as the givenness of nonconceptual content *by way of* concepts required to indicate it.

Givenism, then, can admit not only of intramural disputes about whether we should understand Givenness in direct realist, indirect realist, or phenomenalist terms. There are also disputes within each of these options as to whether to be nonconceptualists about both the content *and* the vehicle of perceptual experience or—in accordance with a one-world Kantianism—to be nonconceptualist about the content only, while holding onto conceptualism about the vehicle or mode of presentation by which nonconceptual content is conveyed to our contemplative and moral-practical reasoning. The direct realist Givenist can regard reality as a mind-independent domain whose direct nonconceptual presentation to us can only be identified by way of our concepts; the indirect realist Givenist can regard the world's direct bearing on us as causally responsible for nonconceptual representations that resemble or "mirror" a mind-independent reality but which similarly require the further mediation of conceptual identification before we can respond to them in thought, word, or deed; finally, the idealist/phenomenalist Givenist can hold that the nonconceptual content that shows up in our conscious awareness just *is* "reality," but reality standing in need of conceptual constitution in order to have any epistemic significance (good or bad).

Despite the attractions of Givenism as an explanation of how observational thinking can be ultimately tethered to reality itself, McDowell wants us to see that the very notion of the Given as nonconceptual mental content is "in fact useless for its purpose" because it does not allow us to make sense of *either* conceptualist or nonconceptualist views about perceptual experience as a vehicle of intentionality.[40] We can put the worry like this: Givenism concedes that to have a concept of something is, at a minimum, to place (or be capable of placing) that thing within the normative context of our beliefs and judgments, one susceptible of rational evaluation about what follows from what and about what counts as a good reason for what. Our ordinary observational beliefs or dispositions to believe, therefore, are rationally assessable or evaluable in virtue of belonging to the system of rational relations that makes them answerable to our evolving system of concepts.

But if our internalizing of the Given furnishes us with a form of content that is nonconceptual, it is in the relevant sense by definition and ex hypothesi alien to the normative context of our beliefs and judgments. From the point of view of the conceptual framework that gives intelligibility to our thinking, a Given is not a rational presentation but a "bare presence"—something that, as Sellars puts it, "presupposes no other knowledge either of particular matters of fact or of general truths."[41] How, therefore, would it be possible for our observational concepts to be *answerable* to the Given, or for the Given

---

40. McDowell, *Mind and World*, 7. McDowell's worries about nonconceptual content are only worries aimed at the sort of content required to make sense of experience as a basis of *intentionality*. This does not necessarily commit him to antagonism about the idea of nonconceptual mental content per se, when the notion of content is serving some other putative purpose. See José Luis Bermúdez, "What Is at Stake in the Debate on Nonconceptual Content?" *Philosophical Perspectives* 21, no. 1 (2007): 55–72, 58; and Jeff Speaks, "Is There a Problem about Nonconceptual Content?" *Philosophical Review* 114, no. 3 (2005): 359–98.

to become answerable to our concepts? The very idea of a Given is the idea of something excluded from the "logical space" of concepts that normatively govern thought, and the idea of internalizing a Given therefore cannot be the idea of taking in anything that could possibly serve as the normative basis for an observational judgment. To receive the Given would not be to supply our observational thinking with content susceptible of rational assessment. But that is precisely the role the Given was theorized to play.

If, however, we follow the weak conceptualism of a one-world Kantianism in placing an intermediary step between the nonconceptual Given and our intentional responses to it—that of a necessary "conceptualization"—we only push the same problem back a step. We end up confusing the labeling of a problem—that of "conceptualizing the Given"—with the solving of that problem, since it is precisely the notion of "applying" the normative structure of a concept to a nonnormative or "brute" content whose coherence is at issue. So the very idea that there is such a thing as a Given—a form of mental content that both exerts a normative force on our thinking and remains external to the normative framework of concepts that forms the basis for our reason-giving—is nonsensical, a myth. Following Sellars, McDowell characterizes the myth of the Given as "the idea that the space of reasons, the space of justifications or warrants, extends more widely than the conceptual sphere. The extra extent of the space of reasons is supposed to allow it to incorporate non-conceptual impacts from outside the realm of thought."[42]

Since conceptual thinking designates a domain governed by the relations of rational accountability, the Givenist commitment to a form of thought content alien to our conceptual thinking

41. Wilfrid Sellars, *Empiricism and the Philosophy of Mind*, intro. Richard Rorty and study guide by Robert Brandom (Cambridge, MA: Harvard University Press, 1997), 127–96, 68–69.
42. McDowell, *Mind and World*, 7.

straightforwardly implies that our empirical concepts cannot become rationally accountable to Givens. But suppose we take this to be a tendentious conception of Givenism and stipulate that whatever sort of nonconceptual content the Given furnishes us with *is* rationally assessable in the relevant way, that it does bear the relevant structure that makes it capable of figuring into human systems of rational relations. If so, then we are hard-pressed to say what we could mean by calling the Given "nonconceptual"—that designation comes to seem like "mere word-play."[43] Perhaps the idea is not that such content fails to exhibit any intrinsic capacity for involvement in rational relations whatever but rather that it displays a form of rational assessibility independent of any *humanly devised* system of rational relations. Surely, though, this cannot be the right idea. The rational relations constitutive of human conceptual thinking only range over the concepts subject to those relations, and Givens either fall within the scope of those relations or do not. If they do, then they are conceptual in the ordinary sense. If they do not, then they are nonconceptual in the only relevant sense.

So, it is incoherent to suppose that empirical thinking is rationally grounded in the Given, that nonconceptual content can inform and ground our observational concepts and judgments by supplying them with nonconceptual reasons. Might we suppose instead that our empirical thinking is nonrationally grounded by the Given? Suppose that internalizing the Given is not a matter of establishing a rational connection between the nonconceptual impressions we receive and the empirical concepts and judgments we take to arise from them.

43. McDowell makes the inverse of this point for those who wish to talk of conceptual capacities as operative in experience, while denying that the operation of those capacities involves our "spontaneity"—the norms of "responsible freedom" governing our rational revisions in our evolving picture of the world. To acknowledge that experience is intrinsically capable of being taken up by "conceptual capacities" while denying that it is intrinsically constituted by "spontaneity," McDowell says, is "mere word-play." Ibid., 13.

Instead, our observational thinking can be thought to be merely *occasioned* by our receptivity to the Given. McDowell draws the analogy to the person who has been discovered in a location from which she had been banished, but only because she was picked up and deposited there by a tornado.[44] While it is true that she cannot be held responsible for where she ended up, the tornado does not constitute a reason for her to be there—it fails to make contact with any normative considerations relevant to the terms of the banishment.

Similarly, the mere occasioning of our observational concepts and beliefs by our internalizing of the Given would not rationally *answer to* the nonconceptual content of the Given but would arise from them in a way that is literally rationally unaccountable. But it is precisely the notion of rational accountability that the Given was meant to secure. As that which our frameworks of empirical thinking are "about," the Given was supposed to furnish us with a standard of correctness against which such thinking is to be judged (as correct or incorrect, warranted or unwarranted, accurate or inaccurate, and so forth). But if thought is not rationally accountable to the Given, if it cannot "answer to" the Given in that sense, then it cannot direct us on what is Given in the right way to constitute the "aboutness" of an intentional relation. As McDowell puts it:

> Now perhaps this picture secures that we cannot be blamed for what happens at that outer boundary, and hence that we cannot be blamed for the inward influence of what happens there. What happens there is the result of an alien force, the causal impact of the world, operating outside the control of our spontaneity. But it is one thing to be exempt from blame, on the ground that the position we find ourselves in can be traced ultimately to brute force; it is quite another thing to have a justification. In effect, the idea of the Given offers exculpations where we wanted justifications.[45]

44. Ibid., 8.

If we are committed to the idea that our perceptual relation to the world involves the internalizing of some content that it impresses upon us, the only available option left to consider is the idea that we are given fundamentally conceptual content. But if we concede that point, then we have just given up on a key feature of the problem that Givenism was supposed to address, and thus a key feature constitutive of Givenism itself. The problem with which the Givenist begins is how the layout of reality *conceived of as a domain itself not conceptually structured* can make itself available to our conceptual thinking. A conceptualist account of the Given that maintains P2, described earlier, just pushes the problem of rational answerability back a step, forcing us to ask how a world construed in nonconceptual terms manages to afford us conceptual Givens. The idea that the world can supply a Given that it does not have to give is no more coherent than the idea of a nonconceptual (or nonconceptually grounded) reason. Thus, whereas Givenism requires that conceptually structured thinking can draw on nonconceptual mental content to make the world available to us, it is in fact impossible to make sense of that idea. Givenism is therefore not merely false but incoherent. It does not even succeed in putting before us a claim whose candidacy for truth or falsity we can begin to consider.

3.5 Coherentism and the Problem of Friction

"Coherentism" figures in McDowell's thinking as a family of theories addressed to the problem of perception whose unifying feature consists precisely in the rejection of Givenism. Coherentists agree that the Given is a myth and that the intentionality of our empirical

45. Ibid.

thinking therefore cannot consist in an intentional relation to it (whether construed in direct realist, indirect realist, or phenomenalist terms). But rather than giving up on the question of how "experience" makes the nonconceptual layout of reality available for our conceptual thinking, they offer explanations that attempt to do without any appeal to the notion of a mind-internal fit between the Given and our concepts. Instead, the Coherentist claim is that our conceptually structured thinking can make reality available to us without positing any mentalistic access to the world as it is independently of the particular frameworks of concept use ratified by our actual discursive social practices. We can understand that which informs or justifies our intentional mental states entirely in terms of the relations that hold among the constituents of our conceptual thinking. The Coherentist, then, picks up just where Givenism left off, with the apparent need to concede that the bearing of the world on our thinking must be an irreducibly *conceptual* bearing. It must belong to the normative context of responsible freedom constitutive of our rational thinking if it is to inform and justify our observational beliefs.

Our conceptual capacities are constitutive of our agency—our capacities to recognize and respond to what we regard as good or bad *reasons* as motivators for what we think, say, and do. But when we try to imagine our observational thinking entirely in terms of our agency, we worry there is no place for *receptivity* to the world to constrain our conceptual thinking. If the world's bearing on us is conceptual, and if the freedom of our conceptual thinking is sufficient for determining what counts as a reason to think, say, or do X, then perceptual experience cannot be intelligibly regarded as a form of *receptivity* to any reality external to thought. To identify experience with our concept use thus threatens to "degenerate into moves in a self-contained game," and "what was meant to be a picture of thinking with empirical content threatens to degenerate into a picture of a frictionless spinning in a void."[46] In identifying our empirical thinking with the exercise of conceptual capacities, Coherentism seems to meet the Givenist problem of "fit" between two radically different forms of mental content—the nonconceptual and the conceptual—but confronts us with an apparent problem of friction: how to secure the world's external constraint on human agency in our observational thinking.

McDowell's treatment of Coherentism centers on the attempts to meet that difficulty proposed by various American postpositivist empiricists and pragmatist philosophers of this century and the last—most notably Quine, Sellars, Davidson, and Brandom. But, in fact, there are at least as many versions of Coherentism as there are of Givenism. I have already schematized the intramural debates among Givenists in terms of three different types of Givenism—direct realist, indirect realist, and phenomenalist. Since Coherentism consists principally in the denial of Givenism in all its forms, it can likewise be understood as developing anti-Givenist versions of each sort of theory. What exactly do Givenists of each type hold that Coherentists deny? As we saw, Givenism handled the question of accounting for the objective purport or "world-involving" character of experience by theorizing what sort of nonconceptual content we receive by internalizing the world's impressions on our conceptual thinking.

Coherentism therefore explains the sense in which our empirical concepts and judgments can be "world-involving" without needing to appeal to the internalization of nonconceptual content as construed by each version of Givenism. That gives us direct realist, indirect realist, and phenomenalist versions of Coherentism. McDowell's treatments of Coherentism tend to center on the direct realisms of Davidson and Brandom.[47] That is entirely appropriate

46. Ibid., 5, 50.

because direct realism is widely regarded by contemporary philosophers as the most promising theory of perception.[48] But it is worth noting phenomenalist/idealist as well as indirect realist strategies as well. Each is an attempt to address the apparent difficulty of how our empirical thinking can be constrained by realities external to thought without endorsing some form of Givenism.

The phenomenalist strategy is simply to dismiss the difficulty as merely apparent and to propose instead that we do without the notion of a reality external to our conceptual thinking altogether. The central claim of phenomenalist or idealist Coherentism is therefore that we are not entitled to any notion of receptivity that is not reducible to the rational relations exhibited by human conceptual activities and therefore reducible to human agency as defined by our giving and receiving of reasons. This amounts to a crass form of constructivism about perceptual experience—the form most often repudiated and the form Coherentists themselves tend to take the least seriously. It is not hard to see why. It is incapable of functioning as a coherent theory about how our observational concepts and judgments can succeed in being "about" the world because it cannot allow our concepts and judgments to be about anything. The domain

47. Davidson's way of advancing on Quine's scheme/content distinction forms his main target in *Mind and World.* See Donald Davidson, "Quine's Externalism," *Grazer Philosophische Studien* 66, no. 1 (2003): 281–97; and Davidson, "The Myth of the Subjective," in *Subjective, Intersubjective, Objective* (New York: Oxford University Press, 2001). Much of McDowell's subsequent refinement and defense of his position against Coherentism, however, has come in the form of his engagements with Robert Brandom's "inferentialist" program. See Steven Hendley, "Answerable to the World: Experience and Practical Intentionality in Brandom's and McDowell's 'Intramural' Debate," *Theoria* 76, no. 2 (2010): 129–51; Robert Brandom, "Non-Inferential Knowledge, Percpetual Experience and Secondary Qualities: Placing McDowell's Empiricism," in *Reading McDowell on Mind and World*, ed. Nicholas H. Smith (New York: Routledge, 2002), 92–106; and John McDowell, "Brandom on Representation and Inference," *Philosophy and Phenomenological Research* 57, no. 1 (1997): 157–62.

48. That is, much of the contemporary literature in the philosophy of perception consists of disputes between Givenist and Coherentist versions of direct realism. Philosophers who hold some version of the other two types tend to act as instigators or discontents with the emerging consensus that direct realism (and its attendant problems) are the most fruitful way forward.

of concepts is thus self-referential. In denying that there are Givens, we are left without any appeal to a mind-internal relation to nonconceptual content that our conceptual thinking could be directed on. In denying that there is a world external to thought, we are left without a mind-external relation to the nonconceptual world for our observational thinking to be directed on. It follows that our conceptual thinking does not succeed in making anything available to thought other than thinking itself; the only thing that our observational concepts and judgments could be "about" are those concepts and judgments themselves. But it is not possible to make any coherent sense of that idea.

Suppose that the rational relations characteristic of our conceptual frameworks are all there is and that we should reject the very idea of "the layout of reality" independent of our discursive activities, not just as an epistemic notion of our access to such a reality but as an ontological notion of there *being* any such reality. This straightforwardly implies that the way things are is identical with the way that discursive agents or communities of discursive agents conceive them to be. But there are discursive agents or communities (I dare say, most of them) who conceive of the way things are as precisely *not* reducible to the way anyone conceives them to be. It follows that the way things are both is and is not the way we conceive them to be. It is even possible for the very same thinker to hold and act on inconsistent beliefs about the way the world is, such that one and the same person simultaneously affirms both that the way things are is identical to the way we conceive them to be and that the way things are is *not* identical with the way we conceive them to be. But if the affirmation of phenomenalist Coherentism entails its own denial, then we could have no idea what it *means* to affirm or deny it, and as such we can make no more sense of its falsity than we can its truth. It is not merely false, but unintelligible.[49]

Direct realist and indirect realist Coherentism both differ from crass constructivism in one crucial respect. Both take it that there is such a thing as a mind-independent and nonconceptually constituted layout of reality. Further, both take it that such a reality guides and constrains the way we introduce and use observational concepts. What differentiates both versions from their Givenist cousins is the story they tell about how the external world's bearing on us secures the necessary guidance and constraint on the normative context of our empirical thinking. Givenists are *internalists* about this question, believing that we "take in" the world's bearing on us in the form of an impression that can inform and justify our empirical concepts. Direct realist and indirect realist Coherentists, on the other hand, are externalists. On an externalist account, the nonconceptual world's bearing on us in experience is not a mentalistic affair at all.[50]

Rather than internalizing an impression, externalists picture our acquaintance with the layout of reality as operating outside the domain of our intentional thinking while remaining in some way externally correlated with it. Our receptivity to the world's impingements on us, which takes place outside the domain of thought, tracks "side by side" with that domain, tethering the normative context of concept use to the nonnormative context of the world. Our observational concepts and judgments may therefore evince, exhibit, or embed those impacts on us, since to have an

---

49. This is why it often figures as the conclusion to a *reductio* in disputes about how the world bears on thought, and functions mostly as a foil in philosophical discussions of that sort. Often what we find are philosophers such as Rorty or Derrida, to name two examples, who seem to urge on us something like a crass constructivism until confronted with the patent incoherence of that view, at which point they retreat to a more moderate (but also less radical or interesting) form of constructivism, protesting the failure to understand the subtlety of their views. When met with surprise about how tame such positions seem, they then shift their weight back to the other leg, as it were, and protest that their interlocutors have failed to understand how radical their views really are.

50. Tim Crane, "Is There a Perceptual Relation?" in *Perceptual Experience*, ed. T. Gendler and J. Hawthorne (New York: Oxford University Press, 2006), 126–46.

empirical concept presupposes such impacts. But the impacts or worldly impingements themselves do not constitute or represent a form of mental content that we possess independently of our conceptual thinking.[51] Direct realist and indirect realist Coherentists differ principally in the way they picture the coordination between the world's mind-external impingements on us and the observational concepts associated with them.

On one way of picturing that coordination, our minds are so constituted that the world's impingements on us give rise to empirical concepts, and those empirical concepts, not any feature of the world itself, figure into our observational thinking. This is the view traditionally attributed to Kant, who (on this reading) pictures the external world's relationship to the mind as impinging upon it with the result that we are saddled with empirical concepts. But, on this picture, whatever external objects impinge upon us and whatever the nature of the impingement might be is entirely unavailable to us—neither is ever represented in any way in what appears to consciousness. Rather, what appears to consciousness are our empirical concepts, whose modes and content are determined entirely by the shape of our receptivity itself. In experience, then, the mind is "itself the lawgiver of nature."[52] This is sometimes called a "two-world" reading of Kant, precisely because it fundamentally distinguishes between two domains, each containing fundamentally different sorts of objects.

On the one hand, there is the realm of mind-independent objects, or "noumena," that constitute things as they are "in themselves" (*Dinge an sich*). On the other hand, there is the mind-dependent domain of conceptualized objects, or "phenomena," that constitute

---

51. William P. Alston, "Externalist Theories of Perception," *Philosophy and Phenomenological Research* 50 (1990): 73–97.
52. See Immanuel Kant, *Critique of Pure Reason*, trans. Norman Kemp Smith with intro. by Howard Caygill (New York: Palgrave-MacMillan, 2003), A127.

the empirical world, the world as it is experienced by us. A mature human mind consists mainly in an interconnected framework of concepts—rules or specifications that gather together various features of the manifold into unities, synthesizing or organizing it in various ways. Concepts can therefore be seen as facilitating an indirect relation between the phenomenal world of the mind and the noumenal layout of reality itself. While Kant himself held that human minds share a basic underlying structure such that our conceptual apparatus gives rise to a common stock of empirical concepts, others have since tended to gravitate toward the idea that our social-practical and cultural formation gives rise to irreducibly different systems of concepts and thus incommensurable forms of observational thinking.[53]

While, on this picture, there remains such a thing as the nonconceptual layout of reality,[54] the impingement of that reality on us only affords access to the conceptual "outputs" of that impingement. We are thus not capable of any "sideways" perspective that would allow us to *observe* our modes of receptivity to the manifold (our "intuitions"), much less the objects on the other end of those sensory modes of receptivity. Instead, we rely on the empirical concepts generated in the mind by this realm beyond it, the qualitative concepts in virtue of which we experience phenomenal objects *as* having observable properties—like experiencing my coffee

---

53. One way of glossing this debate is whether we ought to follow Kant in regarding the most fundamental rules governing our relation to the manifold as natural or acquired, uniform or diverse, conventional or nomological (law-like).

54. There remains a question, however, about how to properly characterize that nonconceptually constituted reality. We might take it to consist of an arena of noumenal objects, properties, and relations that transcend thought and give rise to the manifold of experience, or we might "shave off" the noumena themselves and strictly identify nonconceptual reality with the "manifold" itself. Husserl and many figures in the phenomenological tradition are often read in this latter way, such that their talk of the Given (*Gegebenheit*) is not talk of our direct awareness of the manifold but the ways in which it is presupposed by our phenomenal consciousness. An alternative line is to construe *Gegebenheit* as a form of mental content that enters into our direct awareness; this falls under "phenomenalism" as I've characterized it.

as having a bitter taste, my three-month-old *as* having a shrill cry, and so on. Those concepts mediate between us and the noumenal world, acting as mental representations (*Vorstellungen*) not of that world as it is in itself but precisely of the world's bearing upon our conceptual capacities via our synthesizing of the manifold.[55]

Two-world Kantianism readily acknowledges that the objects, properties, and relations that appear to us stand at a remove from the objects, properties, and relations that obtain in the world itself. The question is whether it is possible for the proposed connection between the phenomenal and noumenal realms to make sense of the idea that our observational (phenomenal) concepts make ultimate (noumenal) reality available to us, even indirectly. Here the Coherentist version of indirect realism appears to be stuck with a more radical difficulty than the Givenist version. The Givenist's indirect realism can explain the relevant form of indirectness by which our concepts direct us on reality by appealing to *representations*: we are meant to picture a kind of *isomorphism* or *resemblance* that holds between what is "Given"—the nonconceptual content of our perceptual experiences—and the nonconceptual layout of reality itself.

The representation is supposed to be nothing less than a mentalistic re-presentation of reality, making our empirical concepts representations of representations, since the job of such concepts is to identify or pick out the relevant aspect of our nonconceptual representation and incorporate it into the evaluative context of our observational reasoning. The Givenist version of indirect realism therefore has at least a surface plausibility in specifying what goes right and what goes wrong in our perceptual experience. Illusion and hallucination can be analyzed either as a failure of isomorphism

---

55. That is, the conceptualization of the manifold as it is received by our sensory receptivity, such that "all our intuition is nothing but the representation of appearance." Kant, *Critique*, B156.

between the representational Given and the world or as a failure of our concepts to properly incorporate the Given into our observational thinking. Veridical perception can be analyzed as successful on both counts, properly internalizing a resemblance and incorporating it into our conceptual framework.

We have seen already that indirect realist Givenism, like Givenism in general, cannot possibly succeed in this latter task—that of incorporating the representational Given into conceptual thought. Indirect realist Coherentism, however, remedies that problem. Since the empirical content that we derive from the world is always already conceptual content, our experiences can figure directly into the rational relations of our conceptual frameworks. But we only gain this suitability of "fit" between empirical content and our observational concepts by giving up on our "friction" with the world—by abandoning the idea that the impact of reality on our sensibility somehow "shows up" in our conceptual thinking. For it belongs centrally to the two-world picture that the inputs of the manifold impressed upon us by the noumena are of a radically different sort than the resultant conceptual output. Clearly, therefore, we cannot say that our empirical concepts—the exercises of our conceptual capacities upon the manifold—*resemble* the manifold. Nor is it coherent to regard our observational thinking are "representing" the manifold by "organizing" it, "categorizing" it, or otherwise breaking up and schematizing it by way of our phenomenal concepts. As Donald Davidson rightly points out:

> We cannot attach a clear meaning to the notion of organizing a single object (the world, nature etc.) unless that object is understood to contain or consist in other objects. Someone who sets out to organize a closet arranges the things in it. If you are told not to organize the shoes and shirts, but the closet itself, you would be bewildered. How would you organize the Pacific Ocean? Straighten out its shores, perhaps, or relocate its islands, or destroy its fish. . . . How about the other kind

of object, experience? Can we think of a language organizing *it*? Much the same difficulties recur. The notion of organization applies only to pluralities.[56]

If what shows up in the phenomenal domain of ordinary experience on the two-world picture cannot be seen as individuating anything determinate in the noumenal realm or the manifold it gives to sensibility, then we are not entitled to see thought as permeable to the world's bearing on it.[57] Nothing "of" or "about" the noumenal or its bearing on us as a manifold actually enters into our observational thinking or tracks with our empirical concepts in any way that entitles us to regard those concepts as representational "proxies" for the layout of reality. The two-world Kantian picture thus leaves us with the picture of the "world of experience" constituted by phenomenal concepts as walled off from reality. Our concepts form a "veil" between ourselves and the noumena,[58] and we are incapable of directing ourselves on anything beyond the veil, whether directly by presenting them to us as they are in themselves or indirectly by imparting representations of them. But if phenomenal concepts are unable to do the representational work of indirectly referring us to reality that, for instance, Givenist "resemblances" purported to do, then in what sense *can* we regard them as putting us in touch with reality itself?

---

56. Donald Davidson, "On the Very Idea of a Conceptual Scheme," *Proceedings and Address of the American Philosophical Association* 47 (1973–1974): 5–20, 14. The idea of the "manifold" as the indeterminate "material" that is presented to thought as conceptually "formed" trades on the image of a kind of homogeneity, which is what makes it congenial to illustrations involving lumps of Play-Doh pushed through screens or a pie being carved up. They mask the difficulty Davidson identifies by making the numerical plurality of objects we find in the world stand in for the plurality in the types of objects that we find in the world.

57. On the present picture the manifold is given—not "Given"—to capacities of sensibility because what we receive is not internalized or conveyed to the mind independently of our concepts. Instead, we should think about the bearing of the manifold more along the lines of Quine's notion of "surface irritations." See W. V. O. Quine, "Two Dogmas of Empiricism," *Philosophical Review* 60, no. 1 (1951): 20–43.

58. Indeed, the wall runs between our empirical selves and our noumenal selves as well.

Two-world Kantians tether the phenomenal world of empirical objects, properties, and relations to the noumenal layout of reality by appealing to a *transcendental* relation. The noumenal world is the "condition of possibility for" our phenomenal world, and phenomena are therefore what they are *in virtue* of the layout of reality. It would seem that a relation between two nonidentical sets of objects X and Y in which X is a *condition of possibility* for y and which implies that y is what it is *in virtue* of X must be a relation of *causal interaction* between X and Y. The idea that the noumenal is the condition of possibility for the phenomenal is just the idea that the noumenal can serve as a causal explanation for the phenomenal. This transcendental cause from the causal relations is different from what we ordinarily predicate of our phenomenal concepts because we are in principle unable to individuate causes in the noumenal domain and match them up in any localized way to their phenomenal effects. We can only identify the noumenal domain as a whole as that realm the content of which is in principle unavailable to us and then go on to claim that that unspecifiable domain is causally responsible for the phenomenal domain as a whole.

Kant himself is often cagey about identifying the transcendental relation as a globally causal relation between the noumenal and phenomenal worlds, and with good reason. To ascribe a causal property to the noumenal order—whether explicitly or as an implicit presupposition—requires that we have the capacity to pick out that order as that to which the property is being ascribed. But the conceit of the two-world picture elaborated above is precisely the denial that we have any such capacity. If the phenomenal world, the "world of experience," is identical with our observational concepts, and if the noumenal world is incapable of being either presented or represented by the world of experience, then it straightforwardly follows that we cannot think "about" or become directed on anything external to the phenomenal world, much less predicate of it a relational property (that is, "being the transcendental cause of phenomena"). Alvin Plantinga is thus right to say that "Kant's thought founders on the fact that the picture requires that he have knowledge the picture denies him."[59]

But this epistemological incoherence is only a consequence of the deeper incoherence about intentionality. It is not that two-world Coherentism requires us to get something right about the layout of reality itself that our picture stipulates we cannot possibly get right. It is that the picture we are considering does not allow us to get a fix on anything we could call "the layout of reality itself," leaving nothing "about" which we might say anything, whether correctly or incorrectly. Now deprived of the notion of a nonconceptually constituted reality that can act as a mind-external (that is, non-Givenist) constraint on our empirical concepts,[60] all we have left to work with to articulate a mind/world relation are our phenomenal concepts, and this throws us back on the incoherence of phenomenalism described earlier. The Coherentist version of indirect realism thus appears irremediably incoherent.

But if we have to externalize the relation that tethers our observational concepts to the nonconceptual layout of reality, we need not do so by means of a transcendental relation between two distinct worlds. Instead, we can acknowledge a single world, the nonconceptually constituted world as it is in itself, and conceive of that world as having a direct bearing on our formation of empirical concepts. The Givenist version of direct realism involved nonconceptual *presentations* of the world before facing the familiar problems of incorporating those presentations into the normative

59. Alvin Plantinga, *Warranted Christian Belief* (New York: Oxford University Press, 2000), 20.
60. That is, we have been deprived of the concepts of both noumena and the manifold as candidates for what our phenomenal concepts are "about."

context of our empirical concepts. The Coherentist, likewise, if she is to be a direct realist, needs some notion of a direct presentation of nonconceptually constituted features of reality to our capacities of receptivity. But in order to do so in a way that rejects Givenism, the Coherentist cannot characterize direct presentations in terms of the internalization of some nonconceptual mental content. Instead, she must both retain the idea that our observational thinking is a purely normative affair of rational relations that govern our conceptual framework and specify how such thinking is guided and constrained from outside the domain of our responsible freedom by the direct bearing of reality upon us in experience.

In *Mind and World*, Donald Davidson attempts to achieve these desiderata. On Davidson's view, "experiences" do not function as "reasons that extend more widely than the conceptual sphere" but rather as details in the causal history that gives rise to our beliefs. McDowell's gloss on Davidson is that he "thinks experience can be nothing but an extra-conceptual impact on sensibility. So he concludes that experience must be outside the space of reasons. According to Davidson experience is causally relevant to a subject's beliefs and judgments, but it has no bearing on their status as justified or warranted. Davidson says that 'nothing can count as a reason for holding a belief except another belief' (p. 310), and he means in particular that experience cannot count as a reason for holding a belief."[61]

What belongs fundamentally to a Coherentist version of direct realism in this description is the idea that the surrounding environment exerts a direct *causal* constraint on our empirical beliefs and the denial that this causal underpinning of our belief gives it its normative status as part of the evaluative context of our conceptual

---

61. McDowell, *Mind and World*, 14.

framework. That is, the modes of receptivity by which the world bears on us in experience are both causally direct and necessary for a *genetic* explanation of our empirical concepts. The stimulus-response mechanisms of my visual system might well be a necessary ingredient in explaining why, upon seeing my scarf, I was inclined to think or say "my scarf." Since the objects or events of the world are embedded in those causal conditions that gave rise to the concept, we can have no trouble regarding the words or thoughts as being "about" my surrounding environment.

While a causal and genetic account of the world's bearing on sensibility suffices to show how the world itself constrains my observational beliefs, it is not an adequate explanation of the *content* of those beliefs. We should not think of our mental or discursive commerce with the world as trading in "experiences"—those are only the causal underpinnings of our observational beliefs, not what such beliefs are "about."[62] When I think or say "my scarf," I do not have in mind a process of retinal biology (that is, an "experience"). Nor is my scarf itself—the "bare presence" of the physical object—a constituent in the word or thought. Instead, the concept of a scarf encodes a complex and interrelated system of norms and practices that determine the various ways we are permitted or obligated to respond when the object we call a scarf is perceptibly present to us—that is, when its bare presence bears causally on our systems of receptivity in the appropriate way. But we must not conflate an analysis of the nonnormative context of experience to which

---

62. See Davidson, "The Myth of the Subjective," 45: "It is an empirical accident that our ears, eyes, taste buds, and tactile and olfactory organs play an intermediate role in the formation of beliefs about the world. The causal connections between thought and objects and events in the world could have been established in entirely different ways without this making any philosophically significant difference to the contents or veridicality of perceptual belief" (45). The obvious exception here is when my beliefs are directed not on external objects but on my experiences. But the same point would hold in that case—namely, that the causal mechanisms by which I am directed on my experiences are not themselves objects of experience.

nonconceptually constituted objects or "bare presences" belong with the normative context of experience to which our use of observational concepts belongs.

We must instead analyze perceptual experience as coordinating these two irreducibly distinct aspects or dimensions, one having to do with the particular forms of causal influence that external objects have on my receptive capacities and the other having to do with the normative context of my concepts and beliefs. We thus have a "two-ply" analysis of perceptual experience that coordinates two distinct systems in a neatly identifiable division of labor. Since the normative system is explicable as a responsiveness to my causal relationship with my environment, we can regard its guidance and constraint by the world as direct—an immediate relation to objects themselves. But since the normative system is the only one to which we can appeal in order to inform and justify our observational concepts and judgments, we do not encounter any problems about how to "incorporate" any nonconceptual mental content into our conceptual thinking. We therefore seem to have a Coherentist form of "friction" that Givenism was after without confronting its problem of "fit" between two different sorts of mental content. While Davidson's articulation of such a two-ply view has been influential, it is by no means the only one.[63]

---

63. Many contemporary philosophers have developed some sort of two-ply account, which analyzes our observational concepts as precipitating out of our causal embeddedness in the world, in order to maintain both that our empirical thinking belongs in an essentially normative context and that it evinces a causally direct relation to the world. See, e.g., Willem A. deVries and Paul Coates, "Brandom's Two-Ply Error," in *Empiricism, Perceptual Knowledge, Normativity and Realism: Essays on Wilfrid Sellars*, ed. Willem A. deVries (Oxford: Oxford University Press, 2009), 131–46. In chapter 5 I argue that Wilfrid Sellars takes a two-ply view as well. Similarly, we can discern such a view in Rorty's appropriations of Davidson. Whereas they agree about the two-ply structure, they differ significantly from one another in how to properly draw the distinction between the causal and normative dimensions and the way in which perceptual experience evinces a coordination between the two.

McDowell raises an important objection to direct realist Coherentism, particularly its "two-aspect" externalism about empirical content. While his immediate target is Davidson's account of perceptual experience, what he finds objectionable is the two-ply structure common "to all such accounts."[64] Specifically, he complains that, on such accounts, "experience is causally relevant to a subject's beliefs and judgments, but it has no bearing on their status as justified or warranted." As a result, "[this] picture depicts our empirical thinking as engaged in with no rational constraint, but only causal influence, from outside."[65] McDowell's point is that while a two-aspect externalism allows that the bearing of reality on our experience is direct, the directness is of the wrong sort. It is *merely* causal, which is to say it is a nonnormative or nonrational guidance or constraint that the world imposes on our observational concepts. But if the world's direct bearing on us in experience is merely causal in this sense, then we are not entitled to conceive of our observational concepts as putting us in touch with reality at all. Once we are denied conscious internal access to the causal mechanism by which the world produces our conceptual responses, it becomes hard to see how we could possibly know that our responses succeed in tracking with what we are supposed to be responding to.

Suppose that we are on opposite sides of a wall. On my side is a series of buttons and on your side is a series of lights. When I push a button, one of your lights goes on. Thus, there is a sense in which what you experience in your room corresponds or correlates with what is happening in my room. But nothing that happens in

---

64. For example, I see something like the following complaint undergirding McDowell's critique of Rorty in McDowell, "Towards Rehabilitating Objectivity," in *Engaged Intellect* (Cambridge, MA: Harvard University Press, 2009), 204–24, and of Brandom in McDowell, "Knowledge and the Internal Revisited," *Philosophy and Phenomenological Research* 65, no. 1 (January 2002): 97–105.

65. McDowell, *Mind and World*, 14.

your room reveals the way things actually are in my room. Causal externalism gives us no reason to think that something like this is not true for our experiences as well. Our embeddedness in the causal network of the world disposes us to think, say, and do certain things. But since the causal bearing of the world on us that disposes us to form our normative beliefs and judgments is external to our consciousness, it functions like my room with the buttons, whereas the space of my normative judgments functions like your room with the lights.

For you to take in the beliefs or concepts that the nonconceptual world imposes on you as reasons to form further beliefs and concepts is for you to be rationally responsive to the lights in your room, not to anything that happens in my room. So in what sense can we say that the experiences that are the proximal causes of your beliefs (that is, the configuration of lights in your room) could possibly direct you on their distal causes out in the world (the configuration of buttons in my room)? They simply cannot, and empirical responsiveness to the world, on this picture, is accordingly necessarily incapable of securing the world-involving character of our observational thinking.

3.6 Fit, Friction, and a Minimal Empiricism

Givenism and Coherentism represent philosophical puzzlements about the same thing: how does perceptual experience enable a concept-free reality to enter into our conceptual thinking via "experience"? Givenism in its various forms answers that question by appealing to concept-free mental content imposed on thought independently of our conceptual capacities. Whether construed as nonconceptual presentations/representations of a mind-independent reality or as the nonconceptual component of a strictly mind-dependent relation, the Given is supposed to serve as the nonconceptual basis for our observational concepts. But while furnishing the mind a point of contact or "friction" with something outside the normative space of the conceptual, Givenism fails to be able to make any use of what it gives, for we can make no sense of the idea of the normative space of reasons to which our observational concepts belong somehow "incorporating" nonnormative content or "bare" presences. Givenism therefore saddles us with an intractable problem of "fit" between two radically different sorts of mental content.

Coherentism, on the other hand, remedies this by asking us to conceive of the content of experience as wholly normative through and through. Refusing to picture our observational concepts as "grounded" in any concept-free conveyances to the mind thus solves the problem of fit, since empirical concepts are not conceived as bearers of nonconceptual content. But this saddles Coherentism in its various forms with its own intractable problem, that of establishing "friction" between our norms of observational thinking (that is, our empirical concepts) and the nonconceptual world that such thinking is supposed to be "about." How can we be entitled to regard "experience" as constrained by how things are in contrast to how we (or anyone) happen to think they are? We might attempt to renounce any need of such extrinsic constraint, or we might attempt to secure it indirectly via a transcendental relation to the layout of reality or directly via some merely causal coordination between that reality and the rational ordering of our concepts. But whichever option we take, we wind up unable to formulate any coherent sense in which our empirical concepts are rationally informed by the world.

By framing the problem of perception in this way, McDowell is attempting to establish a gestalt in which the fundamental incoherence that drives Givenist theorizing is also precisely that which motivates the Coherentist alternative to it, and vice versa. Whereas Givenism's need for a coherent fit between conceptual content and nonconceptual content appears to be shored up by Coherentism's pure conceptualism about content, this necessarily comes at the expense of the friction Givenism hoped to provide. Likewise, whereas Coherentism's need to secure friction between our concepts and some nonconceptual reality beyond them appears to be shored up by Givenism, this necessarily comes at the expense of the fit between concept and content that Coherentism hoped to provide. Each strategy of theorizing therefore has what the other needs, but since neither strategy is capable of coherently satisfying its desire for what it lacks without giving up what it has, the philosophical theorizing is forced to continue unabated, viciously oscillating within and between these two equally inadequate poles.[66] The attempt to "solve" the problem of perception thus turns out to be like trying to cover a king bed with a queen-sized fitted sheet. Pull it to one side, and the other inevitably comes up short.

The problem of perception has thus given rise to this "seesaw" between two equally incoherent ways of accounting for the world's availability to thought in experience.[67] The interminable oscillation between Givenism and Coherentism reveals that we cannot make sense of our ordinary observational thinking apart from some sort of cooperation between our empirical concepts and whatever features of the world we take those concepts to be "about." The varieties of Givenism and Coherentism surveyed above are incoherent precisely

---

66. That is to say, whereas one can address the problem of perception by taking up an indirect realist, direct realist, or phenomenalist/idealist version of Givenism or Coherentism, the inadequacies of any version one chooses can only lead to one of three equally unsatisfying alternatives. One can either attempt to defend what is ultimately an incoherent view, or move to an equally inadequate version within the same pole of the Givenist/Coherentist oscillation (e.g., from an indirect realist to a realist version of Givenism), or migrate toward some equally inadequate version of the opposite pole (e.g., from a direct realist Givenism to an indirect realist Coherentism).

67. McDowell, *Mind and World*, 9.

insofar as they are capable of securing only one element to the exclusion of the other. Thus, while Givenism rightly aims at an appropriate friction between mind and world, a Givenist friction is incoherent as an analysis of what our observational concepts are "about" precisely insofar as Givens are incapable of fitting into the normative context of our conceptual thinking. Likewise, Coherentism rightly preserves the idea that we must regard our empirical thinking as fundamentally and irreducibly suited to the normative context of conceptual thinking. But a Coherentist analysis of that suitability or fittingness is useless as an explanation of what our empirical concepts are "about" precisely insofar as it either must posit a reality external to thought while making it impossible for our observational concepts to direct us on that reality or must attempt to deny that there is any such reality, an idea that cannot even be intelligibly formulated (that is, without falling into a self-referential incoherence).

The oscillation between Givenism and Coherentism reveals that the very attempt to understand our observational thinking requires that we presuppose a relation between empirical concepts and content that can coherently manifest both fit *and* friction. When we fail to include both dimensions, the result is not merely a *false* view of experience, but an *unintelligible* one—we cannot make any coherent sense of norms of observational thinking unconstrained by any relation to a reality outside of thought, nor can we make coherent sense of observational thinking as incorporating any form of mental content that falls outside the normative space of reasons governing observational thought. If we are to extricate ourselves from speaking nonsense in order to formulate an intelligible gloss on what we mean by the world-directedness of "experience," we are at a minimum required to presuppose some relation between our empirical concepts and their empirical content that coherently evinces both fit and friction.

The logical inseparability of fit and friction therefore constitutes what McDowell calls a "minimal empiricism."[68] As such, the necessity of regarding our perceptual experience as both a fitting and frictional relation between mind and world does not constitute a *contestable theory* about the nature of perceptual experience. Such assumptions are instead what we depend on to fix the topic of perceptual experience; they mark out its fundamental grammar. Such logical inseparability is an "empiricism" because it is a claim about the underlying structure implicit in all the various forms of observational thinking or reporting, logical forms with which we are all quite familiar: for instance, "S perceives (sees, hears, smells, and so on) that P," or "S perceives that X is F," or even the thoughts and reports whose logical form is simply "P" or "X is F," where a perceptual experience gives rise to those thoughts or reports.[69]

The logical inseparability of fit and friction constitutes a *minimal empiricism* in the sense that it is analytic in our empirical thinking as such, a minimal requirement for the intelligibility of observational thinking and reporting. Denying the claim that fit and friction are interdependent dimensions of experience is thus much like denying that bachelors are unmarried. To affirm such a thing of bachelors is not to posit a contestable philosophical theory about the nature of bachelors but to state a trivial truism. To deny it is therefore not to raise a genuine problem on the basis of which we can propose a rival philosophical theory (for instance, an account of the married bachelor). To issue such denials or contravening theories is just to

---

68. Ibid., xi.
69. That it was a perceptual experience rather than, say, an inference that served as the basis for such thoughts or reports is easily determined by imagining how the subject would reply to an inquiry about why she thinks that P, or that X is F—a request for her source of information or her justification for such a claim.

speak nonsense, to refuse a trivial truth that constitutes the grammar of our talk about bachelorhood and, as such, is logically necessary.[70] In just the same way, McDowell characterizes the problem of perception as an attempt to problematize the trivial truth that experience must coherently incorporate both fit and friction, a truth constitutive of the grammar of perception.[71]

Givenism and Coherentism, much like rival theories of bachelorhood, thus turn out to be philosophical attempts at denying a trivial or logical truism, but one that holds for perceptual experience instead of bachelorhood—namely, that experience is a way of "taking in the world," a way of incorporating the impacts of a mind-external reality on us into the normative context of thought. It follows that to reaffirm a minimal empiricism in the face of Givenism and Coherentism cannot be regarded either as the positing of a philosophical solution to the problem of perception or indeed as a philosophical theory at all. Instead, it could only be a *reminder* of a trivial truth about our observational thinking.[72]

The need for a reminder, however, is not only parasitic on the fact of forgetfulness but also always indexed to the type and degree of forgetfulness in play. This feature of the reminder reveals an important dimension of the dynamic relationship between the futile (but often vigorous) attempts to impugn a minimal empiricism and the corresponding ability of the truism embodied by minimal

70. A truth that, surely, you already implicitly acknowledge. If you were to protest, I could only assume that you had been led into a serious confusion or perhaps that there had been a breakdown in communication between us. Charity would demand that I conclude either that you were unaware of speaking nonsense or that you were saying something intelligible but that one or both of us is using language in a nonstandard way. See Donald Davidson, "Radical Interpretation Interpreted," *Philosophical Perspectives* 8, Logic and Language (1994): 121–28.

71. To ask the "how possible?" question as if it required a philosophical explanation, a theory of perception. See McDowell, "Experiencing the World," 245.

72. Ses Marie McGinn, *Elucidating the Tractatus: Wittgenstein's Early Philosophy of Logic and Language* (New York: Oxford University Press, 2006), for the significance of Wittgenstein's reminders that "language itself reveals how it functions" (13). See also McDowell, "How Not to Read *Philosophical Investigations*: Brandom's Wittgenstein," in *Engaged Intellect*, 96–114.

empiricism to keep pace with those attempts. My elaboration of McDowell's picture of the oscillation is a bit finer grained than the one he himself offers in *Mind and World*. I elaborated on his discussion of Givenist and Coherentist strategies addressed to the problem of perception in terms of the three substrategies I take to be internal to them: direct realism, indirect realism, and phenomenalism/idealism. But this elaboration is fairly coarse insofar as it deals with the misguidedness not of individual theorists and theories but of *types* of theories. We could attend to the most exquisitely sophisticated bits of philosophical machinery that have been crafted and deployed to address the problem of perception. Were we to do so, the demands on a McDowellian therapy to reveal what appears to be serious philosophy as incoherent nonsense would mount accordingly.

Another way to put the point is to say that anyone whom I might be inclined to label a "Givenist" or a "Coherentist" will no doubt reject the designation, either because she does not acknowledge the problems of fit or friction or because she does acknowledge such problems but takes them to be tractable and thus takes *her* particular account to escape the relevant difficulties. For such a person, the effectiveness of a McDowellian therapy consists not in flatly denying or altogether sidestepping the pseudophilosophical materials out of which she has constructed her simulacrum of a minimal empiricism. Instead, we must engage her theoretical construction in its particularity in order to reveal it *as* pseudophilosophical.[73]

---

73. There is a strong family resemblance between a therapeutic deconstruction of this sort and Derridean deconstruction. The two are decidedly different, however, insofar as the platform from which a therapeutic deconstruction proceeds is a trivial truism, on the basis of which theoretical constructions can be dispatched via a *reductio ad absurdum*. The Derridean conception, on the other hand, purports to make the deconstructive moment intelligible without any platform whatever, as a kind of *groundless* exercise. See Jacques Derrida, "Et Cetera," trans. Geoff Bennington, in *Deconstructions: A User's Guide*, ed. Nicolas Royle (London: Palgrave Macmillan, 2000), 282–305: "Each time that I say 'deconstruction and X (regardless of the concept or the theme),' this is the prelude to a very singular division that turns this X into, or rather makes appear in this X, *an impossibility that becomes its proper and*

McDowell's therapy issues the reminder of a minimal empiricism's trivial truism by going *through* philosophy rather than by standing alongside it and calling out: "Nonsense! Experience is just taking in the world in some way (visually, orally, and so forth)!"[74] His redeployments of various bits of conceptual machinery taken from the likes of Plato and Aristotle, Kant and Frege, Wilfrid Sellars and Gareth Evans are therefore best seen as strategic reappropriations aimed at illuminating some feature of the trivial truism of minimal empiricism against its wrongheaded philosophical detractors.[75]

As a consequence of this, however, McDowell is routinely read as advancing a positive philosophical thesis about the intentionality of "experience" rather than simply reminding us of what we must assume to mark out or deploy the very idea of experience. This confusion about the therapeutic character of McDowell's claim is not helped by the fact that McDowell himself is often happy to align himself with what sound conspicuously like positive philosophical stances or views. But in each case, it is simply a minimal empiricism—a necessary commitment to the inextricability of friction and fit—that is functioning to deflate the entire tradition of philosophical theorizing addressed to the problem of perception. Such a deflation cuts through various theoretically high-flown conceptions of experience by revealing them either as mere logical entailments of a trivial and incontestable truism about experience or

---

sole possibility, with the result that between the X as possible and the 'same' X as impossible, *there is nothing but a relation of homonymy*, a relation for which we have to provide an account" (300, my emphasis). The necessary homonymy of the impossible and the possible (marked here by "sole" and "nothing but") implies that nothing is safe from what I've termed the *reductio*, that there is nothing coherently intelligible from which it proceeds. But this is just another version of phenomenalism or "crass Coherentism" discussed above. The very idea of a groundless and exceptionless deconstruction is, strictly speaking, nonsense. Compare this analysis with Martin Stone's comparative study on Wittgenstein and Derrida on deconstruction in *The New Wittgenstein*, ed. Alice Crary and Rupert Read (New York: Routledge, 2000), 83–117.

74. Maximilian de Gaynesford usefully compares the images of "knot unraveling," therapy," and "dissolution" in *John McDowell* (Malden, MA: Polity, 2004), 14–17.

75. See Tim Thornton, *John McDowell* (Montréal: McGill-Queen's University Press, 2004), 1–2.

as incoherent attempts to challenge or deny that truism, whether directly or by challenging or denying one of its logical entailments. Neither mode of engagement with philosophical theorizing counts as advancing a constructive or contestable thesis. The affirming dimension relegates any useful philosophical reflection on experience to a logical analysis of what we implicitly already know (rather than thinking of such philosophical descriptions in the way they are ordinarily presented—as explaining what we do not already know). The critical dimension exposes as incoherent any attempt to problematize what we already know as a genuine puzzle standing in need of a philosophical solution.

The dimensions are different sides of the same coin. There would be no use for any explicit philosophical analysis of our capacities for perceptual experience as a necessarily fitting and frictional relation between our thinking and the world external to it—no use, in other words, for the affirmative dimension—if we had not mistaken whatever it affirms for a contestable claim, a conceivably incorrect understanding of the intentional structure of perceptual experience among other possible accounts. If that were our dialectical situation, we would be left with the task of marshaling arguments on behalf of one such account over against its competitors. But the vicious oscillation between Givenism and Coherentism demonstrates that this is to have gotten the dialectical situation wrong. While this chapter and the two that follow center on the critical and deconstructive dimension, I will pick up the affirmative dimenstion in chapters 5 and 6.

3.7 Theology in the Oscillation

I have already distinguished between two mutually exclusive ways of accounting theologically for our perceptual relation to God:

cataphatic or apophatic. What distinguishes them, you may recall, is whether or not a single unified understanding of the intentionality of perceptual experience in general—*whatever* such an experience happens to be an experience of—is sufficient to accommodate a theological analysis of the way in which our perceptual experiences of God deliver the content for our God-talk, specifying what such talk is about. Cataphatic analyses are those that characterize revelatory experiences—experiences of God as perceptibly present or acting in some way—as experiences in the ordinary sense, as conforming to the same basic structure of intentionality as our familiar experiences of ordinary objects, properties, and relations in the world. Our experiences of God can establish our God-talk as about God (as contentful, as directing us on various features of God's presence or agency) in a manner strictly parallel (or identical with) the way that our experiences of creatures establish our creature-talk as about them. Unique theological difficulties may arise, of course, when considering the forms of transcendence and immanence by which God is related to the world in comparison with the sort of perceptual equipment with which we have been or can be outfitted.[76]

To have a cataphatic theology of religious experience does not necessarily require denying any such difficulties; it requires only that we analyze and resolve them by appeal to the same working picture of perceptual intentionality we take to govern any putative experiences we might have of the world.[77] That is, the cataphatic

76. I mean to signal here the particular relevance of the cluster of issues I connected with a Christian theology of religious experience in chapter 2—namely, divine transcendence/immanence, human capacities to perceive God, and the grounding and operation of those capacities in nature or divine grace.

77. For example, while cataphatic theologians might dismiss as false or wrongheaded those views of divine transcendence that motivate apophatic critiques of "ontotheology," they need not. If there is nothing inherently inconsistent or nonsensical about denying that God belongs to the order of "being" as its highest instantiation, then there is nothing inherently inconsistent or nonsensical about denying it while also affirming a cataphatic account of our perception of God according to which the structure of intentionality belonging to our ordinary experience is

theologian thinks that the relevant theological worries can be given their due on a standard analysis of how it is that "S perceives X as F" rationally informs and guides S's reporting of her observational belief that X is F, such that those worries ultimately pose no barrier to the possibility of revelatory experience. We can have perceptual experiences that God is thus and so that are sufficient for informing and guiding what we think, say, and do only because the presentation of God to our receptive capacities satisfies the ordinary constraints on receptivity.

At just this juncture the apophatic theologian dissents. An apophatic theology of religious experience, as I have characterized it, is one for which the structure of intentionality characterizing our perceptual relation to God is sui generis. The way in which an experience of the form "S perceives *God* as F" rationally informs and guides S's reporting of an observational belief that God is F cannot be accommodated by the same (or the same sort) of analysis requisite to our ordinary experiences. While such an analysis is *necessary* for an account of our perceptual relation to God, it is not sufficient, for in God's appearing to us, the very structure of intentionality that governs our ordinary experiences is undermined, overwhelmed, overturned, or otherwise disrupted. An analysis of our perception of God on such an account therefore consists of two aims. The first is to endorse some understanding of the standard structure of intentionality and show precisely at which points that structure fails to accommodate the relevant theological considerations.[78] The second is to specify the sui generis way in which God's bearing on us manages to rationally guide and inform our God-talk,

---

somehow capable of accommodating both our directedness on items in the order of being and on God who is in the relevant sense "beyond" or "above" that order.

78. Considerations, that is, about the perceptible presence of God's presence and agency given by God's relation to the world or the nature of the perceptual equipment we have or can acquire.

notwithstanding the aforementioned breakdown of our ordinary perceptual intentionality. Crucially for Givenism, there is on such a view a sense in which presentations of God remain available to us, and there is also a sense in which our receptivity to those presentations guides or constrains what we say about God's appearing to us as F.

The "aboutness" genuinely achieved in our God-talk is not achieved by accommodating revelation within the limits of our receptivity but by transgressing those limits, in virtue of the specific way our receptivity fails to accommodate divine self-presentation. The resulting success of perceptual intentionality precisely *in* or *by means of* its failure is what generates the apophatic insistence on an equivocation between ordinary and revelatory conceptions of experience indexed to two corresponding sorts of aboutness by which reality's bearing on our receptivity can inform our intentions. The ordinary conception tracks the way in which the world's nonrevelatory bearing on us enters into thought and language (the way in which, for instance, my perceptual relation to Whitney Yadav ordinarily enables me to fix the semantic content of the singular term "Whitney Yadav"), while the revelatory conception tracks the unique sense in which God's bearing on us remains unsusceptible of entering into language by way of the relevant process characteristic of nonrevelatory experiences. The sui generis bearing that God has on our receptivity is such that the only way such a revelatory experience can enter into thought and language at all is via the failed operation of our intentional capacities upon it (such that, for example, the failure of a perceptual presentation of God to enable me to exercise my conceptual capacities to fix the semantic content of the singular term "God" in the ordinary way is itself what fixes the semantic content of the singular term "God"). This notion of success-in-failure with respect to our perceptual intentionality of

God also explains the characteristic negativity and paradox essential to an apophatic construal of theological discourse.

I have thus far been putting the matter of apophasis and cataphasis in keeping with the traditional (and etymological) focus on how God enters into our *language* by way of revelatory experience.[79] To fix the language of Christian revelation as apophatic or cataphatic is thus to specify how revelatory content—our experiences of God—manages to supply our *utterances* with the content in virtue of which they succeed in being about God. But, of course, what we say is only one way of characterizing our rational responsiveness to revelatory content. Whatever is revealed to us by way of God's self-presentations can equally well be contemplated without giving way to speech; moreover, it can elicit our desire, immediately motivating us to act or attempt to act apart from any prior contemplative thinking (for example, deliberation) or intervening utterances.[80] Our experiences of God therefore give content to our intentional thinking and bodily actions as well as our linguistic utterances. We can thus generalize from the narrower language-oriented emphasis of apophatic/cataphatic analyses of the role revelatory experience plays in rationally guiding and informing our intentional behavior and instead regard both types as aimed at the full range of such behavior:

---

79. Cataphasis caries the idea of "descending" (*kata*) to human linguistic accessibility, versus apophasis, which denotes a way of remaining linguistically accessible only via some kind of "disclamation" (*apophanai*).

80. The traditional emphasis on language would have a particularly appropriate significance if we take linguistic capacities to be constitutive of our capacities to think or to act. Thought, in other words, is or involves an as-yet unactualized disposition to speak (which is or involves reflection or contemplation insofar as the one so disposed is further disposed to take up various stances toward the disposition to say that P *as* a disposition to say that P). Similarly, we might suppose that to act (or refrain from acting) is always to act (or refrain from acting) under some description, wherein language serves as the repository of available descriptions. Still, on this view, we should insist on distinguishing the linguistic expression of contemplation in the articulation of theological discourse from the contemplation itself or from those expressions of linguistic dispositions that are manifest not by way of discursive articulation but by way of bodily action. Thus, capacities of linguistic utterance, even when they are the hinge on which capacities of thinking and acting turn, cannot be strictly *identified* with thought and action.

they are alternative ways of accounting for the structured relations between the content conveyed in revelatory experiences and the thoughts, words, and deeds by way of which we are intentionally directed on the content of those experiences. Moreover, when the apophatic/cataphatic distinction is delineated in the way I suggested, any proposed theology of religious experience—once made fully explicit—is thus ultimately *either* cataphatic *or* apophatic, never both. That is, an overarching and unifying structure of perceptual intentionality is either sufficient to account for our experiences of both God and creatures or it is not.[81]

Having thus enriched the distinction a bit, we can return to the context in which I initially introduced it. In the first chapter, I emphasized that both apophatic and cataphatic theologies of religious experience are constitutively dependent on some conception of "experience in general." For the sake of simplifying the exposition, I said that we cannot explain revelatory perception in either cataphatic or apophatic terms without presupposing some conception of ordinary perception, whether we take revelatory perception to be an instantiation of it or a disruption of it. As a further clarification, this claim about the priority of ordinary perception to revelatory perception does not entail any particular claim about *explanatory priority*. The dependence of any analysis of revelatory experience on

---

81. While we must accordingly recognize the mutual exclusivity of apophatic and cataphatic theologies of religious experience, this is perfectly consistent with recognizing both apophatic and cataphatic elements in either sort of account, although the sense in which the relevant features of the account in question are apophatic and catapathic will depend on or derive from the more fundamental sense in which the account itself is an apophatic or cataphatic one. For example, on a cataphatic account, its apophatic elements may include some acknowledgment that certain features of God are simply unavailable to experience but only indirectly indicated by it, and it may further characterize the respects in which God is unavailable to ordinary experience as involving its insufficiency to inform or rationally justify certain sorts of theological claims, or as generating a paradox or as engendering ascetic discipline or contemplation. Likewise, apophatic accounts can recognize cataphatic elements by emphasizing, for example, the constitutive role of the intentional operations of ordinary perception as a necessary first step in God's entrance into theological discourse.

some analysis of ordinary experience is not explanatory but logical. That is, the notion of ordinary experience is analytic in the notion of revelatory experience, and this is true whichever notion is prior in the order of explanation or understanding. Counterintuitive as it may seem, it is perfectly possible that the intentionality of ordinary experience is ultimately only explicable or intelligible as derivative of a proper conception of the intentionality of revelatory experience. Alternatively, it could be that ordinary experience is the more primitive notion and we have to derive our explanatory account of revelatory experience from it, or that neither notion is an explanatory primitive but that each instead is partially constituted by the other.

Whichever way we take the order of explanation to go—whether the instantiation of one depends upon that of the other and not vice versa, or whether they must be mutually instantiated or not at all—the very same logical relation between them holds: the intentionality of ordinary experience and that of revelatory experience are either fundamentally parallel/identical in structure (cataphatic), or the intentionality of revelatory experience contravenes that of ordinary experience (whether such contravening is analyzed as a derivative notion or a prior one). When we are after a theology of religious experience—the forms of intentionality made possible by revelation—we cannot treat the topic without also and thereby treating the topic of ordinary experience; we cannot manage to say what a revelatory experience is without saying (even if implicitly) what we think an "ordinary" experience is. Because of this logical overlap or constitutive dependence between the notions of ordinary experience and revelatory experience, any analysis whatsoever of the latter will entail some corresponding analysis of the former. It is in this sense that I have claimed we cannot avoid acknowledging that a theology of religious experience *supervenes* upon some conception of ordinary experience. When two theologians disagree about the structured relations by which ordinary experience guides and informs our intentional behavior, they will necessarily disagree about the structured relations by which revelatory experience guides and informs our intentional behavior.[82]

From the supervenience of a conception of revelatory experience on a conception of ordinary experience, it further follows that any putative difficulty we confront about ordinary experience will necessarily and correspondingly confront our theologies of religious experience, whether apophatic or cataphatic. The philosophical "problem of perception" is just such an apparent difficulty: how is it possible for a nonconceptually constituted world—one that stands independent of the normative framework of our concepts—to bear on our sensory equipment in the sort of way required for our thinking to count as "about" the world? The movement from our experiential intake of objects, properties, and relations existing in a nonrational space (one devoid of any intrinsically rational relations) to the various intentional stances we can take toward such objects, properties, and relations (our placing of them within a logical space of rational relations) appears to be utterly mysterious, like something of a magic trick.

But in order to make sense of what it is for Christians to be receptive to revelation—to an experiential intake of God that guides and informs our intentional behavior "about" God—either in cataphatic or apophatic terms, we seem compelled to commit ourselves (even if inadvertently) to some explication of how the trick is done. Only with some understanding in hand of how it is possible for the world's nonconceptually constituted bearing on us to guide or inform our intentional behavior at all can we specify

---

82. The reverse, however, is not necessarily true. It is possible to conceive of two theologians disagreeing about the structured relations that constitute a perceptual intention directing us upon God while agreeing about the structured relations that constitute a perceptual intention of objects, properties, and relations lacking of divinity.

how such a structured relation (or some suitable parallel to it) is either unproblematically instantiated (cataphatically realized) or else disrupted in some sui generis way (apophatically realized) in our perceptual relation to God. The problem of perception therefore directly determines what sort of structured relation between us and God is governing our construal of the intentionality of revelation, whether that construal is cataphatic or apophatic.

There are only two ways of analyzing our capacity to be normatively guided and informed by the world's nonconceptual bearing on us, broadly two sorts of explanations of what such a capacity must amount to: on the boundary-impression explanation, the nonconceptual constitution of reality is internalized in a nonconceptual Given that mediates across the boundary between the nonconceptual world and our conceptual thinking by serving as the empirical content of those concepts. "Experience" is thus a form of cognition that serves as a mental anchor outside the framework of concepts that normatively governs our conceptual thinking, and, as such, the Given allows the nonconceptual layout of reality itself to inform and guide our intentions. On the social-practical explanation, there is no penetration of the nonconceptual layout of reality into the normative domain of our conceptual thinking. We must reject the very idea of a cognition not dependent on the norms of concept use that in fact regulate what we actually think, say, and do. If, however, we wish to recognize this while embracing the idea of the world as a nonrationally constituted space and avoiding any commitment to the idea that the whole of "reality" itself is mind-dependent, our options are limited. We must regard the relevant sense of "experiential intake" by which we comport ourselves to the nonrationally constituted layout of reality as always already embedded within the social and discursive space of reasons that normatively informs, guides, and corrects what we happen to think, say, and do.

All of the recent contestations between apophatic and cataphatic theologies of religious experience, I contend, have accordingly been played out on the field of these apparently rival philosophies of ordinary experience. We therefore appear to be compelled to adopt and defend, whether implicitly or explicitly, either a boundary-impression or a social-practical resolution to the problem of perception in the service of advocating either a cataphatic or an apophatic analysis of our perceptual relation to God. A landscape marked by these options for theological reflection yields four typical views, determined by whether the theorist in question takes (or assumes) a boundary-impression view or a social-practical view addressed to the problem of perception and whether either view is deployed in a cataphatic or an apophatic account of our perception of God.

Of course, when we consider the sheer number and variety of theological analyses attempting to articulate the proper way to conceive of God's entering into the intentional behavior of Christian belief and practice, few actually self-consciously regard themselves as taking up one of the strategies of the fourfold spectrum I have delineated. None of which I am aware recognizes the wider landscape of options as even apparently constituted by that spectrum, much less as actually constituted by it. In this limited sense, I am happy to acknowledge that the fourfold range of perspectives on the matter is merely ideal-typical. But I nevertheless claim that for any particular account of revelatory intentionality, the more explicit it is, the more explicit will be the entanglement of its theological commitments (to apophaticism or cataphaticism) with its philosophical commitments (to a boundary-impression or a social-practical theory of perception). I have already offered four such views in which the intentionality of our experiences of God is made explicit, each an influential example of one possible strategy belonging to the fourfold range.

Thus, I have taken William P. Alston and Jean-Luc Marion to represent, respectively, cataphatic and apophatic proposals underwritten by a boundary-impression view. The view of ordinary experience that Alston takes to be sufficient for his analysis of revelatory experience is one in which the nonconceptual content impressed on us in experience enjoys both a logical and explanatory priority in guiding and informing our normative intentions.[83] While developing a quite different species of boundary-impression view about ordinary experience, Marion's theory belongs to the same philosophical genus insofar as he sees our receiving the givenness of phenomenal content as always both logically and explanatorily prior to the subjection of that content to conceptual control.[84] But contrary to Alston's cataphatic impulse to regard what he calls "Christian mystical perception" as formally parallel or analogous to the intentional structure of our "ordinary" sense perception, Marion takes the ordinary conceptual control over what is given to be necessarily overturned in his apophatic analysis of revelation.

Victor Preller and Kevin Hector, on the other hand, represent, respectively, apophatic and cataphatic accounts determined by a social-practical account of ordinary experience.[85] Both reject the logical and explanatory priority of nonconceptual content as that which rationally informs and guides our intentional behavior, prioritizing instead the process of social learning by which we learn to form and use concepts in which our sensory relation to the nonconceptual layout of reality is inescapably embedded. But

83. Wlliam P. Alston, *Perceiving God: The Epistemology of Religious Experience* (Ithaca, NY: Cornell University Press, 1991).

84. Marion, *In Excess*.

85. Victor Preller, *Divine Science and the Science of God: A Reformulation of Thomas Aquinas* (Princeton, NJ: Princeton University Press, 1967); Hector, *Theology without Metaphysics*.

whereas Preller takes a social-practical account of ordinary experience to be insufficient to account for our capacity to have ordinary experiences of God or to use language to speak about God, Hector has recently advocated the possibility of appropriating a very similar sort of philosophical theory of perception in a theory of meaning, truth, and reference capable of accommodating the full range of intentional behavior by which Christians take themselves to be directed on God.

3.8 Conclusion

Having momentarily departed from the previous chapter's analysis of the landscape in which Christian philosophers and theologians continue toiling over the ground of our perceptual relation to God, we shifted our attention in this chapter to look beneath the surface of that landscape, to assess its philosophical ground. By way of McDowell's approach to the deconstruction of the problem of perception we have seen that, contrary to all appearances, both the Givenism of boundary-impression views and the anti-Givenist Coherentism of social-practical views constitute irremediably bad soil. By failing to coherently hold together the kind of fit and friction necessary for the very idea that our intentional behaviors are intentional—that the world's bearing on us enables our thought, speech, and action to direct us on whatever they purport to be about—both sorts of philosophical strategies turn out to be failed articulations of the minimal empiricism trivially entailed by the very notion of intentionality rather than rival conceptions of the contestable status and role of empirical content in intentionality.

The ongoing (and mutually motivating) contestations between Givenist and Coherentist accounts of empirical content, therefore, do not represent fertile ground for an analysis of the way in which what we think, say, and do manages to be about the world. Nor is the ground merely fallow, perhaps awaiting the proper cultivation by a more adequate analysis of a nonconceptual givenness or of the world's merely causal or transcendental embeddedness in the discursive and practical norms of our language and concept use. Rather, the vicious oscillation between Givenism and Coherentism is generated by the inner logic of each strategy per se, making an allegiance to either broadly defined approach a necessarily fruitless endeavor. Where the working out of either or the mutual contestation between the two has *appeared* to produce fruit, garnering praise or blame as more or less useful elucidations of our capacities for empirical knowledge, what has in fact been produced is nonsense, not so much as susceptible of appraisal *as* fruit. The philosophical elaborations and mutual oppositions in question all take place within a field of theorizing whose very internal structure is incoherent: our intentional directedness on the world, we are told, is made possible either by our receptivity to givens that we cannot get or else through the kind of embeddedness in the world in which the world cannot rationally constrain our intentional responses to it.

We are thus now in a position to return topside to consider anew the four strategies being deployed to account for our perceptual relation to God, by way of Alston, Marion, Hector, and Preller, whom I take to be among their most rigorous defenders.[86] But with a gestalt in place that reveals the absurdity of Givenism and Coherenism, we can now see this same landscape in a very different

86. To illustrate the range of options currently dominating the contemporary landscape of thinking on the matter, I have focused on these four examples, but it is not hard to see how any proposed account might fit the taxonomy. This is not to say, of course, that *every* contemporary approach to the problem of the perception of God is either a Givenist or a Coherentist apophaticism or else a Givenist or a Coherentist cataphaticism, though the most influential and well-worked-out accounts of which I am aware are. Difficult cases, I have found, tend to be difficult only because they trade on a conception of "ordinary perception" whose assumptions have not been made fully explicit.

light. From the fundamental incoherence of the theories addressed to the problem of perception, it follows that the theologies of religious experience incorporating those theories are likewise incoherent—*ex absurditate*, we might say, *absurdum fit*. Any genuinely significant philosophical and theological insights notwithstanding, our attempts to plant any account of our perceptual relation to God within the poisonous soil of Givenism or Coherentism will ultimately make nonsense of that relation. Once the structure of intentionality belonging to "ordinary experience" stands revealed as incoherent, then so too should the proposals about the structure of "revelatory experience" that they model on ordinary experience, whether by cataphatically affirming the structural parity between the two or by apophatically denying that parity via a transgression of one structure by the other. Given the supervenience of our theologies of religious experience upon the problem of perception, a McDowellian deconstruction of the latter entails a devastating critique of the former.

Accordingly, in part 2 I will argue that Marion and Alston occupy, respectively, apophatic and cataphatic versions of the Givenist pole of a theology of revelation, while Preller and Hector take up, respectively, apophatic and cataphatic versions of the Coherentist pole. Despite the incoherence I attribute to each thinker's account, they represent varied and deeply nuanced arguments and insights in which there is much to be valued, were they not crippled by the vicious oscillation. Since it is the peculiar way in which each figure inflects one or the other pole of that oscillation that principally interests me, however, I will not attend to a good portion of their thinking. It will be enough for the ground-clearing purposes of my argument to simply appropriate the McDowellian picture of the vicious oscillation I have sketched in this chapter to unmask the account of "ordinary perception" constitutive of each thinker's

apophatic or cataphatic account as a version of Givenism or
Coherentism.

PART II

The Perception of God in Some Recent Philosophical Theology

4

Marion, Alston, and the Myth of the Given

In part 1, I have argued that contemporary thinking about God's availability to perceptual experience has come to be dominated first and foremost by philosophical reflection on the nature of perception itself. The problem of perception is just the problem of how the world's impacts on us in experience can furnish us with standards of correctness capable of informing and justifying our observational beliefs. One sort of answer—Givenism—has it that the world imparts to us a special form of mental content that is at once free of the conceptual shape of our thinking and capable of conveying to us the mind-independent structure of the world. Another sort of answer—Coherentism—denies that the world imparts us with idea-like "givens" of this sort, and instead holds that the world's impacts on us causally dispose us to thinking and acting in certain ways.

But in the last chapter we saw that Givenism and Coherentism are equally bad theories of perceptual experience, precisely insofar as neither is capable of explaining how it is that experience makes our beliefs rationally accountable to the world. Whereas Givenist theories purport to show us how experience can put our thinking in touch with the world, it conceives of the givens that the world imparts to thought in a way that cannot possibly make us rationally accountable to them. Coherentism, for its part, purports to show how deliverances of experience can take the proper form to make us rationally accountable to the world. But it fails to show us how experiences themselves manage to actually put our thinking in touch with the world, since it conceives of such experiences in terms of the world's merely causal and non-normative impacts on us. Each sort of view has something the other needs but cannot have: Givenism supplies us a kind of rational fit between mind and world but without friction, while Coherentism supplies us with a kind of friction between mind and world but without fit. These two kinds of theories have therefore been mutually motivating, resulting in a vicious oscillation between them in the contemporary philosophy of mind.

The incoherent accounts of perceptual experience that have resulted from this vicious oscillation, I claim, have infected theological accounts of God's availability to us in perception. Those Christian philosophical theologians and philosophers of religion interested in offering an account of God's availability to us in experience have proceeded by endorsing or developing either a Givenist or a Coherentist account of perception per se and applying that account to God. Whether such accounts are essentially apophatic or cataphatic has depended upon whether God, as an object of perception, somehow uniquely undermines or overturns the structure of the perceptual relation, whether understood in a Givenist or a Coherentist way. In this chapter I aim to critique two influential Givenist accounts of perceiving God, one apophatic (Jean-Luc Marion) and the other cataphatic (William P. Alston).

4.1 Jean-Luc Marion and the Phenomenology of Revelation

Jean-Luc Marion's theology of revelation has been increasingly influential as a way of articulating the Christian commitment to God's self-impartation through revelation while retaining the important qualification provided by the mystical tradition that God is not part of the furniture of the universe—not merely another "being" alongside others, even if the highest among them.[1] Instead, God is, as Anselm has it, "that than which a greater cannot be thought."[2] Marion reads the Anselmian dictum to suggest not that God is the instantiation of our concept of maximal greatness but rather that God is necessarily *greater than* our concept of maximal greatness—for any attributive concept of God we possess or in any sense could possess, if that concept presumes to be adequate to pick out God, then it is thereby disqualified from doing so. There must therefore be some intelligible sense in which our concepts of God name (or "denominate") God precisely in their inadequacy to name.[3] Similarly, to be confronted with the content that such concepts purport to pick out is to, in some sense, take in the inconceivable.[4]

Marion offers a phenomenology of how human conscious awareness comes to be directed to anything at all and then derives from this framework an account of the sui generis character of our directedness on revelation, for which he takes Christ to be the paradigmatic instance. Following Husserl, Marion thinks that an explanation of how human awareness directs itself toward objects

1. See, e.g., Merold Westphal, "The Importance of Overcoming Metaphysics for the Life of Faith," *Modern Theology* 23, no. 2 (April 2007): 253–78; and Westphal, *Overcoming Ontotheology: Toward a Postmodern Christian Faith* (New York: Fordham University Press, 2001).
2. Anselm of Canterbury, *Proslogion*, trans. with intro. and notes by Thomas Williams (Indianapolis, IN: Hackett, 1995), 45.
3. Jean-Luc Marion, *In Excess: Studies of Saturated Phenomena*, trans. Vincent Berraud (New York: Fordham University Press, 2004), 144.
4. Marion, *In Excess*, 150–52.

requires that we set aside any and every reference to what does not actually present itself to our conscious awareness—thus, we must bracket all metaphysical transcendences that we infer or presume as a frame for our lived experiences but which do not actually figure constitutively as the stuff of those lived experiences themselves, such as causation, origins, substances, laws, and so forth.[5] Marion takes this subsuming of the distinction between (mere) appearance and reality under a wider phenomenological umbrella of appearing, what I characterized in the previous chapter as "idealism/phenomenalism," to be a principal contribution of the Husserlian project.

Marion attributes to Husserl a radical denial of any conception of reality or the way things are in themselves that posits a gap between how things do (or could) *appear* to us and the way things *are* independently of any actual (or possible) appearances to us. The ways in which things do or could appear, therefore, cannot be analyzed metaphysically, whether as direct presentations or indirect representations of essentially appearance-independent objects, properties, or relations. Instead, the ways things (potentially) appear to us just is the way they are, provided that what we think about them is strictly limited to what is actually *given* in the appearance—that we do not posit anything other than that which "shows up" as a constitutive feature of that which is given.[6]

Therefore, if we are to isolate the proper sphere of our ability to direct our minds to the things we are aware *of*, we must attend simply to what is given in a phenomenon *as* it is given to us. Following Husserl, Marion analyzes our capacity for a directedness on reality in terms of both a faculty of receptivity to the given—"intuition"—and a faculty of spontaneity by which we subsume what is given under conceptual categories and thereby enable ourselves to take up an

5. Ibid., xi.
6. Ibid., 19.

intentional stance toward the content received in intuition. The mutual relations between intuition and intention, he thinks, yield a complete analysis of our intentionality. To specify what is given is to ask what sort of content we receive in intuition, what belongs not to the conceptual capacities that constitute the horizon of the "I" and that are exercised as responsible freedom in what we think, say, and do but rather that which the I suffers as an intrusion into its conscious awareness. Whatever enters into that domain must, by definition, cross the horizon of our conceptual capacities and, as such, must be conceptually "constituted" by us. We can thus analyze that which appears to us as exemplifying some relation between the content of our receptivity and the conceptual form by which the I constitutes it as something that appears to consciousness.[7]

The relation between intuition and intention is one of "evidence" (*Evidenz*) in which the content we intuit succeeds or fails in fulfilling or fitting the shape of our concepts. Intuited mental content is thus involved in a relation of "adequation" to the concept.[8] The adequation of the intuited given to the conceptual intention results in appearances whose epistemological standing is determined by a "reduction"—by whether or not a given intuition measures up to the concept laid down for it as a regulative rule or standard. The meaningfulness, referentiality, justification, and truth of our intentional behaviors are all a function of the evidentiary relation between intuition and intention.[9] Every phenomenon of our lived

7. Edmund Husserl, *Logical Investigations*, trans. J. N. Findlay (New York: Humanities Press, 1970); Walter Hopp, "Husserl on Sensation, Perception and Interpretation," *Canadian Journal of Philosophy* 38, no. 2 (June 2008): 219–46.

8. Jean-Luc Marion, *Reduction and Givenness: Investigations of Husserl, Heidegger, and Phenomenology*, translated by Thomas A. Carlson (Evanston, IL: Northwestern University Press, 1998), 24.

9. This analysis of falsity strictly belongs to *empirical* concepts, however. Marion also recognizes purely "formal" concepts that are not false but "empty," i.e., trivially true precisely in virtue of failing to be susceptible of an evidentiary relation to the world.

experience of the world follows this pattern. Marion agrees with Husserl that these two possible relations apply to what he calls "poor" objects, cases in which the concept fails to be adequated by any intuited given, and "common-law" objects, cases in which what is suffered in intuition is sufficient for meeting the criteria normatively imposed by the concept, which in turn succeeds in having the meaning it purports to have, in referentially singling out what is given, and in making a referential, justifiable, and truthful identification of the phenomenon in question.[10]

But Marion adds a third possible relation between intuition and intention in which our concepts are overcome, flooded, or *saturated* with that which is given in intuition.[11] Following Kant, Marion takes the domain of the conceptual to establish the subjective horizon of the I and thus to serve as the a priori conditions under which anything can appear to consciousness as an object of thought. The conceptual domain as such, Marion thinks, is exhausted by the concepts belonging to the categories of quantity, quality, relation, and modality—each of which serves as an a priori delimitation on the given. The subject's encounter with a saturated phenomenon is one in which either one or some combination of these four sorts of conceptual delimitations is exceeded by the material content given in an intuition. Saturated phenomena thus evince a kind of *over*adequation in which the conceptual schema of intention is overrun and exceeded by a fulfilling intuition that breaks loose of any mastery of the concept over its manifestation.[12] Such phenomena in

10. Although Marion himself never puts the matter this way, I suspect that he would analyze predicative judgments ("That animal over there is a walrus") compositionally, as complex intentions whose epistemological standing (meaning, reference, justification, etc.) is given by the adequation of its constituents (however that is properly to be analyzed, e.g., the conjunction of the intuitively adequated intentions "there is some X over there," "that X is an animal," and "that X is a walrus," perhaps requiring a further analysis of what fulfilling intuitions are sufficient to adequate the intentions of "animal" and "walrus").

11. See Jean-Luc Marion, *Being Given: Toward a Phenomenology of Givenness*, trans. Jeffrey L. Kosky (Stanford: Stanford University Press, 2002), 199–220.

which the space of intuitive evidence exceeds the space of concepts are what Marion terms "saturated phenomena." The possibility of saturated phenomena shows, Marion argues, that the basis of all phenomenality (the ground of all giving intuition) is both prior to and extends more widely than the domain of our conceptual intention.

The four basic types of saturated phenomena correspond to the Kantian categories of the understanding that regulate the objects of common-law intentions, any one of which may be uniquely overrun by the manifestation of the givenness in an intuition of its nonconceptualizable and unobjectifiable indeterminacy.[13] Thus, the "event" or happening is a phenomenon that manifests the priority and conceptual indeterminacy of givenness in its unpredictability and unrepeatability so as to both submerge and defy all quantifying intentions. The "idol" names those phenomena so overwhelmingly and intolerably "bedazzling" that they cannot be adequated by any qualitative concepts. The givenness of oneself to oneself as "flesh" is experienced as incommunicable and incapable of substitution so as to become absolute, and, as such, the phenomena of experiencing one's flesh *as* one's own escapes capture by our concepts of relation. Finally, "iconic" phenomena subvert the constituting gaze of the intentional "I" in which the mode of one's own looks is surpassed by the experience of finding oneself under the constituting gaze of an unobjectifiable Other. Such an encounter requires a mode of presentation that can only be conceived as exceeding my conceptual capacities to subsume or "appropriate" the "otherness" of another under any mode of presentation constituted by my own intentionality.[14]

---

12. "It sees nothing distinctly . . . but clearly experiences its own powerlessness to master the measurelessness of the intuitive given" (ibid., 216).

13. Ibid., 227; Marion, *In Excess*, 52.

14. Marion, *In Excess*, 53.

Such "experiences," in their break with conceptual understanding, run counter to common-law empirical knowledge in that the domain of givenness, the ground of giving intuition or phenomenality itself, gives itself as a kind of "infinitude" of phenomenal content—whether in the immensity of an event, the intensity of an idol, the univocity of the flesh, or the demand of the icon. Since each of the Kantian categories demarcating the conceptual is also constitutive of the horizon of the I, it follows that each encounter with a saturated phenomenon is an inversion of that horizon in which the self's loss of conceptual control over what is given renders it at the opposite end of the constituting gaze of subjectivity—as one perceived, determined, or constituted by the horizon of another rather than as the one whose conceptual intentions effect the perceiving, constituting, or determining.[15] Saturated phenomena are thus not properly designated as "experiences" constituted by prior conceptual intentions, but as "counter-experiences" constituted by counterintentions—the overcoming of concepts by phenomenal content.[16]

Despite their unique character as contrasted with the objects of everyday experience, Marion does not regard saturated phenomena per se as revelatory or even as rare. Our receptivity to them is instead frequent, ordinary, and banal; they regularly appear in our everyday encounter with the world alongside our experience of common-law objects. There are certain classes of experiences that typify commonly experienced saturated phenomena, such as the event, the painting, one's own flesh, and the faces of others. While encounters that fall under these types readily present themselves to us, their appearance

---

15. In this "inversion of the gaze . . . the I loses primacy as soon as 'the servant' [the subject] is not greater than his 'master' [the given phenomenon]" (Marion, *Being Given*, 240).

16. See Jean-Luc Marion, "The Banality of Saturation," in *Counter-experiences: Reading Jean-Luc Marion*, ed. Kevin Hart (Notre Dame, IN: University of Notre Dame Press, 2007), 383–418, 401–2.

to us *as* saturated phenomena is not guaranteed simply by their givennesss to us as saturated phenomena; rather, it requires our openness to receive them as such. If what gives itself is to fully show itself, we must stay our objectivizing hand from refusing what is given as it is given. Thus, Marion argues that *any* phenomenon given to us as a common-law phenomenon can possibly show itself as a saturated phenomenon.

It follows from the structure of his analysis that even when first-order saturated phenomena show up in accord with their givenness as such, the destabilization of our subjective horizon remains merely partial, since the constituting subject can remain firmly grounded along the remaining categories marking out our subjectivity. For example, the counterexperience of an event can appear via the saturation of my capacities to apply quantitative concepts, even while my capacities to conceptualize (and so master) the event qualitatively, relationally, and modally remain intact. So, despite the gradation characterizing Marion's analysis of "ordinary" and "revelatory" experience as an incremental movement along the axis of intention's saturation, there remains the sharpest phenomenological distinction between the two. First-order saturated phenomena, no matter how residual the subject's conceptual mastery over what appears, remain sufficient to anchor a subject's constituting horizon. But for second-order saturated phenomena, there is nothing left of the determining gaze of the subject, only the inversion of the gaze in which one encounters her own subjectivity as constituted from beyond her own horizon—an experience of the givenness of the given as such in which one comes to see oneself as the given or "gifted" one (*l'adonné*).[17]

---

17. Marion, *Being Given*, 442. See also Tamsin Jones's discussion in *A Genealogy of Marion's Philosophy of Religion: Apparent Darkness* (Bloomington: Indiana University Press, 2011), 115ff.

The unfolding of intuited givens from the phenomenal content from which both intending subjects and their intended objects arise as gifts functions for Marion like the Creator/creature relation, but without a metaphysics of transcendence. Accordingly, the saturation of givenness in any one of the four dimensions above can be thought of as the excessive self-impartation—not of a given phenomenal object but of givenness or phenomenality itself insofar as objectifying categories are exceeded by intuited content. When one encounters the excessiveness of givenness in *all four* respects at once, or what Marion calls a saturation to the "second degree," this can be thought of as the self-impartation or intuition of the fullness of givenness itself.[18] The very possibility of such an impartation is what Marion calls "revelation" in the phenomenological sense. When considered theologically, the realization of revelation in this sense is precisely the revelation of God in which our horizon as experiencing subjects is inverted and we know ourselves as beheld by the God from whom we are given the objective world of phenomena and our very selves as phenomenalizing subjects.

When Marion considers the possibility of revelatory experience (as counterexperience par excellence), both in *Being Given* and in *In Excess*, he gives only one paradigmatic illustration of the possibility (even if not the actuality) of second-degree saturation (or revelation): Jesus, whom he describes as exceeding quantity in his unpredictable and unrepeatable advent that overwhelms all possible expectation, exceeding all possible qualitative concepts in the intensity of his light that unbearably floods our senses, exceeding every possible relation in an absoluteness that saturates every horizon he might confront, and exceeding every possible modality in his irregardable face that inverts our gaze and constitutes us as his witnesses.[19] The

18. Marion, *Being Given*, 367; Marion, *In Excess*, 29.
19. Marion, *In Excess*, 113.

counterexperience in which our subjectivities are overwritten by an intuition that exceeds them makes us witnesses of Jesus, in the specific sense that the truth that has appeared is not produced by our object-constituting conceptual capacities and our subjectivity is thus taken aback. A confrontation with Jesus as revealer and revealed renders us incapable of any possible adequacy of conceptual articulation of what has appeared.

Instead, as witnesses in Marion's sense, our speech belongs to an endless or "infinite" hermeneutic.[20] Any quantitative, qualitative, relational, or modal predication we might seek to apply—which is to say, any predicate at all—will always be "overadequated"—finding its fulfillment and yet not properly applying—to Jesus. The revelatory encounter is thus never (and can never be) determined by any determinate concept we might assign to it. Rather, in supplying our conceptual thinking with an inexhaustible supply of evidence, revelatory experience is the radical other to the objective determinability characteristic of ordinary experience, an objectivity whose residue remains even in the banal saturated phenomena (events, art, bodily self-knowledge, other minds, and the like) whose incapability of adequation remains imperfect.

The hinge on which Marion's phenomenological analysis of ordinary and revelatory experiences turns is thus that of the saturated phenomenon. That notion serves as the bridge concept that permits us to recognize the nonobjectivity (the conceptual indeterminacy) of our ordinary experience whose maximum or limit concept is constituted by the notion of a revelatory counterexperience. In regarding revelation (second-degree saturated phenomena) as an inversion of our subjective horizon and an overturning of our ordinary perceptual capacities for conceptual mastery over what

---

20. Ibid., 112; Robyn Horner, *Jean-Luc Marion: A Theo-Logical Introduction* (Burlington, VT: Ashgate, 2005), 43.

appears to us, Marion clearly takes up an analysis that is apophatic in my sense of the term. Whereas the structure of ordinary experience in his phenomenology is indexed by the object-constituting determinacy of adequation to a concept (specifically, a concept belonging to one of the four Kantian categories), the apophatic structure of revelatory experience consists in overturning the ordinary structure of experience—that is, in the loss of all conceptual determinacy.[21]

Arguably, while the formal distinction between ordinary and revelatory experience for Marion is a matter of whether a phenomenon retains any objective determinacy (if yes, it is ordinary, even if partially saturated; if no, it is revelatory), the *phenomenological* distinction between the two[22]—the difference in what it is like to undergo the relevant sort of experience—is marked by its banality. We experience common-law and partially saturated phenomena as retaining something of the banal ordinariness of everyday experience while we experience fully saturated phenomena as utterly revelatory, the wellspring of an originality, exceptionality, and extraordinariness that overwhelms at every turn in every way.[23]

4.1.1 Marion on the Myth of the Given

In spelling out the account I have summarized above, Marion tends to use the language of "intention" and "intuition" in two different ways.

---

21. Marion, *In Excess*, 12, 28–29.

22. I intend "phenomenological" here in the broad sense of what it is like for a subject to undergo an experience as opposed to the narrow sense of some formal postreduction analysis of what it is like for a subject to have undergone it.

23. Marion's description of the "erotic phenomenon," however, fits neither into the category of the ordinariness or banality of first-degree saturation nor the extraordinariness or revelatory character of second-degree saturation. The experience of love is a kind of transgression that approximates but does not quite achieve the status of revelation on his construal. See Jean-Luc Marion, *The Erotic Phenomenon*, trans. Stephen Lewis (Chicago: University of Chicago Press, 2008).

Both terms have a verbal sense that can be used to describe a mental act and a nominal sense that can be used to describe the result of that mental act. The act of intuiting names our mode of receiving what is given, and the receptivity of that act is what constitutes the givenness of the given. What is given in intuition is therefore the intuited content of a mental phenomenon—the content of something that shows up in our conscious awareness. Intending, on the other hand, is the mental act of bringing an act of intuition under a normative concept, or signification.[24] What results from this conceptualizing of some intuited mode of receptivity is an intentional mental content, a conceptualized or signified intuition.

Marion reserves the idea of a phenomenon—roughly, a mental content, something that enters into our conscious awareness—for the content of an intention, the given intuition that our deployment of a concept has attempted to mark out or circumscribe. So a phenomenon on Marion's picture is always an already-conceptualized form of mental content—no intuited content is actually manifest or shows up to consciousness without having first drawn on the requisite operations of our conceptual capacities required to pick it out as the sort of content it is. Marion's claim that in our receptivity to saturated phenomena we intuit phenomenal content that exceeds any possible conceptual identification of it therefore is not a claim to be capable of a conscious awareness of intuited content *independently* of concepts. He does not think we can directly internalize a nonconceptual or preconceptual intuition as a form of mental content to which we then are subsequently able or unable to apply our normative concepts; intuition in the nominal sense is not itself a form of mental content until it is wedded to a corresponding intention.

---

24. Marion, *Being Given*, 197.

In this sense he agrees with Kant and Husserl that our capacities for intending, conceptual capacities are constitutive of the subjective horizon of our consciousness.[25] The idea of "dispensing with a [conceptual, intentional] horizon altogether," he concedes, "would no doubt forbid any and all manifestation."[26] There is therefore for Marion no such thing as a mental content manifest to consciousness that appears apart from drawing into operation the conceptual capacities belonging to an act of intending. The idea of a saturated phenomenon is therefore not the idea of an intuition that has become manifest to us apart from the conceptual constitution of our subjective horizon. It is rather the idea of "using the horizon in another way so as to be free of its delimiting anteriority, which can only enter into conflict with a phenomenon's claim to absolute appearing."[27]

Having clearly specified that all phenomenal content is conceptualized or conceptually constituted content, Marion seems to explicitly denounce precisely the idea that I have taken to constitute the myth of the Given—the idea that perceptual content is a nonconceptual (and as such nonnormatively constituted) form of mental content. It might therefore seem hard to see how Marion's conception of givenness could be confused with the mythical sort of Givenism with which I wish to charge him.

Nevertheless, Marion is aware of such a charge. In his recently published Taylor lectures titled *The Reason of the Gift*, he confesses

---

25. That is, he accepts their "commonly accepted definition of the phenomenon," which is that of a conceptually constituted given. See Marion, "The Banality of Saturation," 383. For an argument that Marion's allowance of an excess of intuition over against intention fails to hew to the conception of phenomenality essential to the phenomenological tradition, see Dominique Janicaud, "The Theological Turn of French Phenomenology," in *Phenomenology and the "Theological Turn": The French Debate*, trans. Bernard Prusak (New York: Fordham University Press, 2000), 3–106.

26. Marion, *Being Given*, 209.

27. Ibid.

puzzlement at it but hopes to allay any residual worries that he is after all a Givenist.[28] Rather than doing so by reiterating his articulation of the conceptualist analysis of phenomenal content that he retains from Kant and Husserl, which I have summarized above, Marion recounts a historical genealogy of the phenomenological concept of givenness that he himself endorses. Central to the story is the idea that "givenness" (*Gegebenheit*) in the mouths of phenomenologists came to be articulated precisely as a rejection of the idea that phenomenal content is nonconceptual or preconceptual.[29] Marion takes any alleged Sellarsian complaints about his Husserlian and Heideggerian commitments to givenness to be outdated. Trapped in a pre-Husserlian cul-de-sac, Sellarsian criticisms of "the Given" (and McDowellian ones as well, as Marion's translator Stephen Lewis is quick to add in his introduction to the volume) mistakenly confuse Marion for a classical empiricist or a Baden-style neo-Kantian.[30]

To sort out this confusion, Marion distinguishes his own commitments to the phenomenological tradition of reflection on the givenness of phenomena from classical empiricism on the one hand and Kantianism on the other. Classical empiricism on his view is identifiable by its commitment to the notion of conceptually "unconstituted givens," most notably in the form of Lockean "sense data." The Kantian objection to classical empiricism, he rightly notes,

---

28. Jean-Luc Marion, *The Reason of the Gift*, trans. with intro. by Stephen E. Lewis (Charlottesville: University of Virginia Press, 2012), 19: "In recent debates, especially within the French-speaking world, we have seen a question reappear that one might have thought definitively settled after the stubborn refutations of what was qualified (or rather disqualified) under the title of the 'myth of the given'—the question, precisely of *Gegebenheit* [givenness]."

29. He thus seeks to take the more "modest path" by "sketching the phenomenological genealogy of the concept of givenness or *Gegebenheit*, as found in certain uses in the early Heidegger and in late Husserl, respectively" (ibid., 20).

30. A phenomenological notion of givenness is thus "not a matter of taking up once again—doubtless one time too many—the debate over the possibility of unconstituted givens, whether they be understood in the manner of sense-data, as in the Lockean tradition; or as the contents of *Erlebnisse* in the debate concerning protocol statements between Carnap and Neurath; or, in the Bergsonian style, as immediate givens of consciousness" (ibid., 19).

is motivated by an epistemological worry—namely, that experiences, if they are to be the sorts of states or episodes that can supply the warrant or reasons for which a judgment might count as a state or episode of *knowing*, must constitutively involve the very same capacities operative in episodes and states of judging—namely, conceptual capacities. It is therefore out of concern for a theory of knowledge (*Erkenntnistheorie*) that the question of the givenness of experience came to be a matter not of an immediate awareness of intuited givens but rather of how to analyze the "modes" or "manner" or "how" of givenness—the conditions under which intuitions are constituted.[31]

Marion further distinguishes the phenomenological concept from the two leading schools of Kantianism—the Marburg school represented by Natorp and the Baden school represented by Rickert. Both held that the givenness of intuition had to be conceptually constituted in order to give us the normative form of mental content that can properly function as an object of judgment and knowledge. But Rickert held precisely what I read Marion to deny, that we first internalize intuitions in the nominal sense as a form of nonconceptual or preconceptual mental content and subsequently apply the concepts necessary to give that content the proper normative shape of a judgment. Natorp, on the other hand, held strictly that the a priori categories of the understanding constitutive of our subjectivity were always anterior to anything that shows up in conscious experience. He took Rickert's view to entail a commitment to the "prejudice of

---

31. "The issue, then, is no longer the immediate given, the perceptive content, or the lived experience of consciousness—in short, of something that is given (*das Gegebene*), but instead of the style of its phenomenalization *insofar as* it is given, or in short, its *givenness* (*donné*) (*Gegebenheit*). . . . Thus the place of the debate, as well as its stake, found itself shifted from the theory of knowledge (*Erkenntnistheorie*) to phenomenality, and thus to phenomenology" (ibid., 19–20).

the given," a return to the classical empiricist myth of immediate and unconstituted givens.[32]

Marion takes Natorp's charge of "prejudice" as presaging Wilfrid Sellars charge of the myth. Both are epistemologically motivated to deny any adherence to the idea of nonconceptual or preconceptual mental content, whether of the classical empiricist or of the Kantian sort. Sellars points out that the myth is not limited to the sense-data theories he critiques in *Empiricism and the Philosophy of Mind* (hereafter, EPM) but belongs to any view that confuses normative states belonging to the context of rational relations of inference with nonnormative states outside of that context.[33] Likewise, Natorp seems to recognize that classical empiricism went wrong not merely in advocating for nonconceptual givens as immediate instances of knowing, but in taking such givens to enter into our awareness independently of any operation of our conceptual capacities, which is the basis for his critique of Rickert's Kantianism.[34]

Far from giving into the prejudicial myth of the Given, Husserl in an important sense sided with Natorp against Rickert on the matter of the conceptual constitution of phenomena. Husserl rightly departed from Natorp, however, in recognizing that the so-called anteriority of the categories under which phenomena appear to consciousness is not in fact an anteriority but a posteriority, manifest alongside or together with their phenomenal content and requiring the reduction to determine the precise nature of its constitution.[35] But this analysis

32. Ibid., 103n26. See also Dermot Moran, "Analytic Philosophy and Continental Philosophy: Four Confrontations," in *Phenomenology: Responses and Developments*, ed. Leonard Lawlor, vol. 4 of *The History of Continental Philosophy*, ed. Alan Schrift (Durham: Acumen, 2010), 235–66; Jean-François Courtine, "Réduction, construction, destruction. D'un dialogue à trois: Natorp, Husserl, Heidegger," *Philosophiques* 36, no. 2 (2009): 559–77.

33. Wilfrid Sellars, *Empiricism and the Philosophy of Mind*, intro. Richard Rorty and study guide by Robert Brandom (Cambridge, MA: Harvard University Press, 1997), 127–96.

34. Marion, *Reason of the Gift*, 28–29; cf. Moran, "Four Confrontations," 244–46.

35. Marion, *Reason of the Gift*, 30ff; cf. Matheson Russell, *Husserl: A Guide for the Perplexed* (New York: Continuum, 2006), 60–61.

of the givenness of phenomenal consciousness as an irreducible correlation between intuition and intention is just the form of conceptualism we saw Marion himself endorsing as compatible with, or even required by, his conception of a saturated phenomenon.

Nor does Marion take Heidegger to reject the phenomenological concept of givenness as the givenness of the correlation itself (rather than the prioritizing of either of its elements, whether the form of the phenomenon or its content). His insight was instead to question whether the intentionality that constitutes a phenomenon belongs most fundamentally to the "theoretical attitude" characteristic of science, and hence whether the formal ("ontic") categories of the Husserlian reduction actually succeed in describing the phenomena that appear to consciousness *as* they ordinarily appear according to the "natural attitude."[36] The most fundamental phenomenological description of, say, the lectern—to use the well-worn example from Heidegger—does not consist in its appearing *as* a particularly coordinated series of planks or a box atop a stand or any mode of appearing to which these are further reducible. Nor does it appear to me *as* a self-conscious subject.[37]

Instead, there are no subjects or objects to be found as phenomenological constituents of any given lived experience of a lectern, only "the lectern itself," which is seen "in one fell swoop," such that "from the outset, and first of all, what is at issue is an 'object fraught with meaning,'" which is a "'a moment of signification' . . . because 'the meaningful is primary and immediately given to me without any mental detours across thing-oriented apprehension.' . . . The meaning is given, because it shows itself without an object and before every objectification."[38]

---

36. Marion, *Reason of the Gift*, 38.
37. Ibid., 43–48.

In his introductory essay, Stephen Lewis, the translator of *The Reason of the Gift*, advances Marion's defense of the phenomenological concept of givenness by attempting to show not only that it is innocent of the Sellarsian attack on nonconceptually constituted mental content but that the Sellarsian attack itself suffers from the same problematic underlying assumptions as the Givenism it attacks. In virtue of his identification with Natorp, Sellars is open to the same charge that Heidegger levels against Husserl, the Kantians, and the classical empiricists. All alike, Heidegger supposes, wrongly conceive of the phenomena that are up for analysis in the "ontic" terms dictated by the theoretical attitude, and as such they approach the reduction precisely by ruling out rather than strictly attending to the intentional structure of what is given as it actually appears. Lewis cites Claude Romano in suggesting that contemporary "analytical neo-Kantianism," like the neo-Kantianism of Natorp, is guilty of the following error:

> Instead of admitting an immediate given that would be the starting point of all knowledge [like the empiricists], [the neo-Kantians] consider this given as already mediated by concepts, put into form by conceptual schemata or symbolic forms that necessarily involve language. More precisely, in critiquing the given of the empiricists, they end up by rejecting the idea of the given in general—and they reject it because they continue to conceive of every given, after the fashion of their empiricist adversaries, as devoid of immanent meaning and structuring. . . . By refusing the tide of knowledge to the given and instead assigning all knowledge to the sphere of judgment, they diametrically oppose facts and values, causality and justification. [39]

---

38. Ibid., 45. The inner quotations Marion takes from Heidegger's *Towards the Definition of Philosophy*, trans. Ted Sadler (London: Continuum, 2008), 57–58.
39. Stephen E. Lewis, "Introduction," in Marion, *Reason of the Gift*, 9–10, quoting Claude Romano, *Au coeur de la raison, la phénoménologie* (Paris: Gallimard/Folio Essais, 2010), 728–29 (translations Lewis' unless otherwise noted).

Moreover, Lewis thinks that because McDowell shares the Sellarsian insistence on resisting the myth of nonconceptual givens as contents of perception, he is also subject to Heidegger's critique. "Like the neo-Kantians," he says, "Sellars and McDowell maintain that the given is necessarily 'devoid of immanent meaning and structure'—phenomena do not appear, like Heidegger's example of the lectern, as given out of an environing world rich in signification."[40] Lewis then cites Romano again to contrast the view of Natorp, Sellars, and McDowell with the phenomenological concept of givenness that Marion develops from Husserl and Heidegger. Those advocating a phenomenological concept of givenness, Romano says, do not claim to

> derive thought from experience, as empiricism would have it, or, on the contrary, to derive the order that governs experience from the order that governs thought. . . . [Instead, phenomenology] postulates that experience is already reasonable [*sensée*] and structured before the intervention of discursive language and thought, that it possesses its own proper order and an immanent articulation, and is in no case reduced to the naked reception of a "given" such as is recognized by empiricism and only *partially* criticized by Kantianism. Instead of criticizing the very notion of the given, and conferring upon it a mythological status under the pretext that such a given would always already be informed by concepts and categories, [phenomenology] strives to broaden the concept of the given itself well beyond *sense-data*, in order to think an *experience* of the world, but also of art, of culture, of human interactions and institutions, of history, and even of language. . . . Phenomenology thus refuses to follow in the footsteps of the neo-Kantian critique of the given, which, in its eyes, bears only upon an atrophied concept of the given, and in no way upon experience in its comprehensive meaning, which phenomenology is concerned to promote.[41]

---

40. Ibid., 10.
41. Ibid., 10–11, quoting Romano, *Au coeur*, 730–31.

Instead of having Marion dead to rights for transgressing the prohibition of nonconceptualism about perceptual content, the boot turns out to be on the other foot. The Sellarsian and McDowellian critics of Marion stand with the neo-Kantians on the same problematic ground—a ground constituted by their shared commitment to an insufficiently norm-governed conception of givenness. Phenomenology has taken its leave from that shared ground and its "atrophied" conception of the given, embracing a commitment to the intrinsic normativity of experience of wider import than the narrowly conceived conceptualism of neo-Kantianism, whether of the historic Marburg sort or more recent "analytic" type represented by Sellars and McDowell.

4.1.2 Marion's Mythical Givenness

Together, Marion and Lewis offer some prima facie compelling reasons to think not only that Marion's phenomenology is innocent of the Sellarsian charge of Givenism but that the neo-Kantian triumvirate who level the charge (Natrop, Sellars, and McDowell) are themselves guilty of an erroneously "ontic" construal of the fundamentally normative structure had by our ordinary experience. Put in terms of Marion's phenomenology, they are incapable of accounting for both the possibility of revelatory experience and the indeterminacy of ordinary experience because they restrict their analysis of ordinary phenomena to that which is in principle fully conceptually determinable or "objective." We have therefore found two strategies available to Marion by way of a response to the charge of the myth. The first—a defensive strategy—purports to offer a conceptual analysis and a genealogy of the Marion's phenomenological notion of givenness that is incompatible with the mythical conception of givenness of which he is accused.

The second—an offensive strategy that Lewis offers on Marion's behalf—claims that the version of conceptualism about empirical content that motivates the Sellarsian and McDowellian charge of Givenism can be undermined by a Heideggerian objection that it misconstrues the normative conceptual structure of phenomenal givens in a fundamentally "ontic" way. But contrary to Lewis's claims, this second strategy is both patently false and irrelevant to the question of whether the charge of Givenism sticks to Marion. I will therefore dispense with it briefly before turning to the more substantive question about whether Marion's defensive strategy succeeds in staving off the myth of the given.

A bare commitment to the idea that it is a myth to conceive of the modes or content of experience as nonconceptual or (better) as lacking any intrinsic normative structure is consistent with many mutually conflicting ways of characterizing the intrinsic normative structure of experience. Natorp's neo-Kantianism is one way of affirming the intrinsically normative structure of experience, Husserl's formalistic construal of the intuition-intention relation is another, and the Heideggerian construal of the Husserlian "correlation" in terms of a practical rationality of "embodied coping" is yet another.[42] Given a conflict among these views, we could follow Marion and take the Heideggerian analysis of the intrinsic normative structure of experience as fundamentally ordinary, practical, and prereflective to be preferable to both the neo-Kantian and Husserlian analyses of the normative structure of experience as intrinsically scientific, theoretical, and formal. Still, this is a dispute about what *sort*

---

42. Hubert L. Dreyfus, "Overcoming the Myth of the Mental: How Philosophers Can Profit from the Phenomenology of Everyday Expertise," *Proceedings and Addresses of the American Philosophical Association* 79, no. 2 (2005): 47–65; Dreyfus, "The Myth of the Pervasiveness of the Mental," in *Mind, Reason and Being-in-the-World: The McDowell-Dreyfus Debate*, ed. Joseph K. Schear (London: Routledge, 2012), 15–40.

of intrinsically normatively structured content perceptual content is, not *whether* it is thus structured.

Clearly, such debates are founded on a more fundamental agreement that the disputants share with one another but do not share with (the relevant variety of) Givenism—namely, that all experience is intrinsically normatively structured with the sort of rational form requisite to a judgment. Heideggerians, for example, take reflective or theoretical judgments to be abstractions from something more phenomenologically fundamental—that is to say, practical judgments analyzed in the Heideggerian way. They therefore construe the form of an experience required to inform practical judgments of the sort privileged in their phenomenology.

While Marion and Lewis (and Romano) are right to regard Sellars's worries about the myth of the given as having much in common with Natorp's worries about the prejudice of the given, it does not follow from this that either Sellars or McDowell would agree with Natorp or with one another about his so-called ontic analysis of the normative structure of the content of experience. In fact, they agree neither with one another nor with Natorp about that. It is a careless reading of Sellars to see his analysis of empirical content as *phenomenologically* reducible to the ontic terms of science.[43] But more relevant among the mischaracterizations that Lewis derives from Romano to bolster Marion's genealogy is the idea that *McDowell's* wielding of the critique of Givenism somehow implies that he endorses an atrophied conception of givenness. Not only does Lewis's implication not

---

43. This irreducibility and the necessity of maintaining the sui generis character of the "space of reasons" is precisely what motivates Sellars's distinction between the "manifest" image and the "scientific" image. See Wilfrid Sellars, "Philosophy and the Scientific Image of Man," in *Frontiers of Science and Philosophy*, ed. Robert Colodny (Pittsburgh, PA: University of Pittsburgh Press, 1962); Timm Triplett and Willem deVries. "Does Observational Knowledge Require Metaknowledge? A Dialogue on Sellars," *International Journal of Philosophical Studies* 15, no. 1 (2007): 23–51; Jay F. Rosenberg, *Wilfrid Sellars: Fusing the Images* (New York: Oxford University Press, 2007), 9–32.

follow, but it also requires him to assume a positively abysmal reading of McDowell's own characterization of the intrinsically normative structure of experience.

McDowell's naturalized platonism on that score differs markedly from that of Sellars and is entirely compatible with Marion's explication of the phenomenological concept of givenness in its Heideggerian mode.[44] What is fundamentally afforded to us in experience by the world itself, McDowell says, are potential reasons for belief and practice—direct awareness of the opportunities provided by the world itself to inform and justify the full range of what we can think, say, and do. To take in the world in terms of such opportunities is characteristic of our distinctively human way of perceptually directing ourselves on the world. Among the reasons afforded to us in experience by the normative structure of the world are its law-governed features that rationally guide the natural sciences and also features that elicit our rational responses "of art, of culture, of human interactions and institutions, of history, and even of language."[45]

So Lewis's offensive strategy on behalf of Marion in response to the Sellarsian charge fails. Naturalized platonism is the particular *sort*

44. Contrary, so it seems, to the assumptions of some Heideggerians, most notably Hubert Dreyfus. See McDowell's response to Dreyfus's complaint, which mirrors the line that Lewis takes, in John McDowell, "The Myth of the Mind as Detached," in *Mind, Reason and Being-In-The-World: The McDowell-Dreyfus Debate*, ed. Joseph K. Schear (London: Routledge, 2012), 41–58. Worries that McDowell neglects the ordinary social, historical, and linguistic situatedness of phenomenal content are especially puzzling given the significance that he places on these very features in *Mind and World*, which I will take up in the next chapter.

45. Nor does this way of putting things mark any distinction between a domain of brute "fact" over against a domain of norms or "values," but only an internal differentiation between different sorts of normative reasons that the world itself gives us to think, say or do some things and not others (scientific reasons to believe scientific claims and engage in scientific practices, aesthetic reasons to believe claims about art and engage in artistic practices, etc.). Further, this sort of logical differentiation should not be taken to imply that the reasons we actually take in in experience are actually individuated in this way, according to their natural kinds, rather than as complexes of reasons which are nevertheless potentially susceptible of being distinguished even if in fact we most often do not so distinguish them.

of commitment to the intrinsically normative structure of perceptual experience that motivates McDowell's worries about Givenism, and this version of conceptualism about what is genuinely given in experience can hardly be described as an "atrophied concept of the given." But even if McDowell's conceptualism failed to offer the relevant kind of "expansion" of the normative structure of perceptual content for which Lewis commends Marion, this would be irrelevant to the question of whether Marion's own phenomenology secures that expansion by holding to some version of the myth of the given. Since the rejection of Givenism implies a rejection of nonconceptualist accounts of perceptual experience rather than a prescription of any particular sort of conceptualism, the shape of one's positive views about the conceptual (that is, normatively structured) character of the phenomenal given cannot furnish us with any rational grounds for "refusing the critique of the given."[46] The only way to determine whether Marion's own account of perceptual intake—whatever its scope—is subject to such a critique is to show that his account of phenomenal or mental content attributes to it the same rational form or normative structure that can potentially figure in a judgment. This brings us back, then, to an evaluation of Marion's defensive strategy.

Marion's defensive strategy consists in claiming that he is not a nonconceptualist about phenomenal content, which he expresses as a commitment to conceptually "unconstituted givens."[47] It seems perfectly clear from Marion's exposition of his views that he means to be taken as a thoroughgoing "conceptualist" about both the modes and content of phenomenal consciousness of any sort, including perceptual experience. Modes of receptivity given in intuition only appear to consciousness—are only manifest as "phenomena" or forms

---

46. Ibid., 9–10.
47. Ibid., 19.

of mental content—to the extent that they are capable of actualizing the conceptual capacities constitutive of the horizon of our subjective awareness. Since the Givenism criticized by the neo-Kantian triumvirate applies only to violations of this rule and Marion's phenomenology admits of no such violation, he cannot be taken for a Givenist.

Marion's account of "saturated phenomena" is the obvious candidate for an alleged violation of the conceptualist rule. While he may not violate the rule insofar as his views coincide with Husserl and Heidegger, we might say that precisely at the juncture of his departure from them—his proposed "expansion"—Marion turns out to hold a commitment to nonconceptual modes of perception as capable of informing and justifying our judgments about, for instance, events, art, other minds, and our bodily self-awareness (in the case of "partially" saturated phenomena) or revelation (in the case of phenomena saturated "to the second degree"). On this reading of Marion, the only way to make sense of the image of phenomenal content that exceeds conceptual grasp or "runs over" the conceptual forms under which that content appears to us is by taking the "material" or content of an appearance to be the sort of thing that we can be aware of over and above the concepts that we use to identify it or pick it out.

That is, rather than seeing the bounds of our phenomenal consciousness itself as delimited by the conceptual structure in terms of which any intuition must appear if it is to appear at all, Marion must take the bounds of our capacity for subjective awareness to be wider than the bounds of our conceptual capacities, otherwise the "overflow" of phenomenal content would never appear or become manifest to us but instead would run "off the sides" of the conceptual structure constitutive of our awareness. His claims that we can become *aware* of concept-exceeding content—that such content counts as *phenomenal* content, content manifest to our subjective consciousness—therefore has to be understood as a violation of the rule. A commitment to the givenness of phenomenal content or appearances that necessarily exceed every possible conceptual determination thus *entails* a commitment to unconstituted givens.

What should Marion say to this argument? Perhaps the most obvious rejoinder is that it involves a misreading of the nature of saturated phenomena. We should not picture the "excessiveness" of saturated phenomena as the overflow of a conceptual form with a nonconceptual mental content, resulting in the idea of a partially "unconstituted" or nonconceptual mental content. To say, for example, that an experience of a state of affairs as an "event" saturates the quantitative capacities of our subjective awareness is not to say that the event enters into our subjective awareness as a certain kind of brute content, some of which is put into normative form by way of our conceptual capacities and some of which particularly exceeds our capacities to put it into quantitative form, leaving in our awareness some bare, unconstituted, and normatively inert "leftovers" of phenomenal content to which we are necessarily unsuccessful at "applying" our conceptual norms.

Rather, Marion holds that he can understand the excess of phenomenal content over intentional concept constitutive of saturated phenomena alongside a thoroughgoing "conceptualism" about the modes and content of phenomenal appearing. On that conceptualism, recall, the unity of some mode of givenness to intuition and a corresponding intentional concept is required for anything to show up to our subjective awareness at all. The phenomenal content that manifests itself or appears to consciousness is thus always intrinsically normatively structured. For mental content to be "intrinsically normatively structured" is for it to determine in and from itself the standard of correctness or conditions of "adequation" under which any concept or judgment we might deploy succeeds or fails at picking out that phenomenon as its content. For our deployment of an intentional concept or "signification" to be capable of directing us upon a phenomenon and to succeed in applying to it, therefore, would be for that concept to be capable of satisfying the standards of correctness or conditions of adequation laid down by the phenomenon—the concept we deploy would enjoy an adequate measure of isomorphism or "match" with the intrinsic normative structure of the phenomenon that it purports to be "about."

In what sense can we take Marion's conception of the "excessiveness" of saturated phenomena to conform to such a conceptualism about phenomenal content? Consider again the "event" that Marion takes to be a phenomenon that saturates every possible concept of quantity. The phenomenal content of an event is normatively structured through and through, and in just that sense it remains a form of "conceptual content." When Marion analyzes a form of phenomenal content that saturates our quantitative conceptual capacities, he thus concedes that events are capable of appearing or manifesting themselves to our subjective awareness precisely because they "show up" as entirely and not merely partially conceptually constituted. The aspect of an event as constituted by the concept of quantity appears to our subjective awareness as having a distinctive *sort* of intrinsic normative structure—a conceptual character with respect to quantity that differs from other aspects of its (entirely) normative structure.

Events (encountered *as* events) saturate quantity in the sense that the normative standard of correctness for our quantitative concepts that constitutes an event is itself an indeterminate or "infinite" standard. As such, the satisfaction of every possible quantitative concept of which we are capable turns out to be a necessary but never sufficient condition of "adequating" it or picking it out. This inexhaustible or "unsatisfiable" normative standard imposed along the relevant axis of our finite conceptual capacities serves as the engine of the "infinite hermeneutic" demanded by saturated phenomena.

This thoroughgoing "conceptualist" reading of saturated phenomena is more consistent with Marion's defensive strategy as I have outlined it. So, does it fare any better against the charge of Givenism than the nonconceptualist reading of him does? Marion's defensive strategy, read in this way, assumes that because the denial of Givenism entails the denial of normatively unconstituted givens, the reverse is also true—rejecting the notion of unconstituted givens also entails the rejection of Givenism. But that assumption does not follow. More importantly, it is false.

I have already suggested in the previous chapter that there is at least one version of Givenism that is "conceptualist" in a thoroughgoing way—that is, conceptualist about both the modes and content of perceptual experience. On that view, we might acknowledge that perceptual mental content is intrinsically normatively structured and that our conceptual capacities are operative in the mode of receptivity to the normative structure of what is given. But such a view might still constitute a mythical Givenism if we characterize the intrinsic normative structure of what is given to us in a way that is alien to the sort of capacities we actually possess to take it in.[48] Suppose, for example, that the capacities of bats to have a sensory consciousness of sonar were intrinsically conceptual capacities, capacities that afforded those bats not merely opportunities to respond to their environment in the relevant ways but opportunities to respond to the world as normatively structured by rational relations. As such, for a bat to take in the world under the sensory modes of presentation given by sonar

---

48. See the relevant discussion in chapter 3 (3.2.1).

would be for it to become capable of detecting reasons afforded to it by the world as a "logical space of reasons."

To engage in this thought experiment is to imagine what it might be like for a bat to be a rational animal and for its sensory consciousness to be the sensory consciousness of a rational animal.[49] In the imagined scenario, both humans and bats are rational animals taking in the same normatively structured world—a world governed by the same rational relations that constrain what both we and our imaginary bats think and believe. Nevertheless, our human sensory consciousness would be configured to take in the normative structure of the world in a fundamentally different way than that of bats. Given this scenario, could we possibly know what it is like to be a bat? Could we possibly experience the world in the same way as a bat?

Quite clearly, the answer has to be no. Despite the fact that the world makes itself available to both us and bats in a normatively structured way and that we both have conceptual capacities capable of taking in that world, the sort of perceptual content we take in supervenes on the way in which our sensory systems are configured. To the extent that we do not share with bats the same sensory capacities for taking in the world's normative structure, to that extent batty experiences of the world are not possible for us. Or, to make precisely the same point from the world side of the perceptual relation on the given scenario, there are features of the world that afford bats certain sorts of perceptual reasons for believing that the world is thus and so (reasons made available by sonar) that the world cannot

49. The example, of course, is taken from the thought experiment in Thomas Nagel's influential "What Is It Like to Be a Bat?" *Philosophical Review* 83, no. 4 (October 1974): 157–74. I've adapted the thought experiment to reflect what I have argued to be the main mistake in Nagel's exploration of the question: the failure to recognize that the sensory consciousness of humans is not merely another configuration of the same sort of sensory consciousness had by bats, but a sensory consciousness of an essentially different sort, one inextricably related to and intrinsically configured for the development and cultivation of human rationality.

afford us because we lack the requisite capacities to detect it under the relevant modes of presentation (those given to sonar).

Suppose someone were to claim that because the world's conceptual bearing on rational animals includes the phenomenon of sonar, sonar was given to us every bit as much as to bats and therefore we too can experience sonar. Such a person would be confusing the givenness of sonar as a rational potentiality of the world with the givenness of sonar to human consciousness. The sonar phenomenon in the scenario would be rationally available, but, in order to exploit its availability, we would have to possess the requisite capacities to do so. Because we do not, such phenomena are necessarily unavailable to us, and our claimant for the givenness of sonar to humans has gone wrong in failing to recognize this. "Givenism" names just this sort of mistake—a failure to recognize that we have to be *capable of receiving* what is given. But conceptualism was manifestly not at issue in the batty Givenism just described.

The problem of Givenism is therefore not properly nonconceptualism but more fundamentally what I've called "the problem of fit"—the problem of positing "the availability for cognition to subjects whose getting what is supposedly Given to them does not draw on capacities required for the sort of cognition in question."[50] The problem of fit entails the falsity of nonconceptualism about (human) perceptual content only because our sensory consciousness names a capacity to make the normative structure of what we think, say, and do rationally answerable to the world, a capacity configured to require rational inputs (that is, reasons). To suppose that we are capable of receiving nonconceptual givens would count as Givenism only because it would require a necessarily conceptually configured capacity to receive nonconceptual inputs.

---

50. John McDowell, "Avoiding the Myth of the Given," in *Having the World in View* (Cambridge, MA: Harvard University Press, 2009), 256.

But it is also a kind of Givenism to suppose that we are capable of receiving *conceptual* inputs to a perceptual system for which we do not possess the requisite sort of *conceptual* capacities.

Marion's conception of saturated phenomena is Givenist in this latter sense. Consider again the case of our receptivity to the saturated phenomenon of "the event" as Marion conceives it. Marion claims to agree to two features of the Husserlian view:

H1: All phenomenal content is conceptual content.

H2: The manifestation of phenomenal content to consciousness necessarily depends upon the actualizing of our conceptual capacities.

Given these avowed commitments, the very idea of a phenomenon whose normative demands or standards of correctness cannot possibly be satisfied or adequated by any deployment of our conceptual capacities for quantification is the idea of a phenomenon that cannot be given or manifest to us as the phenomenon it is. How then can Marion claim that there is any consistency between the possibility of a saturated phenomenon and the conjunction of H1 and H2 above? He does so by deriving two ways that human conceptual capacities might be capable of phenomenalizing an indeterminate or infinite phenomenal content, both of which are consistent with the conjunction of H1 and H2, but neither of which is consistent with the other. Then, rather than holding to one or the other of them, which is what a consistency with H1 and H2 would demand, Marion instead mistakenly conflates them.

First, it is consistent with the conjunction of H1 and H2 to suppose that there could be a phenomenon whose intrinsic normative structure is *potentially* capable of satisfying an infinitude of quantitative concepts while our capacities for quantification are incapable of actualizing its full potential. But in this case, the infinitude would not be actually apparent to us but only potentially apparent. The extent to which the infinitude could appear to us *as* an infinitude, though, would depend on the conceptual capacities with which we are outfitted. More exactly, the *manifestation* of the infinite quantitative potential of an event would depend on the limits of our conceptual capacities to actualize or exploit that potential by way of exercising our conceptual capacities to deploy a quantitative concept. Note that this is not the same thing as saying that we would have to *actually* deploy such concepts in order for the phenomenon to appear to us, only that we would have to be *able* to do so.[51] Nor does it imply that subjects with limited capacities for actualizing quantitative concepts could not know whether an event has an infinite quantitative potential. It implies only that such a potential cannot possibly *appear* or be *manifest* to that subject; it cannot show up to consciousness *as* an infinitude.

There is a second possibility that is consistent with the conjunction of H1 and H2, but it is inconsistent with the first possibility above. This possibility would hold that our conceptual capacities themselves are not finite, bounded, or determinate and that what manifests itself or appears to us in experience is precisely the infinite, unbounded, and indeterminate character of phenomena.[52] In such a case, there would be no limits to what could be phenomenally given or manifest to us, and our perceptual capacities would be fully capable of exploiting the rational potential of any possible phenomenon. Again,

---

51. Put in Aristotelian terms, the actualizing of my conceptual capacities in experience is only a first-actualization, which also constitutes a second-potentiality, the imbuing of my experience with *rational potential.* That potential may or may not reach its second-actualization in the formation of a judgment or an action.

52. It is easy to configure this analysis in harmony with each of the four types of "saturation"—we would just say, e.g., that our *quantitative* conceptual capacities are not finite, bounded, or determinate, and as such what manifests itself or appears to us in experience is precisely the *quantitatively* infinite, unbounded, and indeterminate character of phenomena, and likewise, mutatis mutandis, for qualitative, modal, relational phenomena. Second-degree saturation or "revelation" on this analysis would entail the unqualified formulation given above.

this does not imply that subjects with unlimited capacities for actualizing the infinite quantitative content of an event ever in fact do so, only that they are actually capable of doing so.

Marion's conflation of these two possible pictures holds that our *limited* conceptual capacities are sufficient to manifest the infinite or unbounded content of a phenomenon. But clearly *that* formulation is inconsistent with the conjunction of H1 and H2. What actually follows from that conjunction is that our limited conceptual capacities are *either* insufficient to manifest the unbounded or infinite conceptual content of a phenomenon, *or* our unlimited conceptual capacities are sufficient to manifest such a phenomenon. By confusing those alternatives, Marion proposes an incoherent and therefore mythical form of phenomenal Givenness, a mode of Givenness that he supposes we are able to receive even while denying us the capacities requisite to receiving it.

Moreover, this incoherence in his account of the givenness of saturated phenomena allows him to draw out the alleged "paradoxes" belonging to traditional apophatic accounts of revelatory experience. The possibility for a manifestation to consciousness of boundless rational potential that imposes an infinite hermeneutical demand on limited intentional capacities is not a "paradox of paradoxes" but an incoherent confusion of the notion of conceptual constitution on which the "phenomenological concept of givenness" depends. A confusion, we might say, between the rational potential putatively intrinsic to the conceptual constitutedness of a phenomenon and the rational capacities required to actualize that potential in the phenomenalizing of that phenomenon. Marion therefore asks us to deny something utterly trivial, that receiving the conceptual structure of a mental content requires the sufficiency of our capacities to take in that structure. If we can neither have nor acquire the capacities required for some mode of givenness to become apparent, then what is given cannot possibly appear.

Faced with this difficulty, the only alternative I see readily available for Marion is to deny H1 and make the actualizing of conceptual capacities not a condition for the *appearing* or *manifestation* of a phenomenon, but only and strictly a condition of the *intelligibility* of what anyway appears. Despite the strong conceptualism I have attributed to him from his portrayal of the consistency of his "definition of the phenomenon" with Kant and Husserl and the continuity of his "phenomenological concept of givenness" with Husserl and Heidegger, there is perhaps some evidence for this alternative reading.[53] Marion might accordingly say that what is given in intuition is the contribution of "sensibility" prior to its conceptual constitution; thus, an unconstituted intuition can be *phenomenally* given—manifest to consciousness—independently of the conceptual constitution by which we subsequently interpret or make sense of what has appeared. Marion would therefore hold that the actualizing of conceptual capacities is not a condition for phenomenal appearing but is only the condition for a limited class of appearances, phenomena that appear as intelligible objects, objects we can (possibly) understand.

At the very least, however, this reading of Marion would sit uncomfortably with the genealogical argument he makes in *The Reason of the Gift*. When we emend Marion's definition of phenomenal appearing to include a rejection of H1, he most closely resembles not Husserl or Heidegger but Rickert. Worse, the very claim he appears to be marshaling his genealogy to disavow—that his concept of givenness countenances the idea of "unconstituted givens"—he himself would turn out to endorse. The most damning

---

53. Marion, *Being Given*, 192, 208, 218.

consequence of this line is that the reason Marion gives for disavowing unconstituted givens is his recognition that the idea is a myth. Taking Marion in this direction therefore leaves him holding onto the more commonly held and nonconceptualist form of Givenism that he claims to be following Natorp and Sellars in denouncing. So whereas reading Marion as embracing nonconceptually constituted phenomena leaves him open to Natorp's and Sellars's attacks on the myth of unconstituted givens, reading him more charitably in a manner consistent with the denouncement of unconstituted givens is what landed him in another (conceptualist) version of the myth recounted above.

4.2 William P. Alston and Givenness in the Theory of Appearing

In *Perceiving God*, William P. Alston aims "to defend the view that putative direct awareness of God can provide justification for certain types of belief about God."[54] In his elaboration of a "putative direct awareness," Alston puts forward a "perceptual model": "I shall argue that if we think of perception in the most general way, in which it is paradigmatically exemplified by but not confined to sense perception, putative awareness of God exhibits this generic character. Thus it is properly termed (putative) perception of God."[55] Thus, unlike Marion, Alston proposes a straightforwardly "cataphatic" thesis about the nature of revelatory experience. Far from taking revelation to require any paradoxical disruption or break in the structure of ordinary experience, Alston's analysis is predicated on the parity of the two cases. The structure of our perceptual relation to God is, mutatis mutandis, the same structure exhibited in our perceptual

---

54. William P. Alston, *Perceiving God: The Epistemology of Religious Experiences* (Ithaca: Cornell University Press, 1991), 9.
55. Ibid., 9.

relation to the sensible objects and properties in our everyday experience. But, he supposes, "any such argument will have to employ some particular account of sense perception, and this is a notoriously controversial topic. I shall be advocating my own view of the matter, the Theory of Appearing."[56]

4.2.1 Givenness in Alston's Theory of Appearing

What, then, is the structure of perceptual experience according to Alston's Theory of Appearing (hereafter, TA)? On the story Alston provides in *Perceiving God*, our analysis of a putative perceptual experience must account for three features: (1) the intrinsically phenomenological and mind-dependent character of a putative perceptual experience, (2) the mind-external content or extrinsic purport of a putative perceptual experience, and (3) how the mind-external content putatively given in experience can play an epistemic role for our perceptual beliefs, informing and justifying them.[57]

For our experiences to rationally ground our empirical beliefs, we must have some receptive capacity to register the world's bearing on us as empirical content. Alston explicates that receptivity in terms of the first two features above, the internal and external features of perception. As an account of the structure of receptivity constitutive of ordinary "experience," Alston puts forward what he calls an "internalist externalism."[58] But for the empirical content given to us

---

56. Ibid. This is not to say that Alston's account of revelatory experience necessarily depends upon the viability of the Theory of Appearing, for he also means to "indicate how experiential awareness of God could be construed as a mode of perception in other theories" (ibid.). Indeed, Alston does indicate the possible points of consistency between theoretical alternatives to the Theory of Appearing and a commitment to the possibility of putative experiences of God as epistemic justifications for religious belief. But when he does, he almost always also offers reasons for preferring the Theory of Appearing to those alternatives. Moreover, his advocacy for the Theory of Appearing inevitably shapes what he *means* by "putative experiences of God" as well as the informing and justifying role he takes them to have for our beliefs "about" God.

57. This is how I would summarize the desiderata he lays out in ch. 1 of *Perceiving God*.

in receptivity to become available to the normative context of what
we think, say, and do, we need a supplementary epistemological story
about how experiences become subject to the normative standards
of epistemic evaluation—that is to say, we need the third feature
mentioned above. In order to account for it, Alston supplements
his "internalist externalism" about receptivity with what he calls a
"doxastic practice" approach to epistemology.[59] TA therefore aims to
meet the three desiderata for a theory of the structure of perceptual
experience by coordinating an internalist externalism about empirical
content with a doxastic practice approach to the epistemology of
perception. I will briefly sketch each of these components in turn.

Alston takes himself to be an "internalist" in claiming that a
distinctive feature marking out any perceptual episode as a perceptual
form of cognition (as opposed to, for instance, imagination, memory,
or abstract thought) is its intrinsically nonconceptual and
phenomenological character.[60] His canonical way of singling out this
dimension is by asking us to close our eyes and imagine, remember,
or think about some object before us (for example, my black loafer)
and then to open our eyes. We can mark out a perceptual experience
(in this case, a sensory experience) from nonperceptual forms of
cognition by the distinctively qualitative modes of *presentation* that
distinguish merely thinking about my loafer (with my eyes closed)
from being aware of it (as occupying my visual field).[61]

Alston unapologetically affirms that, as a mode of consciousness,
experience (paradigmatically, *sensory* experience) is intrinsically
nonconceptual. For example, for a balloon to look red to me "is not

---

58. Alston, *Perceiving God*, 3; cf. William P. Alston, "An Internalist Externalism," *Synthese* 74, no. 3 (March 1988): 265–83.
59. Alston, *Perceiving God*, 146–83, and "A 'Doxastic Practice' Approach to Epistemology," in *Knowledge and Skepticism*, ed. Marjorie Clay and Keith Lehrer (Boulder, CO: Westview, 1989), 1–29.
60. Alston, *Perceiving God*, 37.
61. Ibid., 36.

the same as for me to *take it* to be red, *construe* or *conceptualize* it as red, even though its looking red typically evokes those reactions if the subject has the conceptual equipment so to react."[62] The appearance of a red object as red is therefore "a nonintentional relationship by any of the usual tests."[63] For example, if a spherical object appears red to me and the spherical object is a ball, then it follows for TA that a ball appears to me as red. This transitive and transparent relation between the way things are and the way they appear to me is not true of intentional relations to the world such as *believing, conceiving,* or *taking.* Thus, for X to appear F to S is not the same as for S to believe, conceive, or take X to be F. I may *take it* that there is a red ball before me, but just because the ball is also spherical, it does not necessarily follow that I *take it* that there is a spherical object before me. It is possible that I do not have the concept of a spherical object or that, while having the concept, I fail (for whatever reason) to apply it in this case.

Alston makes it clear that this nonconceptual, nonintentional, and mind-internal or psychological dimension of an experience as a mode of consciousness is not something we should identify as the *content* of an experience.[64] Rather, the vividness and phenomenal richness of nonconceptual qualia are just qualitative ways of *presenting* our extrinsic relation to reality—this is the "externalist" dimension of Alston's analysis. The intrinsically phenomenological character of a perceptual experience is a way in which the nonconceptual layout of reality itself shows up to my conscious awareness or "appears" to me. Though Alston regards the *vehicle* of perception as the nonconceptual and qualitative dimension of experience—the dimension that marks it out as a mental or psychological phenomenon—he regards the *content*

62. Ibid., 37.
63. Ibid., 36.
64. Ibid., 54–59.

of perception as the "things themselves," mind-independent things such tables and chairs. On Alston's "internalist externalism" about perceptual experience, therefore, experiences are direct presentations of concrete particulars that appear to us under some nonconceptual qualitative mode of presentation.

4.2.2 Alston on Doxastic Practices

Whereas Marion sought to avoid commitment to the idea of conceptually unconstituted givens as contents of perception, Alston's internalist externalism explicitly endorses the idea. For Alston, both the vehicle and the content of perception are nonconceptual, with nonconceptual states of conscious awareness ("appearances") serving as the vehicle by means of which we are directed on the nonconceptual layout of reality itself ("that which appears").

Appearances, in that sense, are "*given* to my awareness in a way that sharply contrasts with anything I can do by my own devices to conjure them up in imagination, memory, or abstract thought."[65] To suffer an experience is therefore "from the side of the subject . . . called *direct awareness* and from the side of the object . . . called *presentation, givenness,* or *appearance.* It is a mode of cognition that is essentially independent of any conceptualization, belief, judgment or any other application of general concepts to the object."[66]

While Alston is a thoroughgoing nonconceptualist about the modes and content of perceptual experience, he does not take the nonconceptual and nonintentional character of perceptual experience to immediately constitute knowledge, in and of itself.[67] Rather,

---

65. Ibid., 37.
66. Ibid.
67. Ibid., 27; cf. William P. Alston, "What's Wrong with Immediate Knowledge?" *Synthese* 55, no. 1 (April 1983): 73–95.

Alston holds that in order for the empirical givenness of concrete particulars to become objects of perceptual *knowledge*—that is, for the sort of experiencing of X as F constitutive of knowing *that* X is F—we need to deploy concepts that succeed in identifying or picking out our nonconceptual awareness of particulars.[68] It is by way of conceptual identification that nonconceptual experiences can figure into the more general and propositionally structured form belonging to matters of empirical fact. So, while Alston holds that both the "of-ness" and the "as-ness" in S's experience of X as F is nonconceptual, he concedes that S's belief or knowledge that X is F requires capacities for conceptually identifying an X as F.

On Alston's view, whereas the perceptual experience is a kind of act-object relation that most fundamentally takes concrete particulars as objects and presents them to us independently of any putatively rational relations they bear to one another or us, believing and knowing is precisely a rationally normative act-object relation that takes conceptually structured objects (that is, propositions) as objects.[69] For us to have perceptual knowledge, therefore, requires that experiences can figure into the conceptual structure of a proposition such that the intentional stances we take to those propositions are intentional stances toward the contents of experience. One important use to which we put our concepts, Alston thinks, is to mark out empirical objects as intentional and epistemic objects.[70] The fundamental mode of conceptual identification that

68. Alston, *Perceiving God*, 41.
69. See William P. Alston, "Perception and Conception," in *Pragmatism, Reason, and Norms: A Realistic Assessment*, ed. Kenneth R. Westphal (New York: Fordham University Press, 1998), 59–87; Alston, *A Sensible Metaphysical Realism* (Milwaukee, WI: Marquette University Press, 2001).
70. This is not to say, however, that Alston is committed to the idea that concepts do not affect the ways things can or do appear to us, or even that concepts are not necessary for certain sorts of perceptual experience (e.g., experiences of particulars whose phenomenological mode of appearing presupposes background concepts). It is only to say that we do not need to appeal to any operations of our conceptual capacities in order to give a conceptual analysis of perceptual

Alston considers is forming perceptual *beliefs* about the appearances given in experience. Perceptual beliefs get their content by picking out appearances, and those beliefs count as justified or knowledgeable when the appearances satisfy the relevant normative standards for justification or knowledge imposed by those beliefs.

So how does the content of an "experience" as understood in terms of Alston's internalist externalism figure into the content of a perceptual belief, and how does such content serve not only to inform such beliefs but to rationally ground them? Alston's answer to this is his "Doxastic Practice approach" to epistemology. A "doxastic practice" (hereafter, DP), he tells us, is "a way of forming beliefs and epistemically evaluating them."[71] More particularly, it is "a system or constellation of dispositions or habits, or to use a currently fashionable term, 'mechanisms,' each of which yields a belief as output that is related in a certain way to an 'input.'"[72] To be engaged in doxastic practices, then, is to be engaged in "the exercise of a system or constellation of belief-forming habits or mechanisms, each realizing a function that yields beliefs with a certain kind of content from inputs of a certain type."[73]

Our dispositions to form certain sorts of beliefs on the basis of our receptivity to corresponding sorts of inputs from DPs are socially established and involuntary.[74] We are initiated into an irreducible plurality of widely shared ways of doxastically responding to our environment. These responsive dispositions were well in place before

---

experience—to specify the necessary and sufficient conditions for something to count as a perceptual experience (*Perceiving God*, 38).

71. Ibid., *Perceiving God*, 6.

72. Ibid., 153.

73. Ibid., 155.

74. Wolterstorff thinks Alston's preferred terminology of "practice" is a misnomer insofar as he supposes that engagement in a practice presumes voluntary control. See Nicholas Wolterstorff, "Entitlement to Believe and Practices of Inquiry," in *Practices of Belief*, vol. 2, ed. Terence Cuneo (Cambridge: Cambridge University Press, 2009), 99–100.

we arrived on the scene, even if the particular forms of life continue to evolve and remain susceptible of ongoing revision. We acquire the dispositions to respond to particular sorts of inputs by forming particular sorts of beliefs involuntarily, by our prereflective habituation into the various practices into which we are born and raised. These involuntarily learned and socially established responsive dispositions function as belief-forming mechanisms. Such mechanisms can take both doxastic and nondoxastic inputs—"generational" DPs take nondoxastic inputs and spit out doxastic outputs (beliefs) and are thus a "source of radically new information," whereas "transformational" DPs perform strictly formal or content-neutral operations (for instance, logical operations) on doxastic inputs (for example, background beliefs) in order to produce new beliefs.[75]

Since experiences are not propositionally structured or in any other way conceptually constituted for Alston, he takes them to be nondoxastic inputs in a "generational" form of doxastic practice whose outputs are perceptual beliefs. The movement from sense perception, as a paradigmatic form of perceptual experience, to perceptual beliefs is a socially well-established doxastic practice—we are disposed to form perceptual beliefs on the basis of our experiences. Alston is careful to insist that the experience is not an *inferential* basis for the belief because, for TA, appearances do not have the conceptual structure requisite for inference; rather, the disposition ensures that the relevant sensory experience *causes* a corresponding belief about a sensible object. That causal connection secured by the dispositions acquired in a doxastic practice enables propositionally

---

75. This distinction suggests that Alston sees the norms of our "generational" DPs governing our immediate or noninferential knowledge, while the norms of "transformational" DPs govern our inferential knowledge.

structured outputs to succeed in "tracking with" and thereby referring us to the concrete particulars given in experience.

While this gives us empirically contentful propositions that can function as objects of epistemic evaluation and toward which we can take up various intentional stances, it leaves open the question of the normative epistemic status of the beliefs produced by any such mechanisms. A DP might explain how our experiences impose beliefs "about" the world on us, but it does not yet specify what it takes for such beliefs to be rationally *justified* or *knowledge-constituting* beliefs about the world. For that, Alston says, the output belief has to be the product of a particular *sort* of generational process, one reliably aimed at producing true beliefs. Roughly, the degree to which a perceptual belief P is rationally justified is the degree of reliability with which P has been produced by a perceptual DP. If the perceptual practice is sufficiently reliable, then believing that-p counts as knowing that-p.[76]

In putting things this way, Alston strongly emphasizes a level distinction between knowing (or being justified in believing) that-p and knowing (or being justified in believing) that I know (or am justified in believing) that-p.[77] In order to know that-p, it is not necessary for me to know that I know that-p. As such, in order to be justified or count as knowledge, it is only required that my belief that-p *be* the product of a reliably truth-aimed DP, not that I *know* or *justifiably believe* that it is. Moreover, it is a good thing we need not meet that requirement because any attempt to do so faces the problem of what Alston terms "epistemic circularity," the inevitable need to lean on the deliverances of the very sources of belief under suspicion in order to evaluate those sources, and we therefore have "no sufficient noncircular reason for taking them to be reliable."[78]

76. Alston, *Perceiving God*, 102–9, 143–45.
77. Ibid., 301; Alston, "Two Types of Foundationalism," *Journal of Philosophy* 73, no. 7 (1976): 165–85.

Following Reid, we should regard any putative DP, as well as any belief with which it saddles us, as innocent until proven guilty.

The question of whether we ought to trust any given DP or its outputs, therefore, is a practical one: a matter of doing our epistemic duties in *monitoring* the beliefs of any well-established DP in which we participate. This, in turn, requires that we can recognize and respond to putative overriders of its prima facie rationality.[79] If, for instance, we had reason to think that a DP perpetually introduced inconsistency into our system of beliefs and the network of DPs that give rise to them, we might be practically rational in judging that DP unreliable. But in the absence of any such compelling overriders, we remain practically rational in judging our DP to be reliable. On this standard, sense perception, Alston argues, constitutes a well-established and practically rational basis for forming observational beliefs. While the monitoring of our perceptual beliefs often requires us to revise them in various ways, we confront nothing that overrides our thinking that our mechanism for forming sense-perceptual beliefs is a reliable source of new information about our environment.[80]

4.2.3 The Theory of Appearing and the Appearance of God

Alston's account of relations of "appearing" and their role in our doxastic practices—the prime instance of which is sense perception—serves as the model for the phenomenological, referential, and epistemological structure of any perceptual relation we might bear to anything at all. From that starting point, the

---

78. Alston, *Perceiving God*, 146.
79. Ibid., 170. See also Nicholas Wolterstorff's discussion in "Entitlement to Believe," 99–100.
80. Alston, *Perceiving God*, 170–83. For Alston's full-blown argument for the reliability of sense-perception, see William P. Alston, *The Reliability of Sense Perception* (Ithaca, NY: Cornell University Press, 1993).

question he considers is whether anything about that model precludes the putative possibility of a perceptual relation to God. The primary burden of Alston's argument in *Perceiving God* is therefore to establish that possibility (though, like Marion, not its actuality) by demonstrating the consistency of his conception of Christian "mystical perception" (hereafter, CMP) with the perceptual model given in TA. Alston finds no reasons—theological or otherwise—to prohibit us from supposing that CMP involves relations of appearing perfectly in keeping with TA as a straightforwardly nonsensory analogue to sense perception. Further, since both sense perception and CMP constitute doxastic practices that conform equally well to TA, there is no good reason to withhold the very same practical reasons for endorsing the reliability of CMP that lead us to endorse the reliability of ordinary sense perception.[81] There is thus a kind of structural and epistemological parity between the act-object structure of ordinary sense perception and CMP as rational bases of belief.

On the taxonomy I have offered, Alston's account of religious experience in general, and Christian religious experience in particular, is clearly cataphatic insofar as TA provides the common structure that is univocally instantiated in both ordinary experience and the experience of God. That is not to say that Alston acknowledges no differences between the ordinary and more paradigmatic instantiation of TA (sense perception) and CMP, only that those differences are not fundamentally to be accounted for in terms of any systemic disruption or failure in the structure of ordinary experience.[82] Rather, with respect to the relations of appearing that establish the parity of CMP's act-object structure with sense perception, Alston argues that both can meet the requirements of

---

81. Alston, *Perceiving God*, 81.
82. Ibid., 61–67; cf. William P. Alston, "Aquinas on Theological Predication: A Look Backward and a Look Forward," in *Reasoned Faith*, ed. Eleonore Stump (Ithaca, NY: Cornell University Press, 1993), 145–78.

his internalist externalism. The internal requirement is that of having distinctive qualitative nonconceptual modes of presentation. Alston rightly takes holding that God is a nonsensory object to be perfectly consistent with thinking that God can nevertheless present Godself to us as being thus and so (for instance, good, powerful, and so forth) or doing this or that (for example, blessing, forgiving, and the like) by way of *sensory content*. But he argues that it is equally possible to conceive of God's modes of appearing as *nonsensory*.[83]

There is, after all, nothing incoherent in supposing that "phenomenal content may be very different from any that is produced by our external senses and may not result from the stimulation of any physical sense-organ."[84] Moreover, being able to distinguish phenomenological reports of "sensing" God from ordinary reports about external sensory awareness of objects in our distal environment indicates that putative perceptions of God can lack the distinctive qualia of external sensory stimulation. While the distinctive phenomenal character of divine appearing might be difficult to mark out, this does not mean that there is not such phenomenological distinctiveness. That it should be difficult is to be expected, given our ignorance about the stimulus conditions of divine appearing, our relative lack of control over them given divine freedom, and our consequent inability to identify any underlying physiological or psychological mechanisms for them.[85]

With respect to the external conditions, Alston finds nothing about God that in principle bars God from being or becoming perceptibly *present* to us, for there are not, Alston thinks, "any general a priori constraints on what can appear to our experience. We have to learn from experience what we can be experientially aware of."[86] The

83. Alston, *Perceiving God*, 19–20.
84. Ibid., 17.
85. Ibid., 49.
86. Ibid., 59.

credentials of any given mode of perception, sensory or nonsensory, "does not depend on our understanding of how it is effected."[87] Most people are capable of forming beliefs about the relative positions of their body parts, for example, without knowing how to mark out either the faculty or process that accounts for "proprioception" or the distinctive boundaries of its outputs.

Nor does God's transcendence constrain the possibility that the phenomenology of divine appearing is a direct awareness or presentation of God's immediate bearing on us. We need not perceive the undivided fullness or simple essence of God in order to perceive God at all, only some aspect of God as delimited by our finite perceptual capacity.[88] Nor need the relevant aspect of divine presence be or belong to the divine essence itself in order for that aspect to count as a perception "of" God. It need only be a *manifestation* of God—a way that God genuinely *seems*, even if not a way that God really *is*. To truly perceive God therefore does not entail truly perceiving God *as God is* but is consistent with perceiving God "in an imperfect manner suited to our limitations."[89]

As a belief-forming practice, CMP is distinct from sense perception insofar as its internal and external features putatively conform to different subject matter than that with which our doxastic practices of sense perception are concerned. It has therefore quite understandably built up correspondingly different ways of rationally monitoring the beliefs it produces. But, given the differences in subject matter from that of sense perception, CMP is nevertheless an entirely appropriate way of realizing the same generic perceptual model. The relative predominance of a sense-perceptual practice notwithstanding, it would be just as much a mistake to judge the reliability of CMP by

87. Ibid., 60.
88. Ibid.
89. Ibid., 63.

sense-perceptual standards as it would be to judge sense perception by the standards internal to CMP.[90] Alston therefore concludes that CMP "is a functioning, socially established, perceptual doxastic practice with distinctive experiential inputs, distinctive input-output functions, a distinctive conceptual scheme, and a rich, internally justified overrider system. As such, it possesses a prima facie title to being rationally engaged in, and its outputs are thereby prima facie justified."[91]

This parity of practical justification enjoyed by CMP alongside sense perception, Alston is careful to note, holds only in the absence of "overriders": reasons for thinking not merely that this or that putative perceptual belief about God generated by CMP is mistaken or unreliable (the monitoring of which, after all, is built into the practice of CMP) but that CMP itself and per se is a fundamentally unreliable way of forming our beliefs about God. But Alston argues that most of the overriders we might marshal against the reliability of CMP per se (such as naturalistic objections, inconsistencies among doxastic outputs, and conflicts with other DPs) apply equally well to sense perception and that the plausible practical reasons for rejecting skepticism in the latter case compel us to reject it in the former.[92]

4.2.4 Alston's Mythical Givenness

Like Marion, Alston was well aware of the Sellarsian charge of the myth of the given and the impetus toward conceptualist accounts of perceptual experience in contemporary philosophical literature. But unlike Marion, Alston embraces rather than disavows his own commitment to a Givenist account of our putative perceptual relation

---

90. Ibid., 221.
91. Ibid., 225.
92. Ibid., 175–83.

to God. He simply concedes that his internalist externalism about the modes and content of experience and his doxastic-practice approach to the epistemology of perception (jointly constitutive of TA) entail a commitment to Givenism. As such, he grants that TA forms a proper target for a Sellarsian attack. But Alston does not think that Sellars has succeeded in showing that "the given" is in fact a myth and, as such, something to be avoided. More particularly, Alston thinks that Sellars fails to identify anything problematic or defective about the sort of Givenism that Alston himself endorses by way of TA. Thus, in "Sellars and the Myth of the Given," Alston attempts to identify the Sellarsian attack on Givenism (principally as articulated in EPM), then defends TA, his own preferred version of Givenism, from that attack.[93]

While Alston notes that there is indeed a point of conflict between Sellars and himself, it is not easy to locate because there is much agreement between his perspective and that of Sellars in EPM. Both philosophers, for example, reject the sense-datum theories of perception that form the principal targets of EPM.[94] Both also reject the idea that a direct awareness of particulars can of itself constitute a noninferential knowledge of facts. Instead, both endorse a conceptualism about perceptual *knowledge*, since Alston agrees with Sellars that "there is no non-conceptual knowledge that-so-and-so."[95] "But then where," Alston asks himself, "do I dissent from Sellars' attack on the given?" He goes on to name two central points at which

---

93. William P. Alston, "Sellars and the 'Myth of the Given,'" *Philosophy and Phenomenological Research* 65, no. 1 (July 2002): 69–86, 70. See also note 4, wherein Alston wonders whether the "claim to *non-conceptual knowledge that so-and-so*" just *is* the mythical given that Sellars is concerned to reject.

94. Alston, *Perceiving God*, 56ff; cf. Sellars, *Empiricism and the Philosophy of Mind*, 14, §§1–2.

95. Alston, "Sellars and the 'Myth of the Given,'" 70. See also note 4, wherein Alston wonders whether the "claim to *non-conceptual knowledge that so-and-so*" just *is* the mythical given that Sellars is concerned to reject.

he takes Sellars's attack to genuinely confront TA with a putative problem.

The first is over the question of "whether we have a direct (nonconceptual) awareness of particulars, one that constitutes a kind of cognition of a nonconceptual, nonpropositional sort."[96] "Sellars," Alston says, "is concerned to deny this . . . And it is that with which I take issue." [97] Most of what Alston has to say in defending TA from Sellars is devoted to this first issue: he spends the majority of the essay defending the idea that there are such things as nonconceptual sensations of particulars and that sensations thus understood are features of our phenomenal consciousness—we can be aware of them and their distinctively qualitative character. Sellars goes wrong, he thinks, for being an eliminativist about sensations thus understood—the "myth" is precisely that what is given to us in experience is a nonconceptual sensory awareness of particulars.

The second point of contact Alston names, over and above his nonconceptualism about the modes of perceptual experience, is TA's endorsement of the claim that a nonconceptual "direct awareness of X's . . . provides a basis (justification, warrant . . .) for beliefs about those X's. And this is a direct confrontation [of TA] with Sellars' epistemological interest in the 'myth of the given.'"[98] Alston is right to say that what interests Sellars about the notion of a nonconceptual sensory awareness of particulars is the relationship between that sort of awareness and the epistemic role it is supposed to play in the formation and justification of perceptual beliefs that make it possible for those beliefs to count as knowledgeable. On Sellars's view, it is a mistake to think that a nonconceptual awareness could form the content of a belief that gives it both warranted and warranting

---

96. Alston, "Sellars and the 'Myth of the Given,'" 70.
97. Ibid.
98. Ibid.

epistemic status. Moreover, Sellars very clearly signals his principal reason for thinking that nonconceptual episodes of any sort are incapable of either bearing any suitable analogue to a rational warrant or conferring a rational warrant on a belief: "The essential point is that in characterizing an episode or a state as that of knowing, we are not giving an empirical description of that episode or state; we are placing it in the logical space of reasons, of justifying and being able to justify what one says."[99]

If the content of a perceptual belief (or the content of the empirical concepts constituent in it) is nonconceptual, and if nonconceptual content cannot bear a positive epistemic status, then perceptual beliefs cannot bear a positive epistemic status in virtue of their content. If perceptual beliefs cannot bear a positive epistemic status in virtue of their content, then they cannot confer positive epistemic status on any beliefs inferred from them. But if empirical knowledge consists in the positive epistemic status of a perceptual belief and the beliefs inferred from perceptual beliefs, then there can be no such thing as empirical knowledge. Further, if our perceptual beliefs cannot possibly be empirically knowledge-constituting (that is, if they cannot be candidates for knowing anything about the world), then they cannot be "about" the world at all. It follows that if there is such a thing as empirical knowledge, then the contents of our perceptual beliefs cannot be nonconceptual.

Since Alston holds both that empirical knowledge is possible *and* that the contents of perception are nonconceptual sensations of particulars as cognitions in our conscious awareness, he rightly concludes that "understanding immediate cognitions of particulars in this way, there will be a clear disagreement between Sellars and myself."[100] Given the evident centrality of Sellars's "epistemological

99. Sellars, *Empiricism and the Philosophy of Mind*, §36, 76.
100. Alston, "Sellars and the 'Myth of the Given,'" 70.

interest" in the intentionality and epistemic justification of perceptual beliefs for the way he identifies the myth of the given and what makes it mythical, we should expect this second issue to take center stage in Alston's refutation of Sellars. At any rate, we should expect Alston's identification of Sellars's epistemological motivations to play a guiding role in the way he reads Sellars on the first issue, that of Sellars's alleged prejudice toward the very idea of a nonconceptual sensory awareness of particulars.

What we find instead is puzzling. Alston spends nearly the entire article attempting to refute Sellars's prejudice against the idea of a nonconceptual sensory awareness of particulars *without* addressing the epistemological motivation. But for just that reason, Alston fails to properly identify what it is about the idea of empirical content as nonconceptual content that Sellars finds objectionable. Alston writes as if what Sellars rejects as "mythical" is the very idea of qualitative phenomenal content per se, as if he is an eliminativist about "qualia" (however understood) as a necessary and distinctive feature of perceptual experience.

He therefore writes that Sellars "fails to recognize the fundamental place of the intrinsic character of looks that is brought out by phenomenal looks-concepts, since it ignores (or rejects on principle) such phenomenal concepts altogether."[101] But the second issue Alston flagged—Sellars's "epistemological interest"—should have already made it clear to Alston that what Sellars is concerned to eliminate is not the distinctive and intrinsic phenomenal character of an experience. What he seeks to eliminate as mythical is the notion that an awareness of the intrinsic phenomenal character of an experience capable of supplying the warrant for our perceptual beliefs is a *nonconceptual* form of awareness. Alston argues that Sellars "ignores"

101. Ibid., 77.

the idea of phenomenal concepts as a fundamentally noncomparative way of conceptualizing or identifying nonconceptual experiences and that in this he is guilty of the "non sequitur" of concluding from the fact that our concepts are essentially comparative or logically interconnected that our experiences are analyzable that way as well.[102]

But neither of these complaints will do as *criticisms* of Sellars's conceptualism about experience because they just beg the question. Alston has already identified Sellars's epistemological worry as motivating his attempt to explain how it is that our empirical concepts acquire the intrinsic phenomenal character they do without saying that they do so by way of a direct and quasi-intentional relation to nonconceptual sensations. He refuses that route, moreover, on transcendental grounds. The idea that an empirical concept or perceptual belief gets its content from a direct relation to a nonconceptual Given, Sellars thinks, makes empirical knowledge impossible, and so rejecting that idea is a necessary condition for the possibility of empirical knowledge.[103] On *those* grounds, Sellars has good reason to offer an analysis of perceptual beliefs in such a way as to explicate their content without appeal to nonconceptual contents.

So even if the analysis he goes on to offer is wrong, objecting to it on the grounds that he fails to appeal to the nonconceptual (noncomparative) character of experience just begs the question. That is, even if Sellars's alternative explanation for how our perceptual beliefs get their content or his analysis of the semantics of perceptual beliefs rooted in that explanation is inadequate, that does not show that his critique of Givenism is false, only that his own attempt to avoid Givenism does not work. To address Sellars's attack

102. Ibid., 76, 79.
103. Or, running the argument the other way, his analysis takes the form of a reductio; if our perceptual beliefs are grounded in nonconceptual Givens, then empirical knowledge is impossible. Empirical knowledge is possible, so our perceptual beliefs are not grounded in nonconceptual Givens.

on the Given, Alston would have to show that what *motivates* Sellars's alternative analysis—his transcendental worry that a direct relation to nonconceptual content makes empirical knowledge impossible—is itself mistaken. That worry, you may recall, was predicated on the idea that a positive epistemic status is a property reserved for the normative or evaluative character of concepts. Since nonconceptual sensory episodes are supposed to be merely the nonpropositionally structured proximal effects on our conscious awareness that are caused by our relation to our distal environment, our awareness of those proximal effects could not be the candidates for epistemic warrant or justification that they would need to be in order to supply our concepts and beliefs with content.

But rather than tracing Sellars's rationale for this distinction between an epistemic justification and a nonepistemic or "mere" cause, Alston is at best breezily dismissive of the distinction. In the space of less than two pages, he at last turns to address Sellars's worry about the very idea of nonconceptual warrants or justifications. Instead of an argument, Alston offers only frank bewilderment at Sellars's idea that we have to distinguish between nonconceptual causes and normative or rational causes, among the former of which are sensations and among the latter of which are epistemic justifications. Alston recognizes this same distinction in Davidson, but he finds it no more intelligible or plausible there than he does in Sellars: "Of course if positive epistemic status is conferred only by propositionally structured knowledge or justified belief, then it is not conferred by non-propositionally structured experiences. But why should we accept the antecedent? Neither Sellars nor Davidson so much as hint at a reason for doing so."[104]

---

104. Alston, "Sellars and the 'Myth of the Given,'" 85.

Contra Alston, however, Sellars drops a fairly clear hint very early on in EPM as to why he thinks that a positive epistemic status belongs only to episodes or states that are propositionally structured. The identification of epistemic justification with the normative character of reasons arises from Sellars's distinction between "epistemic" facts and "natural" facts.[105] A failure to recognize that distinction, he says, saddles us with a mistake that is "of a piece with the so-called 'naturalistic fallacy' in ethics."[106]

G. E. Moore coined the term "naturalistic fallacy" in the course of defending the idea that the basic evaluative properties that ground our norms—the properties constitutive of goodness—cannot be reductively analyzed or defined in nonevaluative terms.[107] Instead, we have to regard goodness as a sui generis concept. Moore argues that any merely natural or nonmoral property in terms of which we might wish to define moral goodness, such as pleasantness, is compatible with leaving open the question of whether goodness is in fact strictly *identical* with that nonmoral property. If the concept of moral goodness could be analyzed without remainder in terms of the property of pleasantness, for example, then "goodness is pleasantness" ought to display the same logical form as, for example, "bachelors are unmarried men." But whereas the definitional character of "bachelors are unmarried men" guarantees that predicating bachelorhood of unmarried men is necessarily redundant and as such trivial, the same result is clearly not secured by predicating pleasantness of goodness. If we truly grasp the definition "bachelors are unmarried men," then it will make no sense to wonder whether anyone whom we take to be a bachelor really *is* an unmarried man or not, since we recognize that identifying the relevant individual as a bachelor just is identifying

105. Sellars, *Empiricism and the Philosophy of Mind*, §§5; 18–19,
106. Ibid., §5, 19.
107. See G. E. Moore, *Principia Ethica* (1903; Mineloa, NY: Dover, 2004), 9–20, §§10–14.

him as an unmarried man. "*Of course* that bachelor is an unmarried man," we are inclined to say, "bachelors are *by definition* unmarried men!"

In the case of moral goodness, however, even if we grant that something is morally good if and only if it is pleasant, this cannot in like manner count as a definition or an analysis of moral goodness. If we truly understand the predication being made, we can still recognize as a genuinely open question whether this or that pleasurable act is a morally good act.[108] Unlike the case of our identifying something as a "bachelor," it makes perfect sense to wonder whether some act we have identified as pleasurable really is morally good or not, and this lack of redundancy or triviality holds for any and every morally nonevaluative ("natural") predicate we might propose. Predications of moral goodness are therefore unanalyzable in terms of natural predicates.

Whereas Moore focused on *moral* goodness in his discussion of the irreducibility of the good to the merely natural, Sellars's allusion to Moore indicates that he takes the same point to apply to any essentially normative or evaluative terms whatever, including attempts to analyze *epistemic* goodness in nonepistemic terms. Facts establishing a standard of correctness for our epistemic evaluations (epistemic facts) cannot be reduced to facts that do not do so (natural facts).[109] Sellars therefore denies that "epistemic facts can be analyzed without remainder—even 'in principle'—into non-epistemic facts."[110]

Maximilian de Gaynesford helpfully illustrates the fundamental difference in logical or "grammatical" form between "epistemic" and

---

108. This has come to be regarded as the "open question argument" (ibid., 15–16, 13). For a more recent defense, see Caj Strandberg, "In Defence of the Open Question Argument," *Journal of Ethics* 8, no. 2 (2004): 179–96.

109. The distinction between natural and epistemic facts here is just a more particularized instance of the distinction between is and ought.

110. Sellars, *Empiricism and the Philosophy of Mind*, 19, §5.

nonepistemic "natural" facts.[111] He asks us to suppose that an inductive procedure of empirical testing has led us to derive from repeated instances of striking a match the claim that

N1: If a match is struck, that match should light.

If N1 is true, it counts as a Sellarsian "natural" fact, one that serves as a standard of correctness for a certain class of descriptive statements about matches. For example, it entitles us to affirm in the individual case that

N2: When that match is struck, that match will light.

N1 names a natural fact about matches insofar as it serves as a standard of correctness for claims such as N2. But if we should discover that N2 is false—if, that is, we find a counterexample to N1—then we take this to count as a reason to revise N1. So suppose we claim N2 in reference to our attempt to light a wet match. Our recognition of the requirement that N2 conform to the relevant norms leads us to correct or emend N1. We might do that by adding some qualification such as "if a *dry* match is struck, it should light." The word "should" in N1 is descriptive or predictive, not prescriptive. It signals our expectation that the individual match will conform to the state of affairs specified by the antecedent of N1 given the experimental evidence and a principle of induction. If a state of affairs of the sort belonging to N2—one putatively governed by the standard of correctness specified in N1—fails to conform to that standard, then it is the standard itself that needs correcting.

Now consider an example of an epistemic claim that, if true, would count as a Sellarsian epistemic fact, one that can function as a standard of correctness not merely for whether or not the things we claim

111. This example is taken from Maximilian De Gaynesford's useful discussion in *John McDowell* (Malden, MA: Polity Press), 64ff.

about the world are true, but whether we should *believe* that they are true or whether we are entitled to regard any particular believing that such a claim is true as an instance of *knowing* that it is. A relatively uncontroversial candidate for an epistemic fact of that sort (as opposed to a "natural" one) might be the following:

E1: If anyone believes that they strike a match, then they should believe that a match is struck.

Applied to the individual case, we would conclude the following:

E2: If Sameer believes that he strikes that match, then Sameer believes that match is struck.

Now suppose we find that, among the class of statements governed by the putative fact stated in E1, we find an instance that serves as a counterexample. For example, we can imagine a scenario in which E2 comes out false. Perhaps I believe that I strike a match, but I *do not* believe that the match is struck. It may be, as De Gaynesford suggests, that I am perpetually confused about the correct use of the passive voice.[112]

If our recognition of the requirement that E2 conform to the norm specified by E1 had the same logical form as our recognition of the requirement that N2 conform to the norm specified by N1, then when faced with a counterexample we would be led to correct or emend E1. In this case, we would emend E2 to state that if anyone believes that a match is struck and is perpetually confused about the passive, then they *should* fail to believe that a match is struck. But clearly that is not right. What E2 leads me to do is not to bring E1 into conformity with E2, but the reverse. What E1 claims is that if I believe that I strike the match, then—my grammatical malady notwithstanding—I *should* believe that it is struck. If I do not,

112. Ibid., 66.

then I need to revise my beliefs to conform myself to the epistemic norm, not change that norm to conform to my beliefs. The epistemic standard of correctness established by the "should" of E1 is therefore of a radically different sort than that of N1.

Whereas the *natural* "should" indicates my expectation or assumption that my beliefs will conform to a standard of correctness specified by some antecedently established descriptive norm, the *epistemic* "should" indicates my recognition of an obligation to bring about the conformity of my beliefs to a standard of correctness specified by some antecedently established epistemic norm. Understood in this way, Sellars's distinction between the type of rational norms respectively established by natural and epistemic facts mirrors the distinction Elizabeth Anscombe famously illustrated by comparing a shopper in the grocery store with the private detective tasked with following him.[113] While the shopper is attempting to find all the items on his list and place them in his basket, the private detective who follows him is keeping his own list, recording every item the shopper places in his basket. Sellarsian natural facts of the sort described in N1 above take on the perspective of the detective, whereas Sellarsian "epistemic facts" of the sort described in E1 take on the perspective of the shopper. When the shopper's list says "butter" and he gets margarine instead, then it is the shopper who is mistaken, but the detective is not capable of detecting the mistake *as* a mistake—he must simply record "margarine" on his list. Even if the detective succeeds in describing the behavior of someone who is thinking or acting in accord with an epistemic norm, he fails to

---

113. See G. E. M. Anscombe, *Intention* (Cambridge, MA: Harvard University Press, 2000), 56ff., §32. See also Richard Moran and Martin Stone, "Anscombe on Expression of Intention: An Exegesis," in *Essays on Anscombe's* Intention, ed. Anton Ford, Jennifer Hornsby, and Frederick Stoutland (Cambridge, MA: Harvard University Press, 2011), 33–75.

describe that behavior *as* subject to a norm or to capture with his list the normative function of the shopper's list.

Facts about the *norms to which we are subject* (as expressed by E1 and displayed by the shopper) are thus essentially structured with what John Searle calls a different world/word direction of fit than facts merely *describing our subjection to such norms* (as expressed by N1 and displayed by the detective).[114] It is nonsensical or (at best) necessarily false to suppose that the evaluative force of "should" as it is employed in the stating of epistemic facts such as E1 could be captured, defined, substituted, or translated—even "in principle"—by the descriptive force it has in natural facts such as N1. Any shift from the stating of a fact about our rational answerability or accountability to a norm to the stating of a fact about the properties or patterns of behavior that enable or follow from our accountability to a norm therefore fails to represent a shift from the identification of an epistemic fact to an *analysis* of that fact in terms of natural or nonepistemic facts. Such a shift just changes the subject.

There is an irreducible logical difference between facts about what we "should" think, say, and do in response to the relevant rational norms to which we are subject and facts about what we "should" think, say, and do as anticipations, predictions, or descriptions of the relevant natural laws or nonrational patterns of behavior to which we are subject. From that difference we can derive two correspondingly distinct notions of "reasons," "causes," and "explanations" that are irreducible one to the other. Suppose that as you approach the door I open it, allowing you to come in. When asked *why* I opened the door, I might reply that I saw that your arms were full and, seeing that you needed help getting through the door, I opened it for you. Even where my act is instinctive and involving no deliberation, it is

---

114. John Searle, *Expression and Meaning* (Cambridge: Cambridge University Press, 1979), 97, 122.

possible that in responding this way I have correctly cited the *reason* that I opened the door. Moreover, the reason I offered (seeing that you needed help), coupled perhaps with my desiring to help, *explains* my opening of the door, and accordingly what I saw (your needing help) *caused* me to open the door. When I cite a causal explanation of this sort as the "reason" I opened the door, what I am explaining is why I "should" have opened the door in the evaluative sense of "should" expressed in epistemic facts of the sort illustrated by E1 above.[115]

Contrast this way of citing what I saw as the reason I opened the door with the following alternative reply: I opened the door because my retinas registered the impacts of the patterns of light arising from your posture and relative distance in my distal environment, and this occasioned the relevant electrical impulses from my brain, which in turn caused the coordinated flexing and relaxing of various muscle groups in my back, arm, and hand, enabling me to extend my arm, grasp the door, and pull it toward me. This (admittedly crude) citation of the neurobiological mechanisms involved in my opening of the door could just as well correctly identify the reason that I opened the door, the cause of that act, and as such an explanation for it. But when I cite a causal explanation of this sort as the "reason" I opened the door, what I am explaining is why I "should" have opened the door in the descriptive sense expressed in a natural fact of the sort illustrated by N1 above.[116]

This distinction between epistemic (or "rational") and natural ("merely causal" or "nonrational") reasons for acting extends as well to different sorts of reasons for belief. Sellars claims that when we

---

115. See Donald Davidson, "Actions, Reasons and Causes," *Journal of Philosophy* 60 (1963): 685–700.
116. Davdison describes this difference between the rational character of agent causation and the law-governed character of natural causation in terms of the "anomalism" of the mental. See his "Mental Events," in *Experience and Theory*, ed. Lawrence Foster and J. W. Swanson (London: Duckworth, 1970), 79–102.

characterize ourselves as "knowers" and when we characterize various states or episodes of ours as "knowings," we are characterizing those states or episodes as belonging to the "logical space" of reasons in the *epistemic* sense—as *rational* reasons, *rational* causes, *rational* explanations. By way of contrast, when we characterize any state or episode as having a *merely* causal reason, a nonrational cause or explanation, we cannot characterize any such state as an epistemically good state—one constitutive of knowledge or justified belief. What justifies my beliefs or constitutes them as knowledgeable is my possessing a *rational* entitlement or warrant for that belief, even if I do not or need not possess an entitlement for my entitlement.

Alston on more than one occasion criticizes Sellars's insistence on "logical" (epistemic, rational) reasons as opposed to merely causal ones as the relevant domain in which epistemic justification is conferred on our beliefs. His standard charge is that the insistence is motivated by Sellars's confusion between the *activity* of justifying (in which we are called to evaluate the rational credentials of a belief via the sort of activity that Sellars describes as "placing it in the logical space of reasons, of justifying and being able to justify what one says") and the *state* of *being* justified (for which the giving and receiving of reasons in his "epistemic" sense is not necessarily required).

But this cannot be right because Sellars's characterization of epistemic justification as belonging to the logical space of reasons includes a specification of the priority of the state to the activity of justification in the form of the possession of a *capacity* to engage in the activity. The sort of capacity he has in mind is nothing so grand as one's preparedness to marshal a carefully reasoned case for the veridicality of one's perceptual beliefs. It is rather merely a capacity to place one's perceptual beliefs in the logical space in which the notion of a rational entitlement is intelligibly applicable. If, for example, I claim that the sky is blue but I am utterly incapable of saying why I think that is so, and I further fail to recognize any entailments of the claim I have made, such as its incompatibility with the idea that the sky always and everywhere appears red or that "sky" refers us upward, not downward, and so forth, then in what sense could my belief intelligibly be regarded as enjoying a state of epistemic justification?

Without some minimal capacity to place my beliefs in the logical space of reasons, those beliefs are not susceptible of justificatory states. However, it is possible to possess relevant conceptual capacities without exercising them, since I can potentially recognize a minimal conception of what follows from my beliefs or why I hold them even if I am never called to actually invoke such a recognition in the activity of justifying what I think, say, or do.

Whatever properties or patterns of behavior enable or follow from our accountability to the logical space of normative reasons, that accountability makes our beliefs susceptible of justification or knowledge. This is what McDowell calls Sellars's "master thought" in EPM—namely, that "the conceptual apparatus we employ when we place things in the logical space of reasons is irreducible to any conceptual apparatus that does not serve to place things in the logical space of reasons. So the master thought as it were draws a line; above-the-line are placings in the logical space of reasons, and below it are characterizations that do not do that."[117]

In other words, when we move from considering my above-the-line reason for opening the door for you (or, for instance, my reason for believing that I am obligated to open the door for you) to considering a below-the-line natural reason enabling me to open the door for you, what goes missing in the latter characterization is the idea of an *agent*-cause, and with it the normative status of that agent as a knowing subject, that is, as someone attempting to bring

---

117. McDowell, "Sellars on Perceptual Experience," in *Having the World in View*, 5.

his acts into conformity with a norm. Alston takes this Sellarsian and Davidsonian distinction between two different characterizations of our bodily or psychological states or episodes as "reasons" (only one of which is epistemically efficacious) as a way of "plumping for an incompatibility of causal and epistemic functions."[118] But this evaluation gets Sellars (and Davidson) wrong on two counts. First, they both regard above-the-line and below-the-line characterizations as *irreducibile* to one another, not *incompatible* with one another, as is clearly illustrated in the compatibility between the neurobiological explanation and the rational explanation for my having opened a door for someone. Second, they both take it to be appropriate to think of both sorts of explanations as causal, even if the notion of epistemic efficacy clearly belongs to the category of a rational or epistemic cause and not a nonepistemic or *merely* causal one.

Alston is therefore surely right when he says that the question of whether a causal explanation shows that a belief is justified or why a belief is justified "depends on what kind of cause is in question."[119] But he fails to recognize that he himself has assigned an epistemically justificatory role to the wrong *sort* of causes; that is, to the states or episodes characterized in a merely causal and nonrational way. Sellars schematizes the two sorts of characterizations we might give for a perceptual state or episode, the first corresponding to a natural conception of an experience and the second an epistemic conception:

> (1) The idea that there are certain inner episodes—e.g., sensations of red or of C# which can occur to human beings (and brutes) without any prior process of learning or concept formation and without which it would *in some sense* be impossible to *see*, for example, that the facing

---

118. Alston, "Sellars and the 'Myth of the Given,'" 84.
119. Ibid.

surface of a physical object is red and triangular or *hear* that a certain physical sound is a C#.

(2) The idea that there are certain inner episodes which are the non-inferential knowings that certain items are, for example, red or C#, and that these episodes are the necessary conditions of empirical knowledge as providing the evidence for all other empirical propositions.[120]

As we have already seen, Alston is wrong to think that Sellars's complaint about TA lies simply in its claims that there are such things as identified by (1). Sellars is not an *eliminativist* about the states or episodes of "sensibility" described in (1). Rather, Sellars insists that a satisfactory analysis of the role it plays in perception requires that we coordinate the natural facts about our capacities of "sensibility" identified by (1) with epistemic facts about our capacities for "understanding" or empirical knowledge identified by (2), without conflating or dissolving the distinction between epistemic and natural reasons. Just as the normative force of the shopper's list as an evaluation of the shopper's achievement would be impossible if we had to substitute it for (or derive it from) the detective's list, so too would empirical knowledge become impossible if we had to derive our normative standing in the logical space of reasons (above the line) from characterizations of nonconceptually Given inner states or episodes of sensation outside of that logical space (below the line).[121] That is the transcendental worry undergirding Sellars's "epistemological interest" in the Given.

But the notion of an "experience" Alston defends in TA is a "mongrel resulting from the crossbreeding of [the above] two ideas."[122] In attempting to attribute normative epistemic properties

---

120. Sellars, *Empiricism and the Philosophy of Mind*, §7, 21–23.
121. In fact, just as the norm-governed behavior of shopping is primary and the detective's act of describing has to be understood as secondary and derivative from it, so too our natural characterizations are parasitic on and derivative of our normative ones.
122. Sellars, *Empiricism and the Philosophy of Mind*, §7, 21.

of empirical understanding belonging to the conceptual states or episodes above the line to merely natural characterizations of sensation belonging below the line, Alston is guilty of the version of the myth that McDowell characterizes as confusing epistemic justification with what can at best be conferred by a merely natural characterization of our beliefs, an appeal to which can at best secure exculpation for our belief.[123] Think again of the difference between the shopper and the detective as an illustration of the difference between characterizations of someone's rational accountability to a norm and characterizations that merely describe what patterns of bodily or mental behavior enable or follow from one's being subject to a norm. The difference between the shopper's characterization of the way in which his list guided his actions and the description of that guidance available to the detective could be seen in the difference between their respective responses to an act that ran counter to the norm—the shopper's placing margarine in his basket when the list called for butter.

What the discrepancy illustrates, however, is something that remains true even when the shopper and the detective execute their respective tasks flawlessly and there is no discrepancy. Even when they come out with identical lists, it remains the case that the shopper's list functioned to guide his action and the detective's list functioned merely to reduplicate the shopper's list. The shopper's success is evidenced not by the list but by what is in his basket, whereas the detective's success is evidenced precisely by whether his list matches that of the shopper. Even if the lists are identical, the shopper's list remains a list of items that determined a standard of correctness for the shopper's shopping (a list of items that the shopper "should" have placed in his basket, in the normative sense

123. McDowell, *Mind and World*, 8.

of incurring, for instance, self-recrimination for having forgotten) while the detective's list remains merely a list of items that the shopper managed to put in his basket (a list of items that, if correct, we can expect the shopper to have put in his basket and, in that sense only, a list of items that he "should" have put in his basket). So even if the items on the lists do match, they fundamentally differ in how they characterize the same acts in much the same way as do the neurobiological and the rational characterizations of the reasons that I opened the door for you.

Alston describes experiences in such a way as to provide us with only a detective's account of how Sellars's first sort of characterization of a perceptual state or episode above causes us to form a perceptual belief. In virtue of having an inner episode (which Alston characterizes as a direct sensory awareness of a particular) that is nonconceptually given independently of any prior learning, our established doxastic practices involuntarily dispose us to convert those experiential inputs into belief outputs that have the intrinsic phenomenal character of an extrinsic mode of object-appearing as their content, or what they are about.[124] While this sort of world-directedness of experience is sufficient, on his view, to supply our perceptual beliefs with empirical content irrespective of the reliability of the perceptual doxastic practice in question, the further question of whether the belief is epistemically justified requires something further. Justification is precisely a matter of the reliability with which the doxastic practice can be expected to spit out true beliefs, given the relevant sort of experiential inputs.

But this picture presents Alston with two insurmountable difficulties for identifying direct and nonconceptual sensory awareness of particulars as sources of epistemic justification. The first

---

124. Alston, *Perceiving God*, 63–65.

is a problem internal to Alston's story, and the second is a problem about the limited resources his story gives him to address that internal problem, given the Sellarsian distinction between epistemic reasons and natural reasons.

The internal worry is that from what Alston himself says about how perceptual beliefs get their justification, it follows that his focus on "experiences" in his sense is misplaced. Given what he has said, he should identify the source of epistemic efficacy in his account not with experiences but instead with doxastic practices. Perceptual belief outputs on Alston's story do not indicate the "reliability" of nonconceptual experiential inputs but rather the reliability of the doxastic mechanism that takes those experiences as inputs. Whether my toaster reliably spits out good toast or burned toast is no reflection on the bread. Similarly, what Alston should be saying on his own account is that the epistemic goodness or badness of our perceptual beliefs causally springs not from our experiences but rather from the proper form of unity brought about between our direct sensory awareness of particulars and the propositional structure of the perceptual beliefs caused or occasioned by that awareness. The unity in question is a proper one only insofar as it is brought about by socially established practices of belief formation reliably aimed at truth.

There is therefore a parallel between Sellars and Alston regarding an above-the-line characterization of perceptual experience—both take it that an epistemic characterization of our perceptual experiences is constituted by a propositionally structured actualization of our conceptual capacities. For Alston, our perceptual doxastic practices dispose us to find ourselves involuntarily impressed with perceptual beliefs that are causally occasioned by Alstonian appearances. Our nonconceptual sensory awareness of particulars can figure into the above-the-line context in which we evaluate the rational credentials of our beliefs because that awareness conspired in the propositional output of a doxastic practice.[125] My formation in sense-perceptual practices, therefore, might dispose me to immediately and involuntarily respond to the visual appearance of X as F with the propositionally structured belief *that X looks F*, which, if the practice is reliable, might be a sufficient basis for epistemically justifying the further belief *that X is F*. For Sellars, our sensory and conceptual capacities are united in the course of the conceptual learning that belongs paradigmatically to our initiation into language. The conceptual capacities that we ordinarily draw on in our free exercise of judgment are the same as those that are passively and involuntarily drawn upon in our sensory experiences. The concepts thus actualized by our sensory awareness are thus "so to speak, evoked or wrung from the perceiver by the object perceived."[126] On Sellars's story, therefore, sensations figure above the

125. It is true that Alston takes "phenomenal looks concepts" (whose content is an Alstonian appearance) to have a logical priority to "comparative," "doxastic," and "epistemic" looks concepts (Alston, *Perceiving God*, 44–48), but irrespective of whether that analysis is sustainable, it does not count as an analysis of how appearances justify perceptual beliefs but only as an analysis of how the empirical concepts constituent in those beliefs get their content. A lesson to be drawn from the problems attaching to Givenism and Coherentism as I characterized them in the previous chapter is that separating one's semantic story about perceptual content from one's epistemological story about the rational credentials empirically contentful beliefs must have to count as justified or knowledgeable is not a good idea. Alston has only the most obscure things to say about how we acquire capacities to form phenomenal looks concepts (much less the sense in which we can possess concepts the comprehension of which is "beyond our powers," which occupy a "conceptual space somewhere even if not accessible to us"). Alston, "Sellars and the 'Myth of the Given,'" 77. Such obscurities notwithstanding, Alston seems to think that a doxastic practice is to function as a reliable mechanism whereby an appearance occasions or disposes us to believe that-*p*, where p is a propositionally structured claim involving empirical concepts, however the empirical concepts constituent in p get their content.

126. Sellars, *Empiricism and the Philosophy of Mind*, 40, §16. But whereas Alston seems to consider only those instances in which doxastic practices succeed in saddling us with beliefs, Sellars considers cases in which they saddle us only with the propositional content of a belief without necessarily imposing upon us any particular propositional stance or attitude toward it. In other words, Sellars simply takes something analogous to Alston's doxastic practices as an analysis not only of how perceptual beliefs get their justification, but also as an analysis of how they get their content. As I have shown, however, Alston fails to see what Sellars is up to in his analysis of "looks" talk, and he accordingly fails to recognize how Sellars's analysis might allow Alston to bring into a coherent unity his commitment to the phenomenal character of "appearing"

line, in the logical space of reasons, insofar as the world's sensory impressions on us actualize our conceptual capacities so as to involuntarily impose their claims on us precisely in and by activations of sensory consciousness.

Given this structural parallel between Alston's analysis of justification and Sellars's own analysis, it follows that Alstonian appearances, just like Sellarsian sensations, are intrinsically epistemically inert. Alston's experiential inputs to a perceptual doxastic practice, just like Sellars's "inner episodes" of sensation, can come to play a justificatory role for our perceptual beliefs only insofar as they are conceptually constituted, whether by way of the "conceptual learning" to which Sellars alludes or by way of our participation in the socially established perceptual "doxastic practices" that Alston describes.

Alston nevertheless thinks that his story gives him some resources to maintain the epistemic efficacy not merely of the doxastic mechanism that spits out perceptual beliefs but also of the experiential inputs to that mechanism. Alston takes his crediting of Alstonian appearances with epistemic efficacy to be licensed by the conjunction of two features of his account: first, appearances are the proximate causal grounds for our perceptual beliefs, even if that grounding is ultimately secured by way of a doxastic mechanism, and, second, to be in possession of an appearance is to be directly aware of the proximate causal ground of one's perceptual belief. From this he concludes that, provided they figure in the appropriate doxastic practice, the nonconceptual givenness of appearances cause our perceptual beliefs.

Promising as this line might initially seem, it faces an insurmountable difficulty that Alston might have avoided had he

that he mistakenly takes Sellars to deny, the epistemic role of doxastic practices that he already endorses, and a clearer conception of how our empirical concepts acquire empirical content.

exploited the parallel between his account and Sellars's and located the epistemic efficacy of appearances as belonging to the role they play in the above-the-line characterizations of experience that figure in the logical space of reasons occupied by perceptual beliefs. Alstonian perceptual-looks beliefs or Sellarsian perceptual claims wrung from us in experience saddle us with propositional content that belongs in the logical space of reasons and, as such, allows experiences to serve as epistemic (rather than merely natural) causes of our perceptual beliefs. But what about Alstonian appearances? Are they epistemic causes or natural causes?

It seems fairly clear that they are merely natural causes—they furnish me a reason for my perceptual belief in much the same way that a contraction of the abductor and flexor muscles of my hand furnishes me with a reason for grasping the doorknob. Any direct access we have to appearances considered "in themselves"—that is, considered independently of the perceptual-looks beliefs they occasion as the distinctively experiential *way* that those beliefs are urged on us—can only supply us with below-the-line or natural characterizations of experience in the Sellarsian sense. As we have seen, however, it is a category mistake to identify, substitute, or reduce an epistemic cause to a natural cause. So whatever explanatory power TA might have, it cannot explain how experiences epistemically justify perceptual beliefs because it cannot explain why a perceptual-looks belief *should* follow from an experience in the normative sense of "should," but only in the descriptive or natural sense. The idea that the latter can imply or serve as an inferential basis for the former is a version of the "naturalistic fallacy" that Sellars identifies as a myth—a commitment to the ability of experiences to rationally justify beliefs despite a kind of ill-fittingness between experience and belief that makes a justificatory characterization of experience impossible.

Once saddled with some class of perceptual-looks beliefs (whether those of sense perception or CMP), and recognizing that it is our participation in particular socially established doxastic practices of perception that has paired our perceptual beliefs with the nonconceptual appearances that causally occasion them, we can ask whether or not we ought to have participated in the relevant doxastic practices and thus whether or not some relevant class of appearances should causally occasion the corresponding perceptual-looks beliefs that they do. Given the characterization of perceptual experiences as merely natural causes for our perceptual-looks beliefs, the best that Alston can give us is an exculpatory ground for those beliefs. Recall McDowell's tornado from the previous chapter: if picked up by a tornado and deposited in a place from which I have been banished, I may be afforded an exculpatory reason for being there—I could not help it—but this does not provide me with a justification relevant for addressing the question of whether I *ought* to be there, whether it is good from a normative point of view.

Alston appeals to "practical rationality" in TA to supplement his account of the merely causal reason for holding our perceptual-looks beliefs with an account of our rational entitlement to those beliefs as outputs of a perceptual doxastic practice. All of his arguments to the effect that it is "*prima facie* rational (practically rational) to engage in a socially established doxastic practice" succeed only in elaborating the exculpatory grounds furnished by the natural causes for our perceptual-looks beliefs.[127] Suppose we recognize that, given the doxastic practices we have in fact participated in, we could not help but hold the relevant class of perceptual-looks beliefs as well as the further belief that the way of forming those beliefs prescribed by the practice makes them likely to be true. Could I on that basis be

127. Alston, *Perceiving God*, 175.

entitled to the belief that the practice *is* reliable and that the resultant class of perceptual-looks beliefs *are* likely to be true? Alston concedes that I could not.[128] But he nevertheless thinks that in the absence of any relevant defeaters, I might nevertheless have no reason to deny that my initiation into the relevant doxastic practice has indeed placed me in an epistemically favorable situation.

But at best, then, I seem entitled only to an agnosticism about the doxastic practice in question and therefore an agnosticism about whether the relevant class of appearances justifies the corresponding perceptual-looks beliefs from which they spring. The agnosticism, moreover, stems not from having insufficient practical reasons to hang onto my belief in the reliability of a doxastic practice or the (likely) truth of its outputs, but rather from the irrelevance of practical rationality for the question of whether I ought to hang onto that belief. If my doxastic aim is truth, then upholding any epistemic duties I take myself to be responsible for and recognizing the nonepistemic prudence of my present doxastic situation are insufficient conditions (either singly or jointly) for believing that I ought to continue forming perceptual-looks beliefs as I have or believing that the perceptual-looks beliefs I have already formed are justified by the corresponding appearances on which they are based. These practical considerations are insufficient precisely because the truth of the matter regarding whether or not my perceptual doxastic practices are reliable and their outputs are (likely) true—which is surely what I am aiming at—is *insensitive* to whether or not those conditions are met. That is, even if the perceptual DP in question is in fact unreliable and its outputs are (likely) false, it might be just as nonepistemically prudent to (falsely) believe the opposite, and doing

128. See his discussion of "overriders" in ibid., 170–73.

so need not introduce any massive inconsistencies with the outputs of other DPs.[129]

With respect to CMP, then, Alston's account of its parity with sense perception leaves us without any rational entitlement to our perceptual beliefs about God. Where we wanted an analysis of how putative experiences of God might inform and justify our theological beliefs, we got instead an analysis of how such experiences might exculpate our theological beliefs. "An Alstonian appearance made me believe it" is no more capable of serving our epistemological interest in experience as a source of justification than "the devil made me do it" is capable of serving our moral interests, and for the same reason: neither suffices to make us rationally accountable to a norm.

4.3 Conclusion: Marion, Alston, and the Sellarsian Critique

On the Sellarsian story, if empirical knowledge is to be possible, our sensory capacities ("sensibility") must become indissolubly united to our conceptual capacities (our sui generis capacities for normative understanding) such that the world's actualizations of our sensory capacities give rise to actualizations of our conceptual capacities. The resultant perceptual states or episodes must thus be characterized as sensory modes of directedness on the world that already "contain claims" and can function in the "above-the-line" logical space of epistemic reasons that normatively guide what we think, say, and do. The "must" in Sellars's analysis signals the transcendental character of his epistemological interest in conceptualism about the content of experience. Namely, if our experiences cannot be placed in the logical space of reasons, wherein the very same conceptual capacities

---

129. For a somewhat different argument for the inevitability of an agnosticism of this kind in Alston's account, see Alvin Plantinga, *Warranted Christian Belief* (New York: Oxford University Press, 2000), 103–15.

paradigmatically exercised in judgment are passively drawn into operation in sensory consciousness, then it becomes impossible for experiences to be the sorts of states or episodes that could provide us with a noninferential epistemic justification for our empirical beliefs. And if our empirical beliefs are not thus rationally answerable to the world, then they cannot be "about" the world at all.

To suppose, on the other hand, that experience does make us answerable to the world but that what is given in experience is some form of perceptual content intrinsically alien to the form of our understanding is to fall prey to the myth of the Given, the myth that experiences can somehow furnish us with something to know that does not itself draw on the very capacities requisite to knowing. Marion's phenomenology of givenness appropriates a version of that idea in order to make possible an apophatic form of revelation that exceeds all possible understanding, while Alston's Theory of Appearing appropriates another version of it to make possible a cataphatic form of revelation that accords with the univocal structure of experience. In their reliance on the myth, neither succeeds in offering so much as a coherent analysis of our perceptual relation to God, much less a true one.

5

Preller, Hector, and Sellarsian Coherentism

Just as Marion and Alston can be read as collapsing in apophatic and cataphatic ways, respectively, into the Givenist pole of the vicisious oscillation McDowell delineates, Victor Preller and Kevin Hector can be read as collapsing into its Coherentist pole. Preller has been an important figure in the emergence of an analytic Thomism that has contributed to the recent revival of interest in apophatic approaches to theological language. Hector's recent challenges to that revival—and to Preller's contribution to it in particular—have culminated in his forging of an account that integrates some work in analytic philosophy with a theological synthesis of Barth and Schleiermacher to arrive at a cataphatic alternative to contemporary apophaticisms. But aside from this mutual opposition between an apophatic and a cataphatic deployment of analytic philosophy, their accounts are linked in another important way.

I contend that both accounts depend on a view about how experience grounds our intentional activities that employs a strategy best articulated by Sellars. In Preller's case, the dependence on Sellars is overt, while for Hector the parallel is more a matter of structural resemblance than straightforward appropriation. The trouble, however, is that the underlying Sellarsian commitments shared by Preller and Hector turn out to be a version of Coherentism. In order to see that Preller and Hector are both "Sellarsians" in the relevant sense, that the Sellarsian commitments in question are indeed Coherentist, and that Preller and Hector are therefore both Coherentists, we must first have a grip on Sellars's approach to perception.

5.1 The Sellarsian Approach to Perception

Sellars's conceptualism about perceptual content is in one sense consistent with the minimal empiricism I briefly summarized at the end of chapter 3. McDowell's minimal empiricism, like Sellars's model, arrives at the necessary unity of sensibility and understanding in the intentionality of human experience transcendentally, by way of an inquiry into the conditions of possibility for our ordinary empirical knowledge. Once we have seen that human experience is necessarily constituted as a unity of sensibility and understanding, we might follow a naive realist account of the ability of experiences to be "about" the world simply because the sensible world itself is also structured by intelligible properties, intrinsically constituted with a capacity to serve as direct epistemic causes for belief and action as well as nonnormative causes of merely natural events. We can therefore understand the (putative) standards of correctness implicit in our experiences as direct presentations of the world itself impressing its own rational "claims" on us, which we register sensorially in experience and which our conceptual capacities can actualize as epistemic reasons for what we think, say, and do. When such experiences are veridical, our rational responsiveness to the world can be constitutive of empirical knowledge, whether practical or reflective.

For Sellars, however, the situation is more complicated because he does not consider that the normative content of "epistemic facts" might just be a direct apprehension of the normative structure of the world itself rather than being only about the distinctively normative character of our thinking. Given that assumption, if we can rightly regard our experiences as "about" the world itself and not merely about ourselves, we have to regard epistemic facts about our above-the-line experiences—facts about the conceptual shaping of sensory consciousness—as grounded by natural facts about our nonconceptual sensory relation to the world. As McDowell puts it:

> This picture of visual experiences as conceptual shapings of visual consciousness is already deeply Kantian, in the way it appeals to sensibility and understanding so as to make sense of how experiences have objective purport. But Sellars thinks that to be fully Kantian, the picture needs a further element. He thinks this idea of conceptual shapings of visual consciousness is something we can entitle ourselves to only by means of a transcendental postulation, according to which these conceptual goings-on are guided by manifolds of "sheer receptivity" occurrences in visual consciousness that are not conceptually shaped. Only so, Sellars thinks, can we legitimately take perception to yield conceptual representations of objective reality. If we do not acknowledge that the conceptual goings-on in perception are guided by "sheer receptivity," then no matter what we do toward purporting to equip ourselves with an object of perceptual awareness, the supposed object can be no better than a projection of our mental activity.[1]

As we have seen in the previous chapter, Sellars clearly refuses a reductive *analysis* of "experience" as an epistemic episode belonging to the logical space of reasons rather than a natural episode in our sensory consciousness. To identify an epistemic "should" with a

---

1. John McDowell, "Intentionality as a Relation," *Journal of Philosophy* 95, no. 9 (September 1998): 471–91, 471.

natural one is to be guilty of an analogue of the "naturalistic fallacy."[2] But recognizing this is nevertheless consistent with supposing that we can explain how experiences thus analyzed succeed in directing us on the world solely in nonepistemic terms, by appeal to the "natural" or nonnormative causal relations that govern the world's bearing on us. That is just what Sellars proposes.

The immediate and noninferential experiences of the world that we enjoy as possible affordances of perceptual knowledge are always already constituted as unities of sensibility and understanding—sensorially evoked conceptual or "claims-containing" states or episodes within the logical space of reasons. But while this epistemic dimension of experience is immediately "wrung" from us or evoked noninferentially and directly by activations of our sensory consciousness, those activations of sensibility themselves do not have their home in the logical space of reasons, but below the line, as merely natural happenings. Our external environment is fundamentally constituted not by the normative properties and relations characteristic of our concepts but by natural, nonnormative, or "merely causal" properties and relations. Our natural capacities for sensibility enable our experiences to track with the world. In other words, the operations of mere sensibility, our below-the-line capacities of responsiveness to our environment, are the transcendental guarantors of the world-involving character of our above-the-line experiences. Below-the-line nonnormative sensory causes are the conditions for the possibility of the world-directedness of above-the-line normative perceptual causes.

Sellars denies we can have any direct awareness of the transcendental grounds of experience. That would be to have a direct awareness of the operations of mere sensibility apart from its cooperation with understanding whereas, on pain of falling into the

---

2. Recall the discussion from chapter 3 (3.2), above.

myth of the Given, we have to say that what immediately, directly, and noninferentially appears to consciousness is always sensation inextricably bound to a passive activation of our conceptual capacities. We can, however, indirectly and inferentially identify the nonnormative ground of our intrinsically normative experiences. Isolating in thought the sensory contribution to experience from its conceptual contribution, Sellars thinks, takes a form reminiscent of the reasoning that we earlier saw Alston deploying to single out the distinctively phenomenal or qualitative dimension of experience, a form Paul Coates helpfully designates as a "subtraction argument."[3] To represent to oneself or have the concept of a "bare" sensation is to have the concept of an ordinary experience minus the normative claims noninferentially afforded or urged on us by that experience. We thus derive natural facts about the "descriptive content" of a perceptual experience (compare what Alston called "phenomenal looks-concepts") from epistemic facts as a residue of merely descriptive claims that remain after the rational demands of such claims on what we "should" (in the epistemic sense) believe or do have been abstracted out.[4]

In *Empiricism and the Philosophy of Mind*,[5] Sellars claims that our desire to explain "the facts of sense perception in scientific style"—that is, as merely natural facts about how things are as opposed to any normative demands they make on us—requires us to deploy the

---

3. The claim that Sellars's notion of experience as involving nonconceptual sensory episodes takes the form of a "subtraction argument" is ably defended by Paul Coates in *The Metaphysics of Perception: Wilfrid Sellars, Perceptual Consciousness, and Critical Realism* (New York: Routledge, 2007), 35.

4. This is the point of the "as if" character of the logic of "looks" in his analysis of looks concepts in *Empiricism and the Philosophy of Mind* as a withholding of belief in consideration of what it is that appears to rationally compel it. Contra Alston, his point is not that there is no such thing as phenomenal character, or even that such character cannot be directly and causally "given," so long as its merely causal givenness is not accorded an epistemic role. See Wilfrid Sellars, *Empiricism and the Philosophy of Mind*, intro. Richard Rorty and study guide by Robert Brandom (Cambridge, MA: Harvard University Press, 1997), 22, 50–51.

5. Sellars, *Empiricism and the Philosophy of Mind*.

nonepistemic concepts of mere causation to describe the sensible content of our experience rather than deploying the epistemic concepts of rational causation to describe the content of an experience as conforming to a norm.[6] "Scientific" thinking about the merely sensory conditions for the possibility of our experiences, however, is not a particularly special way of thinking distinct from ordinary thinking. Scientific observation is rather just a disciplined way of carrying through the same kinds of subtraction inferences implicit in much of our ordinary perceptual thinking as well—that is, those thoughts in which we subtract from our picture of how things are in general their particular significance for our purposes or how they matter for us.

We require talk about the merely descriptive content of our experiences to distinguish between perceptual episodes that noninferentially draw on our conceptual capacities in similar (or identical) ways, even while differing in the way in which the world's bearing on us gave rise to them.[7] In those cases for which a visual experience of, say, a rabbit-shaped rock "wrings" from me the same doxastic response (my belief that there is a rabbit over there, my act of holding out a carrot to coax it to me) as would be evoked by a visual experience of a rabbit, what accounts for the difference between the two experiences may not be anything about the claims evoked by the experience, but only the nonconceptually structured phenomenal or causal relations that govern the relation of our external environment to our sensory systems below the line.[8]

---

6. Ibid., 22, §7.

7. Ibid., 85ff., §45.

8. In "Sellars on Perceptual Experience," in *Having the World in View: Essays on Kant, Hegel and Sellars* (Cambridge: Harvard University Press, 2009), 3–22, McDowell wonders why Sellars should advert to anything in consciousness like "sense impressions" to play this explanatory role, since the only relevant below-the-line causal relations he needs are those describable in terms of subpersonal causal relations such as "patterns of light impinging on retinas" (15). But there need not be anything puzzling here. Instead, there may be a legitimate debate as to what residue remains when the "claims" of a noninferential perceptual episode are subtracted

While Sellars claims that our initiation into the space of reasons affords us the capacities to attribute sensations to ourselves and others as that which anchors our experiences to the world,[9] he emphasizes that it is not our *conceptual identification* of sensation in virtue of which our experiences count as responsive to the nonnormative structure of the world itself, but sensation itself below the line playing its transcendental role of grounding above-the-line experiences. The transcendental role of sensibility described above entails our capacity to indirectly place the transcendental grounds of experience into the logical space of reasons—the space of justifying and being able to justify what we think, say, and do—by deriving natural facts about descriptive content from the normative concepts evoked in experience. It follows that the capacity to have an above-the-line experience at all requires being able to justify our empirical claims. It does not follow that we *do* so justify them, but that we *can*.

from that episode. We can marshal intuitions on both sides of an ambiguity with which it is possible to construe the form of conscious "awareness" involved in perception: should we imagine our "awareness" as cleaving to the conceptual or the sensory element of the unity that actually immediately appears to consciousness? Sellars own way of resolving the ambiguity, I think, is actually the more intuitive of the two possibilities. That is, Sellars seems right to attribute the distinctive form of awareness involved in perceptual states to sensibility rather than understanding, and to conclude that the theoretical construct yielded by a "subtraction" of the noninferential content wrung from our conceptual capacities in experience is that of a "brute" sensation, along with all of the causal mechanisms that enable it. But in the overall structure of Sellars's story, not much hangs on which way we go here. All that matters is that we mark out the relevant feature of "sensibility" that belongs below the line as the specification of a natural fact, whether it is a form of non normative "awareness" that exists below the line or strictly unconscious causal goings on below the line. The fundamental structure of his story can remain intact whichever turns out to be the better candidate.

9. Sellars invokes the Rylean "Myth of Jones" to illustrate our acquisition of that capacity (*Empiricism and the Philosophy of Mind*, 90ff., §48. The point of the myth, however, is not to argue that an analysis of above-the-line experiences can do without the idea of a direct sensory awareness of our environment, but an illustration of why we need not think that we *first* become aware of the sensory dimension of experience isolated from the understanding and *then* "apply" concepts to it, on the basis of which we attribute that same procedure to others in order to credit them with like capacities. Rather, our attributions of "mere" sensation to ourselves and others can be seen as secondary and derivative, functioning against the background of the conceptually shaped sensory consciousness we have already acquired.

Still, natural facts about sensation are not observation reports about our immediate awareness of sensations; they are instead inferences—post facto and by way of our accepted conceptual norms—about the nonnormative or natural facts in virtue of which our experiences can be thought to be conceptual responses to the world as it is "in itself." This derivation of natural facts about the nonnormative and merely causal sensory relation to the world is a kind of theory construction (or prototheory construction). It should not be confused with an immediate introspective awareness of "mere sensation" or a noninferential knowledge of our sensory consciousness "in itself." While our merely causal sensory responsiveness to the objective (that is, "natural" or nonepistemic) layout of our environment is primary and fundamental in the order of *being*, it is secondary and derivative in the order of *knowing*. Accordingly, from the epistemic point of view, our access to the merely causal relations by which the layout of the world itself determines our sensibility is necessarily indirect and a matter of inferential justifications, while our access to the normative conceptual and doxastic results of that determination is direct and a matter of noninferential experiences.

James O'Shea has aptly described this approach to the structure of empirical thinking as a kind of "logical irreducibility–*cum*–causal reducibility."[10] We have already seen how the "logical irreducibility" bit works. Our capacity for experiences as epistemic reasons, causes,

---

10. In this I follow James O'Shea's reading of Sellars's "A Semantical Solution of the Mind-Body Problem," which O'Shea sets forward in *Wilfrid Sellars: Naturalism with a Normative Turn* (Malden, MA: Polity, 2007), 21; See also O'Shea, "On the Structure of Sellars' Naturalism with a Normative Turn," in *Empiricism, Perceptual Knowledge, Normativity and Realism: Essays on the Anniversary of 'Empiricism and the Philosophy of Mind'*, ed. Willem de Vries (New York: Oxford University Press, 2009), 187–210. McDowell at points seems to resist the idea that Sellars is interested in offering any causally reductive account of the space of reasons. See, for example, his arguments against Brandom's "inferentialist" reading of Sellars in the same volume, "Why Is Sellars's Essay Called '*Empiricism* and the Philosophy of Mind'?," in de Vries, *Empiricism*, 9–32.

and explanations within a logical space of reasons constitutes the distinctive form of immediate conscious awareness that marks out a human way of engaging the world. Any attempt to reduce, translate, or substitute the idea of a sui generis logical space constitutive of our higher consciousness into nonnormative terms of analysis necessarily screens out the very idea that is supposed to be contained in the reduction, communicated in the translation, or preserved by the substitution: that is, the idea of our rational responsiveness to experiences as epistemic reasons for belief or action. The transcendental role of our "lower" sensory consciousness as nonnormative causal processes below the line is just that of constraining and guiding the irreducible unity of sensibility and understanding in our above-the-line experiences. The world-involving activations of sensibility below the line are the ostensible nonnormative or "natural" explanations for the normative character of our above-the-line experiences of the world. In order to justify the beliefs or practices about the world noninferentially evoked by our experiences, we appeal to natural facts about those experiences themselves from which, if true, the noninferential claims afforded in the experience would follow.

Clearly, the level distinction between the normative character of conscious awareness as the navigation of a logical space of reasons and the nonnormative character of merely causal processes is logically fundamental to Sellars's account of experience as a source of information or justification about the way the world is. His analysis is necessarily "two-ply" insofar as the norms governing our perceptual experiences require merely causal relations rooted in sensibility in order to be world-involving, and our descriptions of the merely causal relations constitutive of sensibility depend on the norms governing our perceptual experiences in order to be actualized in consciousness as a (putative) noninferential awareness *that* things are thus and so. But as O'Shea points out, "the *reducibility* side of Sellars' position is supposed to apply to *the distinction of level itself*; that is, to the distinction between the normative conceptual and the non-normative or pre-conceptual that constitutes the difference between 'man' and his 'precursors.'"[11]

So while the level distinction between norm and nature is logically irreducible in an explanation of the intentionality and epistemology of perception, that distinction itself is not ontologically ultimate. Sellars's view is rather that the norm/nature distinction constitutive of a two-ply approach is itself causally reducible to the level of natural reasons, causes, and explanations. He thinks it possible to show how the normative character of the logical space of reasons that marks out an above-the-line characterizations of experience can precipitate out of nonnormative or natural causes. Below-the-line occurrences are thus doubly transcendental on the Sellarsian approach: they provide the conditions for the possibility of anchoring the above-the-line conceptual shapings of our sensory consciousness to the natural (nonconceptually constituted) world, and they also provide the conditions for the possibility for our having conceptual capacities at all. Sellars thus thinks that we should account for our capacity to place things within a logical space of normative reasons, causes, and explanations in contradistinction to natural or nonnormative reasons, causes, and explanations by telling a story about how the former ultimately emerges from the latter.

Both Preller and Hector appropriate just the sort of two-ply analysis of experience as logically irreducible–cum–causally reducible to "natural" causes that we find in Sellars, one that consists of logically irreducible relations between norm and nature together with a reductionist story about how the normative character of experience

11. O'Shea, "On the Structure of Sellars' Naturalism with a Normative Turn," 192–93.

arises from some class of essentially nonnormative or natural causes. The primary difference between Preller and Hector is simply that Preller exploits the Sellarsian strategy in favor of an apophatic analysis of our perceptual relation to God, while Hector exploits the same strategy in favor of a cataphatic analysis. The problem, however, is that the Sellarsian approach is just a direct realist version of Coherentism,[12] as evidenced by the fact that it entails what I described in previous chapter as a "problem of friction." In what follows, therefore, I will briefly characterize the way the Sellarsian strategy is deployed in Preller's account and the problem to which it gives rise. I will then show how Hector's account manifests that same basic strategy (albeit without the explicit dependence on Sellars we find in Preller); because of this, he confronts the very same sort of problem.

Before turning to that task, however, it is worth considering a possible objection to this overall line of criticism. The objection is that it seems strange to read Preller and Hector as swallowing the whole of what I am calling a "Sellarsian approach," given the explicit *naturalism* of Sellars's logical irreducibility–cum–causal reducibility

---

12. Given the emphasis on the transcendental role of natural causes in directing us on the world and accounting for the intrinsically normative shape of experience, it might seem intuitive to characterize Sellars's views as a kind of indirect realism about perceptual content. After all, he thinks that our knowledge of natural facts—whether about the world in its nonnormative constitution (as it is "in itself") or our nonnormative sensory relation to it—can only be had indirectly by way of inference. But the difference between Sellars's transcendentalism and an indirect realist form of transcendentalism is that the latter regards the objects, properties, and relations of the world "in itself" as not merely transcendental—as the merely causal conditions for the possibility for what is directly manifest to us—but also as transcend*ent*, as not constituent in our experience in any sense and as in principle unavailable as objects of knowledge in any sense, whether directly or indirectly. Our talk "about" those conditions is therefore necessarily indirect—any notion we deploy to identify the transcendental dependence of our experiences upon the transcendent domain, including that of "cause," or "condition of possibility," or "transcendental dependence," turns out to be talk about the phenomenal domain, not the (posited) noumenal one. But Sellars does not think that the nonnormative layout of reality structured by relations of natural or mere causation is a transcendent domain indirectly related to our experiences. He thinks that the world "in itself" is constituent in our experiences by way of sensibility in its union with the understanding phenomenally present in our above-the-line experiences. We are just not directly aware of the world *as* it is "in itself" except by way of inference from the intrinsically normative way in which that same world appears to us.

view. It seems strange because belief in God is obviously incompatible with the idea that the world is constituted most fundamentally by nonnormative causes between sensible objects, properties, and relations, yet the structure of our perceptual relation *to God* is precisely what Preller and Hector are attempting to analyze and explain.

On the surface, there is something to be said for this objection. Sellars paradigmatically delineated the ultimacy of natural causes in terms of a strict realism about the deliverances of the natural sciences, particularly the physical sciences.[13] The "causal reducibility" bit of Sellars's approach is therefore often equated with the "scientism" of his views. Thus, we find him distinguishing between the "manifest image" constituted by the holistic, conceptual, and normative shape of our thinking and the "scientific image," constituted by both transcendental roles that Sellars assigns to below-the-line merely causal processes. The sciences aim to identify all of the nonnormative objects, properties, and relations that indirectly guide our conceptual norms and finally determine what they are "about." Such an achievement would also reveal the more radical transcendental role of natural causes, that of identifying the merely causal processes ultimately responsible for the development of the norms evinced in the manifest image and hence providing a scientific explanation for the "special creation" of the logical space of reasons itself.[14]

The philosopher's task of "fusing the images" of our manifestly normative thinking and our scientific explanations is a stereoscopic one: given the reducibility claim, science can in principle furnish us with a complete and exhaustive naturalistic explanation for the

---

13. See Wilfrid Sellars, "Philosophy and the Scientific Image of Man," in *Frontiers of Science and Philosophy*, ed. Robert Colodny (Pittsburgh, PA: University of Pittsburgh Press, 1962), 35–78.

14. O'Shea speculates that this could be had by a true scientific theory about "the ultimate evolutionary origins of natural languages" ("On the Structure of Sellars' Naturalism with a Normative Turn," 191n4).

conceptual norms that govern our experiences, but, given the irreducibility claim, the *causally* reductive scientific descriptions could not themselves function as reductions, translations, or substitutions of the *logical* role belonging to the norms to which they give rise.[15] But as a sort of nonreductive materialism, it is hard to see how Sellars's stereoscopic vision leaves any room for God. On the contrary, the materialism built into his picture of fusing the images appears to screen out any such possibility in principle. It seems implausible to think that Preller or Hector would take on board a Sellarsian naturalism in their attempts to articulate our perceptual relation to God. But since his naturalism is an essential feature of his overall approach, it therefore seems implausible to read Preller or Hector as appropriating the Sellarsian approach as I have characterized it above.

Against this sort of objection, it is important to note that Sellars's scientism is in fact an entirely derivative feature of his overall strategy, and it is perfectly well possible to adopt his brand of "naturalism" without it.[16] As we have seen, Sellarsian naturalism requires only that we assign the following doubly transcendental role to the idea of natural causes: (1) we must construe our sensory capacities as merely natural causes in order to explain how our intrinsically norm-governed experiences can nevertheless be regarded as (putatively) world-involving, and (2) we must explain how the epistemic causes of norm governance in the logical space of reasons characteristic of a self-conscious human awareness precipitate out of merely natural causes. The first requirement gives the idea of a natural cause its transcendental role in the "logical irreducibility" of the two-ply account, and the second requirement gives it its transcendental role

---

15. Jay Rosenberg, *Wilfrid Sellars: Fusing the Images* (New York: Oxford University Press, 2007), 78–103.
16. Rosenberg, however, tends to depict Sellars's brand of scientific realism as integral to his philosophical views. See Rosenberg, *Wilfrid Sellars*, 12–14.

in the "causal reducibility" of the level distinction to its most ontologically ultimate terms.

Note, however, that neither requirement necessitates that we construe "natural" causes as limited to the sorts of explanations proffered by the physical sciences, or any of the sciences per se. Rather, the notion of a natural cause is just the notion of a *nonnormative* or "mere" cause—one restricted to the descriptive use of "should" characteristic of Anscombe's detective we encountered in the last chapter.[17] If they are understood in that way, we might well regard the deliverance of the hard sciences as an overdetermined or overly narrow conception of "natural facts." Indeed, invoking God, angels, or the soul as the "mere" causes is perfectly consistent with a fact's being "natural" in the relevant sense. Thus, for example, natural facts about angels' impacts on sensibility below the line may ground a large swath of our everyday experiences of the world above the line, and all of our norms may precipitate out of our merely causal sensory relations to the fundamental ontology of the world, included among which is the proliferation of angelic beings.[18]

Still, we need not suppose that natural facts about angels are accessible to scientific inquiry in the strict sense of the physical sciences. Exactly not, insofar as we take angels to be nonphysical entities. What belongs most basically to the Sellarsian strategy, therefore, is not a stereoscopic vision aimed at fusing the manifest image with the *scientific* image, but only one that aims at fusing the manifest image of the norm-governed experiences that inform and justify what we think, say, and do with the *natural* image of nonnormative causes that are the conditions for the possibility of

17. G. E. M. Anscombe, *Intention* (Cambridge, MA: Harvard University Press, 2000), 56ff., §32.

18. Descartes's evil demon comes to mind as an explanation of what he took to be a nonphysicasl and yet a nonetheless "natural" and law-governed constituent of the world, along with, e.g., souls. See René Descartes, *Meditations on First Philosophy*, ed. John Cottingham with intro. by Bernard Williams (Cambridge: Cambridge University Press, 1996).

what is manifest to us. What I have said about angels in this context in principle could therefore just as easily be said mutatis mutandis of, for instance, leprechauns, thetans, phlogiston, fairy dust, or any other manner of putative causal forces to which we might appeal as nonnormative explanations for the world-directed and intrinsically norm-guided character of the rational accountability that characterizes our intentional thought.

5.2 Preller on the Apophatic Science of God

So where do we find the Sellarsian irreducibility-cum-reducibility of norm and nature in Preller's apophatic account of our experience of God? In *Divine Science and the Science of God*, Preller's explicit aim is to "translate the epistemological doctrine of the *Summa Theologiae* into a fairly contemporary mode of discourse highly dependent on the insights and terminology of Wilfrid Sellars."[19] The Thomist epistemological doctrine in question is what Kevin Hector has called Aquinas's "apophatic rule," according to which "in this life, God is radically unintelligible."[20] A proper understanding of the radical unintelligibility of God, Preller thinks, is the key to understanding Thomas's distinction between the two types of theological "knowledge" (*scientia*): the *scientia divina* (the "knowledge related to divine matters") and the *scientia dei* (the "knowledge of God"). For Preller's Aquinas, the *scientia divina* is the knowledge of God available to us by the "natural light of reason" as exemplified by the "five ways" traditionally regarded as proofs for the existence of God in question 2, article 3 of the Prima Pars of the *Summa*. The *scientia dei*, on the

---

19. Victor Preller, *Divine Science and the Science of God: A Reformulation of Thomas Aquinas* (Princeton, NJ: Princeton University Press, 1967), 36.
20. Kevin Hector, "Apophaticism in Thomas Aquinas: A Reformulation and Recommendation," *Scottish Journal of Theology* 60, no. 4 (2007): 377–93, 380.

other hand, is the knowledge of God available to us only by divine grace through faith in the revelation given in sacred Scripture.

On Preller's reading of Thomas, we must understand the natural knowledge of God and the revelatory knowledge of God as two different ways of encountering God's radical unintelligibility prior to our beatification, two different applications of the "apophatic rule" to our putative cognitions of God. Contrary to those construals of Thomas's "natural theology" that take him to hold that we can have some (admittedly limited) positive knowledge of what God is like independently of revelation, Preller takes the five ways to be aimed precisely at a natural knowledge of God's transcendence of our natural capacities for knowing. "Aquinas," Preller says,

> stands firmly in the tradition of Augustine, Pseudo-Dionysius, and . . . Nicholas of Cusa. To claim to know God in this life is to confess a mode of nonknowledge or learned ignorance: "God as an unknown is said to be the terminus of our knowledge in the following respect: that the mind is found to be most perfectly in possession of knowledge of God when it is recognized that His essence is above everything that the mind is capable of apprehending in this life: and thus, although what He is remains unknown, yet it is known that He is."[21]

Natural knowledge of matters related to God, for Preller's Aquinas, is just knowledge of the limited intelligibility of the world according to any conceptual system of which we are capable, a knowledge of the partial absurdity of the world that can be demonstrated by the inevitable frustration that results when we attempt to trace its ultimate intelligibility—whether by way of motion, modality, being, or efficient or final causality.

That the world bottoms out in an apparent requirement of a transcendental condition for the possibility of worldly motion, cause, and so on demonstrates only "that there *is* an area of reality to which

21. Preller, *Divine Science*, 28.

the mind cannot carry us," and the truth that the five ways makes available to us is "the frustrating fact that man's mind is ordered to know that which it cannot discover."[22] The knowledge of this unknown is the *scientia divina*, the knowledge of that "which all men call God."[23] To identify this frustration of the human intellect at the unknown, which the pagans happen to call "god," with the God of revelation, however, is "a function of *theology*, not of philosophy."[24] The *scientia divina* counts as a knowledge of *God*, therefore, only against the background of the *scientia dei*, the knowledge of God given in revelation. Our revelatory knowledge of God is what marks out the necessary frustration of our intellects at the ultimate absurdity of the world as a "divine matter." Considered apart from the background knowledge given by faith in sacred Scripture, the natural knowledge Thomas identifies in the five ways is merely knowledge that "our conceptual categories do *not* exhaust the nature of the real."[25]

The Sellarsian approach takes center stage in Preller's reformulation of Aquinas in trying to make sense of the structure of the more fundamental form of theological knowledge—the *scientia dei*, or revelatory knowledge of God. Preller deploys a Sellarsian approach to show how the structure of the *scientia dei* in Aquinas exhibits its own conformity to the apophatic rule. What interests me is not so much whether Preller's reformulation succeeds in capturing Thomas's views,[26] but whether it can make sense of the perceptual

---

22. Ibid., 29.
23. Thomas Aquinas, *Summa Theologiae: Volume 2, Existence and Nature of God 1a, 2–11*, ed. and trans. Timothy McDermott, in *Summa Theologiae*, ed. Thomas Gilby (Cambridge: Cambridge University Press, 1964), 17, 1a, q.2, 3, ad. 2.
24. Preller, *Divine Science*, 29.
25. Ibid., 30.
26. For an interesting recent dialogue on that question, compare the criticism of Preller's views as failing to capture the function of Thomas's *via negativa* in Hector, "Apophaticism in Thomas Aquinas," 377–93, with the defense of Preller's reading as faithful to Thomas in Adam Eitel,

relation to God involved in revelation.[27] The structure of revelatory knowledge, on Preller's rereading of Thomas, is a special case of our ordinary empirical knowledge, since there is, as Thomas puts it, "nothing in the intellect unless [it is] first in the senses."[28] But to understand the special case, we need to have a grip on the structure of empirical knowledge in the ordinary case.

In spelling out the structure of our ordinary empirical knowledge, Preller articulates the three key features of the Sellarsian approach as I have characterized it. First, he offers on Thomas's behalf a renunciation of the myth of the Given. Thomas, Preller says, "has no doctrine of an immediate given or noninferentially *cognizable* content of sense experience."[29] Second, he offers a two-ply analysis of experience that assigns a transcendental role to our below-the-line causal relations to concrete particulars—that is, that of securing the "empirical significance" or object-involving character of our above-the-line conceptual episodes. He construes "sensation" as a "composite" act consisting in operations of the intellect coordinated with a "physical alteration of the sense organs."[30] While the "physical" responsiveness of our sensory organs registers our relation to objects in our environment, it is not any sort of "conscious state" or intentional relation in the mind, but rather the causal correlate of a conceptual episode that is the "intelligible form" of a material sensory relation to external objects. As Preller puts it, "The important point . . . is that the . . . 'form' of the sensible object is not merely a *given*

"Making Motions in a Language We Do Not Understand: The Apophaticism of Thomas Aquinas and Victor Preller," *Scottish Journal of Theology* 65, no. 1 (2012): 17–33.

27. Indeed, that concern is more in keeping with Preller's interests as well: "I am not interested only (or even primarily) in what Aquinas thought—as a matter of historical curiosity—but in what can be made at the present time of the *methodology* of Aquinas in explicating the status of natural language about God in relation to revealed language" (Preller, *Divine Science*, 36).

28. Preller, *Divine Science*, 37.

29. Ibid., 38.

30. Ibid., 39.

of sense experience, but is *produced by the soul itself* and is *ordered to* the operations of the intellect. . . . At the very first moment of conscious cognition there is an intentional interpretation of the object of experience, ordered to the intelligible categories of the mind."[31]

Preller denies that the correlation between our intentional concepts and the nonintentional and merely "physical" or "material" causal relation to particulars is one in which we simply read the concept directly off its sensible properties: "The concept of 'what the object is' (its true nature) is never merely 'given' in sense experience. The 'real form' of the external object does not inform the intellect—the intellect *informs itself*, on the basis of sense experience, of that which sense experience does not actually contain—the nature of the external object."[32]

Our normative conceptual system has its empirical significance or world-involving character in a nonintentional and merely causal way. The system of truth-evaluable concepts and their rational relations by which our intellect informs itself is logically separable from the material and merely causal relations by which the concepts in the system are indexed to the sensible objects in the world that they are "about." Preller's device for illustrating the logical distinction between the conscious and intentional dimension of our experiences and their preconscious and referential, or object-involving, dimension is a "man-angel."

In fact, Preller, says, "man could not possess an actual conceptual system if he were not having sense experiences," but, on analogy with Thomas's idea of angel intellects unconditioned by material sensibility, we can as a thought experiment "treat man like a temporary angel."[33] Man-angels are purely immaterial beings who

31. Ibid., 38.
32. Ibid., 42.

possess the very same conceptual system that we do, but without any material relations to the world such as those evinced by our sensory relations to it. They would therefore possess a system of intentional concepts that the "agent intellect" impresses on the "passive intellect" but without the *empirical significance* of those concepts conferred by their indexing to the sensory connections that their possessor bears to the material world. Such a being, Preller says, would possess a conceptual *syntax* without its *semantics*: "Such a system would be entirely formal—it would have no material content."[34]

To ask whether any of our empirical concepts is "meaningful," therefore, creates ambiguity between 1) an inquiry about the syntactic role it plays in our conceptual system of "what is a reason for what" and 2) an inquiry about the proximal registering of "sensible accidents" on our physical sensory systems by an external object in our distal environment. The notion of a man-angel thus helps us demarcate the division of labor between above-the-line conceptual contents constitutive of our subjective self-consciousness as knowers and below-the-line nonconceptual and merely causal relations to the world that determine the semantic relations of our conceptual knowledge as a conceptual knowledge *of* the world.

But the *logical* independence of a conceptual syntax and its extensional semantics should not be taken to imply its *actual* independence. In fact, in the case of our ordinary perceptual relation to the world, the semantics are fused to the syntax in the developmental process by which we are initiated into our first and native language.

> In sheer response to the stimuli of our social environment—like little behavioristic machines—we learn to make the sound of "red" at certain times and to avoid it at others. Our use of the physical token may

33. Ibid., 44.
34. Ibid., 45.

be correct from the point of view of one who knows the syntactical-semantical laws of the English language—and people may say, "Ah, look, he knows what 'red' means"—but we *do not* know what "red" means until we understand the rules which govern the use of "red" and learn consciously to obey those rules. Merely to act in a way that happens to conform to the intelligible laws that someone else understands is not to know what we are doing when we utter "red." It is true that there must be something going on "in our minds" when we use the word. We are responding in some fashion to the physical state of our sensory system. But we do not yet know what is going on, and therefore nothing is consciously going on. We do not know *why* it is correct to say "red" at certain times or *how* the statement "Red!" signifies an intelligible aspect of our experience of reality. We do not yet know what it means for a thing to be red or what it is that we are naming when we say it (We do not even know what "naming" means in the language we are learning).[35]

So whereas a syntactic-semantic fusion accounts for our ordinary perceptual relation to the world as both an intentional and referential relation, that fusion itself has its explanatory ground in the nonnormative and causal below-the-line processes that govern our language learning. Ultimately, our norms are explicable in terms of complex stimulus-response patterns by which we are disposed to exhibit linguistic behavior without understanding it *as* linguistic behavior. Here Preller draws on Sellars's illustration of the "syntactical dance" of the honeybees by which various bumps and grinds ostensibly function to signal to one another the relative distance of a clover or the orientation to the hive. Such material moves constitute a "language," but exhibited only as "physically programmed into their nervous systems by the genetic laws of their strain" and not as intentional moves in conformity with norms according to which they could correct one another or hold one another accountable for deviant performances.[36] The training by which we become capable

35. Ibid., 266.

of uttering "red" (aloud or in a language of thought) in the presence of red objects is a kind of know-how that does not yet rise to the level of the syntactico-semantic conscious awareness of red objects characteristic of our ordinary empirical knowledge. It begins much like the training of a dog to lift a paw when offered a hand.

But that, Preller emphasizes, is not a consciousness of red, precisely because the merely causal evoking of linguistic behavior does not of itself evince accountability to a norm. The child no more succeeds in *asserting* that something is red than the dog succeeds in literally participating in the customary norm of greeting.[37] A below-the-line utterance of a linguistic term does not represent the *use* of that term but at best an unintentional *mention* of it. The above-the-line conformity to norms required for shaking hands or a conscious awareness of one's physical states *as* representing states of the world requires a further ability possessed by us but not the dog. The ability in question is to "understand the rules which govern the use of 'red' and learn consciously to obey those rules."[38]

Human capacities to become consciously aware of the world therefore arise because we are capable not merely of becoming disposed to exhibit complex patterns of differential responsiveness to the world tracked by a holistic and interrelated system of prelinguistic utterances that form the protosyntactic terms of our language but also of forming higher-level dispositions to respond normatively to our merely causal responses. Our below-the-line dispositions to respond to the world become above-the-line conscious perceivings of the

---

36. Ibid., 267.
37. Such participation requires *understanding*. But this is not the same as saying that it requires *reflective reasoning*. Recall the baseball player from chapter 2—a swing of the bat can evince a practical understanding, which is what differentiates it from, e.g., a mere muscle spasm.
38. Preller, *Divine Science*, 266. For a discussion of the significance of the use/mention distinction in Sellars's functionalist account of meaning, which nicely parallels Preller's story, see James O'Shea, *Wilfrid Sellars*, 57–63.

world *as* thus and so when the object of those responsive dispositions is the protosyntactic system of utterance that tracks our causal relation to the world. Thus, "when we introspect our experience in terms of the formal rules of our conceptual system . . . we are able to use the formal elements of that system to 'note' or 'become aware of' repeated patterns within our experience and to interpret them in intelligible terms."[39]

To make one's experience intelligible to oneself in this way is "to express the isomorphism that exists between one's experience and one's conceptual system by *utilizing* that system as a means of consciously perceiving and informing that which one experiences."[40] Preller's point is that our ability to use the language, to place the physical states indexed by the interrelated terms of the language in "the logical space of reasons," is what marks the distinction between the protolinguistic system of utterance as a below-the-line and merely causal phenomenon and its function above the line as the expression of our conscious awareness. That ability to track the "formal significance of our descriptions of reality" is constitutive of the "agent intellect" or the "light of reason."[41] To know what reality is like is therefore essentially to "judge one's experience in terms of one's conceptual system. There is no means of short-circuiting the process and 'taking a look' at the world *in its own terms*."[42]

We can further ask what grounds the ascent from our below-the-line merely causal responsiveness to the world to our above-the-line rational responsiveness to our responses to the world. Preller's answer to that question evinces the third feature of his account of ordinary experience that he shares with Sellars—namely, that "the forms by

---

39. Preller, *Divine Science*, 53.
40. Ibid.
41. Ibid.
42. Ibid.

which we judge experience are not learned *from* experience, but result from the natural tendency of the mind to use the 'first principles of the intellect' in interpreting experience."[43] In other words, it is not only that the semantic content of our experiences is fixed by causal relations to the world evinced by our linguistic behavior below the line. The first principles of the intellect govern our above-the-line capacity to respond to our own linguistic responses to the world in our normative uses of language, and this is how we are able to judge our experience in the light of reason. But those first principles are themselves below-the-line principles. The power of the agent intellect to create intelligible forms is a "natural power" of the human constitution.[44] It is neither an extrinsic power, given to us by our below-the line sensations, nor an intrinsic power to actualize any rational potential objectively had by the world.[45]

Instead, it is an intrinsic power of the agent intellect to measure the world against intelligible forms that it creates according to below-the-line causal laws that are not immediately available to us. We can no more directly inspect the natural or below-the-line causal basis for the normative principles of the intellect than we can directly inspect the below-the-line causal basis of our material sensations.[46] Descriptions of the merely causal grounds for the linguistic norms we are disposed to create, Preller thinks, are just as much a matter of indirect inference and theory construction as our descriptions of the merely causal grounds of our sensory experiences. It follows from this, though, that our ordinary experiences do not bottom out in any ultimately *rationally justifiable* syntactico-semantic correlation that we could discover. This is the sense in which Preller takes our intentional relation to the world in experience to be "radically analogical"—the

43. Ibid., 54.
44. Ibid., 55.
45. Ibid., 54, 73.
46. Ibid., 73.

"being" of the interrelated objects and properties of the world and our intellective relation to it is proportionally related to, but not constitutively conveyed by or transparently depicted within, our language. The adequacy of our conscious awareness *of* the world *to* the world is a merely proportional isomorphism to it.[47]

Preller therefore summarizes his conception of our ordinary empirical knowledge as "a matter of reflection on the 'material moves of the mind.'"[48] Such a capacity of reflection assumes that

> we have assimilated enough of the matter of language for the "agent intellect"—whatever power or disposition that names—to take over and conceive immanently in our intentional being the rules of the game we blindly played for so long. At that moment . . . a light dawns and we *know* what we were saying and why. Other members of our human community can and must teach us the material moves justified (as *they* know) by the conceptual system, but no one can teach us that insight which comes with the possession of a conceptual system. That must be conceived within us by the dispositional nature.[49]

So in what sense does Preller take the *scientia dei*, our revelatory knowledge of God in this life, to be a special case of our ordinary empirical knowledge, thus understood?

Preller's claim is that the language of *sacra scriptura* presents us not with a human syntactical system but with a divine one. To be sure, its syntactical terms are borrowed from the language *we* use to express the material moves of *our* conceptual system. But the ordered relations by which those terms are proportioned to reality—the realities of God, ourselves, and the world—belong not to the intentional being of *our* agent intellect, but God's. Sacred Scripture therefore presents us with the material moves of the language of God, the syntactical expression of God's Logos or Word. But while

47. Ibid., 68.
48. Ibid., 267.
49. Ibid., 268.

Scripture presents us with "analogues in our natural language of the first principles of *scientia dei*," we do not possess these analogical terms of God's language in the same way that we possess the terms of our own natural language.

With respect to our natural language, we have ascended from our below-the-line dispositions to elicit the material moves of the conceptual system (our habituation into an unknowing mention of its terms) into an above-the-line conscious conformity to the syntactical norms of our agent intellect in the *use* of those terms. But with respect to the supernatural syntax expressed in Scripture, the best we can achieve in this life is the below-the-line relationship to its terms: "We are now learning, Aquinas would have it, the 'material moves' of the language of God. Our mode of participation here and now in *scientia dei* is the making of motions in a language we do not understand. Submitting to the pedagogy of *sacra doctrina*—mediated through the teaching *magisterium* of the Church—we perform the liturgical bumps and grinds of a syntactical dance that will—we hope—orient us to our supernatural source of life and delectation once we leave the darkness of human life *in via*."[50]

Only God enjoys an intrinsic and fully self-conscious above-the-line possession of God's intentional being and the form of insight capable of rationally justifying those words and actions that sacred Scripture, under the guidance of the church, proposes to habituate in us. The beatified saints enjoy an above-the-line capacity to render revelatory language intelligible in a conscious awareness of God, but they do so "not through created forms, but through God himself."[51] That is, the *beati* enjoy a materially direct relation to God—one of "vision"—that enables them to make the level ascent that we cannot here below. They possess the syntactical principles of the *scientia dei*

50. Ibid., 278.
51. Ibid., 239.

in intelligible form. We, on the other hand, "possess the *scientia dei* [in] . . . a mode appropriate to faith alone, and not to *vision*. . . . [W]e possess only created and nonintelligible propositional analogues of those principles."[52]

The infusion of faith by divine grace is the means by which God, upon our hearing of the word in the church, allows us by way of our natural language to place the material moves learned from *sacra scriptura* into the space of *faith* rather than the space of reasons. The "light of faith" allows us to judge that the unintelligible syntactical dance in which we have been made to participate is proportional to the intentional form of God's language. Thus, the material moves of revelatory language refer us to the mind of God only by the disposition of faith infused in us through an act of divine grace.[53] But this intelligibility of faith remains unintelligible to the light of reason: "The believer does not possess a form of intelligibility which corresponds to the judgement of faith, but only a form of faith itself, conceived *by God* within the soul of the believer—not by the believer himself. How [, for example,] the resuscitation of a dead body could possibly cause his own beatitude, the believer cannot possibly comprehend—although he hopes to comprehend *in patria*. In that respect, the apostles—who saw the empirical result of the resurrection—were no better off than the contemporary believer."[54]

Whereas Sellars's scientism about the natural grounds of our normative directedness on the world motivated his vision of the fusion of natural language exhibited by the manifest image to the language of the scientific image as a regulative ideal for our knowledge of the principles governing our mental relation to reality, Preller substitutes the fusion of the manifest image of our natural

52. Ibid.
53. Ibid., 245.
54. Ibid., 248.

language to the divine image of God's language exemplified in Christ (the human Word of God) as the regulative ideal.

> Some, like Sellars, assume that one day science will tell us in intelligible terms what we are referring to when we say "The mind," and they await the eschatologically perfect theoretical language of next-century's neuro-physics with the same myth-making expectation that Aquinas reserves for the Beatific Vision. But the point is that *now*—whether we mean the *now* which is previous to the first coming of the Good Scientist or the second coming of the Good Shepherd—we do not know how we know or how what we know is related to how things "really" are.[55]

5.3. Hector's Cataphatic Therapy and the Spirit of Recognition

One of the central aims of Hector's *Theology without Metaphysics* is to propose an alternative to an underlying metaphysical commitment that he takes to motivate apophatic accounts of the meaning, truth, and reference of language that purports to be "about" God. The metaphysical commitment in question is what Hector calls "essentialist correspondentism" (henceforth, EC), which is comprised of "*essentialism*, the supposition that that which is fundamentally real about an object is an idea-like 'essence' (which stands at a remove from that which one experiences); and *correspondentism*, the claim that human minds or words are in touch with this reality in virtue of their enjoying a kind of privileged access to it."[56]

On Hector's diagnosis, the conviction that an EC model of God-talk courts idolatry compels many toward an apophatic account of the way that God-talk secures its meaning, truth and reference. The idea that God has an "essence" to which our concepts could

---

55. Ibid.
56. Kevin Hector, *Theology without Metaphysics: God, Language and the Spirit of Recognition* (New York: Cambridge University Press, 2011), 45–46.

correspond amounts to "ontotheology"—a kind of idolatry in which one "does violence to God" by cutting God down to the size of our predetermined conceptual categories.[57]

Rather than challenging EC as the criterion that would have to be met for our language to be meaningful, true, and referential, the impulse of apophaticism is to *accept* EC as a correct picture of what it would mean for our language to "reach out" to put us in touch with its objects, while denying that language in general—and particularly our language about God—could possibly meet the criterion. If we are to be regard our theological talk as meaningful, referential, and true and yet nonidolatrous, we therefore seem to need an explanation that both respects the necessary gulf between God *in se* and our theological language and explains the sense if any in which such language nevertheless manages to meaningfully and truthfully refer us to God.

"Apophatic anti-metaphysics" is Hector's term for describing such theories. Jean-Luc Marion and John Caputo are Hector's chief exemplars of "apophaticism" thus construed,[58] as both illustrate how

---

57. Ibid., 100.

58. The primary use of "apophatic" and its variants in Hector's argument is to mark out a perfectly general picture of concept use in natural languages—a picture according to which we must posit some sort of ontological gap between language and its objects. "Apophatic theology" in Hector's usage therefore fails to mark out anything formally distinct or sui generis about the meaning, truth, or reference of theological discourse in distinction from any other ("ordinary") discourse. But, on the face of it, what Hector calls "apophatic theology" does not count as "apophatic" theology on my way of marking the distinction, but rather as "cataphatic" theology. For, on my characterization, apophatic theology does not circumscribe any particular theory of meaning, but the exceptional and sui generis analysis of theological meaning that is required by the exceptional and sui generis character of God that our theological language purports to be "about." By my lights, then, if all of our language is "apophatic," then none of it is. But perhaps it is possible for my way of marking the distinction to accommodate Hector's usage. For even if the proponents of "apophatic antimetaphysics" posit a single and perfectly general account of the world-directedness of language, still, that account itself is marked by an irreducible contrast between EC as a regulative ideal for our language use and the necessary failure of any attempt to instantiate that ideal in our actual language use. Insofar as the index of our language use is a kind of disruption or failure of the regulative ideal, it counts as apophatic on my usage. The fact that the regulative ideal that would putatively mark out the "ordinary" structure of intentionality is uninstantiated (even necessarily so) can be

the assumption of EC can motivate the apophatic approach insofar as both hold that "language, and especially concept-use, is essentially correspondentistic and so violent, in consequence of which each assumes that one can resist such violence only by maintaining distance between language and its objects (particularly God)."[59]

Rather than accepting the picture offered by EC as the way in which language would have to relate to its objects to count as meaningful, true, or referential and then rejecting the possibility that language (whether theological language in particular or language in general) could meet that standard, Hector's "therapeutic" proposal is that we leave behind the EC picture altogether. If we can manage to put in its place an account of our ordinary linguistic practices of applying a concept to an object that does not require us to "assimilate that object to an antecedently defined, essence-like category" as EC does, then the problem of "ontotheology" would never arise in the first place and we would have no need for an apophatic approach.[60] Hector, therefore, aims to displace an EC metaphysics of concept use "by setting alongside it a picture which takes ordinary practices and experience as its explanatory basis."[61] Hector's strategy for avoiding the problem of cutting God down to the size of our human concepts is to claim that concept use in general does not work that way and, on that basis, to build an account of theological concept use that parallels the structure of ordinary concept use.[62] Hector's account is therefore decidedly "cataphatic" by my lights.

As is the case for Preller, the structure of the perceptual act is important for Hector's non-EC alternative account of the meaning,

accommodated by my usage, since my way of spelling out the distinctions between "ordinary" and "sui generis," "standard" and "nonstandard," etc. constitutive of the distinction between apophatic and cataphatic takes no account of scope of instantiation, but only formal structure.

59. Hector, *Theology without Metaphysics*, 25.
60. Ibid., 49.
61. Ibid., 46.
62. Ibid., 25.

truth, and reference of concept use in natural languages insofar as he endorses the broadly Kantian account of a "concept" as "a rule by which one orders the manifold of one's experience . . . by judging certain aspects of that experience to be relevantly similar to other aspects."[63] By way of "experience," the concept use evinced in our language use comes to be world-involving, or bound up with objects. The question of how our ordinary uses of language can make God intelligible to us, direct us upon God, and assert truths about God without "doing violence" to God is reducible to the question of how the norms governing our theological discourse come to be God-involving, or bound up with experiences of God, without involving any allegedly idolatrous identification of God with the meanings, referents, or truths expressed by *our* use of "God."

The account of ordinary concept use that Hector develops to accomplish that aim is extraordinarily complex, and he draws on a host of philosophical resources to construct it. But what is most interesting for my present purposes is how closely it approximates the essentials of the Sellarsian approach that Preller deployed in his apophatic account. That is, while Hector does not appeal directly to Sellars or claim to appropriate him nearly to the extent that Preller does,[64] the account he offers is essentially structured by all three of the features of the Sellarsian approach I have attributed to Preller: (1) a renunciation of the myth of the Given in the explication of conceptual content, (2) an irreducibly two-ply analysis of observational concepts consisting in an above-the-line dimension that supplies their normative "syntactical" meaning and a nonnormative below-the-line dimension that supplies their "semantic" meaning or object-involving character, and (3) a

---

63. Ibid., 54.
64. Rather, Hector assimilates Sellars's approach into a strategy that incorporates, among others, Brandom, Davidson, Dummett, and Quine. See Hector, *Theology without Metaphysics*, 106n3.

reductive account of how the irreducibly normative content of our observational concepts arises out of our nonnormative relation to the world.[65] Consider some evidence for his commitment to each.

First, having identified concepts as norms that unify the "manifold of experience" by way of a particular kind of discursive social practice, that of discharging one's responsibility to "go on in the same way" as precedent does in our own use of a term, Hector confronts the question of what determines what counts as "going on in the same way" in any particular use of a concept. Common to the proposals he rejects is the idea that we can "derive normativity . . . from a supposedly un-normed fact."[66] We "must not," he says, "try to derive norms from some (supposedly) un-normed 'given.'"[67] To appeal to nonnormative facts about, for instance, regularly recurring patterns in precedent uses of a concept or to nonnormative inclinations or dispositions of precedent users of that concept in our linguistic community as that which determines whether or not our ongoing use of a concept counts as "going on in the same way" evinces precisely what Sellars identified as an analogue of the "naturalistic fallacy in ethics."

Second, Hector gives us a two-ply analysis of the division of labor by which concepts both evince trajectories of normative meaning and track our empirical relation to external objects in our environment. In other words, his account evinces a logical independence of meaning, truth, and reference as determined by inferential relations between intrinsically norm-governed discursive behaviors from the nonnormative circumstances in virtue of which those norm-internal relations succeed in tracking with the objects,

---

65. Significantly, these commitments are shared to a greater or lesser extent by almost all of the philosophers from which Hector draws to construct his account (including, for example, all those listed in the previous note).
66. Hector, *Theology without Metaphysics*, 59.
67. Ibid., 60.

properties, and relations of our external environment. The normative dimension corresponds to the above-the-line character of thought—what Sellars identified as the essentially "epistemic" character of the logical space of reasons and Preller designated as the "syntax" constitutive of our conscious awareness. The nonnormative dimension corresponds to the dual transcendental role of our merely causal relation to the world—what Sellars identified as the essentially "natural" explanation for the world-involving character of our norms as well as the "natural" ground of that normativity, and what Preller identified as the causal ground of the "semantics" for our syntactical system.

With respect to the above-the-line dimension of our concept use, Hector claims to account for the meaning, reference, and truth of our concepts as irreducibly constituted by our recognition of the norms that govern our ordinary discursive practices. Thus, as regards meaning, for example, Hector denies that our concepts derive the semantic role they have in our discursive practices from any nonnormative and discourse-external facts. If conceptual meaning were constituted by a relation of our conceptual categories to the nonnormative facts that they "contain," then we would have to confront the idea that our concepts of God must "contain" or describe the discourse-external facts about God in order to be meaningful. Instead, Hector recommends that we understand the structure and meaning of concepts by embedding "an inferentialist semantics in a pragmatic theory of meaning-as-use, and . . . explain this pragmatics in terms of intersubjective recognition."[68]

So, rather than seeing our use of concepts as attempts to subsume discourse-external facts under the normative standards of our discursive practice, we can see our concept use simply as a form of responsiveness to the norms internal to our discursive practices.

68. Ibid., 106.

Concepts just are a species of norms "by which one orders the manifold of one's experience . . . by treating certain aspects of the experience as the same as other aspects."[69] Since what we are willing to count as sameness in our mutual recognitions "is neither uniform nor predictable,"[70] our use of concepts must be understood in terms of the evolving normative trajectories of intersubjective linguistic performance. The meaning of our linguistic expressions thus precipitates out of this pragmatic theory of concept use as a species of mutual recognition. An agent's words "mean" X if and only if X is capable of being recognized to carry on "the normative trajectory implicit in a series of precedents."[71]

Similarly, Hector takes the notion of reference—the world-directedness or "intentionality" of our concepts—to be an irreducibly normative, discourse-internal, or "syntactical" relation. Words refer insofar as our use of referring expressions inherits a precedent commitment in a chain of use-instances that stretch back to the original institution of the social practice of naming.[72] Reference can therefore be spelled out fully in terms of the discourse-internal norms governing our use of anaphora, our attempt to go on with our use of a term "in the same way" as members of the linguistic community involved in the initial use or "baptism" of a referring term.[73] Roughly, my use of "God" refers to God only if I commit myself in my use of the term to picking out the same semantic function that the term "God" had in the preceding use-instances that I recognize as fixing a normative standard of correctness (that is, as authoritative

69. Ibid., 72.
70. Ibid., 69.
71. Ibid., 105–6.
72. Ibid., 165.
73. Ibid. Cf. Saul Kripke, *Naming and Necessity* (Cambridge, MA: Harvard University Press, 1980). Here Hector deploys Kripke's analysis of proper names as rigid designators to secure the causal relation involved in the Davidsonian "triangulation" by which our terms succeed in singling out features of our external environment.

or "canonical"). The "nontriviality" of the identity claim implicit in my anaphoric use of "God" means that subsequent recognitions of "sameness" in my current use of "God" with the relevant preceding ones can count as genuine discoveries, and in that way the normative trajectory of referring terms can undergo change across time.

A Christian's use of "God" can be judged successful in referring to God only if, first, she commits herself to inheriting a chain of canonical references that stretches back to Abraham, Moses and Jesus; second, she discharges that commitment in her use of the term *God* by trying to go on in the same way as the authoritatively recognized uses, trying to attribute to it the same "meaning" (that is, the semantic role as described above) as the canonical uses specified earlier in the chain; and, finally, her uses of "God" implicitly license others to hold her accountable to the identity claim and to appropriate her uses in their own identity claims—her use thus enabling others to fix their own references to "God" by taking her uses as anaphora.[74] Since this discourse-internal conception of referring to an object does not require any unique correspondence between one's ideas and an object itself, it poses no special problems for our capacity to refer to God in the ordinary way.[75] Since Christians refer to the Spirit as the one who makes it possible for what we think, say, or do to direct us upon the God of Abraham, Moses, and Jesus, Christian God-talk can be seen as referring us to God in the ordinary way through the church's evolving intersubjective recognition of the normative spirit of Christ.

Finally, Hector thinks we should analyze the "truth" of an expression in terms of "the ordinary practice of taking-true."[76] We can regard the evolving norms that govern our "taking as true" as simultaneously restricted to a function of rational relations among

---

74. Hector, *Theology without Metaphysics*, 178.
75. Ibid., 199.
76. Ibid., 243.

our held beliefs. The same discourse-internal dynamics that account for meaning and reference serve to account for the concept of truth, not as a kind of correspondence that holds between beliefs and discourse-external states of affairs but as a discourse-internal feature of the kind of rational accountability implicit in the use of our concepts to refer. The practice of "taking-true" can be analyzed as a conformity of our beliefs to their referents as a normative standard of correctness. But since both the meaning and the reference of our concepts has already been explicated in terms of normative relations internal to our discursive practices, it follows that the truth of our beliefs is determined by relations internal to our discursive practices. Our beliefs are true when they "get their subject matter right," and they get their subject matter right when they go on in the same way as precedent beliefs that have been recognized as getting that subject matter right.

Applied straightforwardly to the theological case, we can say that "a belief about God is true, then, if it gets Christ's subject matter right, and it gets Christ's subject matter right if it goes on in the same way as precedent beliefs which have been recognized as getting it right. Hence if one says, 'God justifies the ungodly,' one's statement is true if it gets its subject matter right, and it is recognizable as such if it carries on the Spirit of precedent beliefs."[77] Since a non-EC conception of the truthfulness of our ordinary discourse does not require any "metaphysical relationship" of correspondence or isomorphism between our claims and what they purport to be about, a conception of ordinary discourse poses no special problems in accounting for the truthfulness of discourse that purports to be about God.

Now there is an obvious objection to Hector's account as I have characterized it thus far. We might concede that he has succeeded in

77. Ibid., 242–43.

understanding meaning, reference, and truth in terms of the norms internal to our discursive practices. Such norms serve as the irreducible explanatory primitives in terms of which each of those notions can be analyzed. But precisely insofar as meaning, truth, and reference are to be understood as irreducibly discourse-internal norms, it is hard to see how they have anything to do with the external world. "Semantic" relations, on Hector's inferentialist account, are merely "syntactical" in Preller's sense.

If we look to his account of reference for an extensional semantics to connect the norms governing our discursive practice to the world itself, however, we find that the extensions of referring terms are just the intensions of the anaphoric terms that serve as the canonical uses in a chain of reference. So our concepts have as their content our conformity (or failure to conform) to the norms of a discursive practice, but the singular referents of our concepts—what it is they pick out—are also just instances of our conforming (or failing to conform) to our established discursive norms. If we attempt to "break out" of this syntactical system of meaning and reference in order to specify its truth conditions in terms of states of our external environment as over against states of our conceptual system, then we find that truth conditions too are conceived in terms of warranted assertability, in terms of the norms of our established practice of taking-true. So, on the face of it, Hector seems to give us an alternative to EC only by cutting us off from the world.

Fortunately, this is not all Hector has to say about meaning, truth, and reference. He is not a crass constructivist. Instead, he is fully cognizant of the fact that defining our notions of concept use "syntactically" in terms of the norms implicit in our discursive practices requires him to say something about how those practices are constrained by the discourse-external context of the world itself. In order to supply that discourse-external constraint, Hector supplements his irreducibly norm-governed analysis of each of the three notions—meaning, reference, truth—with some sort of discourse-external constraint. This account of external constraint constitutes the "second ply" of Hector's story—his version of what Preller calls the "semantic system" that is externally correlated to the "syntactical" system and in virtue of which we are entitled to regard our concepts as genuinely world-involving.

Hector's account straightforwardly follows the Sellarsian approach in accounting for the world's constraint on meaning by appealing to the stimulus-response conditions or "material moves" under which "syntactic" terms are first introduced in the acquiring of our native language. We first learn how to use concepts by learning, for instance, how to think or say "heat" "when and only when heat is sensibly present" and by further inviting normative assessment in our attempts to conform our patterns of thought or utterance to the standards of correctness internal to our discursive practices.[78] The world-involving character of meaning therefore consists in its supplying the "stimulus condition" or *occasion* for acquiring conceptual norms. Hector finds recourse to this explanation in his account of how perceptual experience enables us to apply concepts to the world. When we "become reliably disposed to respond non-inferentially to certain objects by applying the appropriate concepts," we "automatically perceive . . . such objects *as* thus-and-so."[79] Clarifying a bit more, Hector says, "Once one has mastered a concept . . . the appearance of whatever it applies to causes one non-inferentially to apply it, in consequence of which one need not think of concept application as introducing an intermediate, inference-like step between an object's presence and one's perception of it."[80]

---

78. Ibid., 60–61.
79. Ibid., 188.
80. Ibid., 189.

In other words, our habituation into the relevant stimulus-response patterns as we learn our native language enables "sensibility" to play a causal role in evoking or "wringing" from us the relevant concept in the appropriate circumstances. Hector speaks of objects in our external environment as being "bound up" with the normative discursive practices that constitute the meaning and reference of those concepts. He identifies the responsive dispositions inculcated in us by way of our initiation into the discursive norms with Schleiermacher's conception of *Gefühl*: "the immediate presence of whole, undivided existence (sensible as well as spiritual), the unity of a person and his or her sensible or spiritual world."[81]

Hector's description of this "pre-reflective harmony or at-oneness between oneself and one's environing circumstances," which "includes a kind of comportment to or disposition toward those circumstances," is akin to what Hubert Dreyfus has described as the Heideggerian conception of "embodied coping" that we encountered earlier in Marion's account as well.[82] Much in the same way as Marion's and Dreyfus's Heidegger conceives of embodied coping, Hector seems to think of Gefühl in terms of the entanglement between oneself and one's external environment that is exhibited by the dispositional capacities that result from the internalization of a *skill*.[83] Think, for example, of the baseball player whose instinctive comportment of his body to the sensible (visual) stimulus of an approaching ball is immediately wrung from him. That baseball

---

81. Ibid., 77.
82. See Jean-Luc Marion, *The Reason of the Gift*, trans. with intro. by Stephen E. Lewis (Charlottesville: University of Virginia Press, 2012), 34ff.
83. See Hector, *Theology without Metaphysics*, 77ff.; Kevin Hector, "The Mediation of Christ's Normative Spirit: A Constructive Reading of Schleiermacher's Pneumatology," *Modern Theology* 24, no. 1 (January 2008): 1–22. Cf. with the account of Heidegger that Hubert L. Dreyfus gives in *Being-In-The-World: A Commentary on Heidegger's Being and Time* (Cambridge, MA: MIT Press, 1990) and "The Myth of the Pervasiveness of the Mental," in *Mind, Reason and Being-In-The-World: The McDowell-Dreyfus Debate*, ed. Joseph K. Schear (London: Routledge, 2012), 15–40.

player is free from any deliberative or inferential reasoning—he is "at one" with the bat and does not thematize his relation to it as subject to object or take up any cognitive stance *over against* it. Similarly, we acquire our above-the-line capacity to navigate our environment according to the logical space of reasons by cultivating an "at-oneness" of our habits of language use and our comportment to the world.

The crucial difference is that the baseball player acquired that prereflective harmony by a process of habituation—a form of training—that required him at an earlier stage to thematize his relation to a bat and a reflective stance toward what he was doing with it ("Now, keep your eye on the ball and as it approaches, think about where your hips are. . . . No, no, adjust your stance *this* way."). But that prior reflective stance (the one needed for him to acquire his subsequent prereflective dispositional stance), itself required a yet-prior prereflective stance. So the Gefühl he acquired in his initial acquisition of the language required for his subsequent reflective stance toward his bodily position and swing and the yet further subsequent elimination of that reflective stance in his eventual learning of at-oneness with the bat. Our cultivation of the linguistic at-oneness with the world that secures the object-involvement of our above-the-line and discourse-internal practices of expressing meanings, intending referents, and taking-true is, on Hector's account, rock bottom. The entanglement of our linguistic behavior with our external environment is brought about without any prior reflective understanding on our part. Rather, we acquire our above-the-line capacities to inhabit a logical space of reasons through our initial training in the discursive practices of a particular linguistic community.

Since our discursive practices are thus entangled with mind-external objects as the circumstances in which we learn what concepts mean and how they apply, the intrinsically and irreducibly syntactical "subject matter" of our discursive practices of "taking-true" succeeds in incorporating all the "objectivity" or object-involvement we could want.[84] So the "syntactical" norms of discursive practice that irreducibly constitute meaning, reference, and truth in Hector's account are tied to the world itself in virtue of its supplying the stimulus conditions under which we become disposed to apply those norms—the circumstances under which our external environment elicits the recognitional capacities that enable us to respond to it meaningfully, to refer subsequently to prior meaningful responses, and to take some among those meaningful responses as true. Insofar as divine presence and agency can be among those features of our external environment that reliably dispose us to noninferentially apply the relevant theological concepts, we can therefore regard our normative theological discourse as causally constrained by God's availability to us in the world.

This account of the object-involving character of our discursive practices explains how the inferential structure of our conceptual system might come to track with states of the world external to that system. My prior linguistic training disposes me to reliably, differentially, and noninferentially respond to various objects, properties, and relations in my external environment by applying the relevant concept drawn from my syntactical system. But it raises a question about the status of the system-internal norms that determine their correlation with the system-external world. Does Hector understand Gefühl—our "second-nature" prereflective dispositions to respond to the world in terms internal to the normative syntactical system we have acquired in our language learning—to explain merely how we become capable of detecting normative features of the world

---

84. Hector, *Theology without Metaphysics*, 214–17.

that are there anyway, as in a naive realism? Or, does he wish to align himself with the Sellarsian approach, which says something much stronger—namely, that the second-natural normative responses to the world made possible by Gefühl can explain what norms *are* and where they come from in terms of our discursive practices? On that view, norms are not features of the world that are there anyway and that our discursive practices merely enable us to detect. Instead, norms are themselves creatures of our discursive practices—the form of our responsiveness to nonnormative realities, not the form of reality that our discursive practices resonate.

On a naive realist reading of Hector's view, he regards the "attunement" of Gefühl as an attunement of our conceptual capacities to the intrinsic conceptual structure of the world. In contrast, on the "Sellarsian" reading, Hector regards Gefühl as *our* norm-generating "attunement" to the nonnormatively structured world. Elsewhere, Elsewhere, I have criticized Hector's account as incompatible with the naive realist picture.[85] In reply, Hector has been unwilling to concede the incompatibility, hoping instead to preserve a reading of his account that does not commit him to denying McDowell's approach.[86] I continue to maintain, however, that Hector has failed to recognize the consequences of his stated views. McDowell's way of handling object-involvement in the noninferential activation of our normative conceptual capacities in perception entails several positions that Hector's account explicitly denies in favor of the same sort of Sellarsian approach taken by Preller.

85. Sameer Yadav, "Therapy for the Therapist: A McDowellian Critique of Semantic Externalism in Kevin Hector's *Theology without Metaphysics,*" *Journal of Analytic Theology* 1, no. 1 (May 2013): 120–32. What I am characterizing as the "naive realist" picture, in other words, is precisely what Hector's "therapy" seeks to displace. It is part of the view he (mistakenly, on my view) takes to have become embedded "common sense" and that needs to be "overcome" (Hector, *Theology without Metaphysics,* 1).

86. Kevin Hector, "Responses to *JAT's* Symposium on *Theology without Metaphysics,*" *Journal of Analytic Theology* 1, no. 1 (May 2013): 140–47, esp. 144–45.

In defense of this reading, recall the status of norms on McDowell's naturalized platonism, according to which we must regard norms as properties of the world itself. The formation of a dispositional rational responsiveness to our external environment by the uniting of sensibility with understanding in our initiation into a language therefore has to be understood as the formation of capacities to detect and comport ourselves to the rational demands of reality itself. In cases of veridical perception, then, the sensory activation of our conceptual capacities by our environment can be seen as a direct *presentation* of the world as it is in itself. When our linguistic training unites our capacities for sensibility and understanding in the right sort of way, we become equipped to receive the impacts of our environment on us not merely as *sensible* impacts but as *intelligible* ones, effecting a *rational* and *intentional* sensory awareness of the world. As such, our environment itself, by way of the senses, gives us noninferential reasons for believing that things are thus and so or for acting in such and such a way.

Note, then, that to thus receive and respond to the normative conceptual structure of the world is to exhibit an isomorphism, or correspondence of form, between the concepts we actualize in belief or practice and the objective rational norms that inhere in the world—norms the world is already prepared to impose on any creatures properly equipped to actualize them, *whether or not there are in fact any such creatures.* Norms are thus not features of linguistic communities but rather features of the world capable of exerting rational demands on creatures capable of detecting them. The various ways in which different linguistic communities in fact exhibit and actualize human capacities for language acquisition therefore do not *explain* the origin of norms or normativity per se but only the origin of our capacity to directly apprehend or "take in" those norms and noninferentially respond to our perceptions of their demands.

Hector, on the other hand, tells us that "norms are implicit in, *and creatures of*, everyday social practices."[87] He wishes for his account of "everyday social practices" to "count as an adequate account of *norms*" themselves, and he therefore commits himself to explaining how "such practices" can "supply an objective standard according to which we could all be wrong."[88] Like Preller, and in keeping with the Sellarsian approach, Hector purports to explain what norms are—not in terms of the structure of the world, but in terms of the social behavior to which humans are disposed to responding to the world. That explanatory ambition is on display in Hector's response to the following objection that he fails to show how our discursive norms answer to any standard of correctness outside of those norms themselves:

> We have merely shifted the explanatory burden from the source of one performer's norms to the source of another's norms. We were wondering about the standard by which one's performances might be assessed, and we answered that this standard is supplied by previous performances which have been recognized as precedential. But whence the normative standard by which *these* performances are to be assessed? If one answers "from the performances of those from whom he or she learned the practice," it would appear that one is locked into an infinite explanatory regress.[89]

The objection is well put. Moreover, it is a shibboleth to expose whether one takes a naive realist or Sellarsian approach to normativity. The naive realist reply is that the world itself halts the regress and serves as the standard of correctness for what we think, say, and do. The inextricable linkage of our sensibility with the conceptual capacities acquired in language learning can enable us to immediately actualize the world's rational potential in the perceptual

---

87. Hector, *Theology without Metaphysics*, 60.
88. Ibid.
89. Ibid., 69.

act itself. Perception therefore names the way in which our norms are made subject to the tribunal of the world as our standard of rational assessment. But that is decidedly *not* the way Hector attempts to halt the threatened regress. Rather, he opts to avoid the apparent regress by explaining "how norms might be instituted 'out of nothing.'"[90] More specifically, he says that norms emerge through a process that begins with "the differential responsiveness characteristic of both organic and inorganic objects."[91]

Our relation to mind-external objects is thus fundamentally embedded within our discursive practices in the same way that, for example, an ice cube's relation to heat is embedded in its melting, or a sunflower's relation to the sun is embedded in its leaning sunward, or the relation of a capillary to an increase in body temperature is embedded in its dilation.[92] What distinguishes our normative relation to the world from the nonnormative relation borne by ice cubes and capillaries is that we are not limited to responding to objects in our environment; we also have metaresponsive capacities: we can reliably respond not only to the warming effects of the sun on us but also to our responses to that response.[93] The norms of concept use exhibited in our linguistic behavior thus precipitate "out of nothing"—that is, out of a dispositional relation to our environment that is itself nonnormative, a disposition toward metalevel operations upon a type of causal relationship to the external world that we share with mindless objects.[94]

90. Ibid.
91. Ibid., 71.
92. Ibid.
93. Ibid., 72.
94. Hector thinks that invoking this passage to illuminate his account as holding to a kind of externalism about the world's constraint on the norms internal to our discourse—and thus to illuminate its incompatibility with a McDowellian story—is to take it "badly out of context" (Hector, "Responses," 145), but he neglects to say how. On the contrary, an attempt to externalize the world's influence on the norms of our discursive practice is Hector's explicitly stated aim and conclusion, as I have shown in my exposition above.

Hector's account thus exhibits a kind of "naturalism" about the nature of normativity intrinsic to our above-the-line experiences. Of course, he is not a *scientistic* naturalist—he does not identify the nonnormative, below-the-line, or *merely* causal relationships out of which our discursive norms emerge as restricted to the sorts of objects, properties, and relations described in the physical sciences. Rather, he includes God among those causes, and he is careful to extend the worldly properties to which we are "attuned" by Gefühl as "spiritual" and not only "sensible." Still, he endorses the dual transcendental role of mere causes. Our discourse-internal norms of meaning, reference, and truth are tethered to the world itself only because states of the world served as the merely causal occasions for our acquisition of those norms. But this worldly constraint is necessarily a discourse-*external* constraint—one that guides our acquisition of norms "from without," and not as any kind of discourse-internal relation to nonnormative givens. Moreover, while this discourse-external causal constraint on our conceptual system of meaning, reference, and truth explains how a purely "syntactic" system can be genuinely world-involving, the norms constitutive of the syntactic system can themselves be explained in terms of their arising from discourse-external, nonnormative, and merely causal relations we bear to our environment.

5.4 Preller, Hector, and Sellarsian Coherentism

What differentiates Preller's story from Hector's, therefore, is not the account of our ordinary perceptual relation to the world. Both, I think I have shown, hew closely to the Sellarsian approach. Rather, what principally differentiates them is that Hector thinks that a Sellarsian approach to the ordinary perceptual relation to the world evinced in our ordinary discourse is sufficient to account for the perceptual relation to God evinced in our theological discourse, while Preller denies this. Preller's apophaticism can be diagnosed by Hector's lights as motivated by a kind of "essentialist correspondentism." Preller is an "essentialist" insofar as he thinks that what is fundamentally real about an object is an idea-like essence that stands at a remove from that which one experiences.[95] As we saw, Preller takes the idea-like essence of an object to be the syntactical role it plays in God's "language," which stands at a remove from the empirical significance of objects in our language by an analogical relation of proper proportionality. While he is not a correspondentist about our ordinary discourse, Preller counts as a correspondentist about our theological discourse. He holds that the capacity of our agent intellect to make the sensible world intelligible by a metaresponsive reflection on the "material moves" involved in our language learning is "adequate" for our purposes in this life. In that respect, his account of ordinary experience is just like Hector's and "noncorrespondentistic" in the same sense that Hector claims for himself. In ordinary experience, we do not require any privileged access to the "essences" of things in order to know them "adequately."

But Preller also holds that our syntactical system requires a privileged access to essences—a privileged access to the syntax of God's own self-knowledge and knowledge of creation. Such access requires that our agent intellect acquire the capacity to derive the intelligibility of the divine language from a sufficient understanding of its "material moves"—the appropriate stimulus conditions for the correct application of its terms. To understand the causal impacts on our agent intellects made by God and creation in such a way as to yield a syntactic system that corresponds to God's own syntax would be to possess the *revelatory* knowledge shared by God and

---

95. Hector, *Theology without Metaphysics*, 12.

the beatified *in patria*. Such a conceptual system of revelation was exemplified in Christ and is made available to us through the church's initiation of its members into the language of *sacra scriptura*.[96] What makes Preller an apophatic theologian in Hector's sense is his claim that we cannot without an idolatrous equivocation take ourselves to be capable of intentionally *using* revelatory concepts and thereby meeting the correspondence requirement. We can only mention words by infused faith—a faith reminiscent of children who, when still learning the stimulus conditions in which they are disposed to say "red" in the presence of red objects, are not yet *using* the concept of red.

On the face of it, we should take Preller to be a prime candidate for Hector's brand of "therapy." That therapy sought to render EC optional by offering what he described as an *alternative* account of ordinary concept use to the sort offered in EC. Interestingly, however, Hector's account of ordinary concept use is very much the same sort of account as Preller's. So if Preller already endorsed the same sort of view that Hector proposes, what accounts for Preller's insistence on apophaticism over against Hector's provision for cataphaticism? The answer lies in a difference in Preller's apparent conviction that the merely causal stimulus conditions out of which our norms of theological discourse emerge are insufficient to give rise to the metaresponsive dispositions constitutive of those norms. In other words, they disagree about whether the below-the-line conditions required for us to form an above-the-line perceptual relation to God have been or can be satisfied in this life. This amounts to a difference in the "reductive" bit of the transcendental story of a Sellarsian approach. Hector thinks that an account of ordinary perception can accommodate our perceptual relation to God insofar

---

96. Preller, *Divine Science*, 232.

as we can plug God into the stimulus-response dispositions that causally influence the shape of our conceptual system in the ordinary way. Preller thinks that the development of the stimulus-response dispositions required to causally influence our conceptual system in the ordinary way are necessarily retarded by the lack of an ideal material relation to God in this life. The language of revelation, therefore, has to be understood as evincing a conceptual system that *would* emerge from the proper material relation to God but that we now possess in advance of having sufficiently mastered the material moves on which it is founded and which are required to make it intelligible as *our* conceptual system. Through the infusion of faith and the Spirit's guidance of the church's pedagogy, we learn the conceptual system of revelation as a second first language, but one that cannot be fully assimilated into our first first language because it is founded on a wider base of causal relations to God and the world.[97]

What could adjudicate between Preller's apophaticism and Hector's cataphaticism? Is our theological discourse genuinely God-involving because our below-the-line causal relations to God have given rise to our theological concepts in the ordinary way, or is it genuinely God-involving only because God affords a special provision of grace to initiate us into the material moves of a language we do not (yet) understand? Which story of causal influence accounts for the possibility of meaningfulness, intentionality, and truth in our God-talk? Neither. The trouble lies not with a particular story about the causal constraint on a syntactical system but with the fact that the sort of causal constraint required is a *merely* causal constraint. In their endorsement of the Sellarsian approach, each of these stories is merely

---

97. For a parallel treatment of the analogy of learning conceptual systems with the acquiring of a second language in terms of one's native language, see Alasdair MacIntyre, *Whose Justice? Which Rationality?* (Notre Dame, IN: University of Notre Dame Press, 1988), 375ff.

a different way of instantiating the "problem of friction" that I have characterized as constitutive of direct realist versions of Coherentism.

Direct realist Coherentisms, you may recall, are accounts whose relating of norm to nature in perceptual experience evinces a "two-aspect" Kantianism insofar as they identify the normative space of reasons with a distinctively human way of responding to the world and account for the world-involving character of human norms, and ultimately normativity itself, in nonnormative terms. Direct causal relations therefore enable the world itself to tether and shape our norms but without allowing these nonnormative causal relations to be directly internalized as the content, the ostensive referents, or the epistemic standards of our concepts. The problem, however, is that when we imagine the division of labor between norm and nature in this way, it becomes impossible to conceive of our concepts as capable of putting us in touch with the world at all. Two thought experiments help bring out this worry.

First, suppose that in my perceptual experiences of the world the coordination of the causal and normative dimensions are functioning just as the two-ply Coherentist envisions: our immediate environment is just as we ordinarily assume it to be, so that when in the presence of a table, my sensory systems prompt me to think and act with the relevant discursive output—the word or concept *table*. But we might equally well suppose that this very same system of norms has arisen not out of any causal relation to tables, but out of an entirely different sort of underlying stimuli. Our conceptual thinking could equally well be just as it is even if we (or perhaps even our entire discursive community) were in fact free-floating brains being kept alive by a mad scientist in an external environment that consists of a vat of chemical soup. We might suppose in such a case that the causal mechanism that connects our observational thinking to our environment is one consisting in the molecular effects of the chemical soup on our neocortices and patterns of electrical stimulation with the scientist's probe. While the conceptual content would remain identical in both this situation and the one we ordinarily assume,[98] the actual objects in the external world from which such content arises in each case would differ radically. In the ordinary scenario, the relevant object causally corresponding to our observational concept—what that concept is "about"—is a table, while in the mad-scientist scenario it is not a table but a probe or a chemical reaction. Despite the difference between the soupy environment and the environment we ordinarily suppose ourselves to inhabit, the patterning of our purely causal responses to our environment might well be identical in both instances.

This scenario shows that the same dispositional response patterns that externally guide a normative framework can be equally well generated by very different configurations of reality (as illustrated by the scientism of the Sellarsian story, the eschatological ideal in Preller's story, and the trajectory of the "Spirit" in Hector's story). Nor is this a merely "epistemological" worry, since what is at stake is not primarily the question of whether I could have any genuine *knowledge* of tables but rather whether it is possible for me to know what table-talk *means*, or what it could mean for such talk to be *true*, or how such talk could succeed in *referring to* or being *about* tables.

We can consider a second thought experiment that establishes the same point from a slightly different direction, one McDowell draws from Michael Dummett.[99] He asks us to imagine an alien world whose inhabitants possess an external environment in every respect

---

98. That is, the two cases exhibit a type-identity both with respect to dispositional response patterns and with respect to their patterns of governance by discursive norms.

99. John McDowell, "Motivating Inferentialism," in *The Engaged Intellect* (Cambridge, MA: Harvard University Press, 2009), 296, and drawing upon Dummett's *Frege: Philosophy of Language* (Cambridge, MA: Harvard University Press, 1973), 295ff. I've modified the illustration slightly in service of the point at issue.

like the one we inhabit. Furthermore, the denizens of this world possess a behavioral repertoire of linguistic moves and transitions in the social practice of holding one another accountable that exactly resembles ours, with one crucial difference. For them, the entire framework of discursive norms (type-identical to ours to the minutest detail) is governed by a further metabelief that we do not have—namely, the belief that the normative system of discourse in question is precisely meant to be a game and nothing more. That is, the sole distinguishing feature between their social-practical lives and ours is that they do not intend any of what they do to point to anything outside the game of holding one another accountable for discursive activities. There is for them simply no point to playing the game external to the game itself.

Thus, whereas *we* take up our normative framework of linguistic moves and transitions with the intention of asserting things about the way the world is external to our norms and informing one another about it, they have no such aims. On the two-ply account, an alien's thought or utterance of "here is a table" would involve mind-external tables in just the same way ours does. But unlike us, they never intend to predicate any meanings of tables or refer to tables or assert any truths about tables. They are concerned not with tables but with keeping track of patterns of usage that deploy the word or concept *table*, and what matters exclusively for them is the normative status of the discursive players and not how anything stands outside the game. Whereas the mad-scientist scenario reveals the inability of a two-ply account of empirical content to track with mind-external objects in the way we ordinarily presuppose, the alien scenario reveals such accounts to imply the irrelevance of object-involvement to our concept use altogether. Either scenario, however, suffices to show that what I have called a "merely causal" explanation of how mind-independent objects figure into thought and speech is incoherent.

Such an account leaves us without the possibility that our thought and speech track with the world.

5.5 Conclusion

Despite their opposition along the theological axis of apophaticism or cataphaticism, the accounts offered by Preller and Hector fail for the very same reason, one rooted ultimately not in matters of theological substance but only in their mutual commitment to the Sellarsian approach to the structure of ordinary perception. While something similar can be said for Marion and Alston—they fail not on any interesting theological grounds but only because of their respective commitments to Givenism—that fact is exhibited with a touch more irony in Preller's and Hector's Coherentism. In his attempt to circumscribe the empirical significance of our conceptual system, Preller's analysis implies that perhaps even God is in the end a "man-angel"—the possessor of a syntactical system in principle incapable of directing us on what that system purports to be "about."

Hector, for his part, paradoxically offers us a therapeutic proposal that not only fails to dissolve the ontotheological problem—the problem of how our concepts can refer us to God—but democratizes that problem, making it difficult to see not only how our concepts can intentionally refer us to God but how they can refer us to reality as a whole. We seem to be thrown back not merely on an apophatic account of theological discourse but on an "apophatic" account of discourse per se—an unintelligible account of the objective purport of our intentional relations to the world. In that case, the therapeutic cure turns out to be worse than the disease, since we lose touch not only with God but with the world as well.

PART III

Toward a Theological Empiricism

6

McDowell's Naturalized Platonism as a Minimal Empiricism

In part 2, I showed how McDowell's deconstruction of the problem of perception can function as a wide-ranging critique of the theorizing that Christian philosophers and theologians have taken up to make sense of our perceptual relation to God. Much contemporary theological thinking about the structure of intentionality in virtue of which what we think, say, and do manages to be about God turns on a prior commitment to one of the poles in the vicious oscillation between Givenism and Coherentism. More particularly, contemporary theological debates about whether to construe the perceptual grounds of such intentionality in apophatic or cataphatic terms turn out to be nonstarters. They fail to present us with a coherent candidate for an account of religious experience whose theological merits we might then go on to evaluate.

6.1 A Minimal Empiricism

Thus far, I have been focusing attention on the critical dimension of McDowell's views, his rejection of the mutually motivating oscillation between Givenism and Coherentism, seeing them as incoherent ways of denying the necessarily fitting and frictional intentional relation between our thoughts and the layout of reality. The incoherence of both poles of the vicious oscillation uncovers the fact that, at a minimum, our ordinary conception of experience requires us to hold together, on the one hand, a proper fittingness between our perceptual intake and the normative concepts by way of which we are responsive to that intake in what we think, say, and do and, on the other hand, a proper friction between our perceptual intake and the world. To say that in experience we are capable of taking in the world in such a way that we think, say, and do can (but need not always) successfully direct us on the world and that in experience the world itself determines the correctness or incorrectness of what we think, say, and do is not to espouse a theory. Rather, it merely restates a trivial truism about experience—on the order of "bachelors are unmarried." It reminds us of a triviality that we cannot sensibly deny, and each pole of the oscillation is an object lesson about the sort of nonsense we fall into when we attempt to deny it.

The oscillation itself thus functions for McDowell as a criterion for a minimal empiricism—a minimally required commitment to fit and friction without which we lapse back into the oscillation. To avoid the problem of perception is thus not a matter of solving any prior philosophical problem or giving a philosophical *explanation* of how it is possible for our human perceptual capacities to deliver the world to thought and to find in it reasons to think this or say that or do the other. It is instead simply to give an analysis of what we must minimally affirm to properly fix the notion of "human perceptual capacities" in the first place as a capacity for the conjunction of fittingness and friction that Givenism and Coherentism only manage to disjoin (thereby failing not only to explain such a capacity but also to locate a coherent explanandum in the first place).[1]

6.1.1 Fit, Friction, and a Minimal Empiricism

So what conception of the logical inseparability of fit and friction are Givenists and Coherentists nonsensically attempting to deny? Coherentism affirms the fittingness between our empirical concepts and empirical content by refusing the idea that the world's bearing on us in experience furnishes us with nonconceptual mental content that we then somehow convert or incorporate into the normative context of our system of concepts. But in so doing, it denies that empirical thinking can put us in touch with the world at all, since it forces us to understand the world either as a nonconceptual domain that serves as a causal determination external to the reasons we might have to think, say, or do anything or as reducible to our own socially constructed system of concepts and attitudes. Givenism, on the other hand, affirms the friction between our empirical concepts and the empirical content afforded by the world itself by allowing us to internalize the world's immediate impacts on us, allowing them to function as an imposition on our thinking from the side of the world outside the domain of thought. But in doing so, it denies the irreducibly norm-governed character of our observational thinking as a space of reasons by supplying it with a form of mental content

---

1. For a helpful illustration of the distinction between an analysis and explanation, see Wilfrid Sellars, *Empiricism and the Philosophy of Mind*, intro. Richard Rorty and study guide by Robert Brandom (Cambridge, MA: Harvard University Press, 1997), 29–32, §9.

alien to the space of reasons constitutive of our concepts, beliefs, and judgments.[2]

The oscillations between Givenism and Coherentism make nonsense of our observational thinking by affirming either a fit between perceptual content and belief content incapable of securing friction with the world (Coherentism) or else a friction with the world incapable of securing a fit between perceptual content and belief content (Givenism). To bring this oscillation to rest would *at a minimum* require that we hold together the friction that Givenism supplies with the fittingness that Coherentism supplies. Such a minimal empiricism would thus involve a single unified understanding of experience that holds onto *both* that which Coherentism affirms about the normative character of fittingness between perceptual content and belief content without thereby denying friction between perceptual content and the layout of reality itself, *and* that which Givenism affirms about the friction between perceptual content and the layout of reality itself without thereby denying the normative character of fittingness between perceptual content and belief content. Each pole of the oscillation, it would seem, possesses not merely a half-truth, but half of a logical or grammatical *truism* regarding the notion of perceptual experience. If we are to make any sense of the idea that in experience the world as it is anyway, whatever anyone happens to think about it, somehow directly presents itself to us in a manner capable of entering into thought, both bits must be coherently coordinated into a single picture.

In order to avoid the incoherence arising from a denial of friction, the Coherentist must acknowledge with the Givenist that our norms of observational thinking are constrained by the world external to

2. John McDowell, *Mind and World*, 2nd ed. (Cambridge, MA: Harvard University Press, 1996), 8–9.

thought not merely causally but by our capacities to receive and internalize its impacts on us and incorporate them into our normative thinking. And in order to avoid the incoherence arising from the denial of fit, the Givenist must acknowledge that the form of mental content the external world gives to thought is susceptible of such internalization and incorporation—not ill-suited to the normative character of thought. On McDowell's diagnosis, both the Givenist and the Coherentist are prevented from acknowledging the relevant neglected dimension of experience by having taken on board the same faulty assumption.

The assumption in question is that the world itself—the layout of reality independent of anything we think or say about it (if it exists at all)[3]—must be a *nonconceptual* reality, a domain that does not intrinsically possess the sort of normative character we find in it.[4] Therefore, either we must deny that our experience of the world is intrinsically conceptually structured, or, if it is, we must take our experience of it as so structured as to be ultimately grounded in a function of human thought rather than in the world itself. This assumption, moreover, is itself constitutive of the problem of perception; it is what generates the very philosophical puzzlement to which Givenism and Coherentism address themselves as responses. Once we assume that a reality that exists independently of all exercises of human conceptual capacities is itself inert of any intrinsically normative structure, we can rightly come to be puzzled about how a reality *like that* could possibly inform or justify our observational concepts. But if the layout of reality itself is

3. Insofar, of course, as what we have in view is not itself constituted by what we think or say. The point of identifying "the world" with the world independent of exercises of human conceptual capacities, however, is twofold. First, it is to stress that on an exhaustive inventory of what there is, conceptually constituted realities name only a subset (indeed, a relatively small subset) of that inventory. Second, it is to emphasize that the layout of reality external to our exercises of conceptual capacities is in some sense more fundamental than those exercises themselves.
4. McDowell, *Mind and World*, 9.

nonconceptual, then it *could not* inform or justify our observational concepts—the very idea is impossible, and the attempt to entertain it results in nonsense.

The engine that gets the problem of perception going, therefore, is the idea that the empirical world itself is disenchanted or intrinsically inert of meaning and value. If, as we have seen, the presumption of disenchantment prevents Givenism and Coherentism from holding fit and friction together, thereby making nonsense of experience, then a minimal empiricism must deny that assumption. McDowell's claim is that the minimal affirmation required to get us off the seesaw and return us to our ordinary and trivial conception of experience—one that includes both the fittingness of our thought with the content of experience and the friction of that content with the world—is the affirmation of a naturalized platonism.[5]

The purpose of this chapter, therefore, will be to articulate the sense in which a naturalized platonism counts as a minimal empiricism—a reminder of the conception of experience that we already trivially know. McDowell's naturalized platonism supplies us with an analysis of what has gone missing in the Christian philosophers and theologians discussed in earlier chapters—what they have forgotten in their failed attempts to make sense of our perceptual relation to God. Insofar as a naturalized platonism articulates a minimal empiricism, we should take it to be a minimal criterion by which to assess what counts as a *candidate* for a theology of religious experience. With that criterion in place, we can ask whether it is possible to articulate a theology that meets it. I take up this latter question in the final chapter. For now, the task is to establish the criterion itself by setting forward McDowell's conception of a naturalized platonism.

5. Ibid., 91.

6.1.2 Naturalized Platonism as a Minimal Empiricism

Rather than seeing the problem of perception as confronting us with an impossibility—the impossibility of conjoining fit and friction on a disenchanted conception of the world—philosophers have mistaken that impossibility for a theoretical challenge: a call to articulate how a nonconceptually constituted world *could* constrain our normative empirical thinking so as to establish such thinking as directed on the world. On pain of acquiescing to an intolerable mysteriousness about how our thought manages to put us in touch with reality at all, philosophers have been forced to address themselves to the challenge either by positing some form of nonconceptual content by which we internalize the nonconceptual bearing of the world on us (Givenism) or by coordinating our conceptual thinking to a nonconceptually constituted reality without any recourse to such nonconceptual content (Coherentist realism). Or, conceding the nonconceptualism about a mind–independent reality but wishing to escape the pressures of the challenge, they deny that there *is* any such thing as a mind–independent reality, anything external to human conceptual activity (Coherentist phenomenalism).

In order to secure the necessary friction between the world itself and the content of experience that it impresses upon us, we must say (contra Coherentist phenomenalism) that there is a mind–independent world, but in order to secure the proper fit between the sort of thing we can experience and the sort of thing that we can think, say, and do, we must suppose (contra Givenism) that what that world gives to us in experience is *conceptual* content. Finally, if the world's imparting of conceptual content is to supply the particular *sort* of fiction required to establish our thoughts as directed on or about the world, then we must hold (contra Coherentist realism) that being furnished with such conceptual content does not tether us to reality in a merely causal way but constitutes a direct presentation of reality itself, a way of internalizing the world's own conceptual structure.

Thus, in order to escape the oscillation and to make sense of our observational thinking, we must regard as a trivial truism that reality itself possesses a conceptual structure, a structure that does not depend on any human exercise of conceptual capacities but imposes itself on us in experience. This way of picturing the relation between the world's impacts on us and our empirical thinking involves a kind of platonism that allows us to sidestep the problem of friction that renders Coherentism unintelligible insofar as it both admits of a mind-independent reality and construes that reality as an intrinsically rational order.[6] Such a platonism also allows us to sidestep the problem of fit that renders Givenism unintelligible, insofar as it implies that the content of an experience can be *identical* with the layout of reality. If reality itself has a conceptual structure, then the sort of thing that is the case—a state of the world—can also be the sort of thing that one thinks. If experience makes the form of the world directly available to the normative form and rational relations of our thinking, then the world independent of our thought must nevertheless exhibit the normative form and rational relations with which our thinking is capable of resonating.

Such a view succeeds in avoiding the problem of fit, however, insofar as it is capable of affirming (contra Givenism) that the conceptual capacities drawn on in experience are not radically alien to the ordinary conceptual capacities we actually possess and actively exercise in our thinking and judging. If human capacities for

---

6. McDowell restricts his use of "platonism" to a small *p* platonism as a gesture that brackets the question of whether it is in keeping with what Plato himself thought, as well as for the purpose of avoiding association with the sort of view that is ordinarily (and falsely, he thinks) attributed to Plato, which is the idea of the empirical world's conceptual structure as eternally existing abstracta in a heavenly domain of Forms. See Ibid., 77n7.

experiential intake in the broad sense are a species of conceptual capacity—modes of receptivity to presentations of the conceptual structure of reality—then the content given in experience can only succeed in informing and justifying our beliefs and practices if the concepts they make available to us belong to the very same conceptual repertoire we have acquired through our initiation into the language and social practices of a particular human community. What we say in the case of Marion's Givenism is that we can court Givenism not only when the content delivered to thought by our sensory capacities is nonconceptual—not governed by rational norms—but when we imagine that the normative relations implicit in reality that our experience makes available to us fall outside the scope of the rational relations governing *our* frameworks of belief and practice. Conceptual content like that would be just as useless for putting our thinking in touch with the world as a nonconceptual Given proved to be.

So while the world has to be conceptually structured if it is to be conveyed to us in experience as the sort of thing we can think, the concepts it conveys to us in experience also have to be "the sort of thing we can also, for instance, judge" if we are to avoid the problem of fit.[7] The world's impositions of its own conceptual structure on our thinking can therefore be as incongruous or surprising or novel as you like, but our capacity to receive them and incorporate their incongruity, novelty, or surprisingness into the framework of our empirical thinking depends on the particular forms of intelligibility we have received in the various forms of social learning to which we are ordinarily subjected.[8] Putting this in Kantian idiom, McDowell thus characterizes a minimal empiricism as a necessary cooperation

---

7. Ibid., 9.
8. The requirement that empirical content be connected with some conceptual mode of presentation can accommodate both novel and finely grained experiences if we allow not only established descriptive concepts in our repertoire but also demonstrative concepts. See John

between "receptivity" and "spontaneity" in which "receptivity does not make an even notionally separable contribution to the co-operation."[9] Our conceptual capacities are paradigmatically those actively exercised in our practical and theoretical judgments. Clearly, experiences are not active exercises of our responsible freedom by which we direct ourselves on the world, but passive ways of suffering the world's impact on us. But if our receptivity to the world is to be capable of making its conceptual structure available to thought, that receptivity must somehow draw on the same capacities operative in judgment.

My *seeing* my cup as red is therefore not identical to my *taking* the cup to be red, *claiming* that it is red, or even *supposing* that it is red. My experience passively saddles me with a form of conceptual content that I can exploit as the content of my takings, claimings, and supposings. But it is also entirely possible that while the cup presents itself to me as red in my experience of it, I for whatever reason refrain from exploiting that content in any judgments or actions and fail to make any *use* of what the experience nevertheless has made available to me. The difference between S's experiencing that X is F and S's taking X to be F is the difference between our being merely or unreflectively aware of X and our raising that awareness to reflective consciousness in some way.[10] To respect both points—that my experiential intake has to involve operations of my conceptual capacities while also being a passive way of taking in the world's own meanings—we must at a minimum say that the very conceptual capacities we exercise in our judgments are passively and

McDowell, "Singular Thought and the Extent of Inner Space," in *Subject, Thought and Context*, ed. Philip Pettit and John McDowell (Oxford: Clarendon, 1986), 137–68.

9. McDowell, *Mind and World*, 9.

10. See McDowell, "The Logical Form of an Intuition" and "Avoiding the Myth of the Given," in *Having the World in View* (Cambridge, MA: Harvard University Press, 2009), 23–43, 256–72.

involuntarily drawn into operation by the world's bearing on us in experience.

This emphasizes the other side of the identity claim already canvassed: the way the world is in itself must be identical to the sort of thing *we* can think.[11] But who are "we"? The conceptual capacities evinced in the variety of human communities of discourse and social practice are irreducibly diverse. This, however, does not imply a Coherentist constructivism, according to which there are many different worlds, or an indirect realist Coherentism, according to which there is only one world with many different conceptual veils that mediate between it and us. Neither view presents us with anything that can be coherently conceived as an option. Instead, we must suppose that there are many differing ways of being perceptually receptive to the intrinsic intelligibility of the very same world. In other words, there is a single unbounded space of reasons—the layout of reality itself—that our sensory capacities make available to us, but different communities and individuals are capable of receiving and responding only to those reasons afforded by the capacities for resonating reality that have been conferred upon them by their initiation into that space. It follows not only that our conceptual learning is a necessary condition for taking in the world's intrinsic meaning and incorporating it into our active thinking, but also that it prevents us from taking in some features of the world's meaning that are nevertheless there to be taken in.[12]

11. John McDowell, "The True Modesty of an Identity Conception of Truth: A Note in Response to Pascal Engel (2001)," *International Journal of Philosophical Studies* 13, no. 1 (2005): 83–88. See also Jennifer Hornsby, "Truth: The Identity Theory," *Proceedings of the Aristotelian Society* 97 (1997): 1–24.

12. Does this conception require that there is only one maximally consistent conceptual framework that succeeds in getting the world right? The proper answer to that question depends on what sort of metaphysics one adopts to make sense of the minimally required notion of the world's own "rational potential." What lies on the world side of the identity claim, in other words, may be *more* particulate than any possible conceptual framework of which we are or could be capable, but not *less* particulate.

Such an initiation involves the full panoply of social learning involved in any human being's ordinary maturation. To thus have "one's eyes opened to reasons at large" is to imagine our natural condition as one in which our animal sensory capacities are susceptible of being *trained* to rationally direct us upon reality.[13] To be capable of acquiring such training is not common to all animals that possess sensory capacities, but it is "second nature" to us—the incorporation of our sensory capacities into our conceptual capacities is a distinctively human way of actualizing our animal nature.[14] If the processes of acquiring concepts—learning language, social disciplining and habituating of the body, and so forth—were independent of perceptual capacities to take in the reasons for belief and practice provided by the world, then what the world makes available would remain alien to thought, a conceptualist version of Givenism.

It is incoherent to deny the frictional character of a platonism according to which the world imposes its own rational demands on our beliefs and practices such that reality itself serves as a standard of correctness for what we think, say, and do. But it is equally incoherent to deny a naturalism of fittingness according to which the vast cultural diversity of things that we actually think, say, and do are just different ways of actualizing our rational responsiveness to the real and objective demands imposed on us in experience by the very same mind-independent reality. On the other hand, when we affirm this picture—what McDowell dubs a "naturalized platonism"—the intractable difficulties of fit and friction that afflict Givenism and Coherentism simply evaporate. It leaves us with no need for the Coherentist's austerity that denies us the internalizing of the world's direct impact on us in experience, nor for the Givenist's fraudulent

---

13. McDowell, *Mind and World*, 79.
14. Ibid., 84.

donation of any mental content that denies our experiences the form of contact with the world required to directly inform our ordinary contemplative and practical reasoning. Naturalized platonism, therefore, just *is* a minimal empiricism, the trivial truism that we cannot deny on pain of falling back into the oscillation.

We have thus extrapolated two constituents constituting a minimal empiricism from an attempt to avoid the incoherence of the oscillation—the platonist conception of our perceptual friction with reality and the naturalness of perceptual fit between the concepts imposed by reality and our receptivity to them via conceptual capacities that are second nature to us, acquired in an ordinary upbringing. But having done this, we can further specify what this minimal empiricism involves simply by exploring its logical entailments. Like the wider notion of a naturalized platonism itself, the purpose of such an exploration is not discovery but therapeutic reminder: to further unmask some putatively controversial philosophical theses about perception as pseudophilosophical nonsense and deflate others as philosophically sophisticated restatements of what we have no need of philosophers to tell us—trivialities scarcely worth making explicit were it not for those so confused as to entertain their denial.

6.2 Object-Dependent Meaning

A minimally empiricist platonism, McDowell claims, implies that the world's conceptual structure must be counted among the potential *ways* or *modes* in which mind-independent objects themselves are directly presented to us.[15] The ways the world can be can inform the ways that we think about it precisely because the empirical

15. See John McDowell, "De Re Senses," *Philosophical Quarterly* 34, no. 136 (1984): 283–94.

content of our observational judgments can be identical in form to the layout of the external world—that is to say, that which we think can simply be that which is the case and vice versa.[16] McDowell analyzes this identity of form between the layout of reality and the modes of its presentation to us in experience in terms of Gareth Evans's reading of Frege on the semantic relationship between sense (*Sinn*) and reference (*Bedeutung*)—between the meanings or significances of thoughts, on the one hand, and the mind-external objects, properties, and relations to which our linguistic expressions of those thoughts refer us, on the other.[17] For any subject S and any mind-independent object in the world X and any property F, it is therefore never the case that S simply perceives X as a "bare presence."[18] Rather, S's perceptual directedness on X always appears to S under some mode of presentation such that S perceives X *as* F.

The traditional reading of Frege takes him to elaborate this idea by saying that senses fix their referents *descriptively*, by specifying criteria to be uniquely satisfied by the objects they purport to be about. But while this is correct, it is insufficient as a semantics for our empirical concepts. Taken by itself, it is consistent with an autonomy of the domain of senses from that of their putative referents. For if the mind-independent world determines whether the criteria laid down

---

16. McDowell, "True Modesty." See also Hornsby, "Truth."
17. Gareth Evans, *The Varieties of Reference*, ed. John McDowell (Oxford: Oxford Univeristy Press, 1982), esp. chs. 1, 6, and 7. Giving the proper analysis to the proposed "sameness" of content required by a minimal empiricism is beyond the scope of this study. For a recent treatment of the question, see Susanna Schellenberg, "Sameness of Fregean Sense," *Synthese* 189, no. 1 (2012): 163–75.
18. We can of course regard ourselves as perceiving objects without *reflecting* on their mode of presentation to us. In seeing my car in the parking lot, I can *take* myself to simply see my car, and not see it *as* silver or compact, etc. But in such cases, while I see the car as all of those things and more, I may nevertheless not exploit the ways in which the car appears to me as a relevant dimension of my seeing. For just this reason our observational reporting often lacks any explicit mention of the ways things appear to us, their mode of presentation, but instead takes the abbreviated grammatical structure of "S perceives X." The point, however, is precisely that this is an abbreviation of the underlying structure of the perceptual act.

by senses are satisfied or not, and thus determines the truth-value of the propositions (that is, the *Gedanke* thoughts, judgments) in which such senses figure, then in those cases in which such criteria are *not* uniquely satisfied by anything in the world, we are in possession of senses (or thoughts) that do not involve objects at all—*Sinne* (senses) without any accompanying *Bedeutungen* (referents, denotations, meanings).[19] But if that which determines the difference between a referring sense and a nonreferring sense is extrinsic to senses themselves, then the Fregean view lands us precisely in the semantic externalism that we found to be incoherent in the our analysis of Coherentism. The very possibility that the modes of presentation under which the world appears to us could be just as they are even if the world itself were radically different than it appears to be demonstrates the impossibility of senses to refer us to the world.

Evans therefore takes Frege to hold not only that senses direct us upon referents as their mode of presentation but also, complementarily, that referents themselves determine the potential range of senses that can properly be predicated of them. Senses, in other words, are *object-dependent*—they are the necessarily world-involving modes of presentation made possible by the existence of the object itself.[20] The notion of a Fregean *Bedeutung* is just a gloss on our ordinary assumptions that the world as it is independently of what anyone thinks or says about it is already intrinsically meaningful and that in our experiences of such a world, the meaning it makes available to us (when we are not misled) is nothing but a way of realizing that meaning in thought.[21]

---

19. Tyler Burge, "Sinning against Frege," in *Truth, Thought, Reason: Essays on Frege* (New York: Oxford University Press, 2005), 213–239.

20. Evans, *Varieties*, 22–32.

21. Jennifer Hornsby, *Simple Mindedness: In Defense of Naïve Naturalism in the Philosophy of Mind* (Cambridge, MA: Harvard University Press, 1997), 202–3. There are complications of Frege interpretation to sort out here. Tyler Burge contests the tradition that he finds in Betrand

That is, when we are not misled, what experience delivers to thought is the world's own meaning, its objective properties and relations under some mode of presentation. A corollary of this sort of direct realism is the way in which it compels us to treat the question of perceptual error (for instance, hallucination and illusion). If a successful perceptual directedness on the world is effected by an object-involving sense, then insofar as we are *misled* by our sensory capacities, we cannot analyze the resulting illusion or hallucination as a mode of presentation under which the world itself actually shows up to thought. Perceptual errors therefore cannot be Fregean senses, identifiable with the conceptual structure borne by the world itself, but rather subjective states that *merely appear* to be so identifiable. Illusions are thus *pretend* or *imitation Sinne,* mental states of a perceiver that *seem to her as if* the content of her thought were a state of the world. In other words, failures of reference imply failures of sense.[22]

Russell and Alonzo Church that identifies a Fregean *Gendanke* "thought" with the act of *thinking* (*Denktat*). See Burge, "Sinning against Frege," in *Truth, Thought, Reason: Essays on Frege* (New York: Oxford University Press, 2005), 228–29. This distinction encapsulates Frege's antipathy toward psychologism, the view according to which the domain of sense is that of the mind-dependent products arising from the distinctively human activity of thinking. Against such a psychologistic view of sense, Frege identifies *Sinne* (senses) as mind-independent objects of *Denktaten* (activities of thinking). On this view, *Gedanken* (thoughts) are therefore clearly not merely products of *Denktaten* (acts of thinking) but ways of being directed on mind-independent *Sinne* (senses). A *Gedanke* is therefore clearly nonidentical with a *Denktat*. But this does not imply any rejection of the identity thesis—that the ways the world can be, its sense, can be identical with the *content* of our activity of thinking. When a *Sinn* comes to be the object of a *Denktat*, the result is a *Gedanke*, a thought whose "meaning" or content—its *Bedeutung*—is identical to some state of the world under some mode of presentation.

22. The reverse, however, is not necessarily the case. That is, we can (and often do) pick out objects by means of senses that are not in fact properties of those objects. The canonical illustration here is my picking out the person across the room holding a martini glass by referring to him as "the guy over there drinking the martini" when in fact the person is drinking water from the martini glass and thus in fact not drinking a martini. Keith Donnellan used such situations in order to distinguish "speaker meaning" from "semantic meaning" wherein the latter seems to fail of reference while the former succeeds; i.e., the designation "the guy drinking the martini," while false, turns out to be sufficient for me to succeed in referring to that guy across the room, even if the words themselves are insufficient. See Keith Donnellan, "Reference and Definite Desscriptions," *Philosophical Review* 75, no. 3 (July 1966): 281–304. In such cases, the semantic content intended by the designation, the object-dependent sense in virtue of which

This gives us two irreducibly different conceptions of the appearances that figure into experience. We are capable both of genuine (or veridical) appearances constituted by the way in which the world itself figures into experience, in which some feature of its conceptual structure is manifest to thought under some mode of presentation, and of *mere* appearances in which the world's bearing on us in some way fails to furnish us with a mode of presentation that reveals the world's conceptual structure as it actually is. This categorical difference in the content of our ordinary experiences has been dubbed a "disjunctive" conception of experience since, for any particular experience we might enjoy, the content of that experience—what in fact appears to us—is always *either* a veridical experience *or* a nonveridical one.[23]

Of course, we are often incapable of distinguishing between genuine appearances and mere appearances, but our inability to tell the difference between them does not show that there is no such distinction between contentful experiences and experiences that only *seem* to be contentful. For whereas the question of what the world conveys to thought in experience is a matter of intentionality—our modes of directedness on reality—the further question of whether

the designation succeeds in referring, is the *entire disjunction* (i.e., "the guy over there who either is drinking the martini or merely appears to be drinking it"). Mind-external objects, we might say, determine not only the modes of direct presentation under which they themselves can appear to us, but also the modes of presentation under which they can *merely appear* to appear to us.

23. John McDowell, "The Disjunctive Conception of Experience as Material for a Transcendental Argument," in *Disjunctivism: Perception, Action, Knowledge*, ed. Fiona Macpherson and Adrian Haddock (Oxford: Oxford University Press, 2008), 376–89; McDowell, "Tyler Burge on Disjunctivism," *Philosophical Explorations* 13, no. 3 (September 2011): 243–55. Recall the distinction between epistemology and intentionality in the previous chapter. We might be tempted to see this as a distinction between "the order of being" and "the order of knowing," but that is not quite right because an appearance indissolubly consists in a relation between a knowing subject and an object whose existence does not depend on the subject. What distinguishes the epistemological matter from the matter of intentionality is rather the distinction between what I can attend to in X's appearance to me and what is *there* to be attended to in that very same appearance.

we are capable of certifying the credentials of those conveyances is a matter of epistemology.[24] So whereas I may not be in the right epistemic position or possess the proper epistemic equipment to *tell* which of the two disjuncts actually obtains in a putative experience and thus may be unable to judge whether what appears to me is a direct mode of world-presentation or only the mere appearance of world-presentation, what has *in fact* transpired is this: *either* that I have become directly aware of some state of the world under some mode of presentation (a genuine appearance) *or* that the world has *not* in fact manifested itself to me in that way but merely appears as if it had (that is, the appearance of a genuine appearance).[25]

The alternative to disjunctivism is what McDowell terms the "highest common factor" analysis, according to which experiences are not merely epistemically ambiguous but *ontologically* ambiguous. In other words, what distinguishes veridical and nonveridical appearances—those that direct us on the world and those that in some way misdirect us—is nothing intrinsic to the character of the experience itself, but rather something above and beyond it. So while my seeing a desert mirage and my seeing a water source in the distance might be sufficiently phenomenologically alike so as to be indistinguishable to me, the highest-common-factor theorist would explain this by saying that these two experiences can be phenomenologically *identical*, while the disjunctivist claims that they are phenomenologically distinguishable but in a way *indiscernible* by the perceiver.

24. John McDowell, *Perception as a Capacity for Knowledge* (Milwaukee, WI: Marquette University Press, 2011).
25. Haddock and MacPherson distinguish beween a disjunctivism about perceptual content ("experiential" disjunctivism) and one about empirical knowledge ("epistemological" disjunctivism) and attribute both to McDowell. See "Introduction: Varieties of Disjunctivism," in Haddock and MacPherson, *Disjunctivism*, 1–34.

While the notion of phenomenological indiscernibility without identity seems opaque at first glance,[26] it is just a restatement of the point about object-dependence in a phenomenological key. The very idea of the world-directedness of experience as the basis for our observational thinking is the idea of being passively saddled with a particular class of Fregean senses—that is, those distinctively *qualitative* modes of presentation under which the world appears to us.[27] But this formulation constitutes a grammatical remark, a trivially necessary assumption about what our experiences make available to thought. As such, it is not motivated by any desire to combat skepticism about perceptual knowledge, but it instead articulates a condition for the possibility of their being any *candidates* for perceptual knowledge at all. Disjunctivism is thus a claim about what must be the case if the world external to thought is the sort of thing that could *potentially* be thought about, not a claim about whether we are *actually* in a proper position to exploit that potentiality in any given instance.[28]

Indeed, if the minimal requirement of fit requires that our receptivity to the conceptual layout of reality depend on conceptual capacities acquired in the course of our ordinary initiation to a particular community's way of responding to and navigating the space of reasons, then we can never exit our normative conceptual frameworks in order to get a "sideways" vantage on our situation and determine which disjunct holds true. But fallibility in this sense does

---

26. For example, does it not clearly flout Leibniz's Law, according to which identicals are indiscernible?

27. I will take up the question of how to properly coordinate the notion of a Fregean sense with an analysis of "qualia" in a moment. For now, the important point is that an analysis of "what it is like" to have an experience divides along disjunctivist lines as *either* the qualitative character of a mode of object-presentation *or* the qualitative character of a pseudothought, the mere appearance of directedness on a Fregean sense.

28. Put another way, the disjunctivist commitment to the nonidentity of phenomenological indiscernibles can be analyzed as a commitment to the actual indiscernibility of the potentially discernible. It therefore implies no denial of Leibniz's Law.

not require us to admit that what experiences themselves convey to us is intrinsically defeasible—that is, insufficient of itself to direct us on reality. To have at one's disposal only the resources made available by one particular way of being impressed by and responsive to the space of reasons is entirely consistent with claiming that while we are capable of perceptual error, we must *also* be capable of genuine appearances that are indefeasible. When we are presented with genuine appearances, the way the world actually is with respect to its intrinsic conceptual structure is identical to the way it appears to us, identical to the sensory mode of presentation under which it appears.[29]

By way of contrast, the alternative conception envisioned by the highest-common-factor analysis has a surface clarity that turns out to be incoherent. For in claiming that our experiences cannot succeed in directing us on the layout of reality in virtue of the intrinsic character of the experience itself, the highest-common-factor theorist is compelled to specify some extrinsic relation that our experiences bear to the world that could distinguish veridical from nonveridical appearances. But any such specification commits us to some version of Givenism or Coherentism. If, for example, we picture the world-directedness of experience as extrinsically determined by a causal relation, then our options reduce to a Givenist or Coherentist version of indirect realism or else the merely causal direct realism of Coherentism. As we have seen, none of these views succeeded in rendering intelligible the very idea of the world-directedness of experience.

Mind-external objects, therefore, along with the various relations and events into which they figure, do not exist in a domain outside the space of reasons, outside the space of possible warrants or

29. John McDowell, "Criteria, Defeasibility, and Knowledge," *Proceedings of the British Academy* 68 (1982): 455–79.

justifications we might have for believing or acting. But while affirming an identity of the meanings and rational relations exhibited by the world, passively conveyed in experience and actively deployed in thought, we need to distinguish them from one another as well. McDowell's affirmation of platonism or conceptual realism as a trivial truism has often been mistaken as a way of rehabilitating idealism,[30] the view that the objects, properties, and relations constitutive of the world are mind-dependent or in some sense purely subjective or mentalistic in character.[31] But the idea is not that the world itself is identical with any individual or collective acts of thinking or with the set of all thoughts—we already explicitly denied the intelligibility of that idea in our rejection of the phenomenalist/idealist version of Coherentism. Instead, the triviality in question is that the world is intrinsically constituted so as to be *thinkable*.[32]

---

30. On such a misreading one is tempted to see McDowell as simply a humanistic version of Bishop Berkeley, one in which the rational constraint on our thinking is supplied by resources internal to our spontaneity, rather than by resources internal to the spontaneity of the divine mind. In "Exorcising the Philosophical Tradition," in *Reading McDowell on Mind and World*, ed. Nicholas H. Smith (New York: Routledge, 2002), 25–57, Michael Friedman plumps for something like this reading when he says that for McDowell "the very idea of experience of the world . . . is itself a product of spontaneity. . . . In this way, the crucial notion of *independence* is, in the end, given a purely coherence-theoretic reading" (52n23). "I do not see," he concludes, "how he [McDowell] has fully rebutted the charge of idealism" (35).

31. One way to get a grip on such a claim is to state it in reductively eliminativist terms: with respect to any object, property, or relation there is or could be, there is nothing more to its reality or substance or being than its being a *mental* object, an object of thinking. The question of whether idealism as such is properly to be understood as a global form of metaphysical "antirealism," is a rather more subtle matter than is commonly acknowledged. As Andrew Cortens points out, whether one is or isn't inclined to affix the label "antirealist" to a position often depends on whether one takes up a perspective internal or external to the position itself. Idealists such as Berkeley, for example, insists that he is a realist, that idealism is just what realism amounts to, and thus to deny him "realism" from a perspective external to his views is to beg the question against him. See Andrew Cortens, *Global Anti-Realism: A Metaphilosophical Inquiry* (Boulder: Westview , 2000), 21–24.

32. McDowell, *Mind and World*, 25ff. If McDowell disavows idealism in one sense—that of denying a mind-independent reality—he nevertheless embraces it in another sense. See McDowell, "Conceptual Capacities in Perception," in *Having the World in View*, 143. That is, he thinks that "the world itself is indeed structured by the form of judgment." This is not to *identify* thought with the world, but rather to claim that thought is *at home* in the world, suited to it by a kind of structural *conveniens* or "fittingness."

6.3 First and Second Nature

To say that reality is conceptually structured so as to be thinkable is merely to acknowledge that the entire domain of reality existing independently of human thought confronts our receptive capacities with *potential* reasons for belief or action, reasons that our spontaneity makes us capable of actualizing in the formation of a judgment or the initiating of an intentional action. We must therefore conceive of our receptivity as our capacity for passively conveying the rational structure of the world to thought, a form of awareness of the world's bearing on us that makes some subset of its features (the directly perceptible ones) *available* for us to actively exploit by way of our rational responses to it. A genuine appearance is just a Fregean, object-dependent sense whose bearing on my sensory receptivity has not (or not yet) prompted me to any active exercise of contemplative or practical thinking.

When, for example, I walk down the hall from my office, there are countless features of the world, countless qualitative *Sinne* (object-dependent senses), that present themselves to me as I pass by—the patterns on the carpet, the relative change in ambient temperature, and innumerable other details—any of which *could have* prompted me to think (or say) that X is F or to attempt a bodily performance of A-ing.[33] The modes of presentation under which such objective features

33. A prompting, note, need not be a prompting to believe that X is F or a prompting to attempt an action X; it can also be a prompting to determine whether or not we are being prompted to judge that X is F or to attempt X-ing. For example, in the proper circumstances, seeing that you've undertaken a motion as if to throw something at my face might rationally require that I raise my hand to block or catch it. When my response to the motion you have made is unreflective or "automatic," it is nevertheless a *rational* response to what the situation itself demanded of me, as indicated by the fact that, if asked, I can refer to your having made the relevant motion—the event itself—as my *reason* for raising my hand, as manifesting an intrinsically *normative* (and not "merely causal") prompt for me to react in the way I did. But to be presented with such a prompt need not automatically yield my forming a belief or an intention to act. Knowing that you often merely feign throwing things at me precisely because you find it funny to prompt my bodily reactions, I might take your motion not to be the

of the world directly appear to me, we might say, are not necessarily prompts for my belief or action but *opportunities* to be so prompted, *potential* rational affordances for the relevant beliefs or actions.[34] My experience presents me with the world's own rational potential *calling* on my rational capacities. But I need not take advantage of the rational potential it affords me in experience; I need not respond to its call. We do not—and as a rule we cannot—*notice* or *attend to* most of what an experience rationally affords us. Ordinarily, what we actually pick out in our observational thinking—what our experience in fact makes available for our practical or contemplative judgments—is only a minute fraction of what is in fact *there* to be noticed, attended to, or picked out of our passive receptivity to the world.[35] The world's

undertaking of an intention to throw something at me, but the mere appearance of one. If so, the situation might prompt me not to belief or action, but to a reflective deliberation about belief or action. That is, it might prompt me to *entertain* the practical judgment that *seems* to be prompted by the situation itself, a stance that makes possible either my withholding that judgment or following through on it.

34. For a gloss on the difference between potential affordances and actualized affordance as the Kantian distinction between the conceptual but nondiscursive or nonpropositional content of "intuition" and its actualization as the discursive or propositional content of a "judgment," see McDowell, "Avoiding the Myth of the Given," in *Having the World in View*, 256–72. This represents an important emendation from the account of the conceptual content of perceptual experience in *Mind and World*, wherein the distinction between the "thinkability" of the world and the actualization of the world's thinkability in thought is not fully carried through to a corresponding distinction between the merely articulable content of an experience and the actually articulated content of a perceptual judgment.

35. McDowell distinguishes further between the sorts of conceptual affordances given in an experience itself and those the experience makes noninferentially available. Whereas experience itself strictly speaking involves only that content that arises by "drawing on conceptual capacities associated with concepts of proper and common sensibles," the content of an experience can also noninferentially draw into operation our recognitional capacities and thus passively "wring" from us more than what is strictly speaking manifest to experience ("Avoiding the Myth," 260). Thus, for example, the fact that a bird is before me might figure into the content of my visual experience insofar as the concept of a bird is irreducibly associated with concepts associated with sight (a proper sensible) and the common sensibles accessible to seeing (e.g., shape).In other words, insofar as the unity of significances given by what appears in my visual field actualizes my concept of a bird, then the content of my seeing is a bird. But in cases when I further recognize that the bird is a cardinal and you do not possess the concept of a cardinal, our experience nevertheless has the same content. My experience noninferentially reveals to me that what I see is a cardinal while your experience does not further draw passively into operation any such recognitional capacities. See McDowell, "Avoiding the Myth," 259–60.

genuine appearance, its direct presentation under some sensory mode of presentation, is thus its standing poised for our moral-practical and contemplative responses to its rational affordances. The Aristotelian distinction between a first and second potentiality can help elucidate how we acquire the conceptual capacities that allow us to be afforded the world's own rational potential in some ways and not others.[36]

Consider Regis, the dog (half husky and half wolf) I had in high school from the time he was a puppy well into his adult life. As a puppy, Regis was unable to do anything on command—he could not sit, speak, shake, or perform other tricks. However, as a perfectly normal and healthy puppy, Regis was capable of *acquiring* the ability to do all of these things. In this respect, Regis differs from a rock or an insect, neither of which is capable of, for instance, moving one of its parts on my command. Unlike rocks or insects, Regis as a puppy had the *potential* to acquire the capacity to act in that way. Such unrealized potential is what we can call a first potentiality. Now consider Regis after the first year of his life, during which time I trained him to sit, lie down, bark, and shake by issuing the requisite commands. In so doing, Regis fulfilled a first potentiality—he made

So whereas the conceptual content afforded by a perceptual experience is given in intuition (see previous footnote), an experience may also rationally afford or make available to us more than what is immediately given in an intuition by actualizing recognitional capacities alongside or in addition to perceptual capacities. At the moment, I mean my talk of rational affordances to include *both* the conceptual content of experience sensu stricto (the concepts associated with proper and common sensibles) *and* the conceptual content that experiences can noninferentially reveal to us by way of our recognitional capacities. This distinction between what an experience conceptually *presents* to us and what further content that presentation might conceptually *reveal*, while irrelevant for present purposes, will become important when we consider whether there is any such thing as "value intuition"—i.e., whether value concepts are immediately given as proper or common sensibles of "outer" experience or whether outer experience instead merely puts us in a position to noninferentially recognize value. Part of what is at stake here is whether it makes any sense to say that our perception of value has a distinctively qualitative dimension analogous to the proper and common sensibles associated with, e.g., sight, smell, hearing, etc.

36. See *De Anima*, II.5 (417a22–30). My reading of this section is heavily influenced by M. F. Burnyeat, "De Anima II.5," in *Phronesis* 47, no. 1 (2002): 28–90; and Burnyeat, *Aristotle's Divine Intellect* (Milwaukee, WI: Marquette University Press: 2008).

the transition from merely *potentially* having the capacity to obey those commands to *actually* being capable of obeying them. The training in question facilitated the actualization of his potential to act upon command.

The actualization of Regis's first potentiality to shake—the realizing of his potential brought about by training—can be described in two ways. We can in the first place consider it to be a first actualization: a realizing of the merely potential capacity he had as a puppy to learn how to shake. That is, Regis's actually learning to shake required him to exercise whatever capacities differentiate him from an insect that make him *susceptible* of the training required for him to acquire the ability to shake. In order to realize a potential to shake that he did not yet possess, he had to exercise capacities that he *does* have, such as the ability to respond to what he hears, to move his limbs, and so forth. The realizing of his ability to shake, in other words, is the actualization of the relevant set of first potentialities that *enable* him to shake. But since what is brought about by the exercise of these first potentialities is the acquiring of a capacity that he did not previously possess—the ability to shake—we can also describe what was actually brought about by the exercise of Regis's already possessed first-level capacities (the first actuality of his first potentiality) as equivalent to his having come to acquire a second-level capacity—a second potentiality. For what he acquires by actualizing his first potentialities is precisely a *capacity* to shake, which can be had without the exercise of that capacity. That is, having acquired the capacity, Regis stands *poised* to shake on command, but he does not exercise the capacity until I actually issue the command, at which point his actual ability is fully exercised. His second potentiality is actualized (brought to second actuality) in his reaching out a paw. For Regis to have acquired the ability to shake on command is therefore for him to have a first potentiality to shake on command whose first actuality just is a second potentiality to shake on command that in turn reaches second actuality when he in fact shakes on command.

The difference between the first potentialities and second potentialities involved in Regis's acquiring the capacity to shake by a process of training is the difference between first-level capacities possessed prior to their exercise and second-level capacities that come to be possessed *in the exercise* of first-level capacities—that is, by way of practice, habituation, or training. The acquiring of a first-level capacity—a first potentiality—is thus a two-staged process in which the ability comes to be possessed apart from its first exercise. A dog's capacities to move its limbs or hear, for example, are ordinarily already acquired prior to their first actualization in the dog's very first movements or its registering of auditory stimuli (both of which it acquires in utero). In moving its limbs or registering auditory stimuli, the dog is doing what it was already anyway able to do. But its second-level capacities—its capacities to acquire further capacities by training—require a kind of habituation and practice that is not a two-staged process in which it first acquires the capacity and then exercises it. Rather, as Aristotle has it, our second potentialities are such that "what we need to learn before doing, we learn by doing."[37] The bringing into realization of second potentialities out of first potentialities is, as De Gaynesford helpfully puts it, "instead a single process, one in which it is impossible to extricate implementation of the ability from its achievement, putting the ability into effect from gaining purchase on it. So the term 'habituation' is appropriate, with its related terms 'education,' 'training,' 'breaking in,' 'conditioning.' Unlike a staged procedure with abilities that pre-exist their exercise, there is no expectation of clear temporal boundaries on the

---

37. Aristotle, *Nicomachean Ethics*, trans. Roger Crisp (Cambridge: Cambridge University Press, 2000), book II.1, 23; (1103a–1103b).

habituation process, of signs which decisively mark off the subject's attainment of an ability from their earlier lack of it."[38]

So whereas there was a time when Regis did not possess the capacity to shake upon command (but had only the capacities requisite for acquiring that capacity) and whereas there was a subsequent time at which he clearly *did* possess that capacity, it is difficult to pinpoint precisely when he made the transition from one state to the other. During the period of time in which I was training Regis how to shake—for instance, lifting his paw for him and, once raised, rewarding him with a treat—he regularly both raised his paw independently of my command and failed to raise it upon command. Gradually, however, he honed the coordination of hearing the relevant command ("shake") and making the requisite bodily action (raising the paw) until he became disposed to respond always and only on command.

Having thus crossed whatever threshold of achievement constitutes a mastery of the ability to shake, Regis's possession of that ability thus *became* distinguishable from the use of the ability. While the ability had to be exercised for him to acquire it, it had become so well habituated that he possessed the capacity without requiring any cycle of performance and reward. Apart from and prior to the exercise of his capacity to shake, he remained *poised* to exercise the ability—possessing it in an utterly passive way, such that it could remain unactualized until drawn into operation when his surrounding environment afforded him the proper opportunity (that is, upon hearing my command). As such, his capacity to shake came to exhibit the same two-staged characteristic of his first-level

---

38. Maximilian De Gaynesford, *John McDowell* (Malden, MA: Polity, 2004), 55–56. Mistakenly assuming that one must have a capacity prior to exercising it, on the other hand, generates a puzzle about how it is possible to acquire a "second nature" at all. See David Forman, "Autonomy as Second Nature: On McDowell's Arisotelian Natuarlism," *Inquiry* 51, no. 6 (December 2008): 563–80.

capacities. The effortlessness with which he could shake on command was *as if* he had not acquired it by training but he had it in the same way he had the ability to hear or move his limbs. The "as if" here is important, though, since training in fact *was* required for him to acquire his ability to shake in a way not required of his ability to receive auditory stimuli.[39] Clearly, both capacities are natural to him, in the sense of being ordinary features of a dog's animal life, but we can distinguish Regis's first-natural capacities from the capacities he later acquired: his first natural capacities are first potentialities he has naturally possessed apart from any training whereas his subsequently acquired capacities are second potentialities that he acquired only by training. Nevertheless, once these second potentialities were fully realized they became "second nature" to him, possessed *as if* they themselves were first natural. While actually requiring active habituation via the exercise of the first-natural capacities out of which they emerge, second-natural capacities can be like first-natural capacities in being possessed passively, as abilities that clearly precede their exercise.

6.4 The Rational Affordances of Second Nature

With this Aristotelian distinction between first-natural capacities (first potentialities) and second-natural capacities (first potentialities actualized as second potentialities) in hand, we can return to the construal of human conceptual capacities that McDowell takes to be minimally required to make sense of observational thinking as a

---

39. Of course, a dog's capacity to hear as a first-potentiality is nevertheless also capable of being actualized in a number of second-potentialities, such as being able to discriminate various sorts of auditory stimuli and being afforded the opportunity to respond differently to whatever is picked out by its hearing. Regis's capacity to pick out my command is just one example. But his acquiring of such a capacity is an actualization *of* a capacity—being equipped for auditory stimulation—he had prior to acquiring it.

way of directing us on the world. On the picture thus far, we can only coherently suppose that what we think, say, and do is world-directed—has empirical content—when it actualizes the rational potential made available to us by the world. A genuine thought as opposed to the mere appearance of one—a thought that actually has (rather than only *seeming* to have) something to be about—is therefore one whose content is identical with an object-dependent sense (a neo-Fregean *Sinn*). What we think can be identical with what is in fact the case.[40] But if we must analyze our empirical thinking as a rational response to the reasons that the world stands poised to give us, our responsiveness to reasons *as* reasons, then we must also regard ourselves as *capable* of contemplatively and practically actualizing the world's own meaning, capable of registering the world's own rational potential *as* rational potential. That is, we must assume a kind of identity in form between the world's standing poised to furnish us with the reasons that inform our belief and practices and our ability to receive its rational potential in the sort of way that we could actualize in our reflective or practical judgments. Our actualizing of the world's rational potential implies a prior ability: our ability to stand poised to actualize it. The concept of experience just is the concept of an ability, a capability to become passively receptive to the world's own thinkability.

Thus far, the talk of our ability to receive qualitative modes of presentation under which the rational potential of the world itself appears to us *as* rational potential has been construed as a capacity of our "outer" senses. The world stands poised in a direct *sensory*

---

40. As McDowell puts it, "When one's thought is true, what one thinks *is* what is the case. So since the world is everything that is the case . . . there is no gap between thought, as such, and the world" (McDowell, *Mind and World*, 27). The "as such" hearkens to the disjunctivist qualification implied here—to the extent that one's thought fails to articulate that which is the case (fails of identity with any object-dependent senses), it is not genuinely a thought at all but the mere appearance of one.

presentation for our actualizing of its rational potential. In our seeing, hearing, or tasting (and so forth) X as F or X as desirable for A-ing, X's in fact being F or its in fact being desirable for A-ing can itself rationally require us to believe that X is F or to commence A-ing. We must therefore regard our sensory capacities (seeing, hearing, and the like)[41] as *rational* capacities, qualitative ways of receiving the world's own intelligible form. But the idea that our capacities for outer sense—hearing, seeing, feeling, and so on—are themselves *conceptual* capacities can intuitively strike us as off-key. After all, my three-month-old son Ezra seems incapable of conceptual thinking even while he seems perfectly well capable of a *sensory* awareness of his environment—he can register sounds, visually apprehend objects, and so forth.

The intuition arises from the rather obvious fact that the conceptual receptivity of outer sense is not a first-natural ability, not a first potentiality of our capacities for sensory stimulation by the world. Our sensory systems do not function as operations of conceptual capacities from our infancy, and there is therefore a sense in which the sensory capacities possessed by Ezra are just like those of Regis, my dog. Both Regis and Ezra acquired their capacities of outer sense prior to any exercise of those capacities.[42] The way the world is, moreover, affords both Ezra and Regis opportunities

---

41. There are interesting debates about how many sensory modalities we have and how to enumerate them. See C. A. J. Coady, "The Senses of Martians," *Philosophical Review* 83, no. 1 (1974): 107–25; José Luis Bermúdez, "Categorizing Qualitative States: Some Problems," *Anthropology and Philosophy* 3, no. 2 (1999); and Richard Gray, "On the Concept of a Sense," *Synthese* 147, no. 3 (2005): 461–75. This question, however, is immaterial for establishing a minimal empiricism. A naturalized platonist conception of perceptual experience—the denial of which lands us in nonsense—underdetermines any particular way of enumerating sensory modes of presentation and the qualitative distinctives proper to them. While some proposal on that score may be *false*, therefore, it does not thereby render the very idea of a mode of presentation *incoherent*. I will return to this question as a substantive question about the nature of perception, rather than a matter merely of the grammar of perception, in the final chapter under the heading of whether there are "moral" or "spiritual" sensory modalities—qualitative distinctives proper to moral or spiritual modes of presentation.

to actualize their susceptibility of sensory stimulation in comporting themselves with their respective environments. When presented with the nipple, for example, Ezra has the ability not only to visually discriminate it from the background but also to respond to it by sucking in order to draw milk. The first actualizations of Regis's sensory capacities are likewise capable of directing him on sources of food and eliciting the bodily movements requisite for eating. These are clearly actualizations of first potentialities—exercises of first-natural capacities—insofar as neither Ezra nor Regis required any training in order for their sensory systems to facilitate these respective comportments to the world.[43] Ezra's senses thus afford him the capacity to navigate his environment and to enact his dispositions toward it with intentions to act by, for instance, responding to the presence of the nipple by sucking or smiling and cooing upon hearing his parents' voices (albeit mostly that of his mother). Regis's senses likewise afford him the capacity to navigate his environment by, for example, responding to the smell of meat in the air, marking territory, and so on.

But these are not *rational* affordances in the sense we have been considering, precisely because while Ezra is capable of seeing and feeling the nipple, he does not have the concept of a nipple as something the *meaning* of which includes the demands on his responsible freedom requisite to it—he remains unaware of nipples as supplying normative reasons for believing or doing anything. While the presence of a nipple can give him a reason to believe that there is a nipple before him and while it can further afford him a reason to suck,

---

42. Aristotle puts it thus, "This is clear in the case of the senses, since we did not acquire them by seeing often or hearing often; we had them before we used them, and did not acquire them by using them" (*Nicomachean Ethics*, II.1, 23; 1103b, 4).

43. It is of course possible to be much more nuanced here, insofar as there is a sense in which Ezra needed to *learn* how to properly take the nipple—helping to teach him as well as his mother about how this works is what lactation consultants are for, after all. But such consultants depend on a "sucking reflex" already being in place prior to (and as prerequisite for) such training.

it does not afford him such reasons *as* reasons. Lacking both a rational awareness and the capacity for responsible freedom constitutive of it, he is unable to respond to a nipple as a constituent of the conceptual layout of reality. Ezra's intentions to suck, therefore, are much like the intentions actualized by Regis's sensory orientation to the steak placed in his immediate environment. Even while we recognize that the nipple and the steak might rationally afford Ezra and the dog, respectively, reasons to act (by sucking and masticating, respectively), we also recognize that they are unable to put place their visual presentations in the space of reasons, and neither of them therefore is alive to any normative demands made available to them in their experience.

Our acknowledgment of this is evident from the way in which we use and refrain from using volitives (normative uses of "can," "should," "may," "must"). When Ezra seems uninterested in taking the nipple, I may express my concern by saying, "He should be sucking." So too, when puzzled about why your dog refuses to eat the meat thrown before him, you may think, "He should be eating that!" Contrast those instances with the case of being in the passenger seat of a car and noticing that the driver does not seem to be braking for the upcoming stoplight: "You should stop!" In the cases of Ezra and the dog, my use of "should" is not an expectation that a merely sentient being be alive to any rational affordance imposed by the world, whereas in the case of the stop sign, that is precisely my expectation of the driver. What accounts for the difference is our recognition that babies and dogs are incapable of taking in such reasons by the first actualization of their sensory capacities.

But "incapable" here is ambiguous—it may imply failing to possess a capacity or, more strongly, failing to become capable of possessing it. Whereas dogs are incapable of taking in reasons in the latter, stronger sense, Ezra is only incapable in the former, weaker sense.

Ezra certainly will acquire the capacity to take in reasons if the normal course of human maturation proceeds unimpeded for him.[44] In Ezra's case, the sensory faculties that at first function virtually identically to those of the dog in orienting him to his external environment can gradually *become* responsive to reasons *as* reasons if he receives the proper training.[45] The difference between Ezra and Regis, therefore, is that Ezra is capable of a second potentiality of which Regis is incapable. Whereas Ezra is susceptible of learning to take in reasons and exercise responsible freedom, Regis is no more susceptible of *that* sort of training than an insect is susceptible of learning how to shake.

Learning his first language is central to the form of habituation (cultivation, practice, education) by which Ezra gradually acquires the capacity to take in and respond to reasons *as* reasons. A "natural language," McDowell says, "serves as a repository of tradition, a

44. On the one hand, this qualifying clause allows me to sidestep important and difficult questions about the various ways that the normal process of human maturation might be impeded, such as congenital defect or external damage. On the other hand, the normative conceptions of "normal" and "impediment" implicit in this sort of qualification are sometimes thought to be problematic, either because they involve a kind of "naturalistic fallacy" or because they must ultimately "dehumanize" the disabled. I do not think either represents a prohibitive difficulty in the end, but I cannot argue the case at length here. Suffice it say that against the first sort of objection, a minimal empiricism reveals, if nothing else, that human nature, like nature in general, is either intelligible as intrinsically normatively constituted or not intelligible at all. Against the second objection, the relevant notion of a normal maturation need not imply that it must be actually satisfied in order to reveal any individual to be human, only that it be counterfactually true of any individual that, had her intrinsic capacities for maturation gone unimpeded, she would have been capable of taking in the conceptual structure of the world. See Brian Brock and John Swinton, eds., *Disability in the Christian Tradition: A Reader* (Grand Rapids, MI: Eerdmans, 2012).

45. It is in this sense that Aristotle sees the "appetite" and "desire" that we share with nonrational animals as nevertheless distinctly instantiated in human beings in virtue of their governance by the "rational principle" that marks us out from nonrational animals. "The seat of the appetites and of desire in general, does in a sense participate in principle, as being amenable and obedient to it (in the sense in fact in which we speak of 'paying heed' to one's father and friends, not in the sense of the term 'rational' in mathematics). And that principle can in a manner appeal to the irrational part, is indicated by our practice of admonishing delinquents, and by our employment of rebuke and exhortation generally" (*Nicomachean Ethics*, II.1, 1102b, 18). In other words, human sensory capacities are intrinsically rational in the sense of being *susceptible* of normative relations such as praise and blame, as having functions for which volitive ascriptions are proper.

store of historically accumulated wisdom about what is a reason for what," such that "in being initiated into a language, a human being is introduced into something that already embodies putatively rational linkages between concepts, putatively constitutive of the layout of the space of reason, before she comes on the scene . . . as an already going concern."[46] Unlike the case of Regis, the first actualization of Ezra's sensory capacities results in a gradual growth in his capacity to make the putatively rational linkages that determine what counts as a reason for believing X or for initiating intentions for A-ing. Like Regis's gradual transition from an inability to shake to its becoming second nature, our social and linguistic acquisition of the ability to take in reasons and rationally respond to them is not a two-staged process in which we first acquire the ability and then act on it. It is instead a "single process of learning and doing that has no clear boundaries."[47]

This conception of the first actualization of our outer senses as also and simultaneously their achieving of a second potentiality to navigate the space of reasons is just the Aristotelian way of putting the Kantian point made earlier about the inextricability of our receptivity from our spontaneity. Exercising our conceptual capacities in thinking, saying, or doing only counts as a genuine instance of thinking, saying, or doing when it has the empirical content given in experience (otherwise it is the mere appearance of thinking, saying, or doing), but the empirical content given in experience must be seen as the passive way in which our conceptual capacities are drawn into operation by the impact that the world's own conceptual structure has on us.[48] What the Aristotelian talk of actualizing potentialities can illuminate (and what the Kantian formulation can tend to obscure) is

46. Ibid., 126, 125.
47. DeGaynesford, *John McDowell*, 57.
48. The natural realization of ordinary human perception, in other words, is ineliminably both relational and representational. For a more recent defense of this posture toward perceptual

the necessarily *developmental* and *educative* dimension of the logically necessary interrelation that holds between our spontaneity and receptivity.

6.5 The Training of the Senses

The conceptual capacities we actively exercise in the use of our responsible freedom and passively draw into activation by experience are indissolubly acquired together through the ordinary process of inculturation. Since these second-level potentialities of putatively taking in the world are just ways of actualizing our first-level potentialities, the first-level capacities that facilitate our comportment with the world—our capabilities for sensory intake—are appreciably different from those of nonrational animals, such as dogs. For while Ezra's sensory orientation to the world can now, when Ezra is only three months old, function virtually identically to that of my dog, even now Ezra has the capacity to acquire by training the ability to take in the world, to be initiated into the space of reasons and thereby the space of responsible freedom. Moreover, the ordinary and apparently nonrational first actualizations of his sensory capacities now are radically unlike those of Regis insofar as they are merely nascent steps in the training requisite to his initiation into the space of reasons—early moments in his acquiring a kind of second nature of which Regis is essentially incapable.

To regard Ezra's sensory capacities as intrinsically constitutive of his conceptual capacities does not therefore imply that his ability to sensorily register and respond to reality as a space of reasons precedes its exercise, but rather that the nature of his sensory capacities render him susceptible of being *trained* to do so. For while Ezra's sensory

content, see Susanna Schellenberg, "Perceptual Content Defended," *Noûs* 45, no. 4 (2011): 714–50.

intake is not as yet functioning as a mode of rational intake, by the time he is a toddler its functioning in precisely that way will become for him second nature. One proposed alternative to the idea that our sensory capacities are naturally constituted so as to become incorporated by habituation into our conceptual capacities is to regard those capacities at their first actualization as paradigmatically independent of our growing conceptual capacity. Sensation supplies nothing more than a steady stream of nonrational input for the growing and changing conceptual capacities that are embodied in our increasing linguistic competences.

So while there may be a sense in which the experiences of an adult are ordinarily shot through with concepts so as to make it impossible to actually isolate the conceptual contribution from the sensory contribution to the experience, nevertheless the two contributions remain *in principle* isolable and in that sense independent of one another. But if that is the way it is, and sensory input is thus nonrationally (that is, nonconceptually) constituted, then it is extruded from the space of reasons and we have collapsed back into the vicious oscillation. For such input would have to be either construed as internalized by a conceptual capacity or externalized in a causal correlation with the outputs of a conceptual capacity. But the former is just Givenism, which confronts an intractable problem of fit, while the latter is an externalist Coherentism, which confronts an intractable problem of friction. The only way to avoid this is to reject as incoherent the picture that mistakes our first potentiality of sensation as functionally identical with (rather than merely closely analogous to) that of nonrational animals, and to instead suppose that we are "animals whose natural being is permeated with rationality."[49]

---

49. McDowell, *Mind and World*, 85.

McDowell finds this conception of conceptual capacities as a second-natural initiation into the space of reasons in Aristotle's focus on the formation of *ethical character* by which "the practical intellect acquires a determinate shape" (the habits by which practical wisdom becomes "second nature to its possessors"):[50]

> Aristotle's picture can be put like this. The ethical is a domain of rational requirements, which are there in any case, whether or not we are responsive to them. We are alerted to these demands by acquiring appropriate conceptual capacities. When a decent upbringing initiates us into the relevant way of thinking, our eyes are opened to the very existence of this tract of the space of reasons. Thereafter, our appreciation of its detailed layout is indefinitely subject to refinement, in reflective scrutiny of our ethical thinking. We can so much as understand, let alone seek to justify, the thought that reason makes these demands on us only at a standpoint from which demands of this kind seem to be in view.[51]

Ethical formation, on the story I have been telling, is just one particular instance of the perfectly general way in which the system of putative concepts and rational linkages specifying what is a reason for what that we receive via our upbringing functions to open our eyes to reasons at large. While the practical requirements of reason—the *values* reality can or should have for us—belong to one tract of the space of reasons, those requirements do not exhaust the space of reasons. The way things are places rational constraints not only on what we are permitted or required to do but also on what we are permitted or required to reflectively contemplate.[52]

---

50. Ibid., 84.
51. Ibid., 82.
52. We can distinguish between contemplative and practical meaning by asking whether the rational force of the reasons the world presents to us in experience rationally compels us to entertain or hold a belief or whether it rationally compels us to entertain or carry out an intention to act. "Meanings" and "values"—and "morality" for that matter—are, it seems to me, only terms of art to describe the normative significance of our beliefs or practices.

The indefinitely continuous possibility of rational revision to which this appreciation of the layout of reality is subject arises from two sources. The first has to do with the (at least potential) boundlessness of the reasons the world is capable of affording us as compared with the boundedness of the conceptual capacities available to us to actualize its rational potential in thought. Having established, first, that the very capacity to experience the world's own putative meaning and value can only arise in us by way of the contingencies of our upbringing within a human community for whom the conceptual layout of reality is already a running concern and, second, that the world's rational impacts on sensibility can only passively draw into operation the conceptual capacities we have actually formed, we are never in a position to close ourselves off to the possibility that what we are in fact thinking, saying, and doing exhausts what the world permits or requires of us. This is just a logical consequence of the unavailability of a sideways perspective on the world.[53] Whereas Aristotle acknowledges that "it is of no small importance whether we are trained from childhood in one set of habits or another; on the contrary it is of very great, or rather supreme, importance," he himself was insensitive to the sheer variety of human communities into which we might be initiated into the space of reasons.[54]

For this reason, McDowell appeals to Hans-Georg Gadamer's notion of a *Bildung*—a form of intellectual and moral education or cultivation that, far from being a necessary evil or a bias to be removed in our understanding of the world, forms the

---

53. As we have seen, however, the unavailability of a "brute" or nonnormative directedness on the world cannot coherently be regarded as licensing the thought that the world's own rational potential is unavailable to us. On the contrary, the incoherence of a phenomenalist Coherentism (a crass constructivism) reveals that the idea that we are capable of normative thinking just *is* the idea that our thought is capable of being directed on the world.

54. Aristotle, *Nicomachean Ethics*, book II.1, 24 (1103b, 8)

preunderstanding that is the condition for the possibility of having the world in view at all. A *Bildung* is an Aristotelian second nature, abstracted from the context of a particularly Aristotelian specification of the practical and intellectual virtues that constitute the kind of upbringing properly aligned with the rational demands of reality. It is any form of human cultivation that actualizes some of our first-natural potentialities so as to impart to us the second potentiality of an orientation on the world as a rational order. Like Frege, Wittgenstein, and Sellars, Gadamer stresses the importance of acquiring our first language as an index of our reception of a *Bildung*, our induction into a tradition constituted by an interconnected complex of putative linkages as our mode of directedness on the layout of reality. Like Aristotle, Gadamer fixes on the irreducibly normative character of that initiation as establishing the difference between the mere inhabiting of an environment afforded to animals like Regis and the orientation to the world we are capable of acquiring—a capacity to be rationally directed on its conceptual structure.[55] The Gadamerian fusion of horizons is another way of identifying the identity thesis that McDowell endorses, an identity between the rational potential inherent in the way things are and the availability of that potential to the thinking, speaking, and acting that our *Bildung* allows us to stand poised to receive in experience.

Since no *Bildung* can be intelligibly regarded as failing entirely to direct us on the world's domain of object-dependent sense and thus every *Bildung* makes some features of the world's rational potential available and other features unavailable to the communities of discourse to which they belong, it follows that every community of discourse is inherently open to every other community of discourse

---

55. See Hans-Georg Gadamer, *Truth and Method* (New York: Continuum, 1975): "The concept of *world* is thus opposed to the concept of *environment*, which all living beings in the world possess" (441).

to refine our conception of what the world itself rationally permits or requires of us from within our evolving picture of the world. This triangulation of the necessity of a *Bildung* we have acquired by way of our initiation into a particular tradition and community of discourse, the necessity of our direct perceptual openness to the world by way of receiving a *Bildung*, and the necessity with which we must regard the world's rational requirements as moving beyond its actualization in any particular *Bildung* straightforwardly implies what McDowell calls our "standing obligation to revise" our beliefs and practices according to the dictates of experience: "There is no guarantee that the world is completely within the reach of a system of concepts and conceptions as it stands at some particular moment in its historical development. Exactly not; that is why the obligation to reflect is perpetual."[56]

But that obligation has a second source, which is perceptual error. McDowell is rightly scrupulous in saying that the concepts and rational linkages we acquire by way of our initiation into language are merely *putatively* rational, since adjusting our beliefs and practices to the rational demands of experience can (and often does) reveal that

56. McDowell, *Mind and World*, 40. There are apparently vexing questions here about how to properly characterize the relationship between the notion of a tradition as a "conceptual scheme," the idea of such schemes as direct modes of openness to the world rather than "mediators" standing between us and the world, and the nature of the incommensurability that can exist between the varieties of *Bildungen* exhibited within and across different traditions. One can think, for example, of Davidson's argument against the "very idea" of a conceptual schemes in "On the Very Idea of a Conceptual Scheme," *Proceedings and Addresses of the American Philosophical Association* 47 (1973–1974): 5–20, and MacIntyre's reaffirmation against Davidson of the notion of radical incommensurability as a necessary corollary to the notion of a tradition in *Whose Justice? Which Rationality?* (Notre Dame, IN: Notre Dame University Press, 1988), 370ff.McDowell's formulation, I think, allows us to dissolve the difference between these two sorts of views. On the one hand, MacIntyre's way of articulating the notion of "incommensurability" sometimes seems to flirt with (if not fall into) a version of Coherentism by suggesting that it is possible for traditions to be radically incommensurable in the sense of being in principle entirely mutually unintelligible. On the other hand, Davidson's cogent rejection of incommensurability on this radical construal does not leave sufficient construal for "schemes or perspectives . . . not as *"tertia"* that would threaten to make our grip on the world philosophically problematic," but as "languages or traditions . . . constitutive of our unproblematic openness to the world" (McDowell, *Mind and World*, 155).

some of the rational linkages we have taken to establish reasons—and some reasons we have taken the world to afford us in experience—fail to match the world's own conceptual structure. Given the disjunctivist implication of his platonism, such putatively rational linkages and putative reasons that do not actualize the world's own rational potential are not rational at all—they do not constitute *genuine* reasons for believing that-p or A-ing; they merely *appear* to do so and, as such, are not reasons at all but rational simulacra. For this reason, too, reality demands of us a rational responsiveness of ensuring that our empirical concepts and conceptions pass muster. The flow of refinements on our second nature that our experience continually calls upon us to make is "ongoing and arduous work for the understanding. It requires patience and something like humility."[57] The image of rational revision required by a minimally empiricist naturalism of second nature is that of Neurath's ship, in which "a sailor overhauls his ship while it is afloat."[58]

This overhaul, I have emphasized, is not simply a matter of our initiation and growth into the beliefs and practices of the human communities in which we find ourselves, but it also necessarily involves the *transformation* of our sensory capacities themselves, their subjection to a continual pedagogical discipline or training without which our ordinary observational thinking is not possible.[59] Only within such a process of self-transformation through a use of responsible freedom for the attainment of a second nature are our eyes opened to the demands of reason, which are there whether or not we recognize them. And only within the conceptual resources

57. McDowell, *Mind and World*, 40.
58. Ibid., 81.
59. Sabina Lovibond raises some important questions about the implications of our standing obligations to revise our views and critically queries the radical dependence of such revision on a moral tradition in relation to postmodernist attempts at radical revision on the part of those such as Derrida. See *Ethical Formation* (Cambridge, MA: Harvard University Press, 2002).

made available to us by a *Bildung* are we capable of detecting and responding to those demands as well as meeting our standing obligations to revise what we think, say, and do in light of the world's putatively rational bearing on us in experience.

6.6 Normative Properties as Secondary Qualities

The second natural character of our capacity to take in the normative properties of the world places an important qualification on the sort of platonism we are required to acknowledge. For while it implies that normative properties of meaning and value are objective properties of the world itself, we cannot intelligibly describe those properties as existing independently of our sensitivity to them. In "Values and Secondary Qualities," McDowell makes the comparison between the sort of objectivity we ascribe to norms—including ethical and aesthetic norms—and the sort of objectivity we ascribe to colors.[60] My shirt is blue. The microphysical structure of my shirt in virtue of which it absorbs and reflects light in a particular way disposes it to look blue to creatures with suitably photoreceptive sensitivities. What if that same shirt existed in the absence of any photoreceptive creatures? Would it still be blue?

We have to say yes and no. Yes, it would exhibit the very same properties of light absorption and reflection that singularly determine its disposition to appear bluely to creatures suitably equipped to detect those properties under a blue mode of presentation, but no, it would not exhibit color properties in any mind-independent qualitative display of blue. We can contrast dispositional qualities of this sort with properties of, for example, shape and size, which could be displayed by an object independently of its actualization of any

60. McDowell, "Values and Secondary Qualities," in *Mind, Value and Reality* (Cambridge, MA: Harvard University Press, 2002), 131–50.

sensitivities of an observer that might be suited to detect it. Both color and size are objective in the sense of being properties that objects have anyway, whether or not anyone is capable of detecting them or not, but whereas color is a *secondary* property of an object in virtue of naming a quality it is objectively *disposed* to actualize for the suitably sensitive subject, size is a *primary* property of an object in virtue of naming a quality it objectively actualizes irrespective of the sensitivity of the subject.

The object-dependence of normative properties of meaning and value, McDowell claims, can be understood as secondary properties of the world in a manner analogous to the way in which colors are secondary qualities of objects.[61] The conceptual transformation of our perceptual capacities that comes by virtue of our *Bildung*, then, just describes our acquisition of the sensitivity suitable for actualizing the secondary properties of meaning and value constitutive of the world's own intrinsic rational potentiality.[62]

6.7 Conclusion

This analysis of the affirmative dimension of a minimal empiricism involves a breathtaking integration of philosophical formulations. McDowell articulates a platonism about the conceptual structure of

61. McDowell withholds the claim that our sensitivity to the normative properties of the world is *identical* to a perceptual sensitivity of a secondary quality such as color, maintaining that they are merely analogous. I doubt that there is any good reason to withhold the claim, but the point is immaterial for the present purpose, which is just to establish the idea of value as a secondary *property* made available *by way of* sense perception. In the final chapter, I will pick up the question of whether value can instead be seen as a secondary *quality* made available *in* sense perception. See Anne-Marie S. Christiensen, "Getting It Right in Ethical Experience: John McDowell and Virtue Ethics," *Journal of Value Inquiry* 43, no. 4 (2009): 493–506.

62. This emphasis on the internal relation between our direct and immediate perceptual relation to our environment as prompting our revision McDowell emphasizes as against, e.g., MacIntyre. Contrasting more carefully McDowell's views with MacIntyre's is an important task but not one I shall take up here. For a preliminary treatment, see Kelvin Knight, *Aristotelian Philosophy: Ethics and Politics from Aristotle to MacIntyre* (Malden, MA: Polity, 2007), 204–21.

the mind-external reality to which our eyes are gradually opened; a Sellarsian account of that structure as constituted by the normative relations that structure a logical and sui generis space of reasons; a neo-Fregean and disjunctivist conception of that logical space such that the sense given in an experience is either the conceptual and qualitative mode of presentation determined by the mind-external referent or the mere appearance of a genuine sense; a Kantian conception of our perceptual receptivity to mind-external objects or referents as constitutively dependent on the conceptual capacities involved in the active formation of belief and judgment through the exercise of our responsible freedom; an Aristotelian account of the distinctively rational character of our perceptual capacities to direct us on the rational demands of reality as a second-natural way of actualizing an animal life; a Hegelian analysis of the enabling of a second nature in an ordinary upbringing via our initiation into a *Bildung*; a Gadamerian analysis of rational revision as the result of a fusion of the potentialities imparted via the conceptual horizon of the perceiving subject's *Bildung* with those objective potentialities constituting the conceptual structure of the external world; and a Neurathian conception of our standing obligation to revise our beliefs and practices as a process internal to those beliefs and practices themselves.

Two features of McDowell's pursuit of a minimal empiricism are particularly striking. First, despite the complex and sophisticated synthesis of philosophical insights that he coordinates in order to make sense of the world's availability to thought in experience, his therapeutic aim requires that we regard his achievement as in one important sense utterly philosophically uninteresting. All of the entailments of a naturalized platonism are simply grammatical formulations about the world-directedness of experience: truisms presupposed by our observational thinking that it makes no coherent sense to deny. Far from advancing any philosophical theses, the philosophical formulation of a minimal empiricism can be nothing more than a strategic reminder for philosophers who have been bewitched by the problem of perception and its vicious oscillation between Givenism and Coherentism.

Second, the minimal empiricism McDowell uncovers by attempting to avoid the incoherence of the oscillation also constitutes the strongest possible vindication of common sense. The idea that, when we are not misled, our way of thinking about the world (its mode of presentation to us) can be literally identical to the way the world actually is (that is, can be an actualization of the meaning or value it intrinsically possesses), is just the naive realism the phenomenology of which allegedly gave rise to a problem of perception in the first place.[63] We ordinarily suppose that the world itself can exert rational demands on our thinking—that the way things are can itself be a rational tribunal, permitting or obliging me to form some beliefs and not others; the world itself and not anything anyone happens to think about it can or should motivate me to act (or react) in some ways and not others.

In both our practical and contemplative reasoning, therefore, we often take the world as over against any construal we give it (or could give it) to constitute an intrinsically rational order. It is capable of imposing on rational agents *reasons* for belief and practice precisely because it is an intrinsically *meaningful* domain whose meanings we are properly constituted to either resonate or refuse in our thinking and acting.

---

63. See chapter 2 (2.6).

7

Religious Experience in Modernity

An Exculpatory Explanation

The naive realist view of experience with which this book began, it turns out, is not so much a "folk theory" whose unreflective fragility must surely shatter under serious philosophical scrutiny. Its intuitive appeal does not represent any illicit longing that we should seek to extinguish with philosophical or theological therapy.[1] It is, as I have argued in the previous chapter, an incontestable truism on the order of "all bachelors are unmarried."[2] Denying the openness to reality implied by the naive view is therefore not merely a matter of contravening "common sense" considered as a local and culturally contingent background belief that some human communities might just as well do without, but rather a matter of denying the very intelligibility of human community per se as a social-practical form

1. As, for example, I have argued in the previous chapter that Hector has mistakenly undertaken to do.
2. "Incontestable," that is, not in the sense that it cannot be contested by anyone, for it patently has been. Rather, "incontestable" in the sense that it cannot possibly be *coherently* or *successfully* contested.

of responsiveness to the world. The boot is rather on the other foot. All of the heavy weather that philosophers have made over the nature of empirical content is only a culturally contingent attempt to affirm the impossible. What requires the therapeutic intervention is the philosophical temptation toward a Coherentist or Givenist qualification of our naively held naturalized platonism.

Similarly, I meant for my McDowellian critique of Marion, Alston, Preller, and Hector in part 2 to count as a deconstruction of their views—not merely a claim that their theologies of religious experience are *false*, but rather that their respective construals of the perceptual relation are *nonsensical*. In appropriating or developing the theories that have flowered from the thinking engendered by the problem of perception, their accounts of our perceptual relation to God stand exposed as futile and frustrated expressions of a groundless philosophical anxiety—the equivalent of my son's exasperated suggestions about how to properly manipulate his bears in order to get them all into that jar.

7.1 Whence the Problem of Perception?

But to think that these careful and subtle thinkers—alongside a raft of other philosophers—are capable of denying a rationally undeniable truth about experience in order to espouse incoherent alternatives can seem incredible. Does not the idea that we are rationally required (or even merely rationally *entitled*) to summarily dismiss such an apparently consequential philosophical question and the full range of sophisticated theories addressed to it count as a prima facie reason to reject that idea? Another way to put the objection is to say that some entailments of McDowell's reductio can function as premises in a second reductio, the conclusion of which is the rejection of the first. For if the problem of perception indeed represents the mistaking of a pseudoproblem for a genuine one, the following three claims straightforwardly follow.

First, each philosopher addressing himself or herself to the problem of perception (practically every major philosophical figure since, say, Descartes) is apparently guilty of a massive and overwhelming cognitive blindness. In rejecting the naturalized platonism that McDowell claims undergirds our ordinary and prephilosophical realism about perception, some of the most impressive philosophers in modern Western intellectual history seem unable to recognize an apparently trivial and necessary truth as such. Second, the branch of philosophical inquiry about the modes and content of perception that has resulted from this blindness, while apparently enjoying a rich and fruitful development over the past few hundred years or so, is thus in fact a shocking travesty, a pseudophilosophical cul-de-sac.[3] Finally, those who endorse McDowell's derivation of a naturalized platonism from the dilemma presented by the vicious oscillation are among the privileged few who have somehow (how?) managed to pierce the veil and overcome the relevant form of cognitive blindness that has afflicted (and continues to afflict) so many philosophers working in the intentionality of perception or the problem of intentionality more generally.

On the face of it, none of these claims (much less their conjunction) seems all that likely to be true, and our intuitions about their apparent unlikelihood might threaten to outweigh any sympathies we might have with McDowell's diagnosis about Givenism and Coherentism as caught up in a vicious oscillation, escape from which requires his naturalized platonism. Instead, we

---

3. On McDowell's diagnosis, the denial of a minimal empiricism, amounts to something like the denial of the claim "All bachelors are unmarried." While we may acknowledge legitimate disputes over what *makes* that claim true, or the *significance* of its truth, still no one has been so much as tempted to deny *that* it is true. But I have followed McDowell in holding that the temptations to deny a minimal empiricism have been on that order of cognitive dissonance.

might take the absurdity of those claims to suggest the falsity of the diagnosis. Even if one has the contrary intuition and, taking as dim a view of philosophers as Wittgenstein is often mistakenly thought to have done,[4] one thus finds it eminently plausible and even likely that so many philosophers should be serially guilty of a powerful self-deception, the scale and continuity of the myopia surely requires an explanation beyond one's prejudices about the relative stupidity of philosophers. How could such a fate befall so many otherwise perfectly sane and reasonable people? We can bring the explanatory burden even more clearly into focus when we place ourselves in the shoes of one inclined to recognize the problem of perception as a legitimate and pressing worry.

If I am deeply convinced that there is indeed a problem that merits some serious attention, then I might be relieved to find out that there is in fact no such problem, but I might also be reluctant to avail myself of that relief if it means acknowledging that my assessment of the dialectical situation has been quite that egregiously mistaken. Given a prima facie justifiable presumption of self-reliance in philosophical judgments of the relevant kind, a reasonable aversion to radical changes of philosophical perspective, and a legitimate desire to maintain reflective equilibrium among my already-held philosophical views, I might find it uncomfortable to submit my Givenist or Coherentist inclinations to the brute force of the deconstructive argument already set forth. It would help me significantly if, in pointing out my mistake, we possessed an account of the illusory character of the problem of perception—an explanation that renders my philosophical intuitions about its legitimacy understandable in the same way, for example, that the temptation to

---

4. Mistakenly, in the first place, because both his earlier and later thinking includes a good deal of serious engagement with other philosophers, and in the second place because even when his espoused anti-philosophy is given the most radical reading possible, Wittgenstein nevertheless recognizes an important role for the philosopher qua philosopher.

mistake a mirage for a distant pool of water is understandable. As McDowell puts it, "It matters that the illusion is capable of gripping us. I want to be able to acknowledge the power of the illusion's sources, so that we find ourselves able to respect the conviction that the obligations [to philosophize] are genuine, even while we see how we can, for our own part, reject the appearance that we face a pressing intellectual task."[5]

If, on the other hand, why I should have been gripped by something so obviously and embarrassingly ill-conceived remains mysterious, then the alleged deconstruction will be a much harder pill to swallow. Who wishes to subject herself to a form of therapy in which the only available exculpatory explanation for her misdirected anxieties is simply that she is unaccountably stupid or crazy? The capacity to offer a convincing exculpatory explanation is precisely what enables the deconstruction and critique established in previous chapters to function therapeutically.

Therefore, having applied the McDowellian deconstruction to contemporary theologies of religious experience, we need a corresponding exculpatory explanation to fully realize its therapeutic potential. To be properly suited to the theological subject matter of my argument, such an explanation must be a rationale both for the tendency of philosophers to mistakenly recognize a problem of perception and for the ill-fated connection of that rationale with the modern transformation of the problem of religious experience. McDowell himself has restricted his exculpatory explanation to the former sort of rationale, but for my purposes it is necessary to extend the role of that rationale as implicit in the shifts in background assumptions about religious experience evinced in wider cultural registers.

5. John McDowell, *Mind and World*, 2nd ed. (Cambridge, MA: Harvard University Press, 1996), xi.

On the McDowellian diagnosis, what generates the characteristic mysteriousness that initiates our drive to explain perceptual intentionality in either Givenist or Coherentist terms is the assumption that the impingements of the layout of reality on our sensory systems are first of all nonconceptual—the world itself does not intrinsically exhibit the rational structure that our conceptual capacities enable us to find in it. The apparent incongruity between the nonnormative structure of the world and the normative space of reasons exhibited in what we think, say, and do gives rise to the familiar philosophical puzzlements about the nature of perceptual intentionality. How does our registering of the impacts of such a world in experience serve as the middleman between our conceptual thinking and the world such thinking purports to be about? Having seen that it does not make any coherent sense to suppose there is any such incongruity and therefore that this question simply misfires *as a question*, we can ask what has made it appear so compelling that we could become so bewitched by it.

7.2 Modern Disenchantment as an Exculpatory Explanation

McDowell's answer to that question is genealogical in the Nietzschean sense. He wants to draw attention to the deep historical contingency of the conditions that gave rise to the illusion that we can coherently think of reality as nonconceptually structured. Such an illusion has not always predominated, nor must it inevitably retain its grip on us in the future. But what social and historical considerations have created that illusion? McDowell claims that both the desire to cast doubt on a naturalized platonism and the consequent confrontation with the intractable difficulties it engenders have deep roots in a wide-ranging cultural development of a scientistic conception of nature and a corresponding picture of the world as disenchanted in a sense he attributes to Weber:

> What is at work here is a conception of nature that can seem sheer common sense, though it was not always so; the conception I mean was made available only by a hard-won achievement of human thought at a specific time, the time of the rise of modern science. Modern science understands its subject matter in a way that threatens, at least, to leave it disenchanted, as Weber put the point in an image that has become commonplace. The image marks a contrast between two kinds of intelligibility: the kind that is sought by (as we call it) natural science, and the kind we find in something when we place it in relation to other occupants of "the logical space of reasons," to repeat a suggestive phrase from Wilfrid Sellars.[6]

7.2.1 Weberian Disenchantment

The main lines of the Weberian genealogy have already been introduced in the second chapter: the rise and eventual hegemony of a distinctively scientific understanding of the world and a corresponding prevalence of a technological mode of engagement with the world have conspired to effect a disenchantment (*Entzauberung*) in which the modern world was increasingly shaped so as to appear to us inert of any intrinsic meaning or value. Such disenchantment lay at the roots of the philosophical anxiety about how to put meaning and value back into the world—how to reconcile the disenchanted conception of nature newly uncovered by the natural sciences as a domain governed by natural law with the intentional domain of thought, word, and deed that we ordinarily assume to belong to a norm-governed space of responsible freedom, a space of reasons rather than laws.[7] We have, then, a nascent worry

---

6. Ibid., 70.

brewing about how to reconcile reason and agency with natural law as the primary motivation undergirding the so-called problem of perception.

In enabling us to make the natural world intelligible independently from the meaning and value it appears to have for us, emerging regimes of scientific explanation came to *seem* more fundamental than meaning-explanations and therefore it seemed possible to equate the realm of nature with a realm of objects ordered by the nomological (that is, law-like) relations described by the sciences rather than the normative rational relations that typify religious and humanistic discourses. And this conception of nature as disenchanted or brute makes it *seem* plausible to wonder how nature as such can exert any rational demands on what we think, say, or do. But while the sociological processes that Weber describes gave rise to all the social, institutional, linguistic, and phenomenological infrastructure required to make the problem of perception seem a legitimate and pressing worry for philosophers from the modern period to today, McDowell's deconstructive argument reveals that this seeming was illusory, a mere seeming, for the very idea of a brute or nonconceptually constituted world is unintelligible.

McDowell is careful to note, however, that the rise of the natural (and presumably, humanistic and social) sciences is not to be regretted as a wrong turn rather than a monumental cultural achievement, nor is a disenchanted conception of nature a necessary corollary of science per se. As it so happened, the way in which the natural sciences emerged and developed in modern Western societies happened to mistakenly foment a scientistic conception of nature as disenchanted, but it need not have gone that way.[8] Whereas

---

7. Compare the Sellarsian distinction between epistemic facts and natural facts discussed in the previous chapter.

8. See Brad Gregory's *The Unintended Reformation: How a Religious Revolution Secularized Society* (Cambridge, MA: Harvard University Press, 2012), 1–24.

modern scientism can be identified with a narrowing of the natural to exclude the normative and with the consequent temptation toward a sort of naturalistic fallacy (the temptation to assimilate norms to this restrictive nonnormative conception of the natural), the prescientific recognition of nature as intrinsically normative was arguably guilty of the mirror image of that fallacy. The as-yet undeveloped (or underdeveloped) discipline of sharply distinguishing nomological explanations from normative explanations allowed for wrongly assimilating what we (now) recognize as nomologically explicable phenomena to some communally accepted framework of norms.

A few examples can help illustrate the point. First, Galen, the second-century c.e. physician, developed a theory about sexual differentiation according to which the penis and the vagina were essentially different configurations of the same biological structure (the vagina is just the upturned penis) that were indexed to the "vital heat" produced by an individual body. The greater one's vital heat, the more likely the genital structure was to be forced outside the body. But he also thought that in the "great chain of being" men stood in a higher rank of perfection than women, and he seamlessly assimilated his biological theory to this gradation of gender value.[9] We find a second example in the controversies over Galileo's heliocentrism. The difficulty of accepting his astronomical theory lay not so much in the question of literal versus nonliteral readings of Scripture (whether, for example, to take Ps. 104:5, "the Lord set the earth on its foundations, it can never be moved," literally or figuratively) but in accepting that the normative centrality of human existence in the cosmos did not simply and ipso facto imply or entail its physical centrality in the universe.[10]

9. See Galen, *Galen on the Usefulness of the Parts of the Body*, trans. with commentary by Margaret Tallmadge May (Ithaca, NY: Cornell University Press, 1968), 223ff.; and S. M. Connell, "Aristotle and Galen on Sex Difference and Reproduction," *Studies in History and Philosophy of Science* 31, no. 3 (September 2000): 405–27.

As a misattribution of causal powers, we can see how such conflations of normative explanation with nomological explanation might constitute an important dimension of what we now rightly recognize as superstition. By introducing the logical distinction between the world's nonintentional and law-governed intelligibility and its intentional and norm-governed intelligibility, the formalization of the sciences has exposed (and, in large part, displaced) a real tendency toward this characteristically premodern error. Thus, McDowell clarifies that in reasserting the assumption shared by Plato and Aristotle that nature is intrinsically constituted by rational relations of meaning and value, he is "not urging that we should try to regain Aristotle's innocence." On the contrary, he goes on to say,

> It would be crazy to regret the idea that natural science reveals a special kind of intelligibility, to be distinguished from the kind that is proper to meaning. To discard that part of our intellectual inheritance would be to return to mediaeval superstition. It is right to set a high value on the kind of intelligibility we disclose in something when we place it in the realm of law, and to separate it sharply from the intelligibility we disclose in something when we place it in the space of reasons. But instead of trying to integrate the intelligibility of meaning into the realm of law, we can aim at a postlapsarian or knowing counterpart of Aristotle's innocence. We can acknowledge the great step forward that human understanding took when our ancestors formed the idea of a domain of intelligibility, the realm of natural law, that is empty of meaning, but we can refuse to equate that domain of intelligibility with nature, let alone with what is real.[11]

---

10. Maurice A. Finocchiaro, *Defending Copernicus and Galileo* (Dodrecht: Springer, 2009), 96. Finocchiaro distinguishes several motivating factors for Galileo's opposition, among which he includes "anthropocentrism," but ultimately concludes that ecclesiastical authority over "Scriptural interpretation" was principally responsible for that opposition. What he fails to adequately recognize, however, was the extent to which the traditional reading of Scripture was governed precisely by a prior commitment to a kind of anthropocentrism about naturalistic explanations.

11. McDowell, *Mind and World*, 109.

Conjoining the deconstructive argument with an exculpatory explanation rooted in a genealogy of modern disenchantment, McDowell's therapy furnishes us with the resources for what he calls a "partial reenchantment of nature." It is a reenchantment insofar as the necessity of a naturalized Platonic naive realism reinstates a kind of objectivity for the world's intrinsic meaning and value. We cannot sensibly avoid the idea that there are normative properties that inhere in nature and that this rational potential would exist even in the absence of any particular community's capacity to actualize it. But this, McDowell thinks, can only be a *partial* reenchantment insofar as we must renounce any recovery of the premodern innocence that had not adequately developed the equally fundamental sense in which objects and properties in the world can be rightly understood not as realizations of rational potential manifested by agents navigating the space of reasons but as manifestations of law-like relations.

McDowell's therapy therefore requires us to recognize a distinction between "two kinds of happenings in nature: those that are subsumable under natural law, and those that are not subsumable under natural law, because freedom is operative in them."[12] He takes it to be a particularly modern insight that the world's rational potential—its intelligibility or thinkability—has a dual aspect. We can actualize the world's rational potential as a space of reasons, which "centers on the idea of subjects who aspire to conform to rational norms,"[13] and we can actualize its rational potential as a realm governed by natural laws by adducing nomological descriptions that make no necessary reference to agents navigating the space of reasons. Thus, even if we can imagine the possibility that, say, an electron transfer between two atoms expresses a conformity to a

12. John McDowell, "Response to Graham MacDonald," in *McDowell and His Critics*, ed. Cynthia MacDonald and Graham MacDonald (Oxford: Blackwell, 2006), 238.
13. Ibid. 236.

standard of correctness (perhaps it was the realization of a divine intention), we could nevertheless manage to correctly answer the question of *why* the transfer took place independently of any characterization of it as an intentional phenomenon—independently of whether or not it is the terminus of a rationally motivated exercise of freedom.

7.2.2 The Inadequacy of the Weberian Narrative

So, is McDowell's appeal to a Weberian disenchantment narrative sufficient to account for the mistaken tendencies of philosophers and theologians alike to problematize this tempered form of naive realism in either a Givenist or Coherentist direction? J. M. Bernstein has criticized McDowell for having overly intellectualized the Weberian conception of disenchantment, which (particularly in the hands of Adorno) was intended as a wide-ranging analysis of the social, historical, and material conditions of Western culture. Bernstein concedes that both Adorno and McDowell rightly think (pace Weber himself) that "the very possibility of there being rational knowing and meaning depends upon displacing the disenchanted conception of nature (and so society)."[14] But while Adorno actually does some justice to the complex ways in which that conception is at work in the "actual details of the practices, institutional and non-institutional, that . . . [a reenchanted conception] should be orienting,"[15] McDowell's Wittgensteinian reminder is a merely notional nicety narrowly concerned with "the epistemological upshot rather than the cause of disenchantment," and he accordingly cannot contemplate the "possibility of real re-enchantment."[16]

---

14. J. M. Bernstein, "Re-Enchanting Nature," *Reading McDowell on Mind and World*, ed. Nicholas H. Smith (New York: Routledge, 2002), 217.
15. Ibid., 239.

In his reply to Bernstein, McDowell counters that he does in fact offer a cause for the transcendental anxiety represented by disenchantment—namely, the historical rise of modern science to intellectual prominence. Moreover, he makes it clear that the scope of his project is limited to the way in which the conception of nature as disenchanted serves as the precondition for a particular phenomenon exhibited among a small group of intellectuals in modern society (that is, philosophers), not the whole range of cultural institutions that figure into the analyses offered by Weber and Adorno:

> My focus on scientism is enough for what I try to do. It would surely be absurd to suggest that unmasking a scientistic conception of the natural as a prejudice . . . is not a sensible project until, say, capitalism has been overthrown. But that unmasking is all that the re-enchantment of nature comes to for my purposes. No doubt loosening the cultural grip of that conception of the natural in a general way (as opposed to persuading a few occasional intellectuals that they need not swim with the currents of their time) and undoing all its deleterious effects on modern life (as opposed to showing why a certain sort of activity [i.e., entertaining the problem of perception] is not an obligation for philosophers) would require social change, and presumably something on those lines is Adorno's point. But my purposes do not require such ambitions.[17]

In other words, McDowell himself absconds from the question of how the scientistic conception at the heart of disenchantment in the sense that figures into his antiphilosophical agenda is the conception at work in the disparate forms of cultural disenchantment that command Adorno's attention. Accordingly, McDowell has shown little interest in asking whether his proposed deconstruction of disenchantment or his proposed reenchantment has any wider

---

16. Ibid., 220.
17. John McDowell, "Responses," in Smith, *Reading McDowell*, 298.

implications than the (anti)philosophical ones that we have been canvassing thus far.

Bernstein is indeed surely wrong to think that the notion of disenchantment cannot be deconstructed unless we attend to its cultural manifestations beyond a narrow circle of philosophers. But, as I have characterized it, McDowell's therapeutic approach has *two* components—the deconstructive and the exculpatory. Whereas he is right to say that the deconstructive bit remains unscathed by Bernstein's remarks, we might still worry about the adequacy of his sociological gestures toward Weber to establish the exculpatory bit. The classical Weberian story seems to predict the decline of religion and proffer what Charles Taylor has criticized as a "subtraction narrative."[18]

On that narrative, the increasing tendency toward scientific explanation and instrumental valuation in service of immanent material interests results in the rationalizing and instrumentalizing of societal institutions, such that the ultimacy of value explanations characteristic of magical thinking gradually comes to be devalued. The metaphysically ultimate status of normative explanations guiding social arrangements and infrastructures thus is displaced and supplanted by instrumental meanings and values aimed at efficiency in the systematic control over the mundane matters of daily life.[19] This process of disenchantment, which systematically eclipses any meaning or value that the world could possibly be taken to have in itself by the forward march of natural scientific understanding, is the phenomenon of increasing secularization in the West.

---

18. Charles Taylor, *A Secular Age* (Cambridge, MA: Belknap, 2007), 29.

19. See Max Weber, *Economy and Society*, 2 vols., ed. G. Roth and C. Wittich, trans. E. Fischoff et al. (Berkeley: University of California Press, 1978), 225; and Nicholas Gane, *Max Weber and Postmodern Theory: Rationalization versus Re-Enchantment* (New York: Palgrave-Macmillan, 2002), 23–27.

In appealing to the Weberian conception of disenchantment, McDowell's exculpatory explanation thus depends on a broad and quite general sociological theory of secularization to furnish the reasons that modern and contemporary philosophers in particular were mistakenly tempted to deny a trivial truism—that nature is suffused with meaning and value. Admittedly, this story about the prominence of modern scientific discourses and practices in bringing about a form of secularization in which it becomes plausible to regard nature as disenchanted neatly accounts for the virulence of naturalizing research agendas that infect modern and contemporary philosophy, despite the persistence of various pockets of resistance.

McDowell's particular form of resistance, as we have seen, is quietist insofar as he takes it that we have already conceded too much if we acquiesce to the intelligibility of a disenchanted conception of nature. It is not possible to do any better than to retain our ordinary presumption that in experience we can actualize a rational potential that the world itself imposes on us. The Weberian story, then, exculpates because it describes the social construction of an elaborate and wide-ranging illusion—one that makes a necessary falsehood seem to us like a possible truth.

But the Weberian story is not incontestable. That is, it does not have the same status that McDowell accords to a minimal empiricism—it is at least coherently *conceivable* that Weber's story is wrong without courting any patent contradictions or absurdities. To hold the Weberian thesis that secularization is a process of disenchantment is not to entertain the idea that nature is in fact disenchanted (the incoherence of which, I take it, has been established by the deconstruction). Rather, we are considering just the *sociological* thesis purporting to account for the widespread philosophical commitment to disenchantment in terms of the pervasive influence of scientism. But if the Weberian account fails as a description of the role that a disenchanted conception of nature has played in the secularization of Western societies, McDowell is wrong to appeal to it to explain how it could seem plausible for philosophers to (mistakenly) deny a minimal empiricism.

In fact, there are some prima facie good reasons to reject the Weberian account. Whereas it rightly predicts a fragmentation of societal value-spheres, it also predicts manifestly incorrect societal effects of a secularization driven by disenchantment: for instance, increasingly large managerial and bureaucratic systems and an ever-widening devaluation of norms held across various cultural registers, including both the religious and the scientific.[20] Many scholars who reject the Weberian picture do so because of its apparent inadequacy to explain the modern condition of secularity. They point out that modern adherence to communities of religious belonging can hardly be accurately described as in decline,[21] while fundamental teleologies and forms of ultimately noninstrumental valuation—religious and nonreligious—have migrated and transformed rather than in any way deteriorating or diminishing.[22]

If McDowell's reliance on the Weberian disenchantment narrative should turn out to be misplaced, this would not show that his deconstructive argument is wrong but would severely mitigate its therapeutic value. For we would in that case be returned to our puzzlement about the apparently widespread assumption of an unintelligible conception of nature among modern and

20. See Richard Jenkins, "Disenchantment, Enchantment, Re-Enchantment: Max Weber at the Millennium," *Max Weber Studies* 1 (2000): 11–32.

21. Jeffrey Stout, *Democracy and Tradition* (Princeton, NJ: Princeton University Press, 2004), 101–2, 175.

22. Jane Bennett, for example, argues that science itself can be regarded as a source of "enchantment." See Bennett, *The Enchantment of Modern Life: Attachments, Crossings, and Ethics* (Princeton, NJ: Princeton University Press, 2001). Hubert Dreyfus and Sean Kelly draw on the Western literary canon to recover an enchantment of ordinary life in secular society in *All Things Shining: Reading the Western Classics to Find Meaning in a Secular Age* (New York: Free Press, 2011).

contemporary philosophers—what on earth has motivated them to endorse such a conception in the first place? Once we have discounted the Weberian story, it becomes hard to see why it should have seemed (and continues to seem, for many) rationally *compulsory* to presuppose a disenchanted conception of the bearing that nature has on us in experience when accounting for the perceptual basis of our thinking about the empirical world.

The problem is even more acute in the case of the theological appropriation of the McDowell-style therapy I have been recommending. If it is hard to see why a scientistic assumption could have seemed so plausible as to be simply assumed in philosophical attempts to explain the way that experiences ground intentions, it is all the harder to see why the relevant sort of scientism should seem plausible to philosophers and theologians interested in explaining the way that *religious* experiences ground our intentional relations to God. The idea that those antecedently committed to theism—which includes most early modern philosophers—should have found it compelling to assume the disenchanted conception of nature that gave rise to the problem of perception can seem incredible on its face. Did not Descartes, Berkeley, and Locke, for example, clearly acknowledge the objective perceptual availability of God in nature? Similarly, we would be hard-pressed to find any of the figures discussed in previous chapters explicitly espousing anything but an outright rejection of scientistic naturalism.

Considering both the contestability of the Weberian story and, as Akeel Bilgrami aptly puts it, "how genealogically loaded the term 'disenchanted' is despite McDowell's rather bland use of it," we could do with a more plausible exculpatory explanation for how a disenchanted conception of nature should have become such a widely acknowledged feature of the cultural background of modernity.[23] Is it possible to tell a story that accounts for the disenchantment of nature both in the contexts of professional philosophy and the wider contexts of religious belief and practice? There seems to me to be a more plausible narrative of modernity than the one suggested by the classical Weberian line that McDowell invokes—a narrative that can better account for how the illusion of nature's disenchantment came to seem to us like "sheer common sense" and thus can better explain why philosophers and theologians alike should have acquiesced to it.[24]

The narrative I have in mind is Charles Taylor's magisterial account of the emergence of modern secular social orders from Latin Christendom. Secularity in Taylor's sense "is a matter of the whole context of understanding in which our moral, spiritual or religious experience and search takes place," and as such it is not constituted by any distinct sets of belief and practice but rather on the very "conditions of [religious] belief."[25] Contra Weber, Taylor claims that the modern movement toward secularity does not mark out the gradual loss or marginalization of religious experience and the corresponding subtraction of religious belief and practice from modern life. Rather, the transition to modern secularity names a complex set of *transformations* in the modes and content of religious experience and a corresponding reorientation of the parameters within which religious experience can and cannot inform religious belief and practice.

Taylor's appeal to this global change in the "sensed context in which we develop our beliefs" functions in roughly the same way as a *Bildung* functions in McDowell's account of perceptual experience.

23. Akeel Bilgrami, "The Wider Significance of Naturalism: A Genealogical Essay," in *Naturalism and Normativity*, ed. Mario De Caro and David MacArthur (New York: Columbia University Press, 2010), 45.

24. Such an explanation can tend to be missed even by those who recognize that the world was never *really* disenchanted in the first place. See, for example, Patrick Sherry, "Disenchantment, Re-Enchantment and Enchantment," *Modern Theology* 25, no. 3 (July 2009): 369–86.

25. Taylor, *Secular Age*, 3.

The mutually reinforcing social arrangements constitutive of secularity form the most widely and generally shared context of social formation that contributes to our second-natural capacities to take in the Western world. It follows that the second-natural conceptual capacities we acquire simply by way of an ordinary upbringing and participation in secularized social orders—the capacities for spontaneity that are passively drawn into actualization in the receptivity of our ordinary everyday experiences of the world—are *secularized* conceptual capacities.

On Taylor's account, the disenchantment of nature is a defining feature of the global shift in the sort of *Bildung* that supplies us the conceptual capacities constitutive of a secularized experience of the world. Religion too comes to operate against the backdrop of a disenchanted conception of the world. Taylor's master narrative in *A Secular Age* is principally concerned with (1) giving a conceptual and phenomenological analysis of the disenchantment (rather than decline) of religious experience under the conditions of secularity, (2) telling a story about how social and intellectual movements internal to Latin Christendom (rather than any extrinsic and oppositional forces) came to be responsible for the construction of those conditions of disenchantment,[26] and (3) giving a normative assessment of the rationality of religious belief in its inescapably secularized form.

---

26. Thus on Taylor's view, and contrary to what McDowell suggests, it is not that *science* simply gave us a "naturalistic" explanation of the world and that this sparked the search for alternatives to God as an explanatory basis for "natural" phenomena thus understood. The divestiture of normative significance from the world per se and its relocation in a domain outside of the natural world was a process with Christian motivations and one that began prior to both the Darwinian turn and the seventeenth-century scientific revolution (*Secular Age*, 26). For a similar story about the theological origins of modernity, see Gregory, *Unintended Reformation*; Michael Allen Gillespie, *The Theological Origins of Modernity* (Chicago: University of Chicago Press, 2008); and Marcel Gauchet, *The Disenchantment of the World* (Princeton: Princeton University Press, 1999). Interestingly, each of these narratives draws different lessons from its analysis of the religious roots of modern life.

What makes Taylor's approach to the first and second of these matters—the analysis and genealogy of modern disenchantment—particularly well-suited for my purposes is the centrality of Christian religious life and theological reflection in giving rise to it. Taylor helps us to see the erosion of a minimal empiricism and the pressures exerted on it by a scientistic conception of the natural not as an external force invented by, say, Enlightenment intellectuals whose encroachments on Christian sensibilities about the objectivity of meaning and value were resisted by Christian intellectuals from those days to the present day, but as a more subtle dynamics *internal* to Christian self-understanding. The eventual rise of a secular humanism and even the New Atheism is simply an unintended consequence of incipient maneuvers within the evolving beliefs and practices constitutive of Latin Christendom itself. The philosophical agendas associated with the modern problem of perception that McDowell identifies are thus manifestations among the intellectual elite of what was more fundamentally a shift in the infrastructure of religious life in Western social orders.

Taylor's phenomenological and genealogical story about the alliances of a disenchanted conception of nature with metaphysics, theology, politics, political economy and culture therefore furnishes us with just the sort of exculpatory explanation that my theological use of McDowellian therapy requires—one capable of showing how it might have seemed plausible for theologians and philosophers alike to countenance a pseudoproblem as a genuine one.[27] While it is clearly impossible to do justice to the contours of Taylor's story in such short compass, the roughest sketch will suffice to show how that story can be made to suit the purposes of my argument. My exculpatory use of Taylor's story, however, depends on

27. Bilgrami, "Wider Significance of Naturalism," 45.

characterizing secularity in his sense as in one respect *illusory*: insofar as the *Bildung* constituted by secular social arrangements leads us to construe the world not simply as failing to directly and immediately impose its own rational demands on us but as possibly being such that it is *incapable* of imposing any such demands, it makes an absurdity appear to us a possibility.

But it is not clear that this McDowellian assessment is consistent with Taylor's own normative assessment concerning the fragilizing of the rationality of religious belief in our secular age, the third feature of his account I mentioned above. For on Taylor's account, the ground of that fragilization seems, in part, to be the epistemic necessity, on pain of irrationality, of acknowledging the *threat* of disenchantment—the *possibility* that there is nothing beyond the domain of human making that could be a source of meaning (in the thicker, teleological, and existential sense he calls "fullness"), even if our experiences and inclinations lead us to suppose otherwise.[28] That is, Taylor seems to suppose that, against our shared secular background, we must regard our religious experiences as *defeasible.*

A McDowellian posture, on the other hand, would require us to reject the modern threat of disenchantment *as* a threat, and religious beliefs predicated on taking in the world's meaning and value religiously, as *theological* meaning and value, would have to be regarded as no more or less fragile than they ever were. So after briefly recounting Taylor's phenomenology and genealogy of modern disenchantment, I will say a few words about the revision of Taylor's normative assessment of secularity demanded by a McDowellian appropriation of his descriptive story.

---

28. Charles Taylor, "Afterword: Apologia pro Libro suo," in *Varieties of Secularism in a Secular Age*, ed. Michael Warner, Jonathan Vanantwerpen, and Craig Calhoun (Cambridge, MA: Harvard University Press, 2010), 317.

7.3 Charles Taylor and the *Bildung* of the Secular:
Illusion and Reality

What, then, is the naively and tacitly held background—the *Bildung* constitutive of the conceptual capacities passively drawn upon in experience—that Taylor argues now serves as the condition of possibility for our modern lived experiences of fullness, the presumed framework within which we look to the world for ultimate moral and spiritual meaning and value? He makes that background explicit by contrasting it with the phenomenological structure of the lived experiences of the world prior to the rise of the secular. The contrasting picture is of two differently configured experiencing subjects situated in two correspondingly different conceptions of their natural environment.

7.3.1 The Phenomenology of Secularity

The ordinary subject living in the Western Christendom of 1500, on Taylor's account, occupies a late stage in the evolution of an overall social imaginary or tacit orientation toward the world characteristic of ancient Jewish and Christian communities in general—that of a self particularly permeable, open, or porous in relation to the impingements of an enchanted world in lived experience. The commonly held experience of the world as enchanted amounts to at least three things for Taylor. First, the natural world is conceived as an objectively rational and meaningful cosmos—one that bears its properties of meaning and value as objective powers possessed by nature itself. Nature was therefore taken to be capable of "imposing its meaning on us."[29] Premodern subjects were porous insofar as the line between the world naturally charged of meaning and the

29. Taylor, *Secular Age*, 32–33.

discharge of that world in our words, thoughts, and actions was permeable—the intentional responsiveness of the self to its environment was assumed to be in constant commerce or exchange with the rational power of the world, and this rendered that self *vulnerable* to those powers. Among the internally related objects constitutive of the cosmos, moreover, are nonhuman *agents* whose powers are not merely capable of influencing what we think, say, and do, but whose power to do so is motivated by intentions toward us, whether malevolent or beneficent.[30]

Second, Taylor takes the premodern world to be enchanted in the sense that all of the causal powers exhibited by nature were fundamentally determined by their normative meaning and value. It follows from this that our porousness to the rational significance of any feature of the cosmos forms the basis of our vulnerability to the whole range of things it is capable of doing to us. This is just the sort of assumption that lies behind the conflation between norm governance and law governance that I cited above in relation to Galen and the opponents of Galileo. Taylor highlights in particular how the unity of the self's porousness in the foregoing sense with the conflation being described here explains the central role that magic (good and bad) as well as the spirit world played in premodern life. Love potions, for example, and omens were nonagentive objects recognized as having natural causal powers to impact ordinary life determined by the meanings associated with them. The spirit world, on the other hand, was viscerally feared insofar as it confronted us with rational beings whose powers of agency rendered us vulnerable to the hidden, unpredictable dangers of their influence.

Finally, both general features of the premodern enchantment that Taylor describes were given their particularity of content by the

30. Ibid., 31.

fluid and evolving context of Latin Christendom. Porous subjects of an enchanted world did not inhabit a space of meaning and value in general but a Christian society filled with *theological* meanings and values. The background beliefs about the cosmos as a whole and about the sorts of powers possessed by the objects and agents internal to it were determined by the implicit theological orientation of a Christian social imaginary.[31] For that reason, Taylor can identify the enchanted world of our ancestors as one in which the natural powers of meaning and value immanent in nature were construed as displaying a good beyond human flourishing and were rooted in the intentional power of God.[32] Thus,

> the great events in this natural order, storms, droughts, floods, plagues, as well as years of exceptional fertility and flourishing, were seen as acts of God. . . . God was implicated in the very existence of society. . . . One could not but encounter God everywhere. . . . People lived in an "enchanted" world . . . the world of spirits, demons, and moral forces . . . [and in nonpagan European society] the Christian God was the ultimate guarantee that good would triumph or at least hold the plentiful forces of darkness at bay.[33]

On my reading, we should take this story about the relation of porous selves to the enchantment of the world as an account of the *naive perceptual relation* that premodern subjects bore to the world, even if we take it to be a nonveridical one. It is a phenomenological account insofar as it attempts to make explicit some of the background conditions that govern the way the natural world ordinarily *seemed* to the premodern subject, irrespective of whether the way it seemed is the way it in fact *is*. Moreover, the sort of seeming he marks out is meant to be a perceptual seeming insofar as it describes an

31. Charles Taylor, "Modern Social Imaginaries," *Public Culture* 14, no. 1 (Winter 2002): 91–124.
32. Taylor, *Secular Age*, 20.
33. Ibid., 25.

immediate and prereflective seeming constitutive of the receptivity of the subject. Putting Taylor's narrative in terms of McDowell's account of the perceiving subject, we should say that the picture of a porous self navigating the enchanted world of Christendom belonged to the *second-natural* conceptual capacities possessed by the ordinary subject of Western society as imparted by the *Bildung* of the background beliefs, institutions, and practices constitutive of its social imaginary.

While McDowell emphasizes the Gadamerian insight that our perceptual capacities require a tradition that can furnish us with the second-natural conceptual capacities passively drawn into actualization in experience, Taylor's story specifies the vast social and institutional infrastructure required for one's ordinary experience to be intrinsically *religious* experience. Insofar as experience informs our beliefs about the world, therefore, this made it "virtually impossible not to believe in God" precisely because "so many features of their world told in favor of belief. . . . God was implicated in the very existence of society," and hence "one could not but [putatively] encounter God everywhere."[34] The social and institutional shaping of the ordinary upbringing of a perceiving subject in Western Christendom, the shaping of second-natural conceptual capacities by that upbringing, and in turn the training of one's perceptual capacities imparted by that shaping, together virtually guaranteed regular experiences purporting to have God as their content. The emergence of secularity, on the other hand, marks changes in the social and institutional infrastructure of society that impart "new shape to the experience which prompts to and is defined by belief."[35]

Modern secularity consists in the transition from the picture of the porous self in an enchanted world to that of a buffered self

34. Ibid., 24.
35. Ibid.

inhabiting an immanent frame, one within which we can no longer experience the world as enchanted in the way that our premodern ancestors did. That is to say, the natural world has become for us disenchanted as a matter of our ordinary and naive lived experiences of it. This disenchantment, Taylor emphasizes, is not primarily a matter of decline in religious *belief*, but rather a large-scale change in the social and institutional arrangements that has resulted in a decline in modern *experiences* of the world in the particular sort of way that once informed religious belief—the distinctive sort of way prior to the construction of these social and institutional arrangements. So whereas religious belief persists, the background against which it now exists no longer enables the shaping of our perceptual capacities that makes it inevitably *seem* to us that God is in fact present and active in our midst. The pedagogical conditions for our naive lived experiences of the world to straightforwardly and as a matter of course inform our religious beliefs can no longer be met, at least not as the default and ordinary case.

Our naive conception of the world as an immanent frame and its bearing on us as that of a buffered self results from the attenuation of both senses of enchantment already mentioned. In the first place, Taylor claims, we no longer tend to take for granted encounters with powers of meaning whose origins are nonhuman, whether charged objects or agencies whose powers of intentional agency we experience as common. Rather the cosmos of our lived experience is one "in which the only locus of thoughts, feelings, spiritual élan is what we call minds; the only minds in the cosmos [as opposed to *outside* it, where some of us might perhaps acknowledge a divine mind] are those of humans . . . and minds are bounded, so that these thoughts, feelings, etc. are situated 'within' them."[36] Moreover, the

---

36. Ibid., 29–30.

boundary that separates the meaning we find in things (the inner) from the world in which we find them (the outer) is for us a buffered boundary—one for which "things only have the meanings they do in that they awaken a certain response in us and this has to do with our nature as creatures who are thus capable of such responses."[37]

This distinction between inner and outer and the relative autonomy of spontaneity (our freedom to think, say, and do some things and not others) from our receptivity (the impingements of the world on the mind) comes to be thematized in early modern philosophy, for which Descartes is paradigmatic.[38] It forms the basis of the wranglings about the proper way to conceive the relation across the two sides of the boundary, including the various denials about the very existence of either of the opposing sides, whether in a movement toward the idealist denials of an outer or the various criticisms of a Cartesian inner. This problem of how the outer world is mediated to the inner world of a buffered self, the problem of how to properly relate "Mind and World as separate loci" via "epistemological theories of a mediational type" is the problem of perception as I have characterized it, and Taylor too sees it as setting the agenda for the modern philosophy of mind "from Descartes to Rorty."[39] Crucially, however, Taylor insists that it arises as a worry for philosophers *post facto,* as a reflection on a shift in the social order already underway but one that had been fomenting since the high middle ages.

Secondly, as a result of the movement toward a picture of the self as a bounded one whose mental life is an interiorized evocation of the world external to it, rather than as a self that along with all other entities in the cosmos suffers the all-pervasive and rationally

---

37. Ibid., 31.
38. Charles Taylor, "Foundationalism and the Inner-Outer Distinction," in *Reading McDowell on Mind and World*, ed. Nicholas H. Smith (New York: Routledge, 2002), 106–20.
39. Taylor, *Secular Age*, 539.

determined "fields of force" constitutive of the world's meaning and value, we now "find it hard to be frightened the way they were." Except perhaps by way of a willing suspension of disbelief for the sake of a "pleasurable frisson" (such as our enjoyment of ghost stories and the like),[40] we now tend to think of the premodern "conflation" of natural law with the norms peculiar to human minds *as a conflation*. We are thus capable of deploying conceptions of magic and superstition in different and more deconstructive ways than were evinced by premoderns, even if we remain selective about the class of phenomena that merits the deployment.[41] So we take for granted as our default understanding neither that any meaning and value evoked in us by the world arises from the world itself—that we are open to meanings and values that it has anyway—nor that the meaning that the world somehow manages to evoke in us bears any causal powers other than what it evokes in the inner theater of the buffered self. Once again, however, it is important to recall that for Taylor this sense in which modern life has become disenchanted is not intended to mark any shedding of false beliefs, but rather a change in the phenomenological "way in which people used to experience the world," whether any of these putative perceptions (theirs or ours) are right or not.[42]

Finally, Taylor construes the disenchantment of the world as consisting in its no longer immediately and unproblematically testifying to any transcendent goods beyond human flourishing. We no longer experience the world as a cosmic order whose purposive character imposes itself on us as those who must take our place in that order. The social reality we inhabit rather appears to us most

---

40. Taylor, "Afterword," 303.
41. For example, when Augustine remarks on divinization and magic in ch. 23 of *De Doctrina Christiana*, he is not really denying the possibility of the causal efficacies of such things, but offering a theological rationale for avoiding the relevant causal powers.
42. Taylor, "Afterword," 303.

basically as one made by individuals, reflective of human purposes, and ordered to and by the negotiation of the goods constitutive of human flourishing.[43]

As a phenomenological description, none of this is to deny that anyone (including any intellectual elites) *believes* that the world remains enchanted in any of the senses just described. The claim, rather, is that secularity is marked by a profoundly weakened capacity of modern subjects to *naively experience* the world as enchanted in these ways. That incapacity and loss, moreover, is explicable not in terms of any simple subtraction or deletion of social and institutional arrangements, but their remaking and construction into something new—something that both capacitates and incapacitates us perceptually by training our senses in a fundamentally new way. Significantly, Taylor holds that the modern shape of our perceptual capacities and the secularized seemings that have resulted are not limited to the nonreligious, the humanist or the atheist, but to the religious and nonreligious alike.

7.3.2 A Genealogy of Secular Phenomenology

With this phenomenological claim about the nature of the secular in hand, Taylor then gives us its genealogy. Just as he has construed the Western transition to modern secularity in terms of a shift in phenomenology, his genealogical explanation for that shift in phenomenology is given in terms of the evolution of the social and institutional background conditions required to make that phenomenology possible. What sorts of changes were responsible for an entire cultural complex to construct a wide perceptual pedagogy of religious disenchantment precisely out of a similarly wide

43. Taylor, *Secular Age*, 539.

perceptual pedagogy of religious enchantment? Obviously, it is neither possible nor desirable to rehearse Taylor's (long) story.[44] But two features of it are crucially important to keep in mind. The first is that the story he tells is a story about how a change in phenomenology tracks with a change in the infrastructure required both to give rise to and to perpetuate that phenomenology. The second is that, on his genealogical story, a secular phenomenology of disenchantment was an intrinsically *Christian* development, one with an impetus within Western Christendom and one driven in part by a theological rationale internal to it.

Taylor summarizes the overall schematic of his story about the emergence of a secular age from an age of enchantment in terms of two central things that had to take place: "(1) There had to develop a culture that marks a clear division between the 'natural' and the 'supernatural' and (2) it had to come to seem possible to live entirely within the natural." [45] Roughly, his developmental story argues that the shift from the waning enchantment of the early sixteenth century to the thoroughly secularized disenchantment of the present day was facilitated by way of a transitional stage between them—the halfway house of providential deism in the seventeenth and eighteenth centuries. Taylor describes that stage as one in which the dynamic presence and activity of God in creation presumed by the enchanted picture migrated from its locus in and through created nature itself into a segregated space *outside* of nature, thus producing the first of the two above-mentioned features, a sharp distinction between the natural and supernatural.

This expulsion of God from created nature was not for God to cede the divine role as guarantor of the meaning and value of the cosmos as an objective rational order, but to relocate the locus of the sacralized

---

44. But, as he is right to say, not long enough! (Taylor, "Afterword," 301).
45. Ibid., 304.

significance for the natural world from within it as the intrinsic character it derives from God entirely to a place outside it as bestowed from without. The assumption of nature's essential participation in divine presence and activity that both suffuses and transcends creation shifts to that of nature's relative autonomy as a domain established by a divine presence and activity the transcendence of which is imagined in a disjoined relation to creation—a presence from without who is nevertheless free to break into the providential natural order established at creation. Such interventions construe divine revelation either in terms of what can be inferred about the supernatural by way of the natural order caused by it or in terms of miracles as events within the natural order caused from outside of it to suspend the established natural law or bend it toward the purposes of the divine will.

Still, we can ask: what *motivated* the distinction between nature and supernature? Further, irrespective of what motivated it, while it seems to entail that the natural world fails to intrinsically bear a certain sort of *theological* meaning and value, it does not follow that the world is devoid of meaning and value *simpliciter*. So why did anyone think that placing God outside of the natural world should force on us what Taylor has identified as the picture of the buffered self inhabiting an immanent frame? Taylor's answer to these questions both incorporates McDowell's and moves beyond it. Like McDowell, he points to the scientistic conception of nature that rose to prominence in the seventeenth and eighteenth centuries: "To the extent that a view of the comsos as the locus of spirits and meaningful causal powers declines, this . . . is indeed partly caused by the growth of a picture of the universe as governed by universal causal laws [i.e., as opposed to being determined by norms; '*meaningful* causal powers']. And the post-Galilean conception of these laws, which had no place for purpose, utterly excludes the kind of causal powers supposedly embodied in, say, relics or sacred spaces."[46]

In Taylor's phrase "meaningful causal powers," we see how closely connected the two dimensions of premodern enchantment were to one another. In the enchanted social imaginary undergoing the move toward disenchantment, the assumed idea that the world has its own rational potential it imposes on us (let us call it "E1") was inextricably bound to the assumption that the fact of its intelligibility to us—its rational and moral-practical demands *on us*—is explanatorily basic for any feature it might have (call this "E2"). Moreover, the common assumption of the world's enchantment was inextricably bound to the social and institutional forms of Latin Christendom that underwrote and reinforced it (call this Christianized conception of enchantment "CE"). E1, E2, and CE are not *logically* bound to one another, of course, but they were coinstantiated such that it seems initially plausible to think that the dissolution of E2 made the rejection of E1 and CE compulsory. McDowell claims this is just what happened, and his advocacy of a partial re-enchantment of nature amounts to the claim that while it was right to have rejected E2 and CE, the denial of E1 was literally nonsensical, a "baseless prejudice" we can and must retain on pain of incoherence.

But Taylor introduces a historical complication into this picture. He thinks McDowell is essentially correct in holding that the scientific revolution contributed to the scientistic disenchantment of nature that eventually prevailed, but he adds a considerable nuance to that genealogical picture. Filling out the gap between the apparent leap from the ascendancy of modern science to a widespread scientism about the natural is not a mere luxury for explaining why the problem of perception should have appeared—and continues to

46. Taylor, *Secular Age*, 271.

appear—compulsory for *Christian theologians*. Simply positing the leap makes it puzzling how the ascendancy of science could have its roots *within* a Christian social order, how a scientistic naturalism could have arisen *from* that social order, and how elements of that naturalism could have continued to seem compulsory for Christian thinkers alongside more strictly naturalistic ones.

During the early formation and aggressive rise to prominence of a distinctive domain of scientific rationality concerned with the development of empirical methods for explicating natural law, the disentangling of normative intelligibility from nomological intelligibility did not in fact coincide with any urgent perceived crisis about whether nature itself was meaningful or any corresponding temptation to regard nature as desacralized. People "could and did go on sensing that they were in dialogue with God . . . either as individuals or in groups."[47] In other words, the movement from the disenchantment wrought by the rejection of E2 that eventually brought about the rejection of E1 and CE was not initially confronted as a *threat*. Rather, both the ascendancy of science and the supplanting of E1 and CE with a nature/supernature divide in which the natural was the home of law supernaturally established to evoke the meaning and value we find in it were positive constructions initially moved along by a constructive theological rationale, not merely a defensive one.

The theological rationale that served as the primary engine of disenchantment internal to Latin Christendom is that of *reform*—that is, the impetus to "make over the lives of Christians, and their social order, so as to make them conform thoroughly to the demands of the gospel" by way of "an ascending series of steps to establish a Christian order."[48] The march of Christian reform, Taylor claims, accounts for

47. Ibid., 272.
48. Ibid., 304–5.

the evolving construction of social conditions in the West that led both to the rise of the sciences themselves and to the attractiveness of appropriating a scientistic conception of the natural to contribute to constructing a nature/supernature distinction already underway and well established on theological grounds. In other words, rather than finding scientistic implications in the newly developing natural philosophy and taking these to put pressure on a Christian society to reject E1, E2, and CE and to remake their social order as a providential deism predicated on a nature/supernature distinction, we should turn this explanation on its head.

Taylor identifies a growing dissatisfaction in the late medieval and early modern periods with a "multi-speed" system in which "[lay] masses of people were not going to live up to the demands of perfection" but "were being 'carried' in a sense, by the perfect"—that is, by those with renunciative or mendicant vocations.[49] Both lay and clerical movements became involved with a "rage for order" in the "drive to make over the whole society to higher standards."[50] This impetus toward reform and the overcoming of a multispeed system was not necessarily revolutionary, and the Reformation was only one particularly important phase in which that project was carried out. Particularly significant in the late medieval movement toward a more spiritually demanding Christendom was a "progressive impatience with older modes of postaxial religion in which certain collective, ritualistic forms of earlier religions uneasily coexisted with the demands of individual devotion and ethical reform which came from the 'higher' revelations. In Latin Christendom, the attempt was to recover and impose on everyone a more individually committed and Christocentric religion of devotion and action, and to repress or

49. Ibid., 61–62.
50. Ibid., 63.

even abolish older, supposedly 'magical' or 'superstitious' forms of collective ritual practice."[51]

The individualizing, personalizing inwardness brought on by the spirituality of death and the pervasiveness of guiding judgment according to what "really matters" among lay movements resulted in

> unease at the use of causal powers, even for unexceptionable ends. . . . As long as the sacrament is used for purposes of good influence, to bring us more into the ambit of grace, that is acceptable. But the focus on a scatter of worldly ends, even though good in themselves, diverts us from true piety. . . . The crucial point here, is not so much the practice, but the end we have in view. But of course to follow through on this, a great many practices will straight away fall by the wayside. . . . Most radically of all, a deep theological objection arose to "white magic" of the church, whatever its purpose. Treating anything like a charged object, even the sacrament, and even if the purpose is to make me more holy, and not to protect against disease or crop failure, is in principle wrong. God's power can't be contained like this, controlled as it were, through its confinement in things, and thus "aimed" by us in one direction or another. [52]

The steam of reform movements in the late medieval period and early modern period leading up to the scientific revolution can therefore be seen as congenial to a *religious* or *theological* disembedding of God's meaningful causal power from nature. What results is a distinction between a domain of nature in which it is impious to acknowledge magical power and the supernatural domain of divine freedom from natural constraint.

Within this wider context of a cultural shift toward a theological naturalism, the even more radically disenchanted conception of nature catalyzed by the ascendancy of the sciences could appear not merely plausible but desirable and compelling, even if it remained disputable. Entertaining the possibility that nature is absent of any

51. Taylor, "Afterword," 305.
52. Taylor, *Secular Age*, 72.

intrinsic value or meaning could be imagined as religiously permissible, and even as desirable (albeit for reasons that were as political and economic as religious), as long as God could retain a place as providential designer of the natural order. The disenchantment of nature that McDowell finds underlying the characteristically modern philosophical worries about experience as the mediator between mind and world is first and foremost a *theological* disenchantment, one evolved by Latin Christendom to suit spiritual ends internal to a Christian society.

The scientistic conception of nature is thus a beneficiary of the disenchantment brought about by Christian religious reform. But once developed, it eventually became an irrepressible engine of disenchantment. Once the natural and supernatural were widely presumed to be merely contiguous domains acting on one another rather than to be overlapping domains, it becomes possible to imagine living one's life without appeal to any domain transcending nature, without any particular supernatural guarantor to orient any human pursuit of lived experiences of fullness. A conception of nature as a theater of divine agency is, by way of the rise of providential deism, eventually supplanted by a picture of it as a divine gift of natural resource to be understood and enjoyed to suit the natural and this-worldly ends of human life. In the end, the excising of any necessary orientation to a domain transcending nature as the organizing principle of the institutions and practices constitutive of the political, economic, and moral ordering of Western society was an unintended consequence of the uprooting (or as Bilgrami aptly puts it, the "deracinating") of God from nature.[53]

---

53. Akeel Bilgrami, "What Is Enchantment?," in *Varieties of Secularism in a Secular Age*, ed. Michael Warner, Jonathan Vanantwerpen, and Craig Calhoun (Cambridge, MA: Harvard University Press, 2010): 145–65, 147. Bilgrami, however, tends to make this process sound much more intentionally undertaken than it likely was. The idea that the secularizing or disenchanting impetus of providential deism was *unintentional* is stressed as well by Brad Gregory. But while

The first of Taylor's required conditions for the rise of secularity—the demarcation of the supernatural from the natural—therefore itself accounts for the second, the apparent possibility of living entirely within the natural domain. Secularity as such is therefore best seen as the radicalization of a possibility made available (albeit not necessarily required) by the rise of providential deism.[54] The movements toward intellectual development and the social realization of that possibility have brought about the social conditions required for the experiences of secularity characteristic of life in late modernity—an infrastructure constituted by a "historically unprecedented amalgam of new practices and institutional forms (science, technology, industrial production, urbanization), of new ways of living (individualism, secularization, instrumental rationality), and of new forms of malaise (alienation, meaninglessness, a sense of impending social dissolution)."[55]

Taylor thus provides us with a genealogical account of both the *phenomenology* of secularity and the sort of *Bildung* or pedagogical discipline involved in an ordinary upbringing in our society. The institutional structures, social goods, and forms of malaise that characterize a distinctively secularized experience are those that by default seem to constitute an immanent frame—the outer world that in the ordinary case *seems* to evoke within the interiorized space of modern buffered selves a conception of nature *as* desacralized. This regimen for the secular training of the senses was brought about, first, by the intentional construction of a natural/supernatural distinction

Gregory's narrative is in that respect quite similar to Taylor's, Gregory proceeds in a way that overemphasizes "belief" over against phenomenology in characterizing the emergence of modernity from late medieval Christendom.

54. Bilgrami's example centers on the marginalizing of those voices in the Royal Society in late seventeenth-century England antagonistic to the emerging consensus about nature as a brute domain to be disposed of according to human purposes. See Bilgrami, "What Is Enchantment?," 148ff.

55. Taylor, "Modern Social Imaginaries," 91.

itself motivated by religious reform and, second, by the unintentional consequence of allowing the possibility of living entirely within the natural, along with all of the attendant intellectual and social-practical explorations and problems in Western society.

Taylor acknowledges, however, that local forms of community, including religious community, can in some respects relativize the extent to which this secular seeming pervades our ordinary lived experiences. Even among those who acknowledge the immanence of a transcendent source of fullness—an orientation to the natural world as presenting something that reaches to us from beyond it—that acknowledgment tends to be more pervasive as a religious *belief* than as a lived form of religious *experience*, which is far more fleeting. As such, the religious person living under the conditions of secularity must regard her belief as attenuated or fragilized in much the same way, not merely because of the pervasiveness of religious disagreement but because the representative parties to the disagreement do not hold their beliefs as a straightforward empirical judgment in the way that was manifestly the case in ancient and medieval Christendom. In our case, but not in theirs, we encounter God as breaking in to a disenchanted world—a desacralized domain in which divine presence and activity is no longer recognizable simply by looking.

But Taylor has also shown how a scientistic conception of nature that facilitated the divine retreat from nature remains consistent with a distinctively religious construal of the world and God's relation to it. Accordingly, providential deism enables a perfectly natural religious way of acquiescing to nature as disenchanted, one we see clearly in early modern philosophers such as Descartes and Kant, both of whom continued to remain Christian theists even while thematizing the problem of perception in the wake of the desacralization of nature they took to be implied by the successes of the sciences and the progress of modern political economy. For both, God remained important for providentially ordering the mind to a disenchanted nature in just the sort of way required to enable our norm-governed subjective awareness to direct us upon the nonnormative and law-governed structure of the objects, properties, and relations such thought purports to be about.

But while Descartes and Kant proposed solutions to the problem of perception that each took to be compatible with his Christian theism, their thought conforms to the structure of providential deism in general in that it does not *require* any reference to God in the way that a sacralized conception of nature did. Contemporary philosophers may therefore depart from such forbearers by rejecting their theism, or—like the four figures I have discussed in the immediately preceding chapters—philosophers might instead propose solutions to the problem of perception that remain faithful to Christian theism in much the same way that their modern forbearers attempted to do. Either way, what is common to both approaches is precisely their acquiescing to the philosophical worries that arise from a disenchanted conception of nature that informs the Western philosophical tradition in a way that McDowell elides but that Taylor persuasively shows as having its roots more generally in the evolving *Bildung* of Christendom.

7.4 Conclusion

Taylor's story, as I have tried to show, can be usefully dropped inside the framework of McDowell's therapeutic dissolution of the problem of perception as a peculiarly modern prejudice against a minimal empiricism. That it stands exposed as a mere prejudice follows from his deconstructive critique as I have reconstructed it in chapter 3. That such a prejudice could have become so pervasive is understandable, however, in light of the exculpatory explanation given above. Not only modern and contemporary philosophers and theologians have come, by some perverse act of theoretical imagination, to regard the problem of perception as a compelling one. Rather, for anyone living in a secular age, it should *appear* as second nature, in McDowell's sense, that we do indeed confront the problem of perception. It takes but a little reflection to raise to consciousness the conflict between our presumed picture of a buffered secularized self within an immanent frame and the naive realism necessarily implicit in the grammar of experience, according to which we are open to the meanings and values intrinsic in the world itself.[56] This conflict resulting from our tacit commitments to both the secular social imaginary and a minimal empiricism has informed and animated the modern philosophical imagination. On Taylor's story, we can discern many possible ways of acquiescing to our experience of the world as disenchanted—some religious, some nonreligious, some irreligious.

Our construction of the secular, as well as the phenomenology of religious experience that has arisen from it, Taylor thinks, is on the whole a good thing. The immanent frame can be "spun" either as open to transcendence or as closed, in more or less religious or nonreligious terms. Taylor himself plumps for openness, but he wishes to convey that the condition of secularity is just the condition of being unable to have any defeasible reason for insisting on the legitimacy of one reading of the world over the other. What is required for any party when evaluating sources of fullness or paths of moral and spiritual searching is therefore a "leap of faith," an

---

56. De Gaynesford can thus give a rough and ready presentation of the problem of perception that requires no particular philosophical training, but proceeds instead from what have come to be thoroughly "common sense" assumptions. See Maximilian de Gaynesford, *John McDowell* (Malden, MA: Polity, 2004), 6–9.

"anticipatory confidence" that "leaps ahead of the reasons we can muster for it."[57]

To hold that one's views on such matters are "obvious, compelling, allowing of no cavil or demurral," Taylor concludes, is for one's thinking to be "clouded or cramped by a powerful picture which prevents one seeing important aspects of reality."[58] For any of us as modern buffered selves to succumb to this danger of being "held captive" to one particular reading of the inherently ambiguous picture of the immanent frame as the most "natural" one is, Taylor supposes, to suffer from a kind of disability.[59] It is just that sort of disability we can ascribe, for example, to the New Atheists, but no less to religious zealots.

Rather than taking this as an admonition to an infinite deferral of belief or the illusory possibility of "neutrality," Taylor reiterates that the condition of secularity is a conditioning of our *experiences* that imposes a "cross-pressured" existence "between the open and the closed perspectives."[60] Our default way of taking in the world in lived experience as buffered selves within an immanent frame allows us to feel pulled two ways. To be religious in a secular age, therefore, requires an anticipatory confidence that was not necessary prior to its advent, and in the ideally rational assessment, therefore, the leap of faith seems crucial in order to go on.

However, if McDowell's advocacy of a minimal empiricism is well-founded, then there is a sense in which Taylor's assessment of the secular condition has to be wrong, even if his description of it is right. That is, to the extent that the picture of our perceptual relation

---

57. Taylor, *Secular Age*, 550.
58. Ibid., 551.
59. Taylor invokes Wittgenstein here (Taylor, *Secular Age*, 557). See also Ludwig Wittgenstein, *Philosophical Investigations*, 4th. ed., ed. and trans. G. E. M. Anscombe, P. M. S. Hacker, and Joachim Schulte (Oxford: Wiley-Blackwell, 2009), §115.
60. Taylor, *Secular Age*, 555.

to our environment imparted to us in an ordinary upbringing under the *Bildung* of a secularized society is the picture of a buffered self within an immanent frame, to that extent our ordinary conception of ourselves is profoundly mistaken. For on Taylor's conception, the buffered self is constituted precisely by a denial of openness in the sense that McDowell argues is undeniable on pain of incoherence.[61] Recall that for Taylor the boundary constitutive of the inner/outer distinction instantiated by the buffered self is defined in part by an interiority that regards mental states as merely evoked or awakened by the world rather than as influenced by a world charged with any intrinsically rational power. The buffered self attributes such evocations of the meanings things have for us as a function of our nature and not as a porousness to something "out there."

This denial of our openness to the world implicit in a modern secular social order entails a denial of the platonistic dimension of a naturalized platonism. But, as we have seen, a naturalized platonism is a minimal requirement for avoiding a vicious and incoherent oscillation between Givenism and Coherentism. Taylor, however, preserves that modern secular construction not only as a descriptive account of what it is to be a subject in contemporary Western social orders but also as a perfectly coherent self-understanding, even one that has its own advantages and exerts its own constraints on the observational reasons available to us in our "search for the spiritual."[62]

This is not to say that Taylor leaves no dialectical space within which to appreciate McDowell's argument, however. In fact, he has expressed significant sympathy for it.[63] However, within the

---

61. This raises some important questions about the significance of regarding the vast infrastructure of secularity that Taylor describes as a fundamentally malformed *Bildung*. Clearly that topic cannot be taken up here. My interests are more narrowly fixed on what the incoherence of the *Bild* in question implies for a theology of religious experience and not on the question of the social conditions required for a "second nature" capable of instantiating it.

62. Taylor, *Secular Age*, 3.

framework Taylor articulates, McDowell's argument belongs at the level of "spin"—a permissible rather than required way of reading our relation to the immanent frame as buffered selves. As such, Taylor prioritizes the posture he recommends—that of a leap of faith—in his preference for a partial re-enchantment of nature (the recovery of E1) to its denial, which he also takes to be a rational alternative. The leap is required precisely because our belief in E1 has been fragilized, rendered uncertain, susceptible of reasonable protest given the cross-pressured nature of our lived experiences.

But on a McDowellian analysis, this gets things exactly backward—what the deconstruction of the problem of perception shows is not that coherently conceiving of ourselves as buffered in the relevant sense is difficult, but that it is impossible. While secular formations of the self represent one among many possible traditions within which we are rationally capacitated to take in the world, a minimal empiricism represents a perennial and inescapable feature implicit in any perceiving subject shaped by such traditions, and it can be made explicit in any of them. When confronted with a conflict that arises from making both of these preconditions for our perceptual capacities explicit, Taylor makes the mistake of relativizing the grammar of perception to its secular formation. But if McDowell is right, we ought to go the other way and relativize the secular formation of our perceptual capacities to the grammar of perception. This is just what I have attempted to do by slotting Taylor's story into the place of an exculpatory explanation for the *theological* allure of the disenchanted naturalism I have found and deconstructed in Alston, Marion, Preller, and Hector.

Any recovery of a theology of religious experience which is to avoid that allure must therefore advocate a corresponding partial

63. Charles Taylor, "Retrieving Realism," in *Mind, Reason and Being-In-The-World: The McDowell-Dreyfus Debate*, ed. Joseph K. Schear (London: Routledge, 2012), 61–90.

reenchantment of nature—one that retains E1 without requiring the sort of magic arising from the reduction of law to norms as represented by E2.[64] Clearly, the McDowellian argument does not require that such a reenchantment be a *theological* one. McDowell himself tends to regard a turn back to a sacralized conception of the world as superstitious or magical.[65] He thus fails to countenance a viable theological reading of nature as partially reenchanted, a contest between religious and humanistic readings of a naturalism of second nature, or even the advantages of explaining our openness to the world in a theological way. But while a theological reenchantment is not rationally *required*, Bilgrami is right to suggest that it is certainly not ruled out—it cannot be excluded as inconsistent with a minimal empiricism in principle.[66] The remaining question to be taken up

64. In response to Bilgrami's advocacy for something more nearly akin to McDowell's own nontheological advocacy of partial reenchantment, Taylor responds by claiming that the recovery of E1 apart from E2 doesn't count as "getting back what was lost" but only a distant "analogue" of it. I am not so sure. It seems to reflect his regard for "enchantment" as a conceptual package just because it was a historical one, which is just confused. What remains possible, even if not actual, is the possibility of reconstructing selves more fully capable of regarding their moral-practical relation to the world as "porous."

65. Taylor's narrative actually helps to explain how McDowell could make this mistake. The two ways of dismissing theological accounts of our openness to meaning and value evidenced in *Mind and World* are, first, by associating it with E2, as a "magical" view about meaning, and, second, by associating it with what McDowell calls a "rampant Platonism," which acquiesces to a disenchanted conception in the world precisely by making meaning a "supernatural gift." But the first problem does not rule out CE—a Christian "sacralized" conception of the world's meaning and value as owing to divine activity and presence in the world as such; it only rules out one particular sort of explanatory role that that presence and activity can play. The second problem, on the other hand, does not apply to CE at all, but only to the late medieval and early modern vision of God's relation to the world given by what Taylor has called a "providential deism"—one in which the natural/supernatural distinction was already up and running.

66. "Taylor's [religious] ideal of 'transcendence' happens not to coincide with the more minimal [secular humanist] transcendence that I have urged, but there is no decisive reason to favor my sparer version—we are, after all, not required to be wielding any Occam's razor in this region of thought. It would be quite arbitrary to wield it, since some may experience callings that make normative demands on their agency in terms that are more richly religious than anything I have described in the enchantment I have briefly argued for" (Bilgrami, "What Is Enchantment?," 160). It is tempting to assimilate Taylor on the "cross-pressured" nature of secularity to this contestability of theological versus nontheological readings of a minimal empiricism and a correspondingly reasonable dispute as to whether the meanings and values of the natural world to which we are perceptually open are theologically grounded or not. This is how Bilgrami

in the next two chapters, however, is whether we can imagine a theology of religious experience that is consistent with the minimal empiricism represented by a naturalized platonism.

reads Taylor, but that reading runs into exegetical trouble precisely for the reasons specified in the two previous notes. Taylor seems intent on emphasizing the essential *discontinuity* between the "porous" and the "buffered" selves, and the "analogue" to the former that he recognizes remains the recognition of something *permissible*, not required.

8

Gregory of Nyssa

A Minimally Empiricist Reformulation?

If the argument constructed over the preceding chapters is correct, then we should now be in possession of some good reasons to think that many (perhaps most) of the going accounts of the Christian's perceptual relation to God are mistaken. While I have offered some criticisms of what I take to be the most compelling recent accounts—those of Marion, Alston, Preller, and Hector—the ground of my criticisms runs deeper than the particular views espoused by these figures. Instead, the criticisms in question embrace the *types* of views represented by the four figures: i.e., apophatic vs. cataphatic Givenism and apophatic vs. cataphatic Coherentism, respectively. Following McDowell, I have claimed that these theological views are caught up in the vicious oscillation between Givenism and Coherentism. I have further followed McDowell in specifying a kind of naturalized platonism that is required to avoid that oscillation and in claiming that the minimal empiricism represented by his naturalism of second nature is in fact just a philosophical description or analysis of our ordinary and common-sense view about the intentionality of perception. My central thought—that theologians have gone along with philosophers in attempting nonsensically to deny the kind of naive realism captured by a minimal empiricism—called out for an exculpatory explanation for which McDowell's own gestures proved insufficient.

So, at the end of the previous chapter, I put Charles Taylor's account of the secular to work in a therapeutic story that explains why theologians have mistakenly acquiesced to the modern disenchantment of nature. The illusion of nature's disenchantment that engenders such a mistake, Taylor plausibly shows, is a global phenomenon in the modern West—one that has been socially and institutionally established and reinforced not merely among intellectual elites but more widely across disparate registers of everyday life, including the religious. The scope and pervasiveness of disenchantment constitutive of the cross-pressures of our modern forms of life have brought about a transformation not only of our theorizing about religious experience but also of the structure of religious experience itself according to the pedagogies of a secular social imaginary.

But since that imaginary is predicated on the mistaken idea that we can sensibly entertain a conception of nature as disenchanted, we must suppose that the role it plays in training our perceptual capacities has resulted in a malformation of those capacities. As a result, an ordinary upbringing would likely make it very difficult to develop the conceptual capacities required to perceptually sensitize us to God's presence and agency in the world. The problem of the oscillation in contemporary theologies of religious experience is that in specifying the sort of perceptual relation that holds between us and God, Christian philosophers and theologians tend to retain an underlying commitment to the mistaken pedagogy of disenchantment implicit in what has unfortunately (but not necessarily!) become our ordinary experience.[1]

Determining what it might take to ameliorate the malformed pedagogy is an important question for ethics, and it requires a much finer-grained analysis than the one I have given.[2] But my interests in this work are not that ambitious. I am not herein concerned to rectify the elaborate illusion about the religious disenchantment of nature implicit in modern secular societies or to draw on premodern sources to forge new pedagogical itineraries for the reenchantment of religious experience. My aim instead is to highlight a naturalized platonism focused on the intentionality of experience per se as a necessary presumption for contemporary contestations over a proper theology of religious experience. And there is no reason to suppose that constructing a theological account of the bearing God has on us in experience and the receptivity required to perceptually register that bearing requires that we can enjoy or have enjoyed a direct perceptual relation to God ourselves.

Instead, a theological exploration of the intentional structure of a putative perceptual directedness upon God's presence and action in the world remains possible even if as a matter of contingent fact we have not cultivated the relevant faculties, capacities, or opportunities

1. One of the implications I draw from my McDowellian reading of Taylor is thus that William P. Alston mistakenly absolutizes the historical contingency of the extent to which the ordinary person takes herself to have a genuine and direct perceptual awareness of God. Such an awareness, he thinks, is "a rare phenomenon except for a very few souls." See *Perceiving God: The Epistemology of Religious Experience* (Ithaca, NY: Cornell University Press, 1991), 36.

2. This genre of theological reflection is rare in academic theology but is utterly commonplace within the context of actual Christian communities, albeit in a manner thoroughly unthematized as such by them. Such reflection, in other words, is just part and parcel of our ordinary practical reasoning. Subjecting deliberative reflection of that sort to the intellectual discipline manifest in academic theology remains a largely half-tried and half-hearted enterprise on the part of both constituencies, no matter their overlap as a matter of mere set membership. Genuine confluence of the sort implied by a social "itinerary" is halted by established infrastructures that preclude much continuity between the moral and spiritual pursuits of the theologian and those of the average Christian.

to enjoy (or recognize ourselves as having enjoyed) the experiences we are aiming to describe.[3] We will have to look to other resources, such as the testimony of those we judge to reliably report their own observations of God's presence and action, and the development of previous theological proposals for how to properly analyze the intentional structure implicit in those observations.[4] We would not suppose, for example, that we must be sommeliers ourselves in order to profitably address ourselves to the question of what if anything the sommelier is apprehending when she discerns various features of wine, what capacities she must possess in order for her putative

3. This distinction between what is logically or epistemically possible for us and what lies practically open to us is often neglected by Christian philosophers, particularly those whose posture is primarily defensive. Thus, for example, Plantinga's reformed epistemology may well establish that if Christian belief is true and humans are indeed equipped with a *sensus divinitatis* corrupted by sin, *then* those who find that Christian belief is basic for them are warranted and very likely know that Christianity is true. But even if we grant all this, it is only useful as a defensive strategy for those who in fact find that they hold their Christian belief in a way that is (properly) basic. If Taylor's merely descriptive diagnosis is correct, however, the number of Christians who meet that criterion is likely not all that large or representative. Given that one's epistemic confidence is material to the significance of putative defeaters and entitlements, and the relevance of one's social formation as a belief-forming self that Wolterstorff emphasizes as necessary for Plantinga's account, a mere belief in and even reliance upon a redeemed *sensus divinitatis* may be insufficient to produce warrant. For in Plantinga's terms, what it takes to have a congenial environment for the successful operations of a properly functioning faculty might be a higher bar than he supposes. See Alvin Plantinga, *Warranted Christian Belief* (New York: Oxford University Press, 2000), 357–73; 457; and Nicholas Wolterstorff, "Historicizing the Belief-Forming Self," in *Knowledge and Reality: Essays in Honor of Alvin Plantinga*, ed. Thomas Crisp, Matthew Davidson, and David Vander Laan (Dodrecht: Springer, 2006), 111–35.

4. In other words, as a matter of contingent social and historical circumstances, we might be more reliant upon *testimony* in the justification of our theological beliefs than Christian communities who have come before us or those less profoundly shaped by the sorts of transformations Taylor describes. For some related some worries about the epistemic adequacy of religious testimony, see Jennifer Lackey, "Deficient Testimonial Knowledge," in *Knowledge, Virtue, and Action: Putting Epistemic Virtues to Work*, ed. Tim Henning and David P. Schweikard (New York: Routledge, forthcoming). On my account of what a perceptual relation to God must involve, there is an intimate and internal relation between testimony as a perceptual pedagogy, the contents of perception. This relation has significant implications for the sort of testimonial models of epistemic justification frequently employed in the philosophy of religion, such as those advocated by Plantinga (see previous note) and John Greco. See, e.g., Greco, "Religious Knowledge in the Context of Conflicting Testimony," *Proceedings of the American Catholic Philosophical Association* 83 (2009): 61–76, but working out those implications is beyond the scope of this study.

discernments to be perceptually available to her, and how it is possible for her to have acquired those capacities. Of course, we might successfully account for all of these things and yet remain entirely ignorant of *what it is like* to discern the relevant features of the wine. That is, our analysis would make available only a strictly formal understanding. Likewise, I am after an analysis of the form of the Christian's perception of God, not its phenomenology.[5]

What I have argued to this point is that any theological story we wish to defend about how God's empirical bearing on suitably sensitive subjects might inform and justify their beliefs or actions must be consistent with a minimal empiricism—one that avoids succumbing to the illusion of modern disenchantment that propels us into the vicious oscillation between Givenism and Coherentism. Moreover, we should not regard this requirement as a substantive and contestable criterion that philosophy imposes on the theology of religious experience from without.[6] Insofar as we must recognize consistency with a naturalized platonism as a minimum criterion for the truth of the relevant theological claims, the recognition is a trivial one imposed by the grammar of perception itself (akin to the requirement that any story about bachelors must be consistent with characterizing them as unmarried).

Having cleared the ground of approaches inconsistent with a minimal empiricism, the pressing *theological* question is therefore this:

5. This way of putting things risks confusion for the phenomenologist, who will protest that an account of the structure of any given sort of experience *just is* a phenomenology of that sort of experience. But the disagreement is merely apparent, being entirely traceable to an ambiguity in the term "phenomenology." By "phenomenology" we might mean to refer to the intentional structure that some identifiable type of phenomenon has or would have if it were possible or we might mean to refer to an observation report, a description of what it is like to have encountered a particular instance of some type of phenomenon. My point could equally well be put by saying that in our attempts to understand the perception of God it is possible to produce or contribute to a true phenomenology of religious experience in the first sense without being ourselves capable of producing or contributing to a true phenomenology in the second sense.
6. It does not entail, for example, any denial of the relative autonomy of theological claims from the deliverances of properly nontheological disciplines.

is any theology of religious experience capable of satisfying that minimal conception? To issue a negative reply would be to suppose that whatever relation rationally grounds our intentions of God, it could not be a perceptual relation.[7] I suggested at the close of the last chapter that premodern sources might be a good place to look for a minimally empiricist theology of religious experience, since they represent stages in the development of Christian thinking about the structure of intentionality in our (putative) perceptions of God that tended to presume a naive realist conception of experience. As such, they remained as-yet-unencumbered by any deep entanglement with a disenchanted conception of nature, and they were thus relatively innocent of the temptation to wed their theological stories to a pseudoproblem of perception and the vicious oscillation to which it gives rise.

We also saw in the previous chapter, however, that retrieving, rehabilitating, or reformulating this premodern theological innocence poses its own risk: we might avoid pseudophilosophical nonsense only to run headlong into nostalgia of a particularly myopic and overly romanticized sort. Taking account of that danger requires an appropriate stress on the naturalism of a naturalized platonism—the dependence of our capacity to actualize the world's own meaning and value on the conceptual capacities we acquire via contestable and varying forms of pedagogy inculcated by our social location. But it also suggests an additional criterion for any adequate theology of religious experience—namely, that it resist the paradigmatically premodern mistake of assimilating the world's intelligibility as a law-

---

7. For a denial that the Christian mystical tradition involves anything like an "experience" of God, see Denys Turner, *The Darkness of God: Negativity in Christian Mysticism* (Cambridge: Cambridge University Press, 1998). On my account, Turner's denial is wrongheaded precisely insofar as it requires us to understand "experience" in a Givenist sort of way, such that rejecting Givenism is tantamount to rejecting mysticism as concerned with any paradigmatic Christian religious "experience."

governed domain into its intelligibility as a norm-governed domain. Not all causal relations are grounded by rational potential.[8]

My aim in this chapter and the next is therefore to sketch a reformulation of Gregory of Nyssa's (ca. 335–394 c.e.) theology of religious experience that satisfies the above-mentioned criteria. In so doing, what I hope to show is not necessarily that my proposed reformulation is true, or even true to Gregory (points to which I will return momentarily), but rather that it is possible to conceive of a minimally empiricist theology of religious experience, one consistent with a naturalized platonism and thereby innocent of both Givenism and Coherentism. Rival theologies are perfectly possible. But if my disentanglement of the problem of perceiving God from the pseudoproblem of perception is right, then the contestable substance of the account I offer is not primarily a matter of holding the right constructive philosophical theses (or, for that matter, *any* constructive philosophical theses whatever) about the intentionality of perception. The basis on which we ought to accept or reject the picture I adapt from Gregory is substantively theological and not any philosophical commitment aimed at resolving the long-standing disputes about the nature of experience in general that have mistakenly occupied so much of the territory in recent discussion.[9]

8. What goes wrong with contemporary "science vs. religion" debates is very often either the mistaken tendency to assimilate non-rational causes into rational ones and vice-versa, or to respect the distinction but to map rational causal explanatory grounds straightforwardly onto "religion" and merely causal and non-rational explanatory grounds straightforwardly onto "science." My view implies a version of Gould's "non-overlapping magesteria," but one that requires more nuance than he does about the mapping and about the distinction between modes and contents of discourse in the "religious" vs. "scientific" domains. See Stephen J. Gould, "Non-Overlapping Magesteria," *Natural History* 106 (March 1997): 16–22. Spelling out such a view remains an important task for future work.

9. There are at least two notable exceptions here. The first is Mats Wahlberg's *Seeing Nature as Creation: How Anti-Cartesian Philosophy of Mind and Perception Reshapes Natural Theology* (Umea, Sweden: Umea Universitet, 2009), and the second is Paul A. MacDonald Jr.'s *Knowledge and the Transcendent: An Inquiry into the Mind's Relationship to God* (Washington, DC: Catholic University of America Press, 2009). Both explicitly appropriate McDowell's minimal empiricism into their recovery of theological themes which centrally involves our perceptual

I have suggested that there are three sorts of questions the answers to which are jointly constitutive of a theology of religious experience: (1) What are the perceptible features of divine presence or agency given by the God/world relation? (2) What sort of human perceptual capacities are actualized in our putative perceptual directedness on the relevant features of divine presence or agency? (3) How are the relevant actualizations of perceptual capacities that putatively direct us upon God grounded in nature and grace? In the next chapter, I draw on some relevant writings from Gregory's oeuvre to spell out what I take to be the answers he would offer for each of these questions. I am interested in presenting Gregory's theology of religious experience not merely as an exegetical exercise but as a viable candidate for a normative proposal—one that, if true, gets things right about the intentional structure of our perceptual relation to God.

Showing that Nyssen's account is a viable candidate for a theological explanation of our perceptual relation to God, as I have already mentioned, is not the same as showing that it is the right

relation to God. Wahlberg appropriates McDowell to give articulation to the sort of direct perception of the creative intentionality of the divine mind manifest in "the starry heavens above" that we find in John Calvin, while MacDonald similarly makes use of McDowell in his reading of Thomas Aquinas on the structure of our knowledge of God both here and now *in via* and in the beatific vision of the eschaton. Insofar as both articulate their theological views as predicated on a minimal empiricism, my difference from them is primarily theological. Wahlberg, for example seems to me to unnecessarily limit the scope of his appropriation as having a direct significance only for the doctrine of creation. He does little to defend his claim that "many Christian doctrines can be justified by a perceptual warrant," and that most Christian claims derive their justification instead from "*testimonial* beliefs" (272). Insofar as he suggests that the constraints on the perceptual justification of Christian beliefs are imposed by a McDowellian sort of empiricism rather than strictly on theological grounds, I have taken him to be mistaken. Another worry that distinguishes my approach from theirs is that both Wahlberg and MacDonald tend to deploy McDowell's minimal empiricism as a substantive philosophical theory rather than as merely a therapeutic reminder which has the status of a "grammar." This oversight is not merely rhetorical, insofar as it leads to a disagreement between us about what counts as a good reason for endorsing a theology of religious experience as opposed to what counts as a minimally intelligible one. For example, MacDonald often seems to regard the consistency of Aquinas' account of perception with McDowell's minimal empiricism to count as an argument in favor of Aquinas' theological account of the mind/God relation.

explanation. To defend the truth of the view I derive from Gregory would require a much fuller development than I can give here. But the modesty of my twofold aim—proposing a theology of religious experience that manages to avoid both vicious oscillation and an overly indulgent nostalgia—is belied by the difficulties found in reconciling a theological story to a minimal empiricism.

Before positing my own naturalized platonist reading of Gregory, however, I do some stage-setting in this chapter for the interpretive approach I take in the next. Gregory's thinking is notoriously difficult, and there are many exegetical matters that remain controversial. On more than a few such controversies about how best to understand Gregory's views, I suggest novel readings; this is likely to invite the raised eyebrow of the patristic scholar, who will wonder whether the account I suggest is in any meaningful way attributable to Gregory at all.

At the very least, my appropriation of Gregory invites questions about the sense in which I regard the claims I derive from Gregory to be genuinely attributable to him as opposed to being merely tendentious extrapolations. I can perhaps head off at the pass some potential misunderstandings and objections in this chapter by offering two clarifications about my approach. The first is a clarification about the way I understand the distinction between a merely historical-exegetical description of Gregory and the normative philosophical-theological reading of him that I intend. The second is about my use of sources in framing and addressing the relevant interpretive question, that of how Gregory would have us conceive of our perceptual relation to God.

8.1 Reading Gregory of Nyssa: Historical or Normative?

As I have already mentioned, my purpose in turning to Gregory's theology is to show how it can satisfy some criteria that need to be met for a proposal about our empirical relation to God to be genuine and viable. But Gregory himself never explicitly articulated such criteria, much less attempt to demonstrate how any component of his thinking satisfies them. Simply in virtue of his social and historical location, the notion of a naturalized platonism could not have the significance for him that I have accorded it—that of a minimal empiricism. Moreover, it is not clear what if any connection that notion bears to the sort of platonism Gregory himself embraced in his eclectic philosophical appropriations. Nor do we anywhere find Gregory himself thematizing a theology of religious experience or grouping the three loci I have outlined as constitutive of it.

Does not this suffice to show that whatever reading of Gregory I might propose, it can only obscure or distort Gregory's own thinking by forcing him to speak to concerns alien to his own? Why turn to his oeuvre at all, if it is only to function as a mirror of my own interests? The complaint is one I can imagine being lodged both by patristic scholars and by philosopher-theologians. Both would suppose that my stated normative concerns must unduly control my reading, but the more descriptive orientation of the patristic scholar or historical theologian (insofar as the two differ) and the more normative orientation of the philosopher or theologian would elicit different ways of articulating the complaint.

My imagined patristic scholar would recommend that to the extent that I am interested in appropriating Gregory, I bracket my own normative concerns as much as possible in order to give a reconstruction of Gregory's thinking that is faithful to his context. I should clearly signal when I make the turn to evaluating or appropriating (my reconstruction of) Gregory's thinking so it becomes clear where the proper attributions lay.[10] My imagined philosopher-theologian might suggest that I get on with making the normative claim, presenting and evaluating my arguments for whatever position I believe succeeds in getting things right, without all the unnecessary bloat of textual engagement with Gregory in setting forward those arguments for critical evaluation.

In the end, whether I have gotten things right or not does not depend on whether what I have said is attributable to Gregory or not. Insofar as I am interested in sketching a normative proposal for a theology of religious experience, its genealogy seems largely irrelevant. A brief gesture toward Gregory as the inspiration for the argument should suffice. But against both of these intuitions, I will endeavor to attribute what I say to Gregory himself by way of an engagement with his writings, even while refusing to mark any clean division between my exegetical and normative claims. To those readers inclined toward either of the methodological inclinations just canvassed, my proposal can therefore look like an infelicitous hybrid, a conflation of the distinct descriptive and normative tasks that obscures or weakens the efficacy of each.

In *Gregory of Nyssa, Ancient and (Post)modern*, Morweena Ludlow offers a few considerations that help counter this perspective. She points out that any interpretive use of Gregory's writings—whether historical-exegetical or philosophical-theological—is governed by the interpreter's own norms relative to the use she intends her interpretation to serve. We might be looking at Gregory's theology "in a historical manner to explain how Christian doctrine has got where it is now" or to set it "in contrast with the doctrine of another

---

10. As J. Warren Smith puts it in *Passion and Paradise: Human and Divine Emotion in the Thought of Gregory of Nyssa* (New York: Crossroad, 2004): "It is important to distinguish where Nyssen's argument might have proceeded, or where as a matter of constructive theology . . . we would have liked it to go, from where it does in fact proceed" (17).

theologian in the past" or as "a view to which one should revert" or "an example of an outdated system which should now be corrected."[11] Historical-exegetical descriptions that aim at capturing when and where and to whom Gregory affirmed what within his own sociohistorical context therefore rightly conform to contemporary norms of historical investigation. The norms governing this sort of scholarship, however, are themselves "highly influenced by various theological and philosophical assumptions, albeit tacitly."[12]

Moreover, Ludlow rightly points out that there are many ways to interpret Gregory's writings "on their own terms," and not all of these ways involve engaging them primarily for the purposes we identify with the task of historical reconstruction. Whereas to take Gregory seriously as an instance of early Christian theology involves subjecting his work to norms of history writing evinced in contemporary patristic scholarship, to take him seriously qua bishop or philosopher or theologian in an ecclesiastical and intellectual tradition involves subjecting his work to correspondingly different sets of norms. There is therefore no reason not to "give Gregory up to a full range of readers, indeed to the sort of readers for which his work was originally intended: theologians, priests, men and women of faith, interested sceptics."[13]

To engage him in such ways entails attributing certain views to him as a matter of history, but we need not show determinately that he in fact held those views in order to respect the original intentions in question. For while "there are limits to what Gregory's text can plausibly mean—limits which can be ascertained through the scholarly understanding of his language, and his social, political, and cultural context"—operating within those limits can make available

11. Morweena Ludlow, *Gregory of Nyssa: Ancient and (Post)modern* (New York: Oxford University Press, 2007), 9.
12. Ibid., 8.
13. Ibid., 5.

"several plausible meanings."[14] The different eyes that we bring to Gregory's texts—historical, theological, philosophical—can help illumine novel readings within the range of plausible readings. This is similar to the sense in which a modern-day poet—as far removed as she might be from the context of an ancient poetic text—might yet be uniquely suited to uncover the contours of that text in a way that the literary scholar is not.[15] For this reason, Ludlow concludes, we can "outline a productive relationship between historical and explicitly theological readings of the Church fathers" even when "the boundary between historical and theological reflection is often difficult to perceive."[16]

To get a better grasp on Ludlow's case for the usefulness of a more permissive interpretive approach to Gregory, it can help to consider a parallel case outside the domain of early Christian texts. We can find a recent philosophical analogue in Saul Kripke's reading of the private language argument he finds in remarks 201 and 202 of Wittgenstein's *Philosophical Investigations*. In *Wittgenstein on Rules and Private Language*, Kripke offers an exegesis of the paradox he finds Wittgenstein articulating about the idea that our use of the terms of our language is governed by rules we have internalized that function as a determinate standard of correctness for our usage. The structure of the alleged problem of rule-following itself need not detain us—the point is that Kripke's essay professes an interest in offering a reading of Wittgenstein on the problem.

But in doing so, Kripke wants, on the one hand, to acknowledge that a problem he finds in the relevant passages of the *Investigations* presents itself to him in a way that Wittgenstein himself would likely not recognize as his own. For various reasons having to do with what

14. Ibid.
15. Ibid.
16. Ibid., 4, 8.

he takes to be Wittgenstein's likely philosophical presuppositions, Kripke admits that Wittgenstein "might well disapprove of the straightforward formulation given here." "Nevertheless," Kripke goes on to say, "I choose to be so bold as to say: Wittgenstein holds . . . that [such and such a problem afflicts the notion of rule-following]."[17] What justifies this boldness? Is Kripke claiming that the philosophical problem he derives from Wittgenstein is one that is genuinely *there* in Wittgenstein's text, or did Kripke himself simply put it there? He appears to be attributing his reformulation of Wittgenstein to Wittgenstein himself, after having already admitted that the reformulation is alien to the context of Wittgenstein's own thinking. So which is it? In his introductory remarks, Kripke explains his interpretive intentions:

> In the following, I am largely trying to present Wittgenstein's argument, or, more accurately, that set of problems and arguments which I personally have gotten out of reading Wittgenstein. With few exceptions, I am *not* trying to present views of my own; neither am I trying to endorse or to criticize Wittgenstein's approach. . . . Probably many of my formulations and recastings of the argument are done in a way Wittgenstein would not himself approve. So the present paper should be thought of as expounding neither "Wittgenstein's" argument nor "Kripke's": rather Wittgenstein's argument as it struck Kripke, as it presented a problem for him.[18]

What Kripke is getting at here, I think, is this. The formulation of the rule-following problem that Wittgenstein's text incites Kripke to develop—its ability to strike him in the particular way it does—is only possible because of the different philosophical assumptions and predilections that Kripke himself brought to the table. It may not be possible to make explicit all of the assumptions and predilections

---

17. Saul A. Kripke, *Wittgenstein on Rules and Private Language* (Cambridge, MA: Harvard University Press, 1982), 70–71.
18. Kripke, *Wittgenstein on Rules and Private Language*, 5.

responsible for disposing him to read Wittgenstein as he did (the way it struck him), even if he can identify some of the points at which his reading might be out of keeping with Wittgenstein's own philosophical predilections. Kripke does not aim, however, to adjudicate these differences, whether by criticizing Wittgenstein's presuppositions or defending his own, and in this sense he disclaims trying to endorse or to criticize Wittgenstein's approach. He gives us only the vaguest suspicions about *why* Wittgenstein might have disapproved of his formulation. What he attempts to exegete is not Wittgenstein but his mode of responsiveness to Wittgenstein as it is elicited by the text.

But Kripke does not suppose that his reader response approach to the *Investigations* renders it merely a mirror that reflects his own views, or that the formulation of the problem he finds in Wittgenstein's text is an artifact of his own imagining. This is the sense in which he wishes to maintain that the problem that strikes him from his reading of Wittgenstein is not simply "Kripke's." What he means to disclaim, I think, is merely using Wittgenstein's texts as a convenient platform for elaborating his own views, as if Wittgenstein's way of putting things inspired him to identify a problem about rule-following distinct from Wittgenstein's own. That would be to regard the relevant passages in the *Investigations* as eliciting his reflections in an entirely nonconstitutive way, something like how a stone causes ripples in the water. Kripke's proposed reading would thus be no more "in" Wittgenstein than ripples are "in" the stone.

On the contrary, Kripke plainly wishes to retain the idea that the problem that strikes him remains a *Wittgensteinian* problem, even if not one that Wittgenstein himself would have or could have formulated. Such an idea is bold precisely because Kripke does not himself endeavor (as his subsequent interpreters have done) to determine precisely *where* Wittgenstein ends and Kripke begins. What his essay gives us is therefore neither Wittgenstein nor Kripke but the fusion of their horizons, to employ the Gadamerian image. Recognizing this, philosophers wishing to address themselves to this fusion in the horizons of two distinct subjects have found it convenient to grant the fusion its own fictional persona—that of "Kripkenstein." This portmanteau is useful because it enables us to engage the fusion on its own terms—as a reading of Wittgenstein that genuinely illumines his views while also failing to be any straightforward reconstruction of them. Kripke's essay has had an important influence both on those whose interests are centered on a proper reconstruction of Wittgenstein's later philosophy and on those interested in normative questions about rule-following in natural language.

Whatever impact my reading of Gregory might have, I intend something like the kind of impact exerted by Kripkenstein. To return to Ludlow, I can affirm of my own reading that while it might seem as if I were "subjecting Gregory to criteria which are not only anachronistic, but which fail to capture the best of what Gregory is trying to say," in fact I am simply "using him as a source of good ideas":

> In some ways the plucking of a healthy theological shoot from the past and transplanting it into newer soil—or grafting it onto a newer stem—is less anachronistic than the kind of "return" to the past attempted by some theological conservatism. Furthermore, some of the analytic philosophical uses of Gregory have been the most creative: precisely because of their awareness that one cannot step into the same theological-philosophical river twice, they feel free to use the ideas they find stimulating and reject the rest. Consequently (and rather oddly, given that they seem to share so few philosophical ideas in common with Gregory), they seem to be doing far more justice to Gregory's own concept of the non-finality of theological pronouncements than those who seem to be trying to "recover the past."[19]

In issuing my own Kripkean disclaimer, therefore, the theology of religious experience I suggest in this chapter claims to be neither Gregory's nor my own, but a retrieval grounded by the fusion of our horizons. My exegesis attempts to exposit from his texts the way in which his problems and arguments have struck me, given the entanglement of a theology of religious experience with the problem of perception that I have articulated thus far.

8.2 Sources

My reading of Gregory draws primarily from five texts in his corpus, three from what Jean Daniélou characterizes as the middle period of his career and two from what he identifies as the late period.[20] The late period is marked by what Daniélou characterized as Gregory's two most important works of spiritual theology, both written in the 390s near the end of his life—namely, *Vita Moysis* (*The Life of Moses*, hereafter LM) and *Commentarius in Canticum Canticorum* (*Homilies on the Song of Songs*, hereafter HSS).[21] In both works Gregory offers allegorical readings of Scripture that guide his readers on a spiritual

19. Ludlow, *Gregory of Nyssa*, 276.

20. Jean Daniélou, "La chronologie des oeuvres de Grégoire de Nysse," in *Studia Patristica: Papers Presented to the Fourth International Conference on Patristic Studies*, ed. Frank Leslie Cross (Berlin: Akademie Verlag, 1966), 159–69. Both were written in the early 390s, Cahill suggests between 391 and 394 for *Homilies on the Song of Songs*. See J. B. Cahill, "The Date and Setting of Gregory of Nyssa's Commentary on the Song of Songs," *Journal of Theological Studies*, 32 (1981): 447–60. For the dating of *The Life of Moses* around the same period, see Franz Dünzl, "Gregory von Nyssa's *Homilien zum Canticum* auf dem Hintergrund seiner *Vita Moysis*," *Vigiliae Christianae* 44 (1990): 371–81.

21. Gregory of Nyssa, *The Life of Moses*, trans. Abraham Malherbe and Everett Ferguson (New York: Paulist, 1978). Gregory of Nyssa, *Homilies on the Song of Songs*, no. 13 in *Writings from the Greco-Roman World*, ed. Brian E. Daley and John. T. Fitzgerald, trans. with intro. and notes by Richard A. Norris Jr. (Atlanta, GA: Society of Biblical Literature, 2012); cf. the older and somewhat less reliable translation of Casmir McCambley: Gregory of Nyssa, *Commentary on the Song of Songs* (Brookline, MA: Hellenic College Press, 1987). Unless otherwise noted, I quote from Norris's translation, although for reference and comparison purposes I cite McCambley's translation as well.

pilgrimage through three moments or stages in the soul's ascent to God, which he adapts from Origen's conception of spiritual progress as a journey in the acquisition of virtue (*ethike*) that leads to a spiritual way of perceiving and responding to the natural world (*physike*), which in turn prepares one for a contemplative vision of God (*enoptike*).[22]

While Gregory's version is significantly developed from Origen's (in ways to be explored below), he finds the threefold pattern of ascent repeated in both the calling and subsequent exploits of Moses and again in the bride's relentless pursuit of her bridegroom. Gregory allows the biblical text to shape the contours of the ascent in different ways in LM and HSS. In both texts, however, the basic threefold structure serves as the fundamental form of the Christian's progress in being conformed to the image of Christ by the Spirit through a process of moral and intellectual transformation. Gregory characterizes the transformation of the self enacted in the ascent as our creaturely mode of participation in God's goodness and beauty. In articulating the structure of intentionality involved in the ascent—the different ways in which it manages to direct us upon God—both of Gregory's late commentaries draw heavily on the language and imagery of sense perception.

One way of getting at the problem of properly understanding Gregory's account of our perceptual relation to God is by identifying it with the problem of properly understanding his deployment of perception talk in these two texts. Thus, for example, in the first homily of HSS, Gregory comments that "there is in us a dual activity of perception, the one bodily, the other more divine. . . . [T]here is a certain analogy between the sense organs of the body and the operations of the soul."[23] Whereas the sense organs direct us on

---

22. Andrew Louth, *The Origins of the Christian Mystical Tradition: From Plato to Denys*, 2nd ed. (Oxford: Oxford University Press, 2007), iv.

sensory realities such as the distinction in taste between wine and milk or the sense of touch when "the lips of two persons make contact in a kiss," the "intellectual and apprehending capacity of the soul grasps spiritual realities."[24]

Sarah Coakley's recent discussion of Gregory's theology of spiritual perception has reintroduced the central interpretive question raised by Mariette Canévet in the dictionary of spirituality, which is whether we ought to understand the apprehension of spiritual realities via some faculty or process of spiritual sensing as continuous or discontinuous with the workings of bodily sensation in relation to sensible realities. Regarding the distinction between bodily and spiritual perceptual capacities, Canévet asks whether "the spiritual senses designate a 'spiritual' exercise of our properly corporeal senses through a transfiguration of these very senses, or is the perception of the divine performed by an inner sense that has nothing to do with the bodily senses?"[25]

The Christian's apprehension of God is thus to a greater or lesser extent continuous or discontinuous with ordinary operations of bodily sense perception insofar as acts of spiritual sensing depend on acts of bodily sensing. The former option discussed by Canévet—that of spiritual sensing as involving a transfiguration of bodily sensing—posits some form of continuity or relationship of dependence between spiritual and bodily perceptual capacities, whereas the latter option posits their complete discontinuity or

23. Gregory, *Homilies on the Song of Songs* (Norris), Homily 1, 35; cf. Gregory, *Commentary on the Song of Songs* (McCambley), 52, J34.

24. Cf. Gregory, *Life of Moses*, 156–57, in which the apprehension of God is in some sense not a sensory apprehension but an intellectual one, and yet it remains "possible . . . to come to some perception of the divine concern for us" (215).

25. Canévet, "Sens Spirituel," in *Dictionnaire de spiritualité ascétique et mystique doctrine et histoire*, vol. 15, ed. Marcel Viller et al. (Paris: Beauchesne, 1993): "D'où la question: en raison de l'Incarnation les sens spirituel désignent-ils un exercise "spirituel" de nos propres sens corporels grâce à une transfiguration de ces sense, ou la perception du divin effectuée par un sens intérieur qui n'a rien à voir avec les sens corporels?" (15).

mutual independence. If the latter view is correct and the inner sense by which we apprehend God in Christ operates independently of our bodily outer sense, we may well continue to recognize a parallel structure or family resemblance between one's bodily sensory capacities and one's capacities to apprehend God in Christ. Similarities of that sort are precisely what explain Scripture's frequent deployment of sensory language in contexts of the believer's acquaintance with God. Such uses serve to illustrate an interiorized and nonsensory spiritual awareness of God in the soul by means of parallels drawn from the realm of the corporeal senses, and this is just the sort of analogy that Gregory has in mind. But we should not take this mere resemblance to indicate that exercises of spiritual perception actually themselves involve facts about physical sensations or the corporeal faculties that give rise to them. Rather, there remains a strict separation between the two modes of apprehending. Spiritual-perceptual acts of seeing God's presence and activity in creation through Christ do not in themselves involve ordinary bodily acts of sight—the two are altogether different modes of taking in different dimensions of reality.

Canévet attributes this view to Origen of Alexandria (ca. 185–ca. 254), whom she reads (and who is standardly read) as holding a form of Christianized platonism in which the flesh and spirit are strongly disjoined.[26] Accordingly, for Origen the sensuous character of bodily perception finds its locus in the materiality of the flesh (the physical body) whereas the intellective character of spiritual sense originates in the immaterial soul.[27] On this understanding, one might regard bodily sensing more or less loosely as a metaphor for spiritual sensing. More strongly, one might regard them as related analogically—as

---

26. "Sense Origène penche pour une discontinuité entre les deux modes" (ibid.).

27. Gordon Rudy argues that Origen's belief in an eschatological "spiritual" body which he conceives as having as little as possible to do with our present material form of bodily existence.

conceptually or really homologous with one another such that, for example, one would not be misled by reading off key features of the inner logic or structure of intentionality of spiritual sensing from an examination of the inner logic or structure of intentionality of bodily sensing.

But whichever of these glosses on Origen one prefers (and both of them have their defenders),[28] the relation between corporeal and spiritual perception is at bottom one involving distinct faculties, even if the two are thought to be tightly coordinated.[29] Consequently, the meaning of the term *perception* as used in "spiritual perception" must be understood, strictly speaking, as either analogical to the term's use in "sense perception" or as univocal in both employments but identifying only the abstracted logical structure of intentionality they share but each instantiate in their own sui generis way. Such an analysis of the use of "perception" would apply mutatis mutandis to Gregory's use of perceptual language (and his reading of the scriptural use of perceptual language) more generally, including his use of visual, auditory, tactile, olfactory, and gustatory language of the sensory modalities in their bodily sense as compared with their spiritual sense.

Where an Origenist reading of Gregory posits a fundamental discontinuity between bodily sense perception and the spiritual apprehension of God, the alternative reading Canévet suggests posits

28. In his delineation of the five spiritual senses, and especially in his Songs commentary, Origen often appears to take the stronger view, which is why Rahner and von Balthasar both tend toward a stronger "analogical" identification over a "metaphorical one. See Stephen Fields, "Balthasar and Rahner on the Spiritual Senses," *Theological Studies* 57 (1996): 224–41. But both "metaphorical" and recent attempts to secure more substantial "analogical" views of Origen *both* belong within Canévet's "discontinuity" conception of spiritual perception, insofar as they stop short of regarding spiritual perception as essentially (rather than incidentally) *constituted by* bodily sensing. For a useful discussion on which views were actually held by Origen, see Mark McInroy, "Origen of Alexandria," in *The Spiritual Senses: Perceiving God in Western Christianity*, ed. Sarah Coakley and Paul Gavrilyuk (Cambridge: Cambridge University Press, 2012), 20–35.

29. See Gordon Rudy's helpful exegetical summary of the development of Origen's views in *Mystical Language of Sensation in the Later Middle Ages* (New York: Routledge, 2002), 17–32.

a fundamental continuity. On this reading, Christians apprehend God by a 'spiritual' exercise of our properly corporeal senses. Spiritual perception thus involves the deployment of the bodily senses, but in a spiritual way as opposed to a fleshly way. Taken in this manner, Gregory might read, for example, Paul's rejection of the sight "according to the flesh" by which we behold Christ after the ascension in 2 Cor. 5:16-17 not as a rejection of the sensory capacity of the corporeal body to behold Christ's presence in the world, but rather as a call for the proper *use* of that body, which (as in Gal. 5:16-26) is "according to the spirit" (or better, "the Spirit") when it is governed in accordance with virtue. In the same way that we can read Paul as envisioning the transfiguration of bodily sense by its spiritual deployment, so too does Gregory. Thus understood, the form of continuity Gregory posits between sense perception and spiritual perception is one in which the spiritual necessarily involves, makes use of, or appropriates the body. Since on this reading of the twofold nature of perception, the Christian's apprehension of God necessarily involves a spiritual deployment of corporeal sense, a proper analysis of the structure internal to an act of spiritually apprehending God must make some reference to our ordinary faculties of sense perception. Bodily sensing must somehow facilitate the spiritual act rather than merely being irrelevant to it or even a hindrance or obstacle to it.

Canévet suggests that while Gregory of Nyssa was in many other respects Origen's spiritual successor, he departed from his master's discontinuous reading of the relation between spiritual and corporeal sensing in favor of a claim of continuity.[30] According to Gregory, the practical and theoretical knowledge of the Triune Lord enjoyed by Christians both necessarily involves sensory content and ultimately

---

30. See Canévet, *Dictionnaire de spiritualité*, 24–25, 30, 608–609, 611–12.

draws its justification from human perception functioning in the ordinary way. When deployed in a spiritual as opposed to a fleshly way, those very sensory capacities basic to our human constitution and by which we take in and respond to the world in everyday life become capable of rendering us directly and objectively open to God, both within and beyond creation. The sensory relation to reality must be something incorporated into the spiritual-perceptual act itself rather than merely put to one side as Origen (allegedly) supposed.

Coakley's recent reading of Gregory on the spiritual senses essentially resurrects Canévet's view, which she claims has been inadequately explored because of the subsequent influence of Daniélou's magisterial treatment of Gregory. Coakley claims that while Daniélou rightly recognized the transformative dimension of our perceptual relation to God, he nevertheless remained insensitive to the question raised by Canévet. Rather, Daniélou simply defaulted to the Origenist reading of Gregory.[31] Plumping for something more closely resembling Canévet's continuity claim, however, Coakley thinks it possible to read Gregory's late work in terms of an intimate cooperation between bodily and intellectual capacities, rather than merely as two distinct (even if analogically related) human abilities. Daniélou might not have missed the nature of the continuity, she claims, if he had not cordoned off Gregory's late spiritual works of HSS and LM from his earlier midcareer philosophical writings as sources in the reconstruction of his views on religious experience.

---

31. See Coakley, "Gregory of Nyssa," in *Spiritual Senses*, 36–55. He picked it up, she suggests, from Rahner's influential article on the "five spiritual senses." Karl Rahner, "Le debut d'une doctrine des cinq sens spirituels chez Origene," *Revue d'ascetique et de mystique* 13 (1932): 112–45, published later in shortened form in his *Schriften zur Theologie*, vol. 12: *Theologie aus Erfahrung des Geistes*, ed. K. Neufeld, SJ (Zurich: Benziger Verlag, 1975), 111–36; English trans. Dom David Morland in *Theological Investigations*, vol. 16 (New York: Seabury, 1979), 81–103.

A clearer picture emerges, Coakley suggests, when we more carefully integrate the anthropological insights of those earlier texts into our reading of the perceptual relation implicit in the soul's ascent. The transition from Gregory's earlier works into the maturation of his midcareer thinking is typically thought to be marked by the deaths of his siblings—his elder brother and teacher Basil of Caesarea in January 379 followed less than a year later by Macrina the Younger, the elder sister who had played an instrumental role in raising both brothers and instructing them about the ascetic life. Taking on their mantle, Gregory not only seeks to perpetuate their philosophical and theological legacy but also nuances their teaching and takes them in his own new directions. Coakley herself concentrates her attention on some relevant passages from *De anima et de resurrectione* (*On the Soul and the Resurrection*, hereafter OSR).[32] Coakley's salutary approach brings back to the fore Canévet's earlier line of questioning and contends for an integration of the views espoused in Gregory's earlier works into his later thinking on spiritual perception. Few recent studies have thematized the problem of spiritual perception in Gregory, and fewer still offer any detailed explanation of how his earlier account of the soul's perceptual powers shows up in his later thinking about the form of intentionality involved in the ascent.[33]

But I also think we can improve on Coakley's suggestion by broadening the scope of texts we consider from his middle period.

---

32. Gregory of Nyssa, *On the Soul and the Resurrection*, trans. with intro. by Catherine P. Roth (Crestwood, NY: St. Vladimir's Seminary Press, 1993).

33. Gregory's understanding of the nature and function of our perceptual capacities tends to play a subservient role to a more fundamental object of analysis, such as his view of the passions, as in Smith, *Passion and Paradise*; or faith in Martin Laird, *Gregory of Nyssa and the Grasp of Faith* (New York: Oxford University Press, 2004); or grace in Verna Harrison, *Grace and Human Freedom according to St. Gregory of Nyssa* (New York: Edwin Mellen, 1992). But it is equally possible to place his views on the intentionality of perception as central, and this has not yet been attempted, as far as I am aware.

During the period immediately following the deaths of Basil and Macrina, Gregory develops his most important contributions to a theology of religious experience not only in OSR, but also in *De hominis opificio* ("On the Making of Man," hereafter OMM)[34] and book 2 of *Contra Eunomium* ("Against Eunomius," hereafter AE).[35] Across these three works, all composed between 379 and 382 C.E.,[36] we find Gregory developing his views about each of the three theological loci that I have designated as jointly constitutive of a theology of religious experience.[37]

We can therefore identify across these works Gregory's account of the perceptible properties of God given in the God/world relation, his conception of the reach and limits of human perceptual capacities, and his understanding of the proper relation of nature to grace grounding those capacities. But for the moment, my point is that it is possible derive a composite picture of the structure of intentionality Gregory attributes to our perception of God from these three texts. Assuming that we can find such a picture in Gregory's earlier works, what is the relation between that picture and Gregory's treatment of the soul's ascent to God in LM and HSS? Coakley's complaint about Daniélou's account of the ascent is that it neglects Gregory's earlier treatment of the bodily senses, but while she insists that we must incorporate Gregory's philosophy into his later spirituality, she

---

34. Gregory of Nyssa, "On the Making of Man," trans. Henry Austin Wilson, in *Nicene and Post-Nicene Fathers*, ed. Philip Schaff and Henry Wace, vol. 5, second series (Peabody, MA: Hendrickson, 1994), 386–426.

35. Gregory of Nyssa, "Against Eunomius," trans. Henry Austin Wilson, in Schaff and Wace, *Nicene and Post-Nicene Fathers*, 33–247; and Gregory, "The Second Book against Enoumius (Translation)," trans. Stuart George Hall, in *Gregory of Nyssa: Contra Eunomium II*, ed. Lenka Karfíková, Scot Douglass, and Johannes Zachhuber (Leiden: Brill, 2004), 59–204.

36. Pierre Maraval, "Chronology of Works," in *The Brill Dictionary of Gregory of Nyssa*, ed. Lucas Francisco Mateo-Seco and Giulio Maspero, trans. Seth Cherney (Leiden: Brill, 2010), 153–69.

37. Of course, the rhetorical and polemical contexts of these texts differ significantly from one another and those differences must be taken into account when drawing together Gregory's claims into a composite picture.

does not offer any principled way of determining the sense in which the earlier work might be more philosophical and the later more spiritual. She only insists that we must relate the two aspects of Gregory's thought, whereas Daniélou insulates one from the other. "Implicitly," she says, he seems to have "left that topic of ordinary physiological sensation or perception to some sort of *philosophical* analysis in Gregory, whereas what he is discussing under the rubric of 'the spiritual senses' is what he calls 'la vie spirituelle' [the spiritual life]."[38]

Whether or not Daniélou was in fact guilty of such a thing, Coakley is surely right to reject any view that fails "to hold philosophy and spirituality together."[39] But it would help us determine just *how* to relate Gregory's earlier philosophical thinking to his later views on spirituality if we had a better sense of these *relata*. The three texts of Gregory's middle period—as different as they are from one another in genre, rhetorical purposes, and occasion—evince more similarity with one another as philosophical discourses than they do with the spiritual character of Gregory's late work. Accounting for that difference can furnish us with a heuristic clue about how the views I have culled from OMM, OSR, and AE show up in the theology of the spiritual senses we find in LM and HSS. I propose that whereas we find Gregory giving a conceptual analysis of the structure of intentionality involved in a human perceptual relation to God in the earlier work, in the later texts we find him describing how that same structure comes to be instantiated in anyone's actual enjoyment of that relation.

Put another way, Gregory's treatment of the God/world relation, human perceptual capacities, and nature and grace in the earlier

---

38. Coakley, "Gregory of Nyssa," 42.
39. Ibid., 41. See also Sarah Coakley, "Re-thinking Gregory of Nyssa: Introduction—Gender, Trinitarian Analogies, and the Pedagogy of the Song," *Modern Theology* 18, no. 2 (2002): 431–43, 441.

texts functions like an architect drafting a blueprint for a theology of religious experience. Although the literary forms and occasions for the three earlier texts are different from one another—OMM is an exposition of the creation of humans in the Genesis account written as a supplement to Basil's *Hexaemeron*, OSR is written as a dialogue between Nyssen and Macrina, and AE defends and extends Basil's opposition of Eunomian heresy—all are primarily aimed at describing and explaining their titular doctrinal locutions. OMM is a scriptural account of the theological anthropology Gregory finds in the Genesis account, OSR a dialogical account of the anthropology demanded by our eschatological end, and AE a highly polemical rejoinder to Eunomius's writings about the comprehensibility of the divine nature.

But the rhetorical aim of Gregory's expositions in each case is to identify the proper boundaries for our beliefs. Moral-practical guidance is at best implicit or, when explicit, made subordinate to this wider doxastic aim. By way of contrast, these lines drawn in earlier works function within his late works much like a blueprint functions for the foreman at the construction site—as an action-guiding tool for practical reasoning. As such, the rhetorical aim of HSS and LM is not primarily that of *drafting* a conceptual analysis but rather *implementing* his earlier thinking as a guide for our practical reasoning. Warren Smith has likewise described this as a movement from a structural "diagram" to the dynamics of that structure "at work in response to God's self-revelation."[40]

---

40. Speaking of the relation between OMM/OSR on the one hand and HSS/LM on the other, Smith says that the former "describe the process [of the soul's journey into God] *anthropologically*" by outlining "the dynamics of the human soul to explain psychological mechanisms necessary for the transformation of the passions," while the latter offers instead a "narrative description of the ascent—the intellect's turning of the lower faculties toward the Divine" (Smith, *Passion and Paradise*, 149).

Admittedly, appropriating Gregory's texts in this way implies a significant continuity in the development of his thought. Indeed, I endorse a particularly strong thesis about that continuity—namely, that Nyssen's way of integrating the relevant theological loci into a theology of religious experience in the earlier texts does not substantially differ from the account evinced in the later ones. Coakley disagrees. She holds that Gregory's conception of the continuity between bodily and spiritual sense underwent a significant transformation in the transition from his middle period to his late period.[41] On my view, however, the consistency of his later thinking with his earlier views on our perceptual relation to God emerges once we widen the scope of texts and topics that bear on the question. When we do this, we find that the structure of perceptual intentionality undergirding Gregory's story about the soul's ascent in LM and HSS deploys a picture of the God/world relation, human perceptual capacities, and nature and grace that he had already staked out in OMM, OSR, and AE. His spiritual theology can thus be read as coherently and straightforwardly precipitating out of his philosophical theology.[42]

---

41. On Coakley's story, although Gregory has begun to assign the bodily senses a positive role as susceptible of spiritual transformation in OSR, he still regards our corporeality as subservient to the "higher" regulative function of the rational "eye of the soul" (Coakley, "Gregory of Nyssa," 53–54). By the time we get to HSS, however, Gregory permits the bodily senses to be activated in a perception of God that overwhelms the mind's eye, which is darkened in a sensory relation to Christ in which the "supposedly 'lower' senses, in their transformed and purged condition, seem to topple the higher ones at last" (ibid., 50, 54). The third and final stage of the ascent, on Coakley's reading, effects a reversal of the supremacy Gregory had accorded to the inner eye of the soul in his earlier writings. Whereas he had not yet completely let go of the privilege of the rational "eye of the soul" in his mid-career writings, his late work not only relinquishes that privilege but accords it to the bodily senses instead. Thus in the third and "contemplative" stage of the ascent, the corporeal senses *become* "spiritual senses" while "the mind in its 'seeing' capacity . . . is completely darkened in the intimacy of divine closeness" (ibid., 50). As we will see below, I think this is a misreading of the "divine darkness" trope in Gregory's thinking.

42. This does not imply, however, that the theology—or even more narrowly, the theology of religious experience—Gregory develops over the course of his life is in every way coherent or systematic. I agree with Warren Smith's judgment that Gregory's account is theologically "kaleidoscopic" (*Passion and Paradise*, 51). But it is to say that we can construct a coherent

Changing the metaphor somewhat, what we find in Nyssen's structural diagram are the lexical and syntactical materials for a coherent conceptual *grammar* of Christian religious experience as the soul's ascent to God, whereas what we find in his account of the moral-practical dynamics is instruction on the proper *use* of that grammar, a *pragmatics* of the soul's ascent. I turn now to an elucidation of both.

picture *out of* the resources he gives us, and further that doing so does not force us to read Gregory *against* Gregory in the way it would if, e.g., Coakley's developmental story were right.

9

Christian Religious Experience

A Posttherapeutic Proposal

The aim of this chapter is to spell out both Nyssen's conceptual grammar of spiritual perception and the form of the Christian life he takes it to engender. The picture I offer here is guided by the twin interpretive aims of retrieval I introduced in the previous chapter: (1) remaining consistent with the minimally empiricist requirements of a naturalized platonism and (2) avoiding any conflation between law-governed and norm-governed phenomena.

I proceed as follows. First, to reconstruct what I regard as the conceptual grammar governing Nyssen's account of our perceptual relation to God, I sketch very briefly three theses advanced in his earlier works, each comprising one of the three necessary constituents of a theology of religious experience: the perceptual content given by the God/world relation, the human perceptual capacities of his theological anthropology, and the grounding of our perceptual relation to God in nature and grace. Nyssen's metaphysics of divine and created powers in the God/world relation determine for him what of God he takes to be perceptually available to us in creation. In Gregory's theological anthropology, our perceptual capacities to take in the manifestations of divine power in the world are constituted by capacities for *moral* perception that he takes to supervene on our capacities for sense perception. Finally, Nyssen grounds these capacities to perceive God in created nature, and grounds the activations of such capacities in the grace of divine agency.

Second, with this threefold structural diagram of our perceptual relation to God in place, I contend that my reading remains entirely consistent with the naturalized platonism constitutive of a minimal empiricism. Whatever the other demerits of the view, it illustrates a theology of religious experience apart from the problem of perception and without confronting either a Givenist problem of fit or a Coherentist problem of friction. I then offer a reading of Nyssen on the soul's ascent to God in *The Life of Moses* (hereafter, LM) and *Homilies on the Song of Songs* (hereafter, HSS) as the dynamic outworking of Nyssen's minimally empiricist model of spiritual perception as a distinctively Christian model of practical reason.

Finally, I conclude with some remarks that interpret the significance of Nyssen's minimally empiricist theology of religious experience against the backdrop of my deconstruction of the problem of perception conducted in previous chapters.

9.1 God and World:
Manifestations of Power, Created and Divine

The first question to be addressed if we are to understand Nyssen's theology of religious experience is what of God he takes to be present in or to creation. The question is metaphysical rather than epistemological insofar as it concerns what features of God's presence or agency are in fact *there* to be perceived, whether or not anyone succeeds in acquiring a perceptual knowledge of them. Commentators have often observed that the distinction between creator and creature is the most fundamental feature of Gregory's theological metaphysics,[1] but the more difficult matter has been working out what sort of relation is marked by the distinction. The two most prominent guiding themes in Nyssen's treatment are, on the surface at least, apparently at odds.

On the one hand, he stresses a strong continuity between divine and creaturely being according to which created nature essentially "participates" (*metousia*) in God, insisting that every fundamental property a creature might have necessarily exhibits kinship (*koinonia*) with properties that belong properly to God.[2] On the other hand, he stresses a strong discontinuity between creature and creator, insisting on the absolute separation or "gap" (*diastema*) that exists between the mutable form of creaturely existence bound by space and time and the eternal and immutable being of God.[3] How does he reconcile these views?

In "Against Eunomius," Nyssen relies on a metaphysics of powers and their manifestations to spell out the sense in which properties of God are present in the properties of creatures.[4] Roughly, he holds that substances are individuated by their essential or natural powers,

1. See, for example, Andrew Louth: "For Gregory the realm of the intelligible is divided into the uncreated and creative on the one hand and on the other that which is created—and this is the fundamental divide." *The Origins of the Christian Mystical Tradition: From Plato to Denys*, 2nd ed. (Oxford: Oxford University Press, 2007),78.
2. See David L. Balas, *Metousia Theou: Man's Participatoin in God's Perfections according to Saint Gregory of Nyssa* (Rome: I. B. C. Libreria Herder, 1966); and Balas, "Participation," in *The Brill Dictionary of Gregory of Nyssa*, ed. Lucas Francisco Mateo-Seco and Giulio Maspero, trans. Seth Cherney (Leiden: Brill, 2010), 581–87.
3. So Louth: "The gulf between uncreated and created is such for Gregory that there is no possibility of the soul passing across it" (*Origins*, 79). See also Scot Douglass's extensive discussion of the *diastema*, or "gap," between God and creation in *Theology of the Gap: Cappadocian Language Theory and the Trinitarian Controversy* (New York: Peter Lang, 2005), 29–56.

and the nature (*phusis*), substance, or essence (*ousia*) of a thing is just its fundamental power, that power in virtue of which it possesses whatever powers it has, or that power in virtue of which all of its other powers are united.[5] For something to have a power is for it to have a disposition of a particular sort—namely, the disposition to manifest itself in some characteristic type of event when given the appropriate circumstances required for triggering that disposition and thus eliciting the relevant manifestation.[6] So, for example, for a bottle to possess the property of fragility is for it to be disposed to breaking, a disposition triggered or activated when, for example, it is struck with sufficient force. To talk about any property of a thing is therefore to refer to a power or some unified collection of powers it has.[7] We can thus think of properties of objects as powers and of powers as truth-makers for counterfactuals—descriptions of what that object *would do* in any of the various possible circumstances in which it might find itself.[8]

Attributing the property of fragility to my eyeglasses, for example, names the fact that they possess a nature sufficient to be (part of) the *truth-maker* for those counterfactuals that describe the relative ease with which they might be broken or no longer properly functional given various circumstances that would activate that disposition (for example, if they were stepped on, if I ran over them, if they were fired

---

4. My discussion of powers in Nyssen is adapted from Michel René Barnes, *The Power of God: Dynamis in Gregory of Nyssa's Trinitarian Theology* (Washington, DC: Catholic University of America Press, 2001), which I pull toward discussions about powers that have enjoyed a recent resurgence in contemporary metaphysics.

5. Barnes, *Dynamis*, 282–83.

6. Jennifer McKitrick, "A Case for Extrinsic Dispositions," *Australasian Journal of Philosophy* 81, no. 2 (June 2003): 155–74, 157.

7. Barnes, *Dynamis*, 290. Gregory's understanding that "if the same power, then the same nature," Barnes says, has as a corollary the idea that "common operations [activities or *energeiai*] indicate common natures." See also Michael Rea's discussion of natures as fundamental powers in "Hylomorphism Reconditioned," *Philosophical Perspectives* 25, no. 1 (December 2011): 341–58.

8. Jonathan D. Jacobs, "Powerful Qualities, not Pure Powers," *Monist* 94, no. 1 (2011): 81–102, 92.

out of a cannon, and so forth). My eyeglasses possess the property of fragility, therefore, simply because they are *disposed* to breaking in these circumstances (among others), even if none of those circumstances ever actually obtains and thus the relevant disposition is never triggered in a characteristic *manifestation* of the fragility of my eyeglasses, such as their breaking. So while they need not break in order to be fragile, my eyeglasses are not in fact fragile if there are no possible circumstances in which they *would* break.

This picture of properties as powers allows us to reconstruct Gregory's view that creation participates in God. All created objects partake of God, Nyssen thinks, insofar as every single creaturely property—every disposition or power that creatures do or might possess—is itself just the activation or manifestation of a corresponding divine property—a power or disposition possessed by God. The entire set of divine properties, powers, and dispositions activated or manifest as the properties, powers, or dispositions of created objects are what Gregory refers to as God's *energeia*, or "activities."[9] The powers and manifestations of powers exhibited by creatures, in other words, are themselves manifestations of divine powers. Whereas every creature is freely brought into being ex nihilo by God, the properties and powers borne by creatures—their powers and dispositions to do the various things determined by their respective created natures—are constituted by the uncreated and intentional activities of God. The fragility of my eyeglasses—like the redness of a tomato or the beauty of a sunset or the charge of a particle—therefore names something that God intentionally *does*. My eyeglasses' power of fragility, to take one example, is the manifestation of God's disposition to dispose my eyeglasses to break under certain conditions. Therefore, created natures manifest the

---

9. Barnes, *Dynamis*, 234–40.

presence and agency of God precisely in virtue of manifesting their natural properties.

The multiple and various powers (dispositions, properties) that creatures possess constitute a corresponding multitude of activated powers (dispositions, properties) that God possesses. God, however, is not just a congeries of mutually independent dispositions to manifest the dispositions of created nature, but rather is the fundamental and simple essence, substance, or nature that necessarily unites the divine *energeia*. On my gloss of Nyssen's conception of powers as dispositions to manifest an event-type, given the appropriate triggering circumstances that activate that disposition, the divine nature is that in virtue of which God is capable of triggering or activating dispositions to manifest the divine *energeia* as the properties in which God's created objects participate. Most often, Nyssen reserves the term *dynamis* to designate the singular power of the divine nature that serves as the truth-maker for the manifestation of the divine *energeia* as the dispositional powers of created "works" (or *erga*): "Whether you look at the world as a whole, or at the parts of the world which make up that complete whole, all these are works (*erga*) of the Father, in that they are works (*erga*) of His Power . . . for the acivity (*energeia*) of the Power (*dynamis*) bears relation to him Whose Power (*dynamis*) it is. Thus, since the Son is the Power (*dynamis*) of the Father, all these works (*erga*) of the Son are works (*erga*) of the Father."[10]

The divine activities or *energeia* manifest *in* creation are thus also themselves manifestations *of* the singular, fundamental, and simple power of the divine nature or essence—manifestations of whatever power in virtue of which God is God. The power of the divine nature

10. Gregory of Nyssa, "Against Eunomius," in *Nicene and Post-Nicene Fathers*, ed. Philip Schaff and Henry Wace, trans. Henry Austin Wilson, vol. 5, second series (Peabody, MA: Hendrickson, 1994), Book VI, 187 (hereafter: Wilson, *AE*), quoted in Barnes, *Dynamis*, 293.

manifests itself as divine activities that in turn manifest themselves as the properties of created objects. Creation itself thus manifests the divine nature in a manner parallel to the way in which, for instance, human intentional actions manifest the rational and volitional nature of a human person. What I think, say, and do are direct manifestations of my dispositions toward those thoughts, words, and actions, and those dispositions are in turn manifestations of the sort of thing I am (that is, a *rational agent*) as well as an indication of the particular sort of rational agent I am. As we shall see, Gregory thinks that the case of human intentional activities as manifestations of the nature of human persons is parallel to the case of God's manifestations in creation precisely because the human case is *derivative* from the divine case.[11]

But, in the case of divine manifestation, Gregory seems to confront the problem that this account of creation's participation in God's essential power appears to establish *too strong* a continuity between the dynamis God possesses in virtue of the divine *ousia*, the manifestation of that dynamis in God's creative energeia, and the manifestations of that energeia in God's *erga*, or works, of creation. If God's works are manifestations of God's intentional activities and those activities are manifestations of the divine nature or essential power, then creation turns out to be a necessary manifestation of the divine nature or essence, an emanation of God, or the divine body. Nyssen avoids this result, however, by claiming that while all of God's activities, once undertaken, necessarily manifest God's uncreated and essential power, God's undertaking of creative activities is not itself necessary.[12]

---

11. The structure of the human powers and their relative likeness and unlikeness to God constitutes Nyssen's theological anthropology, to be discussed in this section.
12. See Lucas Francisco Mateo-Seco, "Creation," in Mateo-Seco and Maspero, *The Brill Dictionary of Gregory of Nyssa*, 183–90.

The only truth-maker in virtue of which God's nature is necessarily manifest is God's dynamis. As such, the divine nature is never *merely* dispositional (that is, a mere potentiality). Rather, that essential power in virtue of which God is God is eternally, immutably, and necessarily activated. God's essence therefore neither has nor requires any trigger for its actualization—God is necessarily manifest in and to Godself and necessarily does whatever it is in virtue of which God is God. But the necessary manifestation of God's eternal and immutable power consists at least in part in God's manifestation as a rational agent: a free mind and will of unlimited perfections or virtues requisite to rational agency—perfections consisting of the necessary, immutable, and eternal manifestation of infinite goodness, knowledge, and freedom. The necessarily activated power of divine freedom that belongs essentially to God is manifest precisely as an infinite potentiality—a freedom to act or refrain from acting unconstrained by anything external to the divine nature. The manifestations of God's infinite creative power therefore depend only and entirely on the free exercise of the divine will in actualizing any intention envisioned by the divine mind.

It therefore belongs necessarily to the divine nature that God *can* but *need not* activate any power or disposition to manifest God's intentional action in a created *ergon*, or work. Bringing about the existence of the various natural kinds constitutive of created objects is thus a manifestation of the *freedom* of the divine dynamis as the uncreated energeia manifested as the creaturely powers of created *erga*. The delimitations of the powers constitutive of each natural kind, as well as the essential mutability of the creatures for which those powers are manifested, are explicable in terms of the divine freedom to manifest the power of the divine will. Nyssen can thus deny that it belongs *essentially* to the divine power to manifest itself in the activity of bringing about creation.

In a nutshell, then, Nyssen's picture is that all created powers and their (potential and actual) manifestations are themselves manifestations of God's power to freely enact creative intentions. God's possessing that free creative power, however, is a manifestation of the essential power constitutive of the divine nature—a singular infinite power that is necessarily, eternally, and immutably activated. Gregory therefore takes it that God's objective availability to creation consists in God's free intentional activities and whatever properties of God's dynamis are manifest by way of those activities. By characterizing the created order not merely as *dependent on* but rather more strongly as *constituted by* God's intentional activities (that is, as participant in the creative power of the divine nature), Nyssen is able to conceive of God as present in and to creation in the strongest possible sense—bringing it about, sustaining it in being, and guiding it to the natural ends dictated by God's creative purposes—while maintaining the contingency of creation itself upon divine freedom.

But by picturing the essential dynamis of the divine nature as manifest in creation only under the mode of God's free intentional activities, Nyssen also places a constraint on what features of God creation makes available to us. The mutable, temporal, and contingent powers of created nature constitute the limits within which God freely manifests the divine presence and activity, whereas no such limits constrain God's manifestation of God to Godself. As such, no creature can participate in the fundamentally immutable, eternal, and necessary mode by which the essential divine power or dynamis is manifest in and for Godself.

All of this has important implications for the way Nyssen construes the rational potential inherent in created nature. Creation has meaning and value, he thinks, precisely insofar as it intrinsically manifests God's intentions in creating it. Moreover, since all of God's free intentional activities necessarily manifest those features of the fundamental divine power or dynamis in virtue of which God has powers of creative freedom, God's activities render the rational agency of the divine nature perceptible to anything capable of perceiving the meanings and values of purposive intentions as such. God's manner of presence and action in the world is limited by the contingent and diffuse exercises of God's agency that are constitutive of the internal differentiation of created natures.[13]

Nevertheless, Nyssen does not think of creation as merely *indicating* God's presence, like a contrail indicates the presence of an airplane, but as partially *constituted by* God's presence via God's uncreated energeia, like saline solution mediates the presence of salt. The presence and activity of God are similarly immanent to creation.[14] More specifically, Nyssen marks out two distinct ways in which

13. Gregory of Nyssa, "On the Making of Man," in *Nicene and Post-Nicene Fathers*, ed. Philip Schaff and Henry Wace, trans. Henry Austin Wilson, vol. 5, second series (Peabody, MA: Hendrickson, 1994), XII.9, 398 (hereafter: Wilson, *OMM*): "And here, I think there is a view of the matter more close to nature, by which we may learn something of the more refined doctrines. For since the most beautiful and supreme good of all is the Divinity Itself, to which incline all things that have a tendency towards what is beautiful and good, we therefore say that the mind, as being in the image of the most beautiful, itself also remains in beauty and goodness so long as it partakes as far as is possible in its likeness to the archetype."

14. "There is a Cause of the whole system and structure, on which the whole nature of intelligible things depends, from which it gets its origins and causes to which it looks and returns, and by which it abides. And because as the Apostle says, 'His eternal power and divinity is seen, perceived from the creation of the world,' therefore the whole creation, and above all the ordered display in the heavens, by the skill revealed in generated things demonstrates the wisdom of their Maker. What he seems to me to want to explain to us is the evidence of visible realities that what exists has been wisely and skilfully prepared and abides for ever by the power of the Governor of the universe. The very heavens themselves, he says, by displaying the wisdom of their Maker, all but utter sound as they cry out and proclaim the wisdom of their Designer, though without sound. One may hear them instructing us as if in speech, 'As you look to us, you men, to the beauty and the greatness in us, and to this perpetually revolving movement, the orderly and harmonious motion, I always in the same paths and invariable, contemplate the one who presides over our design, and through the visible beauty let your mind rise to the original and invisible Beauty. For nothing in us is ungoverned or self-moving or self-sufficient, but every visible thing about us, every perceptible thing, depends upon the sublime and ineffable Power [*dynamis*].'" Gregory of Nyssa, "The Second Book against Enoumius (Translation)," trans. Stuart George Hall, in *Gregory of Nyssa: Contra Eunomium II*,

divine immanence is manifest in the various properties of created nature: God can manifest intentional creative activity *sensibly* or *intelligibly*, giving rise to creation's sensible properties and its intelligible properties.[15] First, the materiality of creatures manifests the concepts of materiality eternally possessed by the divine intellect, and in virtue of instantiating those concepts, creatures possess the *sensible* powers that they do.[16] That is, the manifest dispositions of material creatures to occupy space and time and to exhibit their various qualitative features, as well as the unactivated dispositional powers that determine their susceptibility to material change, are

ed. Lenka Karfíková, Scot Douglass, and Johannes Zachhuber (Leiden: Brill, 2004), Book II, §§222–24, 107–8 (hereafter: Hall, *AE*).

15. "The nature of existents is twofold, being divided into what is intelligible and what is sensible." (Hall, *AE*, Book II, §572, 188).

16. See Gregory of Nyssa, *On the Soul and the Resurrection*, trans. with intro. by Catherine P. Roth (Crestwood, NY: St. Vladimir's Seminary Press, 1993), 99 (hereafter: Roth, *OSR*): "So since the qualities which together complete the body are comprehended by mind and not by sense-perception, and the Divine is intellectual, why should not the Intelligible One be able to create the intelligible qualities which by their concurrence with one another have engendered the nature of our bodies?" There has been an ongoing debate about whether in marking out sensible properties as essentially or intrinsically constituted by intelligible properties Nyssen denies the very existence of matter and as such establishes himself as an idealist. This is just what Richard Sorabji suggests in *Time, Creation and the Continuum* (Ithaca, NY: Cornell University Press, 1983), 287–94. Darren Hibbs, in "Was Gregory of Nyssa a Berkeleyan Idealist?," *British Journal for the History of Philosophy* 13, no. 3 (2005): 425–35, has contested that claim, however, noting that it makes no sense to suppose that Nyssen denies the existence of matter when that is precisely what he is appealing to divine concepts to explain: "Gregory is not arguing that material bodies do not exist—he is explaining how they come to exist" (432). Jonathan Hill has recently defended Sorabji against Hibbs, however, in "Gregory of Nyssa, Material Substance and Berkeleyan Idealism," *British Journal for the History of Philosophy* 17, no. 4 (2009): 653–83, claiming that while different from Berkeley's idealism, Gregory was claiming precisely that in the material world "physical things have no reality beyond God's will" (683). Hill is right in holding that Gregory identifies the physical creation as constituted by an act (or, as I am characterizing it, an *activity* or *energeia* of the divine will or *dynamis*). But he is wrong to suppose that this entails any kind of idealism. All it requires is that the sensible properties or powers of physical creation are so constituted. This is compatible with holding that what the divine will brings into being ex nihilo is a contingent material object whose natural powers are extrinsic and derivative. The *analysis* of material and sensible objects as a hylomorphic compound whose matter is traceable to a sheer act of divine will and whose form is traceable to the actualization of a divine idea concept does not require any prior *assembly* of a preexisting "prime matter" with a preexisting creaturely power—a powerful material object can simply be brought about by a single coordinated intentional creative act of divine mind and will.

empirically *observable* to any creatures with suitable and properly functioning sensory powers.

Second, the rational, moral, and aesthetic properties of creatures manifest the essential wisdom and goodness of the intentional powers of the divine dynamis—the virtues of divine agency—and in virtue of manifesting God's free exercise of that agency, creatures have the *intelligible* powers they do. That is, the manifest dispositions of all creatures, including material creatures, to exhibit their intrinsic or natural meaning and value, as well as the unactivated dispositional powers that determine the conceptual, aesthetic, and moral meanings and values they might come to possess under various circumstances, are also empirically observable to any creatures with suitable and properly functioning powers of rational intellection.[17]

It follows from Nyssen's metaphysical picture that sensible properties of the physical domain in created nature manifest the divine energeia by way of which God spatiotemporally, quantitatively, and qualitatively actualizes empirical concepts of the divine mind, while the intelligible properties of created natures manifest the intentionality of the divine energeia that constitutes the meaning and the moral and aesthetic value (goodness and beauty, or *kalon*) of each creature as a participant in the rational ordering of creation. It further follows that on this way of marking the sensibility/intelligibility distinction, there is a sense in which the intelligibility of creation is more fundamental than its sensibility. Nyssen

---

17. See Ilaria Ramelli, "Good/Beauty," in Mateo-Seco and Maspero, *The Brill Dictionary of Gregory of Nyssa*, 356–63. Gregory favors the use of *kalon* to describe the value properties of creation as manifesting the "archetypical" goodness and beauty of the divine nature within the varying limits imposed by the peculiar nature of each creature. Thus, "the most beautiful and supreme good of all is the Divinity Itself, to which incline all things that have a tendency towards what is beautiful and good," and all of creation "partakes as far as is possible in its likeness to the archetype; but if it were at all to depart from this it is deprived of that beauty in which it was" (Wilson, *OMM*, XII.9, 398). As we shall see, the mindedness constitutive of a human nature, on Nyssen's view, is the creaturely delimitation of divine goodness and beauty most capable of manifesting a resemblance to the form of God's archetypal goodness and beauty.

acknowledges that there are creatures (such as angels and God) with purely intelligible natures—substances whose fundamental power consists in uniting only rational, aesthetic, and moral powers. But his metaphysics precludes the possibility of creatures with purely sensible natures—substances whose fundamental power consists in uniting only spatiotemporal, quantitative, and sensory-qualitative powers.

Rather, the sensible powers or dispositions of a creature necessarily manifest the conceptual structure of God's ideas of spatiotemporal, quantitative, and qualitative disposition and manifestation. As such, the sensibility of material creation it itself also intelligible and necessarily so, being ontologically grounded in the intellective properties of the divine dynamis as the basis of God's creative freedom actualized in the divine energeia. Nyssen's identification of the sensibility of material reality as rationally structured by divine ideas thus commits him to the idea that the sensibility of creation supervenes on its intelligibility.

It is important to recognize that, on the foregoing picture, Nyssen conceives both the sensibility and intelligibility of creation as intrinsic and constitutive features of the whole of created nature, not merely as properties of perceivers. If we imagine that all and only those creatures equipped with intellective or sensory powers suitably equipped for intelligibly or sensibly apprehending the creation were annihilated, it would still be the case on his view that the world itself possesses both sensible and intelligible properties—that is, *powers or dispositions* to manifest their intrinsic sensory and conceptual, moral, and aesthetic features to suitably sensitive creatures. However, in the absence of any such creatures possessed of the requisite sensory and intellective powers to actualize that potential—powers to trigger the sensory or intellective manifestations of the relevant creaturely dispositions—creation would fail to *reveal* the intrinsic sensibility and intelligibility it derives from God's energeia.

9.2 Human Perceptual Powers and the Spiritual Senses

On the composite picture I am sketching thus far, the works, or *ergon*, of the created order are constituted both by material and immaterial dispositions, powers, or properties. Whereas all creaturely properties are constituted by intelligibility—dispositions to manifest their meaning and value—only material creation bears powers of sensibility as well. Both sorts of powers borne by creatures (sensible and intelligible) are constituted (each in its own way) by divine activities or energeia that manifest the essential goodness and beauty of the divine mind and will. In his reading of the Genesis creation narrative in "On the Making of Man" (hereafter, OMM), Gregory further claims that God created this world for the sake of humankind. Thus, "when He had decked the habitation with beauties of every kind, and prepared this great and varied banquet, then introduced man, assigning to him as his task not the acquiring of what was not there, but the enjoyment of the things which were there."[18]

In other words the sensible and intelligible properties of creation were structured with distinctively *human* powers of apprehension already in view, and, "for this reason," Nyssen says, "He [God] gives him [human nature] as foundations the instincts of a twofold organization, blending the Divine with the earthy, that by means of both he may be naturally and properly disposed to each enjoyment, enjoying God by means of his more divine nature, and the good things of earth by the sense that is akin to them."[19] Just as the fundamental properties of created nature are twofold—intelligible and sensible—the fundamental power of human nature, according to Nyssen, is twofold, consisting in the union of a divine power with a distinctively creaturely power of sense. He takes this creaturely power

18. Wilson, *OMM*, II.2, 389.
19. Ibid., II.2, 389.

406

of sense by which we are directed on the materiality of creation to constitute our kinship not with God but with the good things of earth.

Nyssen articulates that kinship, moreover, in a standard Aristotelian way by distinguishing between nonliving or inanimate things and living things, and he further distinguishes between three sorts of fundamental powers or natures that a living thing might have.[20] The first sort of creaturely life possesses nutritive powers of the sort belonging to all organic life forms and evinced most simply in vegetative life. The second sort incorporates the nutritive powers of vegetative life into more complex sensory powers of the sort belonging to those organic life forms broadly identifiable with animal life. Animal life is marked out by those living things capable of manifesting their nutritive powers in capacities to regulate their own bodily lives according to a sensory awareness of their surrounding environments. The sensory awareness of animals, moreover, is governed by appetites aimed at whatever sensible goods are requisite to their particular form of bodily life. Sensation for any given sort of animal, then, is ordered by inclinations to pursue what is pleasant and avoid what is unpleasant, where pleasantness and unpleasantness are indexed to the particular sort of animal life.

He further follows Aristotle in characterizing humans as rational animals—creatures whose capacities for bodily self-regulation according to animal inclination toward the material goods on which they are sensorily directed is entirely incorporated into capacities for rational agency. Nyssen fixes on these human capacities for rational agency as the powers in virtue of which humans bear the image and likeness of God. That is, we possess a power of mind and will that both derives from and resembles the goodness, beauty, and freedom

20. Ibid., VIII.4–5, 392–93.

of the divine dynamis manifest in the divine energeia that constitute the sensible and intelligible properties of created nature.

> And if you were to examine the other points also by which the Divine beauty is expressed, you will find that to them too the likeness in the image which we present is perfectly preserved. The Godhead is mind and word: for "in the beginning was the Word" and the followers of Paul "have the mind of Christ" which "speaks" in them: humanity too is not far removed from these: you see in yourself word and understanding, an imitation of the very Mind and Word. Again, God is love, and the fount of love: for this the great John declares, that "love is of God," and "God is love": the Fashioner of our nature has made this to be our feature too: for "hereby," He says, "shall all men know that ye are my disciples, if ye love one another":—thus, if this be absent, the whole stamp of the likeness is transformed. The Deity beholds and hears all things, and searches all things out: you too have the power of apprehension of things by means of sight and hearing, and the understanding that inquires into things and searches them out.[21]

But, unlike God, our powers of rational agency are inseparably bound to and delimited by our essentially vegetative and animal nature.[22] This unity of animality and divinity in human nature explains the dual nature of our capacities for a receptivity and responsiveness both to the material sensibility of the good things of the earth to which our animality is ordered and to the enjoyment of God who is immaterial and purely intelligible.

Significantly, Nyssen pictures this essentially human unity of sensory and rational power not as three distinct powers aggregated or "welded together," but as a fundamental unity or "commixture."[23] Whereas nonhuman animal sensory systems comparable with ours

---

21. Ibid., V.2, 390.
22. John Behr, "The Rational Animal: A Re-reading of Gregory of Nyssa's *De Hominis Opificio*," *Journal of Early Christian Studies* 7, no. 1 (Summer 1999): 219–47; J. Warren Smith, *Passion and Paradise: Human and Divine Emotion in the Thought of Gregory of Nyssa* (New York: Crossroad, 2004), 26ff.
23. Wilson, *OMM*, VIII.5, 392–93.

operate apart from any rational capacity, the intellectual power is necessarily operative in the passivity of human sense perception. In other words, Gregory takes it that ordinary sensation for humans does not take place without the intellectual faculty.[24] He thus subsumes animal sensation under our rational faculties as the passive and receptive side of the free and active capacities of mind and will in virtue of which we resemble God. The conceptual content of human sense perception, in other words, supplies us with the reasons that figure into our intentional activities of belief and practice. He thus regards the mind as a kind of power to organize and inspect the empirical concepts that the world impresses upon us in experience, concepts he associates with the proper and common sensibles of the five sensory modalities: seeing, hearing, touching, tasting, and smelling.[25]

The flip side of this coinherence of the rational and the sensory power concerns not the passivity of perceptual experience in our "reception of concepts from without,"[26] but the active forms of theoretical and practical reasoning that characterize our responsiveness to the conceptual content of perception. Human spontaneity or freedom enables us to proceed from our perceptual intake of the world's rational ordering to the intellectual activity of theoretical or practical reasoning on the basis of that perceptual intake. That is, the rational operation of our senses can "lead us on to the understanding of the super-sensual world of fact and thought," such that our "eye becomes the interpreter of that almighty wisdom which is visible in the universe."[27] Gregory's doctrine of the spiritual

---

24. Ibid., XIV.3, 402: "Thus, neither is there perception without material substance, nor does the act of perception [*aiesthesis*] take place without the intellectual faculty."

25. Ibid., X.6–7, 395: We find, then, by experience . . . with taste, with smell, with perception by touch; each implants in us by means of its own perceptive power the knowledge of things of every kind."

26. Ibid., X.2, 394.

27. Roth, *OSR*, 34.

senses is reducible precisely to this latter implication of the blended character of human sensory consciousness with the rational powers requisite for thought, speech, and action. That is, he thinks that humans just are that sort of creature whose mode of perception is simultaneously rational and sensory and whose perceptual content can be both the sensible and the intelligible properties manifest in creation.

God, unlike us, does not require any passive act of perception to take in the world, nor does God possess the bodily nature suited for animal sensory powers. Nonhuman animals, unlike us, are incapable of taking in the rational structure of the world, either its intelligible manifestations of divine virtues and purposiveness or its sensible manifestations of divine sensory *concepts* of quality, quantity, and spatiotemporal extension. Their mode of sensory receptivity and responsiveness to the world is not *irrational* but *nonrational*, and, as such, their sense perceptions are neither governed by nor inform any conception of the world as a rational order. In this essential likeness and unlikeness both to God and the nonhuman domain of the created order, human nature can be regarded as the midpoint at which the divine and creaturely "touch."[28]

Nyssen's doctrine of the spiritual senses is thus not an ancillary or subsidiary feature of his theology, but rather its very heart—the site at which his theological metaphysics of the God/world relation and his theological epistemology of the human knowledge of God intersect. Human sense perception is capable of orienting us to the sensible world in a way that opens the eyes of our soul to the nonsensory world of meaning and value that grounds it—a world constituted by the activities or energeia of God. Because our sensory

---

28. Wilson, *OMM*, VIII.5, 393: "For this rational animal, man, is blended of every form of soul; he is nourished by the vegetative kind of soul, and to the faculty of growth was added that of sense, which stands midway, if we regard its peculiar nature, between the intellectual and the more material essence being as much coarser than the one as it is more refined than the other."

powers have been taken up into our rational resemblance to God, the ordinary operations of our bodily senses can correspondingly open our intellectual "eye" to the wisdom, goodness, and beauty of God's intentional activity manifest to us in our environment as the natural powers of creation.

Gregory does not intend any deep paradox about this picture of the perceptual availability ("visibility") to thought of a purely intelligible or nonsensible God by way of our perceptions of the sensible world: it just names the perceptible presentation of nonsensible *content* under a sensory *mode* of presentation. When, for example, I witness an injustice such as my older son pushing his little brother onto the ground in order to take away his toy, it is possible for this situation both to be and to present itself to me as *an injustice*. For it to be both would not necessarily require me to *infer* that it is unjust from any more-fundamental features of the situation. Rather, I might simply and literally *see that it is unjust*. Now ,on the one hand, clearly injustice is not a sensible property of the situation on Nyssen's terms. All the same, my perception of the injustice was constituted by what appeared in my visual field—had I been closing my eyes or had I failed to take in some pertinent sensible feature of the situation, I might have failed to see the intelligible content conveyed by that sensible situation: its injustice.

My apprehension of the intelligible property—the injustice of Noah's pushing Ezra—therefore *supervenes* on the sensible properties that constitute my apprehension of Noah's pushing Ezra, on the various sensibles of sight involved. Sufficient changes in what appeared to me at the subvenient level of my sensory apprehension would thus imply corresponding changes in what appeared to me at the supervenient level of my intellectual apprehension. In a similar way, Nyssen regards intelligible properties of God—divine power, purposes, and virtues—as "visible" by the operations of the intellect in sense perception. Like injustice, divine wisdom can be a visible property even if it is not a visual property. So too, presumably, can clumsiness, kindness, and malice. To take another example, sonorousness or abruptness might be audible properties of a song even if they are not auditory properties or proper sensibles of sound in the way that timbre or pitch might be.[29] So while it is the case that intelligible reality "in itself can be known only by the intellect and not by sight," the intellect is passively receptive to intelligible reality precisely "by the very operation of our senses" because the rational power "cannot enter into the bodily life otherwise than by entering through [sense] perception."[30] In other words, the supervenience of sensory apprehension on intellectual apprehension at the level of our perceptual powers therefore corresponds to the supervenience of sensible properties upon intelligible properties at the level of the world's own constitution. Gregory therefore holds that our sensory capacities themselves belong to our rational nature as *rational* senses, thus making the intelligible world available to thought by way of our sensory receptivity to the sensible world. Insofar as he holds that our bodily powers are powers of a more fundamental power, that of a rational soul constitutive of our human nature, Nyssen sometimes speaks of the rational constitution of our sensory capacities as "senses of the soul" (*aestheteteria tes pyches*), that is, soulish or *spiritual* senses.

But Nyssen also holds that what we possess by nature is not an already realized rational shaping of our bodily sensory capacities, but rather the *power* to realize that sort of shaping. That is, our rational nature is capable of gradually acquiring the rational capacities to

---

29. A "proper" sensible is just a sensory quality proper to a particular sensory modality—since sounds are qualitative features available only to hearing, they can be called proper sensibles of hearing. Similarly, colors are proper sensibles of sight. Shapes, however, can be qualitatively discerned both by sight and by touch, and as such shapes are common sensibles of sight and touch.

30. Roth, *OSR*, 34, 35, 56.

form our sensory capacities to take in intelligible reality. A human nature is thus realized in the formation of the spiritual senses. Such a formation, Nyssen thinks, occurs in the natural course of our maturation in an ordinary human upbringing. In *On the Soul and the Resurrection*, Gregory (again, via Macrina) deploys the same Aristotelian conception of the human soul as trichotomous that he set forward in OMM—that is, that to be human is for our vegetative powers to be essentially constituted as *animal* powers of appetite/sensation and for those animal powers of appetite/sensation to be essentially constituted as *rational* powers. But here he uses that analysis not merely to describe the structure of the power that marks out the human soul but to construct a developmental model of the way we come to acquire the rational powers that we possess by nature: "First the power enters into the embryo which is formed within the womb through the capacity for receiving nourishment and growing, but afterwards it brings the grace of sense-perception to the infant which comes forth into light. Then, as an adult plant produces fruit, it gradually reveals the faculty of reason, not all at once, but increasing along with the growth of the child in the normal order of development."[31]

Just as in OMM, Gregory is careful to emphasize that this developmental picture is not one in which our maturation proceeds through the accretion of distinct powers, with an essentially nonrational sensory power welded onto a nonsensory vegetative power and then a rational power subsequently beginning to grow alongside or externally cooperating with sensation. Rather, the unfolding of human powers of nourishment and sensation just *is* the flowering of a rational power, like a seed turning into a husk. Just as the potentiality for becoming a husk is already there in the seed

31. Ibid., 100.

from the beginning, so our potential to express our rational nature is already there from birth.[32]

In "Against Eunomius," Nyssen offers more details about just what *sort* of conceptual shaping of our sensory capacities constitutes a normal order of development. In the course of rejecting the Eunomian idea that God's mode of self-understanding conforms to the discursive means available to humans to understand God, Nyssen claims instead that the intelligibility of the world according to human linguistic conventions is an accommodation to us. What God bestows on us is not a natural inclination to reproduce the names God has given to things but the power of naming by way of which we actualize the rational potential or conceptual content things have in virtue of being divine intentions.[33]

But different communities cultivate this God-given verbally rational faculty in different ways, and hence while "rational speech belongs to all men [*sic*], different words are inevitably used in accordance with differences between nations."[34] We are by nature, as Behr glosses it, an essentially "word bearing animal" whose discursive powers are manifest precisely within the limited contingencies of our bodily lives.[35] The relevant contingencies include not only our first-natural bodily constitution, such as the arrangements of our hands and mouth that suit our bodies for the use of reason, but also the conventions of language acquisition that furnish us with the conceptual repertoire required for that use.[36]

Nyssen appeals to this possibility of internal differentiation of conceptual capacities given in an ordinary upbringing within the

32. Nyssen thus compares our development to that of the grain becoming the ear, "not changing its nature while it is in the soil but revealing and perfecting itself by the operation of its nourishment" (ibid.).

33. Hall, *AE*, Book 2, §§237–246a, 111–14.

34. Ibid., Book 2, §246b, 114.

35. Behr, "Rational Animal," 231.

36. Wilson, *OMM* VIII.8, 393–394.

human community to account for the number of moral-practical and political disagreements that emerge in the deliverances of spiritual perception in comparison to the relatively greater consensus about the deliverances of sense perception. The differentiation might explain why there tend to be fewer disagreements about, for example, proper sensibles of sight such as color concepts than there are about "the affairs which occupy our life . . . which deal with the political and moral sphere of life."[37]

Therefore, our faculties for spiritual sensing can be misshapen in the repertoire of conceptual capacities we have available to be drawn upon by the world's impression on us, thereby leading to the failure of the intelligible world to present itself to the mind by way of the activations of our senses. Such misshapenness is how Gregory explains the spiritual blindness of those such as Epicurus, whose conceptual capacities for a rational intake of the world in experience were constrained by a conception of that world as entirely constituted by its sensibility. Because of this (erroneous) rational constraint on his sensory capacities, he

> completely closed the eyes of his soul and was unable to look at any of the bodiless things which are known by the intellect, just as someone who is shut up in a little hut remains unaware of the heavenly marvels because he is prevented by the walls and roof from seeing what is outside. All perceptible things which are seen in the universe are simply a sort of earthly walls which shut off small-souled people from the vision of intelligible things. Such a man looks only at earth, water, air and fire . . . what it is contained by, he cannot see, because of the smallness of his soul.[38]

Since our spiritual senses work through the world's activations of our sensory capacities to passively draw into operation our conceptual capacities and thereby directly present intelligible realities to the

---

37. AE Book 2§§.571–573, 188–189.
38. Roth, OSR, 31–32.

mind, we will not be properly equipped to receive the intelligible world unless our conceptual capacities have been properly formed. There are two sorts of failures of spiritual perception that Gregory combines here to explain this blindness. The first is that of someone who "voluntarily closes the eyes" to avoid seeing, and the second is that of one suffering an involuntary accident in which one is "deprived of sight."[39] Epicurus closes his eyes to the goods of the intelligible world by choice and, as a result, sustains an injury to the eyes of his soul that diminish his sensitivities to intelligible goods, making him "small-souled" in his capacities for spiritual perception. This is a constraint not merely on his active reasoning but on the rational constitution of his receptive sensory capacities to present him with the intelligible content that one reasons *about*.

The connection between the voluntary and involuntary here signals the way in which Gregory conceives of virtue as the central category for understanding the form of training by which we come to acquire and perfect our capacities of spiritual perception. A knowledge of the intelligible beauty and goodness of God manifest in and through the world consists in the mutually reinforcing capacities of receptivity and responsiveness in which we perceive what is good and the demands that it places upon us: to desire the good in such a way that we are properly motivated to conform to those demands. Both capacities, moreover, are acquired in their exercise and either grow or atrophy by way of habituation. In the formation of our beliefs and practices, therefore, either our spiritual senses are enlarged through increasing sensitization and attraction to the divine goodness and beauty manifest in creation and thereby motivated to act according to its demands, or else, in our failure to do the good, they

39. Ibid., 96.

grow increasingly dull and insensitive to it and we become incapable of perceiving the good.

> Our rational nature came to birth for this purpose, so that the wealth of divine good things might not be idle. A kind of vessels and voluntary receptacles for souls were fashioned by the Wisdom which constructed the universe, in order that there should be a container to receive good things, a container which would always become larger with the addition of what would be poured into it. For the participation in the divine good is such that it makes anyone into whom it enters greater and more receptive. As it is taken up it increases the power and magnitude of the recipient, so that the person who is nourished always grows and never ceases from growth. Since the fountain of good things flows unfailingly, the nature of the participants who use all the influx to add to their own magnitude (because nothing of what is received is superfluous or useless) becomes at the same time both more capable of attracting the better and more able to contain it. Each adds to the other: the one who is nourished gains greater power from the abundance of good things, and the nourishing supply rises in flood to match the increase of the one who is growing. Those whose growth is not cut off by any limit will surely continue to increase in this manner.[40]

In sum, therefore, Gregory holds that the rational intelligibility of creation manifests the intelligibility of the goodness and beauty of God's intentional activity for our sakes. In virtue of manifesting divine powers of reason and freedom as our own creaturely reason and freedom, we can acquire a perceptual capacity for taking in the rational demands imposed upon us by the beauty and goodness of God's activities in creation under sensory modes of presentation, as well as the appetite to motivate a proper responsiveness to God's demands. Further, while we acquire these mutually dependent capacities for intellectual and moral-practical virtue by way of an ordinary upbringing, their growth is entirely dependent upon their

---

40. Ibid., 87–88.

exercise. Such a growth amounts to an ongoing training and deployment of the spiritual senses.

Nyssen therefore develops his account of rational perception—the identification of divine nonsensory intelligible properties as capable of directly manifesting themselves to our intellects under created sensible modes of presentation—in service of an ethics of virtue. But his version of virtue ethics uniquely incorporates an ethical intuitionism and yields a kind of divine command theory. The content of a moral perception is a rational demand upon our intentions (intuitionism),[41] and that demand is an intentional act of divine calling upon us (divine command),[42] the goodness or beauty of which we can only detect and become motivated to properly respond to through our prior habituation in just such a receptivity and responsiveness (virtue).[43]

41. Nyssen's theory thus bears important parallels with some more recent intuitionist accounts, such as, e.g., Lawrence Blum, *Moral Perception and Particularity* (New York: Cambridge University Press, 1994); and Robert Audi, *Moral Perception* (Princeton, NJ: Princeton University Press, 2013). While likewise requiring that moral properties are perceptible, Nyssen parts company from contemporary intuitionism in both his way of specifying the content of moral perception and his moral epistemology. An analysis and evaluation of the relevant differences would be an important task for working out his account more fully but are beyond the scope of the present study.

42. Nyssen's account of the particularity of divine commands as individuated by one's responsiveness to an encounter with God in Christ by the Spirit, and its necessarily uncodifiable character, bears interesting parallels with Barth's version of divine command theory. But perhaps unlike Barth, it also allows the content of a divine command to be recognized and responded to as a rational demand on one's intentional capacities *without* one's having any capacity to recognize such demands *as* God's. Moreover, Nyssen also has a story about the social and historical character of our capacity to receive divine commands that, it seems to me, Barth lacks.

43. Much work on the virtues in theological ethics has failed to specify just what sorts of sensitivities are required and cultivated in the cultivation of character. Nyssen's story allows us to straightforwardly identify such sensitivities as derivative of our ordinary *perceptual* sensitivities. Virtues just *are* such sensitivities to intrinsically motivating reasons presented to us by our environment, while habits are the means for acquiring the requisite sensitivities to them that succeed in motivating us to think or act in accord with what such reasons are reasons *for*. On this view, theologians such as Stanley Hauerwas have mistakenly regarded the virtues as relativizing the significance of experience, rather than as resituating it. See, e.g., Stanley Hauerwas, "Casuistry in Context," in *The Hauerwas Reader*, ed. John Berkman and Michael Cartwright (Durham, NC: Duke University Press, 2001), 268: "I am not at all that happy

While Nyssen thus takes humans to be uniquely capable of perceptual presentations of God's immanence to creation, he also thinks that such perceptual presentations provide an inferential basis for our claims about the divine nature, which transcends God's creative activities. The visibility of God within the universe via divine energeia, Nyssen thinks, "points in itself to the Being who encompasses it." Moreover, the purposive meaning and value exhibited by created nature as existing for the sake of humanity consist precisely in God's intention for our movement from a perceptual recognition of these direct presentations of God's wisdom, goodness, and beauty in creation to what they indirectly indicate to us about the divine nature or essence—what God is like *ad intra* considered apart from the way in which that nature is contingently manifest in God's activities in, to, and for creation. Thus, Gregory says that God "manifests man in the world to be the beholder of some of the wonders therein, and the lord of others; that by his enjoyment he might have knowledge of the Giver, and by the beauty and majesty of the things he saw might trace out that power of the Maker which is beyond speech and language."[44]

Nyssen takes our knowledge of God as "Giver" to be a direct perceptual knowledge of God's energeia, such that God gives *Godself* precisely in giving the gifts of creation's intelligible goods. In our visual apprehension of the material sensibility of creation, we apprehend the immaterial intelligibility of divine beauty and majesty itself under a creaturely mode of presentation. From this perceptual

with an emphasis on experience as an end in and of itself for moral reflection. . . . More important than having had an experience is whether we know how to name it or describe it." Even more radically mistaken, on this view, is Paul J. Griffiths's claim that virtue intrinsically "attenuates" experience, since habit as "second nature" requires the extinguishing of the "inner theater." See Griffiths, "Experience Attenuated: The Proper End of the Liturgical Life" (William James Lecture on Religious Experience, Harvard Divinity School, April 23, 2009). On one reading, Hauerwas's rejection of experience is perhaps subtly tempted toward Coherentism, while Griffiths's is subtly tempted toward Givenism.

44. Wilson, *OMM*, II.1, 389.

presentation of the beauty and majesty of God's energeia, however, we can infer or "trace out" truths about the fundamental "power" or dynamis in virtue of which God's free creative activities are possible. The constraint of our animality upon our rationality implies that nothing intelligible can enter into the domain of our linguistic competence except by way of the senses. The intelligibility of God's essentially unlimited and uncreated power—the essential dynamis in virtue of which God is God—cannot possibly appear to us under any creaturely mode of presentation *as* that sort of power, as it appears to God.

We could not possibly actualize the intelligibility of the divine essence as such by our capacities of thought or speech. This is not to say that our God-talk fails to *refer* to the divine nature, only that we are limited in our talk about God by the correspondingly limited modes of presentation given us by God's contingent intentional activity in creation. What it might be like to be presented with the divine dynamis in just the way God is present to Godself *ad intra* is necessarily beyond our ken. The knowledge of the divine essence that constitutes God's own self-understanding, we might say, represents a class of object-dependent senses by definition not available to creatures—a rational potential incapable of being actualized by conceptual capacities other than those possessed by God (if indeed God knows Godself by way of divine concepts).

Perhaps Nyssen's clearest and most comprehensive statement about the sense in which the divine nature is and is not comprehensible (whether perceptually or in any other way) is given in "Against Eunomius." The thought of Basil, his brother and teacher, Gregory says, "enables anyone, whose vision is not obstructed by the screen of heresy, to perceive quite clearly"[45] that

---

45. This obscuring of nonsensory facts "visible" to the mind by a pedagogical malformation echoes Gregory's condemnation (via Macrina) of those who shut the eye of their soul in stopping at the

the manner of existence of the essential nature of the Divinity is intangible, inconceivable, and beyond all rational comprehension. Human thought, investigating and searching by such reasoning as is possible, reaches out and touches the unapproachable and sublime Nature, neither seeing so clearly as distinctly to glimpse the Invisible, nor so totally debarred from approaching as to be unable to form any impression of what it seeks. By the reach of reason, its goal is to discover whatever that is which it seeks, and in a sense it does understand it by the very fact that it cannot perceive it, inasmuch as it acquires clear knowledge that what it seeks is beyond all knowledge. It detects things which are incompatible with the divine nature, and is not unaware of those which it is proper to attribute to it; yet it cannot perceive what that nature itself is, to which these thoughts apply, but, from the knowledge of the things which are and are not attributed, it sees all that can be seen—that that which rests beyond every evil, and is perceived as possessing every good, must surely be such as is unutterable in word and inaccessible to thought.[46]

The densely compacted picture given here is one in which the *mode* or *manner* of existence of the "essential nature of Divinity"—its intelligibility *as* the essential divine nature—remains unavailable to us. That nature "itself" never presents itself to us, and as such it does not enter into thought by any direct acquaintance with it; our minds "cannot perceive what that nature itself is." However, we can direct ourselves on the essential mode or manner of God's existence indirectly, by way of inferential reasoning on the basis of a *nonessential* mode or manner of God's existence—that is, by way of a direct acquaintance with properties that "can be seen," such as God's freedom from evil and possession of goodness.

It is tempting to think that the perceptual unavailability of the essential mode of God's existence—the ways God is in, for, and to Godself—entails the perceptual unavailability of God *simpliciter*.

---

sensible properties of creation, erecting walls between the sensible universe and the intelligible realities that are beyond it (Roth, *OSR*).

46. Hall, *AE*, 89.

On that reading, we should regard what Nyssen has said about the energeia of God—the traces of the divine essence in God's free creative activities—as insufficient to count as perceptual presentations of God in or to creatures. For example, we might read Nyssen as holding that God's activities merely *indicate* the presence and agency of God, like a contrail can indicate a nearby airplane or the movement of a leaf can indicate wind. Or, again, we might think that the rational demands imposed on us by creation are mediated by creatures as *representatives* of God's demands on us, as creaturely *proxies* in much the same way that an ambassador can represent the intentions of a foreign dignitary in her absence. But whether we imagine our perceptual relation to God as mediated by indicators or proxies, that relation would be at best indirect—it is not God's presence or agency that we (putatively) take in but rather the creaturely effects or divinely appointed representatives of that presence or agency.

On this picture, what precludes any direct perceptual relation to God by way of the divine creative energeia is the absence of any direct *presentation* of God's own self. Just as, strictly speaking, the airplane, the wind, and the dignitary are not present in the experience of the contrail, the leaf's movement, and the ambassadorial speech, respectively, so God is not strictly speaking present in the creatures resulting from the divine energeia. But while tempting, this would be a misreading of the view I am suggesting. There is no good inference from the unavailability of God's *essence* as the content of a perceptual experience to the unavailability of God *simpliciter* as the content of a perceptual experience. For one thing, we never perceive anything *simpliciter*; we only ever perceive things *as* having such and such a property. For another, it is compatible with S's perceiving X as F (or perceiving that X is F) that S succeeds in perceiving X even if X is not in fact F. Alston correctly notes that we have no good reasons to suppose that a necessary failure to perceive God's essence constitutes a failure to perceive God:

> In sense perception we constantly perceive things without perceiving their essences. Even with vision . . . objects present themselves not as *having a certain essential nature*, but rather as having certain superficial features: colors, shapes, relative position in space. . . . People perceived water for many millennia without having any idea that its chemical constitution is H2O. And so it is with those who take themselves to be directly aware of God in mystical experience. They take themselves to be aware of God as displaying certain features—goodness, power, plentitude, lovingness—or as doing certain things—speaking, strengthening, forgiving—not as being aware of the divine essence. To directly perceive X is for X to present itself to one's experience as so-and-so, where the so-and-so is typically not essential. Indeed, it is not even necessary for direct perception of X that X actually have the features it presents itself as having. I can directly perceive a book that looks blue, even though the book is really grey and only looks blue because of the lighting. Our failure to grasp the divine essence does not prevent us from directly perceiving God.[47]

Alston suggests a perceptual analogue to the Thomist claim about theological knowledge, according to which God "accommodates Himself to our limited mode of intellection so that we may gain such knowledge of Him as is possible for us, even though it does not succeed in representing Him as He is. . . . [W]hy should the same thing not be true of human perception of God?"[48]

In a note, Alston refers us to Albert Farges's articulation of the account he finds in the mystical tradition (and particularly the Carmelites) as a possible model for the directness of our perceptual relation to God. On Alston's summary of Farges, "it is by virtue of the mystic's consciousness of the action of God in his soul that

---

47. William P. Alston, *Perceiving God: The Epistemology of Religious Experience* (Ithaca, NY: Cornell University Press, 1991), 62.
48. Ibid., 63.

423

the mystic is able to perceive God Himself."[49] Nyssen's account of our direct perceptual relation to God under the *modi* of God's free and creative actions is a version of the view that Farges suggests. Among the intelligible properties present to us in creation are divine properties, properties belonging properly (even if contingently) to God that can present themselves to us *as* belonging to God insofar as we are cultivating the relevant intellectual and moral-practical virtues in our responsiveness to those presentations. What God's energeia present to us are contingent and creaturely presentations of divine properties or powers *as* divine properties or powers—not merely as their effects—even if these presentations do not disclose such properties of divine goodness and beauty *as* they are fundamentally grounded in the divine essence. God's perceptible traces in creation, therefore, are neither merely effects, indicators, or proxies nor direct presentations of God under an essential mode of presentation; rather, they are direct presentations of God under nonessential modes of presentation.

We can possess a concept of the more fundamental and essential mode of God's goodness present to us in God's free actions by abstracting away from creaturely limitations. As such, Nyssen thinks that we can *infer* truths about the essential mode of God's existence as unbounded by the limits of creation. Abstracting from the divine goodness with which we are directly acquainted leads us to recognize that the essential mode of divine goodness is necessarily beyond our capacity to take in. Thus, the goodness that can be directly perceived nevertheless manages in its limited way to "approach" the divine nature. That is, we never glimpse God's essential mode of existence *as* it is essentially; instead, from our direct acquaintance with that essence *as* the goodness contingently present in and to creaturely

49. Ibid., 62n54. See Albert Farges, *Mystical Phenomena Compared with Their Human and Diabolical Counterfeits*, trans. S. P. Jacques (1926; Whitefish, MT: Kessinger, 2003), 275–78.

being, we can infer in our experience of approaching the mode of presentation, which we are nevertheless incapable of fully receiving, that we can and do indeed touch the divine nature. We can refer to, intend, and direct ourselves on that nature under those modes of presentation in which God's goodness is conveyed to us via a nonessential manner of existence constituted by divine activity in and to created nature.

Gregory trades on a distinction between the entire possible range of senses determined by God's essence (those capable of presenting the divine nature) and the narrower range of senses within it (those capable of presenting the manner of existence of the divine nature itself, rather than its manner of existence in creation). The only experience of God we can have under the latter modes of presentation, Nyssen says, is an acquaintance with an absence—an experience *that* God's essential nature transcends any creaturely capacity of experience, thought, or language. The mutual dependence between the intelligible properties we can "see" (God under the nonessential modes of presentation given by creatures) and those properties we cannot see but must infer (God's essential manner of existence absent all creaturely evil or limitation) enables us to "form an impression" of the divine nature.

A brief illustration can elucidate this way of reading Gregory on the internal relation between our perceptual knowledge of God's energeia and our inferential knowledge of the essential dynamis that grounds it. First, consider my blue pillow. There are two distinct ways of thinking about its color. I can think of its blueness in terms of the underlying microphysical structure in virtue of which its reflection and absorption of light enables it to appear blue to a suitably sensitive observer such as myself. But I can also think about its blueness simply in terms of the quality of blueness under which it appears to me as the relevant sort of observer. This is the distinction between blueness as a *primary* property of the pillow (the microphysical structure it has) and as a *secondary* property of the pillow (the disposition of that microphysical structure to appear bluely to suitably sensitive observers). Now suppose that I am ignorant of the microphysical structure in virtue of which it appears blue to me.

Clearly, my direct acquaintance with the way in which it must appear to an observer configured as I am puts me in touch with its microphysical structure, for being acquainted with the quality *just is* being acquainted with the microphysical structure in the sort of way requisite to my capacities to take it in. Moreover, despite being ignorant of the microphysical structure, I could nevertheless infer from the way it appears to me that there must be *something I know not what* in virtue of which it is particularly disposed to appear to me the way it does. Gregory's picture identifies the manner of existence of the divine essence in itself as the primary property of God, while the divine activities under which that essence is disposed to appear to creaturely like us name God's secondary qualities. This analogy reveals the idea of a singular content (in this case God's essential nature) whose fundamental and primary intelligibility is only knowable as being of a sort we are incapable of actualizing except by way of a secondary and derivative intelligibility.

Is this reading of Gregory's account of the constraints on God's entry into thought and language apophatic or cataphatic in the way I have drawn that distinction? When we draw that distinction in a way that does not follow from the problem of perception, the distinguishing feature of an apophatic theology does not have anything to do with puzzles about how it is possible for what we think, say, and do to refer us to God. The question is rather whether there are any essential properties or features of God whose existence we can know about but whose intrinsic character we can know nothing about and, further, whether that unknowability imposes special constraints on the ordinary way in which God enters into our thinking, speaking, and acting. On that construal, Gregory is clearly an apophatic theologian because he takes the essential sense of the divine essence—the sense it has as the rational potential of God's being that is necessarily actualized by God's own comprehension of it—to be incapable of being actualized by any creaturely powers of rationality. Moreover, as the intrinsic power manifest in the powers of creaturely beings, God's entrance into thought and language in a mode of appearing marked by intentional creative activity is nonstandard. That is, God is the only object whose appearance to us manifests not merely the goodness and beauty of the creature that appears but the very divine creative powers of goodness and beauty themselves in virtue of which that which appears is good or beautiful.

This reading of divine incomprehensibility entails a commitment to divine ineffability, but one not subject to the usual complaint that the very idea of naming an ineffable property is incoherent.[50] Gregory does *not* say that our uses of language are not capable of intending the divine essence *simpliciter* but rather such uses are not capable of intending the divine essence *under a divine mode of presentation*. Moreover, strictly speaking, even here he does not say that such an intention is impossible for us *simpliciter* but only that it is impossible *except* by way of employing language about the limits of human powers of knowing. It is in this thoroughly straightforward and nonparadoxical sense that our knowledge of the divine essence

---

50. See William P. Alston, "Ineffability," *Philosophical Review* 65, no. 4 (October 1956): 506–22. For a response to the Alstonian complaint, see Leonard Angel, "Reconstructing the Ineffable: The Grammatical Roles of 'God,'" *Religious Studies* 14, no. 4 (December 1978): 485–95. For various strategies of defending the notion of ineffable properties more generally, see André Kukla, *Ineffability and Philosophy* (New York: Routledge, 2005). For a more general treatment of the epistemological significance of our cognitive limits, see Nicholas Rescher, *Ignorance: On the Wider Implications of Deficient Knowledge* (Pittsburgh, PA: University of Pittsburgh Press, 2009).

must be a knowing by way of an "unknowing." Such knowing by unknowing consists in that ordinary perceptual knowledge of God's *activities* whose recognition is predicated on a background belief about our ignorance of God's *essence* in the ordinary sense. This necessary presumption of our ignorance about the divine essence stands behind the activities that Gregory has in mind in taking our knowledge of God to require *faith*. Faith involves our acceptance of the speculative belief that our acquaintance with what we take to be the divine activities in fact acquaints us with the divine nature.

Nyssen's view is not that such faith amounts to a mere conjecture that gives something less than knowledge.[51] Nor is it that faith functions analogously to perception in virtue of which we can have a direct reference to a mode of divine presentation akin to a perceptual knowledge directly acquainting us with the divine essence *as* the divine essence. Instead, Nyssen's idea is that the intimate and mutual dependence of what we can know by acquaintance with what we cannot hangs together in such a way that what does not directly appear to us can be confirmed or disconfirmed by way of the empirical evidence constituted by what does.

There is a parallel here between the internal relation between inferential (contemplative) and noninferential (perceptual)

---

51. Such a view has been suggested by Bernard Pottier in *Dieu et le Christ selon Grégoire de Nysse: Etude systématique du 'ContreEunome' avec traduction iné'dite des extraits d'Eunome* Ouvertures 12 (Namur: Culture et vérité, 1994), 209: faith, "ce n'est pourtant pas," he says, "une connaissance." Laird is closer to the sort of picture I commend when he says, drawing on Verna Harrison's account, that she "identifies the function of faith as that of bridging the ontological gulf between the created and the uncreated. Faith 'brings us into a relation with the divine essence.'" Martin Laird, *Gregory of Nyssa and the Grasp of Faith* (New York: Oxford University Press, 2004), 22, quoting Harrison, *Grace and Human Freedom according to St. Gregory of Nyssa* (New York: Edwin Mellen, 1992), 67. But neither seems to describe precisely what sort of relation is involved, whereas I am suggesting a relation between two distinct modes of presentation or Fregean *Sinne* of the same object or *Bedeutung*, one of which names an intelligibility or *Sinn* under which God as its object or Bedeutung is comprehensible to us and the other *Sinn* of which is implied by the first and has as its object the very same *Bedeutung* but which is comprehensible only to God.

knowledge of God that Nyssen stakes out, on the one hand, and a remark of Wilfrid Sellars in *Empiricism and the Philosophy of Mind* about the structure of empirical knowledge in general, on the other.[52]

> If I reject the framework of traditional empiricism, it is not because I want to say that empirical knowledge has *no* foundation. For to put it in this way is to suggest that it is really "empirical knowledge so-called," and to put it in a box with rumors and hoaxes. There is clearly *some* point to the picture of human knowledge as resting on a level of propositions—observation reports—which do not rest on other propositions in the same way as other propositions rest on them. On the other hand, I do wish to insist that the metaphor of "foundation" is misleading in that it keeps us from seeing that if there is a logical dimension in which other empirical propositions rest on observation reports, there is another logical dimension in which the latter rest on the former.[53]

There is, Sellars says, a mutual dependence between the superstructure of empirical knowledge and its observational base.[54] On the minimally empiricist conception of experience McDowell advocates, we only become capable of taking in the world's own conceptual structure—actualizing its rational potential—once we have acquired the appropriate conceptual repertoire by way of the *Bildung* supplied by an ordinary upbringing. Clearly, our acquisition of the requisite conceptual capacities is, at first, neither voluntary nor rational. About that, we must concur with the merely causal or dispositional analysis supposed by Coherentists such as Hector. But once our second-natural responses to the world's impressions on us *become* voluntary and rational—once we become capable of genuinely

52. Wilfrid Sellars, *Empiricism and the Philosophy of Mind*, intro. Richard Rorty and study guide by Robert Brandom (Cambridge, MA: Harvard University Press, 1997).
53. Ibid., 78, §38.
54. See John McDowell's discussion in "Why Is Sellars's Essay Called '*Empiricism* and the Philosophy of Mind'?," in *Empiricism, Perceptual Knowledge, Normativity and Realism: Essays on Wilfrid Sellars*, ed. Willem A. de Vries (Oxford: Oxford University Press, 2009), 9–32.

intentional responses to its bearing on us in experience—we thereby become capable of directly taking in the world's own rational demands in experience and revising what we think, say, and do accordingly.

Having become a party to this self-correcting epistemological enterprise, the content of our experiences is always *both* dependent on our acquired Bildung and dependent on the world, but not in the same way. Our Bildung forms a superstructure for our observational knowledge—a wide conceptual shaping of sensory consciousness that determines what sorts of perceptible properties we are and are not equipped to detect. But our actual experiences of the world—the ways in which the world itself passively draws into operation features of that superstructure—furnish us with a foundational class of noninferential observational beliefs to which the superstructure is fundamentally accountable. Those observational beliefs constitute knowledge, moreover, when the world itself has furnished us with an indefeasible presentation of some way that it actually is—some rational potential I have directly taken in and actualized by my belief. So while my experiences are dependent on my Bildung, my Bildung is made directly accountable to the world in my experiences of it.

The dependence of our knowledge of God's energeia on our ignorance of God's dynamis is of just this sort, with our beliefs about the divine nature forming a feature of our Christian Bildung that enables us to experience the value properties of the world as God's energeia. But there are two ways in which our observational beliefs can be thus dependent on background knowledge. McDowell articulates a difference between a sort of perceptual content whose dependence on background knowledge is *theory laden* and a sort of perceptual content that is not, using the example of perceiving colors versus perceiving mu mesons:

It would be infelicitous to describe the bit of our worldview that is embodied in colour experience . . . as a theory. The general knowledge (so called) that Sellars invokes need not be acceptance of a body of propositions at all, inferentially articulated or not. It might be simply a responsiveness in practice to differences in lighting conditions, a practical rather than theoretical grasp of their significance for the possibility of telling what colors things have by looking. So the dependence of colour experience on background knowledge need not be a case of experience being theory-laden.

But why should we suppose we can draw general conclusions from this case? In a different kind of case, command of a theory— . . . an inferentially articulated body of knowledge—can make it possible for concepts that belong in the theory to figure in the content of someone's perceptual experience. A favourite example of Brandom's is the physicist who can observe *mu*-mesons. Experience of *mu*-mesons is surely theory-laden. Whether the embodiment of a bit of world view in experience of a particular kind reveals the experience as theory-laden depends on the character of the bit of world view that is embodied in the experience. There is no evident reason to expect that one answer will fit all cases.

What does seem plausible is that experience that is, though knowledge-dependent, not theory-laden, like colour experience, is in a certain sense more basic than theory-laden experience, as in the case of the physicist's experience of *mu*-mesons. If the physicist is challenged, she can retreat to a less committal account of what is available in her experience, exploiting the theory in which *mu*-mesons figure to justify the claim that, given that her experience yields that lesser information, she is in the presence of *mu*-mesons. When background knowledge operates in the way exemplified with colour experience, there is no such scope for retreat. So perhaps we can say . . . that fundamental experience of the world is not in any good sense theory-laden, even if there can be experience of the world that is theory-laden.[55]

On my reading, Nyssen takes our knowledge of God's energeia—in contradistinction to our knowledge of sensible properties such as

---

55. John McDowell, "Response to Costas Pagondiotis," *Tiorema* 25, no. 2 (2006): 115–19, 118–19.

colors—to be theory laden in precisely McDowell's sense. *If* we do in fact know that there are mu mesons, then when we directly and noninferentially perceive the relevant patterns of activity in a cloud chamber, we are in fact directly perceiving the activity of mu mesons. Similarly, Gregory holds that our knowledge of God is both theoretical and perceptual—our perception of God's activities ineliminably depends on our belief that our belief in God's essence amounts to knowledge.[56]

9.3 Nature as Openness to Grace

Gregory therefore holds that the content of Christian religious experience is the power or dynamis of the divine essence under the modes of presentation of the goodness and beauty of the free and creative intentional activity or energeia. Our knowledge of that essence apart from its creaturely manifestation, as it is known by God, is limited to an inferential knowledge of its epistemic unavailability to us. Since the intelligibility of God's energeia in creation is accommodated to the distinctive animal rationality of human nature, we are by nature capable of *acquiring* capacities to perceive the beauty and goodness of God's presence and intentions in and through creaturely objects, properties, and relations. That natural acquisition, moreover, comes by way of the ordinary processes of social learning, and, as such, the proper conceptual-discursive and moral-political formation is capable of gradually and increasingly awakening our senses to the intelligible world of God's work in creation and training our desires to actualize that intelligibility in thought, word, and deed. Actualizing the spiritual intelligibility of nature in God's intentional activity enables us to conform our creaturely powers of free and

56. See McDowell, "Sellars's Essay." Obviously, defending the view I am suggesting would require a good deal more elaboration and development than I can give here.

rational agency to the character of the divine agency manifest in creation. Our experiences of God in the world are thus not in any way independent of our receptivity to divine grace in the soul by way of the moral formation that guides our engagements with the world.

Nyssen characterizes the physical world as divinely intended to impose God's intelligible goods on human powers of rational receptivity and responsiveness. He describes human nature as divinely created with rationally constituted capacities of desire, sensation, and agency. The natural aim, or telos, of these powers, moreover, is the cultivation of spiritual sensitivity and virtuous character. Such capacities, he thinks, are required to actualize creation's rational potential in direct perceptual experiences of and intentional responses to God's presence and activity in creation. He takes human nature to play a central role in mediating divine grace to all of creation insofar as our ability to desire, detect, and intentionally actualize its intelligibility marks the realization of God's intentions in and for it.

Nyssen thus conceives of material or sensible creation as bearing the potential of openness to divine grace inasmuch as it supervenes on intelligible goods. In turn, that openness to grace is realized or actualized by human operations of spiritual perception and exercises of freedom thta mirror the virtues of the divine mind and will. God's perceptible calls to us in creation to mirror the goodness and beauty of divine agency in the soul, in other words, are also creation's own calls to us to fulfill its intended purpose. The human resemblance to God in manifesting intelligible goods in and through sensible creation establishes human nature as a creaturely mirror of the divine nature and establishes the physical creation (including our own bodily existence) as a "mirror of the mirror."[57] By encompassing

---

57. Wilson, *OMM*, XII.9, 398.

within our own nature both the material/sensible and the immaterial/intelligible properties of creation, we internalize the relation of mirroring the divine mind and will and manifesting the power of that reflected image (mirroring the mirror) in our own material bodies. As humans cultivate a receptivity and responsiveness to God, therefore, the whole of nature makes an ascent to God and divine grace descends on all of nature.[58]

On Nyssen's picture, are the capacities or operations of the spiritual senses grounded in human nature or divine grace? The question misfires.[59] Nyssen claims that creation is graced by nature, or naturally graced. Creation is naturally constituted by a divine self-gift, as its intelligible and sensible powers are manifestations of God's activities. But all of the delimitations of God's intentional powers that make each creature what it is are ordered to the creature's potential for manifesting the virtues of God's mind and will by way of engaging a human nature that images that mind and will. The actualization of that constitution, therefore, is a receptivity to the imprint of divine virtue, whether as the medium of its disclosure (material creation) or the agent who works in that medium (human creatures). We can therefore distinguish two senses in which Gregory takes created nature to be fundamentally graced. First, nature is actually graced in its natural constitution by admitting a potential *openness* to grace in humans' engagement with their material environments. Nature, as Blowers puts it, "opens out into the frontier between created and uncreated reality extending to eternity; it is the open-ended and 'graced' realm of participation in God."[60] Second,

---

58. He calls this an "anabatic" or "ascending" anthropology. See Behr, "Rational Animal," 231ff.

59. As Paul M. Blowers puts it in "Maximus the Confessor, Gregory of Nyssa and the Concept of 'Perpetual Progress,'" *Vigiliae Christianae* 46, no. 2 (June 1992), Gregory appears not to "operate with a radical bifurcation of nature and grace, as in certain schools of later Western Christian thought" (164).

60. Ibid.

created nature is merely potentially graced in its natural operations by allowing the *actualization* of its constitutional openness to grace in the freedom with which humans navigate their material environment.

From what has already been said regarding the nature of the spiritual senses, we have seen that the sense in which we are naturally constituted for an openness to God is similar to the sense in which a puppy is naturally constituted to shake or roll over (whereas, for example, a rock is not so constituted). That is, we are constituted by a capacity to *acquire* a perceptual capacity to receive and respond to divine grace, a capacity, moreover, that can only be acquired in its exercise and whose acquisition by training depends on an initiation into the proper discursive and moral-political community. Gregory appeals to the misuse of human freedom in Adam that has resulted in our inability both to actualize and to cultivate our constitutional openness to God. We are rendered in need of the redemptive grace of Christ to return us to our original splendor—not to an originary attainment but rather to an uninhibited natural capacity of receptivity and responsiveness to divine grace. Given the damage done to our graced nature by sin, we are dependent on the power of Christ's virtue to give us the spiritual eyes to see and ears to hear God's manifestation in creation. Christ, for Gregory, is the prototype and fulfillment of the divine image in human nature whose power capacitates us by the Spirit through the pedagogy of the church.[61]

9.4 Minimal Empiricism in the Soul's Ascent to God

There are all sorts of reasons we might have for thinking that Nyssen's theology of the spiritual senses is wrong. His analysis of the God/world relation in terms of powers courts legitimate metaphysical

---

61. Wilson, *OMM*, XVI.1–9, 403–404.

controversies and is not clearly compatible with other theological commitments that he has, most notably his doctrine of divine simplicity and his analysis of the Trinity. His account of the powers constitutive of human nature, moreover, leaves open the question of whether it is best accommodated by substance dualism or some version of property dualism about the human person as the possessor of those powers. His account of nature and grace requires a synergism between divine and human agency that many will find objectionable.[62] While framed on radically different terms than those assumed in the dispute between Augustine and Pelagius, it confronts us with similar problems about the distinction and relation between divine and human freedom, along with all the usual metaphysical worries about compatibilism and incompatibilism.[63]

My suggested reconstruction of Nyssen's views is thus both underdetermined and philosophically and theologically controversial.[64] Nevertheless, it seems to have at least one advantage over the views criticized in previous chapters—the theology of religious experience it advances is entirely compatible with a minimal empiricism. That is, it clears a minimal bar that many modern and contemporary accounts fail to clear: it manages to proceed from an intelligible conception of perceptual experience, one that does not succumb—in the way that Marion, Alston, Preller, and Hector do, for example—to the temptation toward Givenism or Coherentism. Instead, it presumes the sort of naturalized platonism constitutive

---

62. See Ekkehard Mühlenberg, "Synergism in Gregory of Nsysa," *Zeitschrift fur die Neutestamentliche Wissenschaft* 68 (1977): 93–122.
63. Christopher A. Beeley goes so far as to suggest, in "The Holy Spirit in the Cappadocians: Past and Present," *Modern Theology* 26, no. 1 (2010): 90–119, that Nyssen loses sight of the Spirit's grace in our divinization precisely because his synergism makes him a kind of "moralist" (107). But see Smith, *Passion and Paradise*, 158–59, which suggests that Nyssen rather holds to a kind of prevenient grace.
64. Not to mention exegetically, although I have attempted to address some worries about that at the outset.

of our naive realism about experience. The empirical content we (putatively) take in belongs to the space of reasons that governs our thinking (thereby establishing the fit between mind and world) and also (potentially) puts our empirical thinking and rational motivations for action in touch with the world's own rational demands on us, with the objective features of the way the world is anyway whether or not we or anyone else are prepared to recognize them as such (thereby establishing friction between mind and world).

Moreover, Nyssen's story manages to affirm the minimal fit and friction constitutive of the very idea of a perceptual experience insofar as he endorses a form of naturalized platonism. His account is platonistic inasmuch as he understands the world as intrinsically constituted by a rational potential that manifests the power and presence of God's intentional activities in and through created nature. Certainly, Nyssen endorses a *theological* platonism, but he does not hold what McDowell calls a "rampant" platonism. On a rampant platonism, one acquiesces to the idea that the natural world lacks any intrinsic rational powers or potential and concludes that the rational potential realized in our intentional activities must derive from a supernatural domain—a realm beyond nature. For this reason, McDowell concludes that "meaning is not a mysterious gift from outside nature"; it is not the case that "our species acquired what makes it special, the capacity to resonate to meaning, in a gift from outside nature."[65] But the movement from the rejection of a rampant platonism to the rejection of a theological conception of meaning as gift is a non sequitur. While the idea that meaning, if there is to be any, must descend on a disenchanted world from on high clearly does not fit the structure of Nyssen's thinking, the idea that nature receives its intelligibility as a gift clearly does.

65. John McDowell, *Mind and World*, 2nd ed. (Cambridge, MA: Harvard University Press, 1996), 88, 123.

That Nyssen's platonism is not rampant is evident in the fact that there is no disenchanted conception of nature in his thinking that would send him looking to a transcendent domain to bring meaning to it. On his account, the sensible world is itself intrinsically intelligible insofar as it is constituted by the intelligible concepts of sensibility entertained by the divine mind and enacted by God's creative freedom. In addition, Nyssen does not hold that merely recognizing the world as a meaningful domain of itself logically entails that it must manifest a supernatural power. That would be to suppose that our acknowledgment of God's presence and activity in the world were a merely a matter of formal deduction. Instead, Nyssen characterizes Christians as those who, having been initiated into the community of faith, have been granted capacities of spiritual perception by way of which they enjoy lived experiences of the world as a theater of divine presence and action that empirically informs the entire range of their beliefs and practices.

In other words, we know the world as well as our place in it to be the manifestation of a creative gift of divine intentionality not merely by some prior argument that we must assume it to be so on pain of irrationality. Rather, we know the world to manifest God's presence to us and God's agency toward us through revelation to those who have eyes to see and ears to hear. For us to entertain the idea that the world is not the way we take it to be, that our putative perceptions are illusory rather than genuine, would therefore not necessarily entail that the world is meaningless but that our theological claims are either false or empirically unfounded. Put in terms of the Fregean and disjunctivist analysis given in the previous chapter, characteristically Christian experiences are not genuinely object-dependent senses—not in fact actualizations of any rational potential had by the world—but instead merely *appear* to be so. Nyssen's theology of the mutually suitable relation between creation that manifests the rational potential for divine revelation and human creatures uniquely suited for resonating and actualizing that potential is a substantive and not a merely formal way of making intelligible a platonistic conception of the world's intelligibility.

This theological conception of the world's rational potential is consistent with a *naturalized* platonism. Nyssen's account is capable of recognizing our capacities of spiritual perception as second-natural in precisely McDowell's sense. McDowell's dictum that we "must not suppose that receptivity makes an even notionally separable contribution to its cooperation with spontaneity" follows straightforwardly from Nyssen's Aristotelian conception of human nature as the incorporation of an animal form of receptivity into powers of spontaneity that resemble God's rational agency.[66] Moreover, he construes human capacities to actualize the rational potential or intelligibility of created nature on which its sensibility supervenes as a power both naturally acquired and cultivated in its exercise through our ordinary acculturation into the moral-practical, linguistic, and bodily disciplines of some human community. He holds that the customs and observances cultivated in the church are those that best initiate and train our senses to detect the rational affordances objectively revealed in creation. Initiation into a Christian form of life, he thinks, furnishes us with a framework for the ongoing project of rationally revising one's belief and practice to best accord with experience, and in that sense he is committed to the idea that a Christian formation or *paideia* is more *empirically well-supported* than a pagan one.

Therefore, as a theological inflection of a naturalized platonism, Nyssen's theology of religious experience is clearly neither insufficiently naturalized nor rampantly platonistic, at least not in the

---

66. Ibid., 41.

relevant senses needed to avoid the characteristically modern collapse into the vicious oscillation, as I specified them in chapter 6. Of course, his theological claim is contestable: that a Christian cultivation of our ordinary perceptual capacities to take in and respond to the rational demands of creation opens our eyes (and ears and so on) to that intelligibility as manifesting the intentional activity of God calling us into conformity with Christ by the Spirit. The contestability of that claim derives in part from its contingency upon experience, upon our capacities to look at the world and find that it is so in experience. An important implication of Gregory's theological empiricism—his view that theological knowledge derives principally from our acquaintance with its subject matter—is that our ability to know the truth of Christian claims about God's relation to the world depend on the faithfulness of the Christian community to nurture the form of life capable of training our spiritual senses to become directly perceptually acquainted with God's presence and action in the world.[67]

67. Stanley Hauerwas has strictly identified the church's capacity to produce "witnesses" to the truth of its claims in its moral-practical form of life with the truthfulness of what it purports to bear witness to per se, and he has accordingly been criticized for holding the apparent absurdity that truths about God somehow depend on whether anyone knows that they are true. A "robust theological description of existence," Hauerwas says, depends on "the way Christians must and should live." *With the Grain of the Universe* (Grand Rapids: Baker Academic, 2013), 38–39. Cf. Paul J. Griffiths's worry about the coherence of thinking that a Christian conviction needs any sort of witness outside of the conviction itself as an epistemological basis for that conviction, in "Witness and Conviction in *With the Grain of the Universe*," *Modern Theology* 19, no. 1 (January 2003): 72. The structure of Nyssen's theology of religious experience can help us articulate at least one way in which to make sense of such a claim: It is necessarily part of the Christian's eschatological claim that God's creative intentions are not merely potential in creation but have been and will continue to be actualized by a community whose form of life serves as a perceptual pedagogy capable of capacitating us to actualize God's perceptible relation to creation. It follows that if there are not or could not be any perceivers capable of bearing witness to the God/world relation, then God's creative intentions for humanity have ceased to be realizable and the Christian's central claim about the God/world relation is therefore false. Denying that there are any faithful witnesses to Christianity would entail denying that Christianity is true. One way to secure that denial might be to show that there is not or could not be any community of the sort required to produce any agents capable of the observation reports that would bear witness to God's manifestation in the world in Christ by the Spirit.

I conclude my explication of Nyssen's view by suggesting that the minimal empiricism embedded within the diagram of his theology of religious experience sketched above is the very same picture at work in the dynamics of his theology as presented in HSS and LM, Nyssen's later commentaries. In those works, he reads both the bride's pursuit of the bridegroom in the Song of Songs and Moses' journey to meet God on Mount Sinai as narratives of the soul's ascent to God. While differing in some respects relative to the contours of the biblical text, he takes both narratives to present us with a model for what Coakley aptly describes as the "refurbishing" of the divine image in us.[68] The model describes our return to humanity's original splendor through the never-ending cultivation of divine virtue in the soul through which we both participate in and uncover God's immanence to all creation precisely through our distinctively human perceptual receptivity and responsiveness to creation as the various modes of God's intentional activity directed toward us.

Accordingly, Nyssen's account of the three stages of the ascent ought to be read as a description of the dynamics of human participation in God that presumes and enacts his earlier theology of the spiritual senses. Readers of Nyssen on the structure of the ascent have disagreed as to whether the three stages should be regarded as temporal moments in the life of the soul to be progressively passed through,[69] or whether instead they represent a more logical ordering of precedence and subsequence.[70] Another

---

68. Sarah Coakley, "Gregory of Nyssa," in *The Spiritual Senses: Perceiving God in Western Christianity*, ed. Paul L. Gavrilyuk and Coakley (New York: Cambridge University Press, 2012), 41.

69. This is what we find in Jean Daniélou, *Platonisme et Théologie Mystique* (Paris: Aubier, 1944), 185–88, as well as Louth, *Mystical Tradition*, 17–18. Morweena Ludlow suggests that the ascent is a "cumulative" picture of a pilgrimage that advances from "earlier" to "later" stages. See her "Divine Infinity and Eschatology: The Limits and Dynamics of Human Knowledge according to Gregory of Nyssa (*CE* II 67–170)," in *Gregory of Nyssa: Contra Eunomium II*, ed. Lenka Karfíková, Scot Douglass, and Johannes Zachhuber (Leiden: Brill, 2004), 235.

exegetical worry has been whether he imagines our progression through the stages to be linear, cyclical, or some combination. Perhaps the most prominent dispute has centered on how properly to understand the intrinsic character of the third stage and its relation of the first two stages as their culminating achievement.

A good many of these exegetical puzzles resolve themselves, however, once we recognize that Nyssen's model of the ascent is a model of cultivating the spiritual senses that accords with the picture already diagrammed in his earlier work. Viewed in this light, I think his three-staged articulation of the dynamics of spiritual perception is neither a strictly narrative presentation of a real-time chronological movement of the human person in the journey toward God nor a strictly formal presentation of the logical elements involved in that movement, but rather a combination of both. That is, Nyssen singles out three formal features of the human perceptual relation to God from his earlier work and then highlights the contribution that each of those features makes to the progress of our actual lived experience of God.

Think, for example, of a football coach reviewing the video recording of a successful play. If the coach recognizes communication, technique, and execution as essentially constitutive of that play and wishes to comment on how it actually unfolded, he might highlight and explicate the significance of communication when reviewing the earlier moments in which the quarterback calls out the intended play, formation, snap count, and so on ("Open right 22 Charley B on 4!"). He might focus on explaining ball-

---

70. Smith emphasizes this feature to a greater extent than the other, chastening the notion of temporal moments of advancement by treating each stage as its own "cycle" of ascent that "spirals upward" to the next (*Passion and Paradise*, 153–54). Ronald E. Heine goes further, relativizing a temporal picture altogether and arguing instead that the "cumulative" picture of the ascent represents *dimensions* of the spiritual life that are always present. See *Perfection in the Virtuous Life: A Study in the Relationship between Edification and Polemical Theology in Gregory of Nyssa's* De vita Moysis (Philadelphia, PA: Philadelphia Patristic Foundation, 1975), 106–7.

handling technique and so on when discussing the middle of the play, from the point at which the ball is snapped to the down. Finally, when considering the down at the end of the play, the coach might discuss the relative merits, problems, and improvisation required in the proper execution of the play.

Clearly, however, more than one of the three formal elements can be instantiated in each moment of the progressive unfolding of the play. We do not have to suppose that there is no communication going on during the middle of the play or no technique at issue prior to the snap. Similarly, I take Nyssen's analysis of the narrative of the soul's ascent to be organized according to three formal elements in his understanding of spiritual perception, each of which is most naturally explicated according to a corresponding moment in the actual unfolding of the soul's communion with God. Consequently, I read the three stages of the ascent that Gregory explicates in HSS and LM to be a description of the temporal unfolding of our lived experiences of God according to the particular role played by three formal features of our perceptual capacities involved in those experiences.

In LM, Nyssen recasts the soul's ascent to God in the Moses' ascent of Sinai, while in HSS the soul is cast as the bride in pursuit of God as the bridegroom. Thus, in the first stage of the ascent, Moses receives the milk of his biological mother even after having been adopted by an Egyptian. Gregory reads this as a preparatory moment in which the soul's initiation into a pagan moral and intellectual context must be supplemented and reoriented by the "customs" (*ta ethe*) and "observances" (*ta nomina*) of the church.[71] Similarly, in Homily 11 of HSS, Nyssen characterizes the first step of the ascent as a preparatory pedagogy in which we withdraw from false opinions

---

71. Gregory of Nyssa, *The Life of Moses*, trans. Abraham Malherbe and Everett Ferguson (New York: Paulist, 1978) II.10–12, 57 (hereafter: Malherbe, *LM*); cf. Smith, *Passion and Paradise*, 155.

and thereby obey the divine command that "orders that this heavy sleep be banished from the eyes of the soul" by reorienting ourselves toward "the true and substantive realities . . . under the guidance of the Word."[72] In both cases, Nyssen emphasizes an educative function of orienting our beliefs and practices to God as true Being whose name we know in and through Christ as revealed in the teachings and disciplines of the church. In LM, he describes the transition to a Christian formation not as an utter discontinuity from a pagan upbringing but rather as an educative reorientation toward the true ground of pagan virtue that opens the eyes of one's soul more clearly to the intelligible world. The "dialectic between the cognitive training and the moral discipline," Smith says, "rightly orders the soul's orientation toward the cosmic hierarchy."[73] Nyssen's emphasis in the first stage seems to be less on the *operations* of our capacities to direct ourselves on the intelligible world than on the proper form of training we require for the *sensitization* or *capacitation* in virtue of which such operations are possible. Thus, he focuses on the susceptibility of our rationally constituted appetite and senses to a training that, by properly inclining us to the intelligible world, can render us "wakeful."[74]

After describing the first stage as preparation, Nyssen depicts a distinct second stage of the ascent as an actual acquaintance with the intelligible world through the cultivation of virtue—receiving and responding to God's presence as an intelligible divine economy manifest within the sensible world through Christ as the arch-principle or Logos who holds the key to that intelligibility.[75] The

---

72. Gregory of Nyssa, *Homilies on the Song of Songs*, no. 13 in *Writings from the Greco-Roman World*, ed. Brian E. Daley and John. T. Fitzgerald, trans. with intro. and notes by Richard A. Norris Jr. (Atlanta, GA: Society of Biblical Literature, 2012), Homily 11, 335 (hereafter: Norris, *HSS*). Cf. Gregory of Nyssa, *Commentary on the Song of Songs*, trans. Casmir McCambley (Brookline, MA: Hellenic College Press, 1987), 199, J317 (hereafter: McCambley, *CSS*).

73. Smith, *Passion and Paradise*, 159.

74. Norris, *HSS*, 334 (cf. "watchful" in McCambley, *CSS*, 200, J 318).

sensitization of our receptive faculties gives way to "lofty perceptions" in which our directedness on the sensible world puts us in touch with the intelligible world as the locus of God's outworking of salvation in Christ by the Spirit. Thus, Christ, who is "the Word," "changes his power in diverse ways to suit those who eat . . . making his message strong meat for the more mature and greens for the weaker and milk for little children."[76] Such revelations of Christ depicted as manna from heaven represent "teachings for the virtuous life."[77] In both HSS and LM, Nyssen pictures the cultivation of virtue as a recognition of the goodness and beauty of creation, which bears the traces of God's own goodness and beauty, and as eliciting a responsiveness to our perceptions of it by mirroring that virtue and becoming beautiful ourselves.[78] In HSS, he depicts the divine manifestations to our spiritual senses in terms of the calling of the bridegroom that is constantly propelling the bride forward from a pursuit to a participation in the virtues of Christ.

Finally, Moses' entrance into the cloud darkness on Sinai represents the third stage, wherein the soul enters into an apophatic and contemplative encounter with God's transcendence of material creation. There God is apprehended as surpassing all comprehension, a luminous darkness in which one sees in not seeing, knows in unknowing.[79] Similarly, in HSS he describes how the soul is "surrounded by the divine night, in which the Bridegroom draws near but is not manifest."[80] In much the same way that the first two stages seem to fit neatly with a conception of the training and

75. Malherbe, *LM*, II.19–25, II.102–61; 59–60, 78–94. See also Smith, *Passion*, 159–64; and Louth, *Origins*, 85–87.
76. Malherbe, *LM*, II.140, 88
77. Ibid., II.141, 88.
78. Norris, *HSS*, 51–52 (cf. McCambley, *CSS*, 60–61, J46–47); 159–60 (cf. McCambley, *CSS*, 118–19, J158–59).
79. Malherbe, *LM*, II.163–4, 95.
80. Norris, *HSS*, 343 (cf. McCambley, *CSS*, 203, J324).

operation of the spiritual senses as I have characterized them from his earlier work, we can bring Gregory's apophaticism in the third stage into line with that reading. Precisely by our direct spiritual perception of what *can* be apprehend of God, we can come to reflect on what we cannot. "[L]eaving behind everything that is observed"—not only sensibles but also intelligibles—we come to recognize through "the intelligence's yearning for understanding" that the divine essence is "unattainable . . . by every intelligent creature."[81]

Moses comes to know by way of contemplation "that what is divine is beyond all knowledge and comprehension," and this is "a kind of darkness."[82] Significantly, Nyssen explicitly marks the contemplative stage of the ascent as one in which we have left perception behind entirely. We do not encounter here a different *sort* of direct awareness of God—one whose invisibility to our capacities of spiritual perception somehow becomes visible in some other way. Rather, the darkness of the intellect centers on the absolute unavailability of the divine essence, which is nevertheless a kind of availability *as* unavailable. We can touch the divine essence without its appearing to us as such only because it *does* manifest itself to us, not as such but under the modes of presentation given by God's activity in and through the divine economy revealed in creation. On this reading, this stage does not offer a phenomenology of mystical *experience* of God that escapes our conceptual grasp, whether as an activation of the senses that bypasses the mind,[83] or an activation of

---

81. Malherbe, *LM*, II.163, 95.
82. Ibid.
83. Both Coakley and Laird represent the third stage as more particularly expressive of the "union" of the soul with God by way of an even *greater* direct acquaintance than was had in the second stage, rather than as an expression of the generative role of God's unavailable modes of presentation as holding promise for greater self-transformation. Thus see, for example, Coakley, "Gregory of Nyssa," 50, who wrongly, I think, reads Nyssen on the embrace of Christ in the "divine night" as envisioning a sensory awareness of God divorced from our

the mind that ceases to depend on the senses,[84] or any nonstandard perceptual encounter on Gregory's model of perception. God is not being represented as perceptibly *present* to Moses at all. It is not, as Nyssen himself simply states, a perceptual form of cognition but a purely contemplative or intellective one that follows from some reasoning about what the goodness and beauty of God would have to be, given a manifestation free from the constraints of created nature.

In what sense is such a recognition of the limits of spiritual perception "luminous"? What Gregory means to indicate by this, I

rational constitution. Laird regards the "grasp of faith" as a means of directing us upon God that is in some respect *more* direct than the knowledge given in the second stage because it bypasses our conceptual grasp to make God present to us, resulting in a "logophatic" speech that is not *about* God but "full of God." See Martin Laird, "'Whereof We Speak': Gregory of Nyssa, Jean-Luc Marion and the Current Apophatic Rage," *Heythrop Journal* 42 (2001): 1–12. As I read Gregory, both of these readings would undermine the entire tenor of his theological anthropology, insofar as they both attempt to disaggregate the rational faculty from another (whether the sense, for Coakley, or faith, for Laird). But Gregory denies that the rational faculty is one element in an aggregate in the first place: our rational faculty is essential and ineliminable for any intentional directedness of which we are capable qua human. Alteration from that view would require a radical revision by the time we get to his late work, and there is insufficient evidence for any such revision, especially when a reading in perfect continuity with his earlier picture is readily available and can be easily accommodated by the text. Or so I've tried to indicate.

84. Smith picks up on Nyssen's emphasis on the indirect character of the relation to God specified in the *theoria* of the third stage: "[The soul] discerns God's presence and knows God *indirectly* through the glory of the sanctuary. While God in his essence remains unseen, as when the face of the sun is obscured in a full eclipse by the moon, nevertheless, the glory of God's activities, his *energeia*, like the glow of the penumbra around the eclipsed sun, is visible" (*Passion and Paradise*, 172). But he is wrong, I think, to locate the receptivity to divine *energeia* by the "spiritual senses" in the third stage rather than the second. Nyssen does not regard the contemplative moment as one in which the soul is "purified of its tendency to conceptualize the Divine by adopting analogues from the sensual world" (172). The trouble is not that Nyssen regards the contemplative moment as a necessary chastening of the perceptual one of the second stage, but rather that the second stage does not merely name the adoption of analogues from the sensual world but rather precisely the enjoyment of the glory of the divine activities revealed in the economy of salvation that Smith predicates of the third stage. But once this bookkeeping is enforced, what role the third stage plays on Smith's reading remains puzzling. If, however, Nyssen is as I suggest contemplating God as the transcendent source of the immanent intelligible goods revealed to us precisely via the rational operations of our senses, then such contemplation always represents a prior dependence *on* the spiritual senses as the basis for moving *beyond* them. The mutual dependence of these two dimensions is much easier to confuse or conflate when regarding them, as Smith does, as *moments* along a temporal path, even if one governed by a "dialectic."

think, is the *generativity* of this contemplative claim for a pedagogy of our spiritual senses and appetites. That is, when we recognize the perceptible manifestations of God in creation as limited modes of presentation of an object of limitless rational potential, then the capacity to grow in virtue described in the second stage of the ascent can never mark an end to the training and operation of our spiritual senses. Instead, given a contemplative recognition of the essence of God, which remains unavailable to us as such, we are led to recognize the limitless availability of God according to our growing receptivity toward the divine. Since "the Good attracts to itself those who look to it," our faith in the limitless content of that essential Good ensures that "the soul rises ever higher and will always make its flight yet higher—by its desire of the heavenly things *straining ahead [epekteinomai] for what is still to come.*"[85] Daniélou coined the term *epectasy* to single out Nyssen's concept of our rational agency as capable of an infinite extension in straining forward toward the inexhaustible fullness of the divine essence.[86] But while the third stage might be regarded as the explicit articulation of an unknowable essence touched only by way of the energeia and comprehended in itself only as a formal notion (as Nyssen had already claimed in "Against Eunomius"), it also forms the very condition for the possibility of the soul's progress in virtue, and, as such, it is a darkness that enlightens. Divine incomprehensibility in Nyssen's sense, in other words, is a transcendental condition for the possibility of our perceptual receptivity to grace—it names the theory ladenness in all the operations of our spiritual senses.

---

85. Malherbe, *LM*, II.225, 113. See also Kathryn Rombs, "Gregory of Nyssa's Doctrine of Epektasis: Some Logical Implications," in *Studia Patristica*, vol. 37, ed. Maurice Wiles and E. J. Yarnold with P. M. Parvis (Leuven: Peeters, 2001), 288–93. Smith, *Passion and Paradise*, 104–25.
86. Daniélou, *Platonisme*, 298.

Nyssen's delineation of the three stages of the ascent is therefore nothing less than an analysis of the training, cultivation, and renewal of the spiritual senses. Given the diagram of spiritual perception given in his earlier work, the significance of each stage for our perceptual relation to God should be evident. Each stage of the ascent lays down a requirement that facilitates our experience of God in conformity to this picture. By way of his articulation of the first stage of the ascent, Nyssen claims that unless we possess the proper repertoire of conceptual capacities, the virtues of God's intentional activities toward us in creation cannot present themselves to our spiritual senses *as* God's virtues. By way of the second stage, he claims that unless those virtues are present to us as such in and through our relation to Christ by the Spirit, we cannot receive and respond to them so as to participate in the goodness and beauty of the divine power of rational agency by our own imaging of it. Finally, by way of the third stage, he claims that unless we recognize the way in which our responsiveness to presentations of divine energeia in pursuit of conformity to Christ depends on a prior acknowledgment of the divine essence as incomprehensible and capable of being grasped only by faith,[87] we cannot continue to participate in God as a source of perpetual growth. Without the recognition of any new outpouring of divine self-gift that we must be poised to receive, our rationally constituted desire will lack the intelligible object required to elicit our openness to God. Divine incomprehensibility in Nyssen's sense, in other words, is a transcendental condition for the possibility of our receptivity to grace.

---

87. Such a grasping, I have emphasized against Laird, is not a means of direct apprehension by way of the forsaking of conceptual thinking per se, but rather an indirect means of apprehension by way of refusing to admit the possibility that any *observational* concepts we possess or are capable of possessing could supply the content for our concept of the divine essence. The concept of the divine essence, however, is one we do possess and that unproblematically refers us to God—but it is one that has a very limited sense, that of a divine agency unlimited in goodness and beauty of the sort revealed by the intentional activities of that agency in and through created nature.

So we have a movement from the training of the spiritual senses to their cultivation in the recognition of and conformity to presentations of divine virtue, then from that cultivation to the more reflective contemplation on the dependence of what the spiritual senses can take in on what they cannot (the dependence, we might say, of the light of revelation on the darkness of divine hiddenness). In what sense might this reading of the three stages count as a *progression*? What sort of succession does Nyssen aim to depict by way of the soul's movement from one stage to the next? On the one hand, there appears to be an element of logical progression evinced by the ascent narrative, since reflection on a perceptual experience of God (stage 3) logically depends on having had a prior perceptual experience of God (stage 2), which in turn logically depends on possessing properly formed perceptual capacities (stage 1). Nyssen's articulation of the threefold dynamic of the ascent is a claim about the internal structure of epectasy—the perfection of human nature consists not in the satiation of our limited desire by the divine essence or the erasure of our creaturely limitation but rather the expansion of appetitive and sensory receptivity to God in fulfillments that produce greater sensitivity and desire and which anticipate even greater fulfillments, ad infinitum.

Should we also view the progression temporally? It seems initially plausible to treat the movement as one thing after another: first we train the senses to encounter God, then we encounter God, then we reflect on that encounter. This seems to me mistaken, however, in the same way that a strict temporal analysis of the football coach's commentary on the play would be wrong. That is, it suggests a strict identification of a logically distinct feature of our perceptual relation to God with temporally distinct moments in the unfolding of that relation. In fact, however, all three features of spiritual perception delineated in the ascent are constitutively present in each. Both the initial and ongoing subjection of our sensory capacities to a pedagogical training for a receptivity and responsiveness to spiritual realities (stage 1) necessarily *involves* the operation of those capacities themselves (stage 2), since, in Gregory's understanding, spiritual capacities are acquired in the exercise of moral and intellectual virtue.

Moreover, our recognition of the content of perception acquired by way of our participation in virtue (stage 2) necessarily involves the assumption that what is received does not exhaust that which is available, an assumption that can only be acquired via contemplation and not acquaintance (stage 3). In other words, the work on the soul effected in the third stage not only logically depends on the others but constitutively incorporates them. What then accounts for Gregory's separating the stages and mapping them onto a narrative (that is, a temporally ordered) sequence? The sequence, it seems, names *phenomenological dimensions* of our spiritual experience rather than strictly logical relations or temporal sequence. That is, the dynamic it unfolds is of the qualitatively rhythmic character of what it is like for the Christian to progressively mature into ever-greater attunement with God's presence and action in the world. Logically, the three stages name mutually constituting features of our spiritual perception. Temporally, each dimension is in play in a much messier way than could be captured in a staged progression of the Christian project of mirroring God in the soul via our conformity to Christ in the Spirit.[88]

But, in our lived experiences, we experience the temporal unfolding of our own participation in that project *as* a movement from one stage to the next. That is, we experience moments in our perceptual relation to God that center more clearly on the

---

88. Such messiness is not captured any better by blurring the stages into one another or complexifying them into a dialectic hierarchy. To the extent that either strategy captures a sequence of mental and moral-practical acts, it can only do so by evacuating the stages to a greater or lesser extent of any ground for distinguishing them in the first place.

pedagogical task of rational revision and moral-intellectual preparation requisite to our encounter with God. Similarly, we often take ourselves to be unself-consciously engaged in actually experiencing and attending to God's demands, simply undergoing rather than reflecting on whatever it is like to be thus acquainted with God. Finally, our experiences of God are punctuated by moments of contemplation on the orientation of our engagements with God to God's necessary transcendence of them. Structurally, the three are mutually interdependent. Temporally, the first two stages unfold together insofar as the training required to apprehend God's virtuous energeia is acquired by the exercise of the relevant capacities for such apprehensions. The interposing of reflection on God's transcendence required for revising, correcting, and motivating the continuation of our training is more circumstantial and sporadic than principled. But a pursuit of God is marked by the clear and distinct *phenomenological character* belonging to each logical dimension constituent in the temporal unfolding of our lived experiences of God.

As we saw from Nyssen's analysis in OMM and *On the Soul and the Resurrection*, our capacities of receptivity and spontaneity, which grow mutually through our pedagogy in, cultivation of, and contemplation on divine virtue, enable us to become intentionally directed on the activities (energeia) of God. Those divine activities, moreover, manifest the power (dynamis) constitutive of the divine essence (*ousia*) and nature (*phusis*). We can therefore trace God's uncreated activities manifest within creation as reaching to us from beyond creation and as existing in a manner unlimited by the constraints of created nature. While that tracing can only hit its mark inferentially and not by any acquaintance or comprehension of the unlimited manner of existence of God's goodness and beauty, Nyssen regards the infinitude of God's essential power to be the source of our modes of apprehension of it in the limited scope of God's creative activities.

The continuous or "epectic" rather than terminating character of the ascent that Gregory describes is thus, as Smith aptly characterizes it, an ever-ascending spiral through the stages of the ascent, but, as I read him, it remains a phenomenological rather than logical or temporal spiral. On the one hand, viewing the ascent as modeling epectasy in our relation to God means that the union with God thematized in the third stage is never a final culmination, not even in the eschatological overcoming of sin. But it also means that Nyssen does not regard the contemplative vision of God depicted in the third stage as an achievement reserved for the few. The path trod by all Christians from the earliest initiate to the exemplars of maturity consists in a phenomenological movement from the training of the spiritual senses to their operation in the pursuit of virtue to the recognition of the absolute transcendence of their object. What differentiates the mature from the immature is the greater or lesser quality of transformation achieved in one's iteration of the threefold cycle, not whether one stage of that cycle, the last one, has for the first time become available after having been sufficiently purified via prior iterations of the first two stages.

9.5 Conclusion

To reiterate, none of this is to say that the story I have derived from Nyssen is without problems or even that it is necessarily the most promising account to develop. While I judge it to be promising (and, indeed, the correct account) and hope to develop it in subsequent work, my reason for invoking it in this context does not require that anyone think it promising (much less correct). Rather, my turn to Nyssen in this concluding chapter has been primarily illustrative of how a constructive theology of religious experience might survive the critique that I have elucidated.

If the McDowellian deconstruction of the problem of perception is correct, then much recent work on the questions of theological realism and antirealism and the problem of how human experiences, thoughts, words, and actions manage to succeed in directing us upon God is irreparably mistaken. Moreover, an exculpatory explanation rooted in the modern processes of disenchantment enables us to see just how long and all-embracing the road to recovery must be if we are not simply to avoid the intellectual temptation to *theologize* from within the pseudoproblem of perception—a freedom from temptation that I have attempted to model in this chapter—but also to construct new pedagogies for training the senses that are inevitably required to open eyes blinded by modern malformations.

Nyssen's account of the ascent suggests an important point of departure for spelling out one form that such a pedagogy might take. It raises interesting questions about what sort of thoroughgoing program of moral *askesis* might be required in order to acquire perceptual sensitivities to the presence and agency of God. We might suppose that the shift in background between premodern contexts and our own implies a corresponding shift in the nature and accessibility of perceptual training available to us from what was presumably available to our premodern forbearers. Our cultivation of second-natural capacities of spiritual perception accordingly depends on very different social and institutional infrastructures that serve as pedagogies for our sensory capacities.

Presumably, the relevant differences enable us to distinguish not merely how things can *seem* to us from how things might have seemed to them, but also which realities were in fact perceptually available to them and which to us. Whatever such a difference amounts to, it admits of a range of pedagogical preparation required to cultivate the requisite perceptual capacity—what one must learn to see *that* the sky is blue does not require any specialized training over and above an ordinary upbringing, whereas to see that this rug is distinct from that one or to taste that this is a merlot and not a cabernet seems to run further in the direction of perceptual expertise. Nyssen's story similarly points us toward the importance of identifying *experts* in spiritual perception.

If the deconstructive and therapeutic thrust of the present study is correct, therefore, then it bears potential for some fairly wide-ranging research agendas. This will no doubt put a good deal of pressure on the prior question: *is* the synthesis I have presented correct? Although I believe I have given some good reasons to think so, McDowell's work, while important in the recent philosophical literature on perception, has also been controversial, and that is no doubt due to some needed refinements of the broadly Wittgensteinian position he takes up. However, I believe that much of the prominent criticism has come from misreading his views, so I have largely opted to bypass such criticisms in my reading of McDowell rather than distracting from my central theological purposes.

More substantively, the critical posture I have taken is directed at theologians and Christian philosophers of religion whose implied rejections of a naturalized platonism in theology have landed them in what I have argued is a distinctively theological version of the oscillation between Givenism or Coherentism, whether of an apophatic or cataphatic sort. I advocate that we eschew the relatively recent puzzles that have arisen as a result of a desperate grasp onto one of these two horns. In the interest of asking and answering meaningful theological questions, we ought to avoid expending needless energy courting the illusory ones.

I recognize an unavoidable irony of my argument. Persuading anyone to avert her gaze from what I have taken to be illusory—the theology's beholdenness to the philosophical problem of perception—has required precisely a strenuous attention to the mirage itself. Nor do I suppose that my argument will effect the hoped-for moratorium on the problem in all its subtle forms. In confronting the hydra, we have to settle for enlisting help in lopping off the heads as they emerge. Or, to shift the image to a more aptly therapeutic one, while a trauma of modernity remains for theologians attempting to imagine a sensible theological empiricism, perhaps this work can begin to help a few go on.

Bibliography

Adams, Robert M. *Finite and Infinite Goods.* New York: Oxford University Press, 2002.

———. "Religious Disagreements and Doxastic Practices." *Philosophy and Phenomenological Research* 54, no. 4 (December 1994): 885–90.

Alston, William P. "Aquinas on Theological Predication: A Look Backward and a Look Forward." In *Reasoned Faith,* edited by Eleonore Stump, 145–78. Ithaca, NY: Cornell University Press, 1993.

———. "Back to the Theory of Appearing." *Philososophical Perspectives* 19 (1999): 181–203.

———. *Divine Nature and Human Language: Essays in Philosophical Theology.* Ithaca, NY: Cornell University Press, 1989.

———. "A 'Doxastic Practice' Approach to Epistemology." In *Knowledge and Skepticism,* ed. Marjorie Clay and Keith Lehrer, 1-29. Boulder, CO: Westview, 1989.

———. "Externalist Theories of Perception." *Philosophy and Phenomenological Research* 50 (1990): 73–97.

———. "Functionalism and Theological Language." *American Philosophical Quarterly* 22, no. 3 (July 1985): 221–30.

———. "Ineffability." *Philosophical Review* 65, no. 4 (October 1956): 506–22.

———. "An Internalist Externalism." *Synthese* 74, no. 3 (March 1988): 265–83.

———. *Perceiving God: The Epistemology of Religious Experience*. Ithaca, NY: Cornell University Press, 1991.

———. "Perception and Conception." In *Pragmatism, Reason, and Norms: A Realistic Assessment*, edited by Kenneth R. Westphal, 59–87. New York: Fordham University Press, 1998.

———. "Perception and Representation." *Philosophy and Phenomenological Research* 70, no. 2 (March 2005): 253–88.

———. *Philosophy of Language*. Englewood Cliffs, NJ: Prentice-Hall, 1964.

———. *The Reliability of Sense Perception*. Ithaca, NY: Cornell University Press, 1993.

———. "Response to Critics." *Religious Studies* 30, no. 2 (June 1994): 171–80.

———. "Sellars and the 'Myth of the Given.'" *Philosophy and Phenomenological Research* 65, no. 1 (July 1991): 69–86.

———. *A Sensible Metaphysical Realism*. Aquinas Lecture Series of Marquette University. Milwaukee, WI: Marquette University Press, 2001.

———. "Two Types of Foundationalism," *Journal of Philosophy* 73, no. 7 (1976): 165–85.

———. "What's Wrong with Immediate Knowledge?" *Synthese* 55, no. 1 (April 1983): 73–95.

Ameriks, K. "Recent Work on Kant's Theoretical Philosophy." *American Philosophical Quarterly* 19 (1982): 1–24.

Angel, Leonard. "Reconstructing the Ineffable: The Grammatical Roles of 'God.'" *Religious Studies* 14, no. 4 (December 1978): 485–95.

Annas, Julia E. *Hellenistic Philosophy of Mind*. Berkeley: University of California Press, 1994.

Anscombe, G. E. M. *Intention*. 2nd ed. Cambridge, MA: Harvard University Press, 2000.

Anselm of Canterbury. *Proslogion*, trans. with intro. and notes by Thomas Williams. Indianapolis, IN: Hackett, 1995.

Aquinas, St. Thomas. *Summa Theologiae: Volume 2, Existence and Nature of God 1a, 2–11*, ed. and trans. Timothy McDermott, in *Summa Theologiae*, ed. Thomas Gilby. Cambridge: Cambridge University Press, 1964.

Aristotle. *De Anima: Books II and III*. Translated by D.W. Hamlyn. Oxford: Oxford University Press, 1993.

———. *Nicomachean Ethics*. Translated by Roger Crisp. Cambridge: Cambridge University Press, 2000.

Asad, Talal. *Genealogies of Religion: Discipline and Reasons of Power in Christianity and Islam*. Baltimore: Johns Hopkins University Press, 1993.

Audi, Robert. *Moral Perception*. Princeton, NJ: Princeton University Press, 2013.

Bagger, Matthew. *The Uses of Paradox: Religion, Self-Transformation and the Absurd*. New York: Columbia University Press, 2007.

von Balthasar, Hans Urs. *Presence and Thought: An Essay on the Religious Philosophy of Gregory of Nyssa*. San Francisco: Ignatius, 1988.

Balas, David L. *Metousia Theou: Man's Participation in God's Perfections according to Saint Gregory of Nyssa*. Studia Anselmiana 55. Rome: I. B. C. Libreria Herder, 1966.

———. "Participation." In *The Brill Dictionary of Gregory of Nyssa*, ed. Lucas Francisco Mateo-Seco and Giulio Maspero, trans. Seth Cherney, 581–87. Leiden: Brill, 2010.

Barnes, Michel René. "Divine Unity and the Divided Self: Gregory of Nyssa's Trinitarian Theology in its Psychological Context." *Modern Theology* 18, no. 4 (October 2002): 475–96.

———. "The Polemical Context and Content of Gregory of Nyssa's Psychology." *Journal of Medieval Philosophy and Theology* 4 (1994): 1–24.

———. *The Power of God: Dynamis in Gregory of Nyssa's Trinitarian Theology*. Washington, DC: Catholic University of America Press, 2001.

Battaly, Heather D., and Michael P. Lynch. *Perspectives on the Philosophy of William P. Alston*. Oxford: Rowman and Littlefield, 2005.

Bauman, Zygmunt, and Leonidas Donskis, *Moral Blindness: The Loss of Sensitivity in Liquid Modernity*. Malden, MA: Polity, 2013.

Beeley, Christopher A. "The Holy Spirit in the Cappadocians: Past and Present." *Modern Theology* 26, no. 1 (2010): 90–119.

Behr, John. *The Nicene Faith.* Vol. 2. Crestwood, NY: St. Vladimir's Seminary Press, 2004.

———. "The Rational Animal: A Re-reading of Gregory of Nyssa's *De Hominis Opificio.*" *Journal of Early Christian Studies* 7, no. 1 (Summer 1999): 219–47.

Berkeley, George. *Principles of Human Knowledge.* New York: Penguin Classics, 1988. Originally published in 1710.

Bennett, Jane. *The Enchantment of Modern Life: Attachments, Crossings, and Ethics.* Princeton, NJ: Princeton University Press, 2001.

Bermúdez, José Luis. "Categorizing Qualitative States: Some Problems." *Anthropology and Philosophy* 3, no. 2 (1999).

———. "Naturalized Sense Data." *Philosophy and Phenomenological Research* 61 (2000): 353–74.

———. "What Is at Stake in the Debate on Nonconceptual Content?" *Philosophical Perspectives* 21, no. 1 (2007): 55–72.

Bernauer, James, and Jeremy Carrette, eds. *Michel Foucault and Theology: The Politics of Religious Experience.* Burlington, VT: Ashgate, 2004.

Bernstein, J. M. "Re-Enchanting Nature." In *Reading McDowell on Mind and World*, edited by Nicholas H. Smith, 217–45. New York: Routledge, 2002.

Bett, Richard, ed. *The Cambridge Companion to Ancient Skepticism.* Cambridge: Cambridge University Press, 2010.

Betz, John R. "Beyond the Sublime: The Aesthetics of the Analogy of Being (Part Two)." *Modern Theology* 22, no. 1 (January 2006): 1–50.

Bilgrami, Akeel. "What Is Enchantment?" In *Varieties of Secularism in a Secular Age*, edited by Michael Warner, Jonathan Vanantwerpen, and

Craig Calhoun, 145–65. Cambridge, MA: Harvard University Press, 2010.

———. "The Wider Significance of Naturalism: A Genealogical Essay." In *Naturalism and Normativity*, edited by Mario de Caro and David MacArthur, 23–54. New York: Columbia University Press, 2010.

Bishop, Jeffrey P. "Mind-Body Unity: Gregory of Nyssa and a Surprising Fourth-Century Perspective." *Perspectives in Biology and Medicine* 43, no. 4 (Summer 2000): 519–29.

Blum, Lawrence. *Moral Perception and Particularity.* New York: Cambridge University Press, 1994.

Blowers, Paul M. "Maximus the Confessor, Gregory of Nyssa and the Concept of 'Perpetual Progress.'" *Vigiliae Christianae* 46, no. 2 (June 1992): 151–71.

Bom, Klaas. "Directed by Desire: An Exploration Based on the Structures of the Desire for God." *Scottish Journal of Theology* 62, no. 2 (2009): 135–48.

Bouchet, Jean-René. "Le vocabulaire de l'union et du rapport des natures chez saint Grégoire de Nysse." *Revue Thomiste* 68 (1968): 533–82.

Brandom, Robert. *Making It Explicit: Reasoning, Representing, and Discursive Commitments* Cambridge, MA: Harvard University Press, 1994.

———. "Non-Inferential Knowledge, Percpetual Experience and Secondary Qualities: Placing McDowell's Empiricism." In *Reading McDowell on Mind and World*, edited by Nicholas H. Smith, 92–106. New York: Routledge, 2002.

———. "Perception and Rational Constraint: McDowell's 'Mind and World.'" *Philosophical Issues* 7, Perception (1996): 241–59.

———. *Tales of the Mighty Dead: Historical Essays in the Metaphysics of Intentionality.* Cambridge, MA: Harvard University Press, 2002.

Brock, Brian, and John Swinton, eds. *Disability in the Christian Tradition: A Reader.* Grand Rapids, MI: Eerdmans, 2012.

Burge, Tyler. "Sinning against Frege." In *Truth, Thought, Reason: Essays on Frege*, 213–239. New York: Oxford University Press, 2005.

Burnyeat, Myles F. *Aristotle's Divine Intellect.* Aquinas Lecture Series. Milwaukee, WI: Marquette University Press, 2008.

———. "De Anima II.5." *Phronesis* 47, no. 1 (2002): 28–90.

Burrell, David. *Aquinas, God and Action.* Chicago: University of Scranton Press, 2008.

Cahill, J. B. "The Date and Setting of Gregory of Nyssa's Commentary on the Song of Songs." *Journal of Theological Studies* 32 (1981): 447–60.

Canévet, Mariette. *Grégoire de Nysse et l'Herméneutique Biblique: Étude des rapports entre le langage et la connaissance de Dieu.* Paris: Etudes Augustiniennes, 1983.

———. "Sens Spirituel." In *Dictionnaire de spiritualité ascétique et mystique doctrine et histoire*, vol. 15, edited by Marcel Viller and assisted by F. Cavallera, J. de Guibert, et al., 14–41. Paris: Beauchesne, 1993.

Christensen, Anne-Marie S. "Getting It Right in Ethical Experience: John McDowell and Virtue Ethics." *Journal of Value Inquiry* 43, no. 4 (2009): 493–506.

Chomsky, Noam. *Syntactic Structures.* Berlin: Walter de Gruyter, 1957.

Cirelli, Anthony. "Re-Assessing the Meaning of Thought: Hans Urs von Balthasar's Retrieval of Gregory of Nyssa." *Heythrop Journal* 50, no. 3 (2009): 416–24.

Coady, C. A. J. "The Senses of Martians." *Philosophical Review* 83, no. 1 (1974): 107–25.

Coakley, Sarah. *Christ without Absolutes.* Oxford: Clarendon, 1988.

———. "Does Kenotic Christology Rest on a Mistake?" In *Exploring Kenotic Christology*, edited by C. Stephen Evans, 246–64. New York: Oxford University Press, 2006.

————. "Gregory of Nyssa." In *The Spiritual Senses: Perceiving God in Western Christianity*, edited by Paul L. Gavrilyuk and Sarah Coakley, 36–55. New York: Cambridge University Press, 2012.

————. "Mingling in Gregory of Nyssa's Christology: A Reconsideration." In *Who Is Jesus Christ for Us Today: Pathways to Contemporary Christology*, edited by Andreas Schuele and Thomas Gunter, 72–84. Louisville, KY: Westminster John Knox, 2009.

————. *Powers and Submissions: Spirituality, Philosophy and Gender.* New York: Blackwell, 2002.

————. "Response to W. P. Alston." In *The Resurrection: An Interdisciplinary Symposium on the Resurrection of Jesus*, edited by Stephen T. Davis, Daniel Kendall, and Gerald O'Collins, 184–90. Oxford: Oxford University Press, 1998.

————. "Re-thinking Gregory of Nyssa: Introduction—Gender, Trinitarian Analogies, and the Pedagogy of the Song." *Modern Theology* 18, no. 2 (2002): 431–43.

————. "Shaping the Field: A Transatlantic Perspective." In *Fields of Faith*, edited by David F. Ford, Ben Quash, and Janet Martin Soskice, 39–55. New York: Cambridge University Press, 2005.

————. "Theological Scholarship as Religious Vocation." *Christian Higher Education* 5 (2005): 55–68.

Coates, Paul. *The Metaphysics of Perception: Wilfrid Sellars, Perceptual Consciousness, and Critical Realism.* New York: Routledge, 2007.

Connell, S. M. "Aristotle and Galen on Sex Difference and Reproduction." *Studies in History and Philosophy of Science* 31, no. 3 (September 2000): 405–27.

Coolman, Boyd Taylor. *Knowing God by Experience: The Spiritual Senses in the Theology of William of Auxerre.* Washington, DC: Catholic University of America Press, 2004.

Cortens, Andrew. *Global Anti-Realism: A Metaphilosophical Inquiry.* Boulder: Westview, 2000.

Courtine, Jean-François. "The Given." In *The Myth of the Mental,* edited by Joseph Schear. London: Routledge, forthcoming.

———. "Réduction, construction, destruction. D'un dialogue à trois : Natorp, Husserl, Heidegger." *Philosophiques* 36, no. 2 (2009): 559–77.

Crane, Tim. "Intentionality as the Mark of the Mental." In *Contemporary Issues in the Philosophy of Mind,* edited by Anthony O'Hear, 1–17. New York: Cambridge University Press, 1998.

———. "Is There a Perceptual Relation?" In *Perceptual Experience,* edited by T. Gendler and J. Hawthorne, 126–46. New York: Oxford University Press, 2006.

Daley, Brian E. "Divine Transcendence and Human Transformation: Gregory of Nyssa's Antiapollinarian Christology." *Modern Theology* 18, no. 4 (October 2002): 497–506.

Dalferth, Ingolf. *Becoming Present: An Inquiry into the Christian Sense of the Presence of God.* Leuven: Peeters, 2006.

Daniélou, Jean. "La chronologie des oeuvres de Grégoire de Nysse." In *Studia Patristica: Papers Presented to the Fourth International Conference on Patristic Studies,* edited by Frank Leslie Cross, 159–69. Berlin: Akademie Verlag, 1966.

———. *God and the Ways of Knowing.* New York: Meridian, 1957.

———. *Platonisme et Théologie Mystique.* Paris: Aubier, 1944.

Davidson, Donald. "Actions, Reasons and Causes," *Journal of Philosophy* 60 (1963): 685–700.

———. "Mental Events." In *Experience and Theory,* edited by Lawrence Foster and J. W. Swanson, 79–102. London: Duckworth, 1970.

———. "The Myth of the Subjective." In *Subjective, Intersubjective, Objective,* ch. 3. New York: Oxford University Press, 2001.

———. "On the Very Idea of a Conceptual Scheme." *Proceedings and Addresses of the American Philosophical Association* 47 (1973–1974): 5–20.

———. "Quine's Externalism." *Grazer Philosophische Studien* 66, no. 1 (2003): 281–97.

———. "Radical Interpretation Interpreted." *Philosophical Perspectives* 8, Logic and Language (1994): 121–28.

de Gaynesford, Maximilian. *John McDowell.* Malden, MA: Polity, 2004.

de Lubac, Henri. *Surnaturel: Etudes Historiques.* Paris: Aubier, 1946.

de Rijk, Lambertus M. *Giraldus Odonis O.F.M.: Opera Philosophica. Vol. 2, De intentionibus.* Leiden: Brill, 2005.

Derrida, Jacques. "Et Cetera," translated by Geoff Bennington. In *Deconstructions: A User's Guide,* edited by Nicolas Royle, 282–305. London: Palgrave Macmillan, 2000.

Descartes, René. *Meditations on First Philosophy.* Edited by John Cottingham with an introduction by Bernard Williams. Cambridge: Cambridge University Press, 1996.

deVries, Willem A., ed. *Empiricism, Perceptual Knowledge, Normativity and Realism: Essays on Wilfrid Sellars.* Oxford: Oxford University Press, 2009.

———. "McDowell, Sellars and Sense Impressions." *European Journal of Philosophy* 14, no. 2 (2006): 182–201.

———. Review of *Wilfrid Sellars: Fusing the Images,* by Jay F. Rosenberg. *Notre Dame Philosophical Reviews,* June 11, 2008. http://ndpr.nd.edu/review.cfm?id=13307.

———. *Wilfrid Sellars.* Montréal, Québec: McGill-Queen's University Press, 2005.

deVries, Willem A., and Paul Coates. "Brandom's Two-Ply Error." In *Empiricism, Perceptual Knowledge, Normativity and Realism: Essays on Wilfrid Sellars,* edited by Willem A. deVries, 131–46. Oxford: Oxford University Press, 2009.

Dolidze, Tina. "The Cognitive Function of Epinoia in *CE II* and its Meaning for Gregory of Nyssa's Theory of Theological Language." In *Gregory of Nyssa: Contra Eunomium II*, edited by Lenka Karfíková, Scot Douglass, and Johannes Zachhuber, 445–60. Supplements to Vigiliae Christianae 82. Leiden: Brill, 2007, 445–60.

Donnellan, Keith. "Reference and Definite Descriptions." *Philosophical Review* 75, no. 3 (July 1966): 281–304.

Douglass, Scot. *Theology of the Gap: Cappadocian Language Theory and the Trinitarian Controversy.* New York: Peter Lang, 2005.

Dretske, Fred. *Seeing and Knowing.* Chicago: University of Chicago Press, 1969.

Dreyfus, Hubert L. *Being-In-The-World: A Commentary on Heidegger's Being and Time.* Cambridge, MA: MIT Press, 1990.

———. "Overcoming the Myth of the Mental: How Philosophers Can Profit from the Phenomenology of Everyday Expertise." *Proceedings and Addresses of the American Philosophical Association* 79, no. 2 (2005): 47–65

———. "The Myth of the Pervasiveness of the Mental." In *Mind, Reason and Being-in-the-World: The McDowell-Dreyfus Debate*, ed. Joseph K. Schear, 15–40. London: Routledge, 2012.

———, and Sean Dorrance Kelly. *All Things Shining: Reading the Western Classics to Find Meaning in a Secular Age.* New York: Free Press, 2011.

Dummett, Michael. *Frege: Philosophy of Language.* Cambridge, MA: Harvard University Press, 1973.

Dünzl, Franz. "Gregory von Nyssa's *Homilien zum Canticum* auf dem Hintergrund seiner *Vita Moysis*." *Vigiliae Christianae* 44 (1990): 371–81.

Eitel, Adam. "Making Motions in a Language We Do Not Understand: The Apophaticism of Thomas Aquinas and Victor Preller." *Scottish Journal of Theology* 65, no. 1 (2012): 17–33.

Esfeld, Michael. "Aristotle's Direct Realism in 'De Anima.'" *Review of Metaphysics* 54, no. 2 (December 2000): 321–36.

Evans, Gareth. *The Varieties of Reference.* Edited by John McDowell. Oxford: Oxford University Press, 1982.

Evans, Gareth, and John McDowell, eds. *Truth and Meaning: Essays in Semantics.* Oxford: Oxford University Press, 1976.

Farges, Albert. *Mystical Phenomena Compared with Their Human and Diabolical Counterfeits,* trans. S. P. Jacques. Whitefish, MT: Kessinger, 2003.

Feingold, Lawrence. *The Natural Desire to See God according to St. Thomas Aquinas and His Interpreters.* Rome: Apollinare Studi, 2001.

Fields, Stephen. "Balthasar and Rahner on the Spiritual Senses." *Theological Studies* 57 (1996): 224–41.

Finan T., and Toomey T., eds. *The Relationship between Neoplatonism and Christianity* Dublin: Four Courts, 1992.

Ferlo, Roger. *Sensing God: Reading Scripture with All Our Senses.* Cambridge, MA: Cowley, 2002.

Finocchiaro, Maurice A. *Defending Copernicus and Galileo.* Dodrecht: Springer, 2009.

Fodor, Jerry. *Representations: Philosophical Essays on the Foundations of Cognitive Science.* Cambridge: MIT Press, 1981.

Ford, Anton, Jennifer Hornsby, and Frederick Stoutland, eds. *Essays on Anscombe's* Intention. Cambridge, MA: Harvard University Press, 2011.

Foman, David. "Autonomy as Second Nature: On McDowell's Arisotelian Naturalism." *Inquiry* 51, no. 6 (December 2008): 563–80.

Friedman, Michael. "Exorcising the Philosophical Tradition," in *Reading McDowell on Mind and World,* ed. Nicholas H. Smith, 25–57. New York: Routledge, 2002.

Fritz, Peter Joseph. "Black Holes and Revelations: Michael Henry and Jean-Luc Marion on the Aesthetics of the Invisible." *Modern Theology* 25, no. 3 (July 2009): 415–40.

Gadamer, Hans-Georg. *Truth and Method.* New York: Continuum, 1975.

Galen. *Galen on the Usefulness of the Parts of the Body*. Translated with commentary by Margaret Tallmadge May. Ithaca, NY: Cornell University Press, 1968.

Gane, Nicholas. *Max Weber and Postmodern Theory: Rationalization versus Re-Enchantment*. New York: Palgrave-Macmillan, 2002.

Gauchet, Marcel. *The Disenchantment of the World*. Princeton: Princeton University Press, 1999.

Gendler, Tamar, and John Hawthorne. *Perceptual Experience*. Oxford: Clarendon, 2006.

Gillespie, Michael Allen. *The Theological Origins of Modernity*. Chicago: University of Chicago Press, 2008.

Good, Justin. *Wittgenstein and the Theory of Perception*. New York: Continuum, 2006.

Gordon, Peter E. "The Place of the Sacred in the Absence of God: Charles Taylor's *A Secular Age*." *Journal of the History of Ideas* 69, no. 4 (October 2008): 647–73.

Gorringe, Timothy. *The Education of Desire: Towards a Theology of the Senses*. Harrisburg, PA: Trinity Press International, 2002.

Gould, Stephen J. "Non-Overlapping Magesteria." *Natural History* 106 (March 1997): 16–22.

Gray, Richard. "On the Concept of a Sense." *Synthese* 147, no. 3 (2005): 461–75.

Greco. John. "Religious Knowledge in the Context of Conflicting Testimony." *Proceedings of the American Catholic Philosophical Association* 83 (2009): 61–76.

Gregory, Brad. *The Unintended Reformation: How a Religious Revolution Secularized Society*. Cambridge, MA: Belknap, 2012.

Gregory of Nyssa. "Against Eunomius." In *Nicene and Post-Nicene Fathers*, edited by Philip Schaff and Henry Wace, translated by Henry Austin Wilson, vol. 5, second series, 57–475. Peabody, MA: Hendrickson, 1994.

———. *Commentary on the Song of Songs*. Translated by Casimir McCambley. Brookline, MA: Hellenic College Press, 1987.

———. *From Glory to Glory: Texts from Gregory of Nyssa's Mystical Writings*. Selected and with an introduction by Jean Daniélou, translated and edited by Herbert Musurillo. New York: Charles Scribner's Sons, 1961.

———. *Homilies on the Beatitudes: An English Version with Commentary and Supporting Studies: Proceedings of the Eighth International Colloquium on Gregory of Nyssa, Paderborn, 14–18 September 1998*. Edited by Hubertus R. Drobner and Alberto Viciano. Supplements to Vigiliae Christianae 52. Leiden: Brill, 2000.

———. *Homilies on the Song of Songs*. In *Writings from the Greco-Roman World*, no. 13, edited by Brian E. Daley and John. T. Fitzgerald, translated with an introduction and notes by Richard A. Norris Jr. Atlanta, GA: Society of Biblical Literature, 2012.

———. *The Life of Moses*. Translated by Abraham Malherbe and Everett Ferguson. New York: Paulist, 1978.

———. "On the Making of Man." In *Nicene and Post-Nicene Fathers*, edited by Philip Schaff and Henry Wace, translated by Henry Austin Wilson, vol. 5, second series, 719–67. Peabody, MA: Hendrickson, 1994.

———. "On Perfection." In *Saint Gregory of Nyssan's Ascetical Workds*, translated by Virginia Woods Callahan, 93–124. Washington, DC: Catholic University of America Press, 1999.

———. *On the Soul and the Resurrection*. Translated with an introduction by Catherine P. Roth. Crestwood, NY: St. Vladimir's Seminary Press, 1993.

———. "The Second Book against Enoumius (Translation)." Translated by Stuart George Hall. In *Gregory of Nyssa: Contra Eunomium II*, edited by Lenka Karfíková, Scot Douglass, and Johannes Zachhuber, 59–204. Supplements to Vigiliae Christianae 82. Leiden: Brill, 2007.

Griffiths, Paul J. "Witness and Conviction in *With the Grain of the Universe*." *Modern Theology* 19, no. 1 (January 2003): 67–75.

Haddock, Adrian, and Fiona MacPherson. *Disjunctivism: Perception, Action, Knowledge.* Oxford: Oxford University Press, 2008.

Hadot, Pierre. *What Is Ancient Philosophy?* Translated by Michael Chase. Cambridge, MA: Harvard University Press, 2002.

Hadot, Pierre, and Michael Chase. *Philosophy as a Way of Life: Spiritual Exercises from Socrates to Foucault.* Oxford: Wiley-Blackwell, 1995.

———. *Plotinus or the Simplicity of Vision.* Chicago: University of Chicago Press, 1998.

Hare, John. *The Moral Gap.* New York: Oxford University Press, 1997.

Harrison, Verna E. F. *God's Many-Splendored Image.* Grand Rapids, MI: Baker Academic, 2010.

———. *Grace and Human Freedom according to St. Gregory of Nyssa.* Studies in the Bible and Early Christianity 30. New York: Edwin Mellen, 1992.

Hart, David Benltey. *The Beauty of the Infinite: The Aesthetics of Christian Truth.* Grand Rapids, MI: Eerdmans: 2003.

Hart, Kevin, ed. *Counter-Experiences: Reading Jean-Luc Marion.* Notre Dame, IN: University of Notre Dame Press, 2007.

Hart, William David. "Naturalizing Christian Ethics: A Critique of Charles Taylor's *A Secular Age.*" *Journal of Religious Ethics* 40, no. 1 (2012): 149–70.

Hauerwas, Stanley. "The Church as God's New Language." In *The Hauerwas Reader,* edited by John Berkman and Michael Cartwright, 142–64. Durham, NC: Duke University Press, 2001.

———. "Casuistry in Context." In *The Hauerwas Reader,* ed. John Berkman and Michael Cartwright, Durham, 267–286. NC: Duke University Press, 2001.

———. *With the Grain of the Universe.* Grand Rapids, MI: Baker Academic, 2013.

Hauerwas, Stanley, and Brian Goldstone. "Disciplined Seeing: Forms of Christianity and Forms of Life." *South Atlantic Quarterly* 109, no. 4 (Fall 2010): 765–90.

Hauerwas, Stanley, and Charles Pinches. *Christians among the Virtues: Theological Conversations with Ancient and Modern Ethics.* Notre Dame, IN: University of Notre Dame Press, 1997.

Healey, Nicholas. "Henri de Lubac on Nature and Grace: A Note on Some Recent Contributions to the Debate." *Communio* 35 (Winter 2008): 535–64.

Hector, Kevin W. "Apophaticism in Thomas Aquinas: A Reformulation and Recommendation." *Scottish Journal of Theology* 60, no. 4 (2007): 377–93.

———. "The Mediation of Christ's Normative Spirit: A Constructive Reading of Schleiermacher's Pneumatology." *Modern Theology* 24, no. 1 (January 2008): 1–22.

———. "Responses to *JAT's* Symposium on *Theology without Metaphysics*." *Journal of Analytic Theology* 1, no. 1 (May 2013): 140–47.

———. *Theology without Metaphysics: God, Language and the Spirit of Recognition.* New York: Cambridge University Press, 2011.

Heidegger, Martin. *Poetry, Language, Thought.* Translated by Albert Hofstadter. New York: Harper Collins, 1972.

———. *Towards the Definition of Philosophy.* Translated by Ted Sadler. London: Continuum, 2008.

Heine, Ronald E. *Perfection in the Virtuous Life: A Study in the Relationship between Edification and Polemical Theology in Gregory of Nyssa's De* vita Moysis. Philadelphia, PA: Philadelphia Patristic Foundation, 1975.

Hendley, Steven. "Answerable to the World: Experience and Practical Intentionality in Brandom's and McDowell's 'Intramural' Debate." *Theoria* 76, no. 2 (2010): 129–51.

Hernandez, Jill Graper, ed. *The New Intuitionism.* New York: Continuum, 2011.

Hibbs, Darren. "Was Gregory of Nyssa a Berkeleyan Idealist?" *British Journal for the History of Philosophy* 13, no. 3 (2005): 425–35.

Hick, John. *Faith and Knowledge.* Ithaca, NY: Cornell University Press, 1966.

Hill, Jonathan. "Gregory of Nyssa, Material Substance and Berkeleyan Idealism." *British Journal for the History of Philosophy* 17, no. 4 (2009): 653–83.

Hopp, Walter. "Husserl on Sensation, Perception and Interpretation." *Canadian Journal of Philosophy* 38, no. 2 (June 2008): 219–46.

Horner, Robyn. *Jean-Luc Marion: A Theo-Logical Introduction.* Burlington, VT: Ashgate, 2005.

Hornsby, Jennifer. *Simple Mindedness: In Defense of Naïve Naturalism in the Philosophy of Mind.* Cambridge, MA: Harvard University Press, 1997.

———. "Truth: The Identity Theory." *Proceedings of the Aristotelian Society* 97 (1997): 1–24.

Hume, David. *An Enquiry Concerning Human Understanding.* In *Enquiries Concerning Human Understanding and Concerning the Principles of Morals,* edited by L. A. Selby-Bigge, 3rd ed. revised by P. H. Nidditch. Oxford: Clarendon, 1975. Originally published in 1758.

———. *A Treatise of Human Nature.* Edited by L. A. Selby-Bigge. 2nd ed. revised by P. H. Nidditch. Oxford: Clarendon, 1975. Originally published in 1739.

Husserl, Edmund. *Logical Investigations.* Translated by J. N. Findlay. New York: Humanities Press, 1970.

Hütter, Reinhard. "Desiderium Naturale Visionis Dei—Est autem duplex hominis beatitudo sive felicitas: Some Observations about Lawrence Feingold's and John Milbank's Recent Interventions in the Debate over the Natural Desire to See God." *Nova Et Vetera* 5, no. 1 (2007): 81–132.

Jacobs, Jonathan D. "Powerful Qualities, not Pure Powers." *Monist* 94, no. 1 (2011): 81–102.

Janicaud, Dominique, et al. *Phenomenology and the "Theological Turn": The French Debate*. New York: Fordham University Press, 2000.

Jenkins, Richard. "Disenchantment, Enchantment, Re-Enchantment: Max Weber at the Millennium." *Max Weber Studies* 1 (2000): 11–32.

Jones, Tamsin. *A Genealogy of Marion's Philosophy of Religion: Apparent Darkness*. Bloomington: Indiana University Press, 2011.

Jones Farmer, Tamsin. "Revealing the Invisible: Gregory of Nyssa on the Gift of Revelation." *Modern Theology* 21, no. 1 (January 2005): 67–85.

Kant, Immanuel. *Critique of Pure Reason*. Translated by Norman Kemp Smith with an introduction by Howard Caygill. New York: Palgrave-Macmillan, 2003.

Katz, Steven T. "Language, Epistemology, and Mysticism." In *Mysticism and Philosophical Analysis*, edited by S. T. Katz, 22–74. London: Sheldon, 1978.

Kelly, Sean D. "The Non-Conceptual Content of Perceptual Experience: Situation Dependence and Fineness of Grain." *Philosophy and Phenomenological Research* 62, no. 3 (May 2001): 601–8.

Kerr, Fergus. *After Aquinas: Versions of Thomism*. Oxford: Blackwell, 2002.

———. *Theology after Wittgenstein*. 2nd ed. Oxford: SPCK, 1997.

King, Rolfe. *Obstacles to Divine Revelation: God and the Reorientation of Human Reason*. New York: Continuum, 2008.

Knight, John Allan. *Liberalism versus Postliberalism*. Oxford: Oxford University Press: 2012.

Knight, Kelvin. *Aristotelian Philosophy: Ethics and Politics from Aristotle to MacIntyre*. Malden, MA: Polity, 2007.

Simon Knuuttila, "Aristotle's Theory of Perception and Medieval Aristotelianism." In Simo Knuuttila, Simo and Pekka Kärkkäinen, eds. *Theories of Perception in Medieval and Early Modern Philosophy*. Studies in the History of the Philosophy of Mind 6. New York: Springer, 2008.

Kripke, Saul A. *Naming and Necessity*. Cambridge, MA: Harvard University Press, 1980.

———. *Wittgenstein on Rules and Private Language*. Cambridge, MA: Harvard University Press, 1982.

Kukla, André. *Ineffability and Philosophy*. New York: Routledge, 2005.

Lackey, Jennifer. "Deficient Testimonial Knowledge." In *Knowledge, Virtue, and Action: Putting Epistemic Virtues to Work*, edited by Tim Henning and David P. Schweikard. New York: Routledge, forthcoming.

Lagerlund, H., ed. *Representation and Objects of Thought in Medieval Philosophy*. Aldershot: Ashgate, 2007.

Laird, Martin. "Apophasis and Logophasis in Gregory of Nyssa's *Commentarius in Canticum canticorum*." *Studia Patristica* 37, edited by Maurice Wiles and E. J. Yarnold with the assistance of P. M. Parvis, 126–32. Leuven: Peeters, 2001.

———. "'By Faith Alone': A Technical Term in Gregory of Nyssa." *Vigiliae Christianae* 54, no. 1 (2000): 61–79.

———. "The Fountain of His Lips: Desire and Divine Union in Gregory of Nyssa's *Homilies on the Song of Songs*." *Spiritus* 7 (2007): 40–57.

———. *Gregory of Nyssa and the Grasp of Faith*. New York: Oxford University Press, 2004.

———. "Gregory of Nyssa and the Mysticism of Darkness: A Reconsideration." *Journal of Religion* 79 (October 1999): 592–616.

———. "Under Solomon's Tutelage: The Education of Desire in the *Homilies on the Song of Songs*." *Modern Theology* 18, no. 4 (October 2002): 507–25.

———. "'Whereof We Speak': Gregory of Nyssa, Jean-Luc Marion and the Current Apophatic Rage." *Heythrop Journal* 42 (2001): 1–12.

Leeds, Stephen. "Qualia, Awareness, Sellars." *Noûs* 27, no. 3 (September 1993): 303–30.

Levinas, Emmanuel. *Alterity and Transcendence*. New York: Columbia University Press, 1999.

Lewis, C. I. *Mind and the World Order: Outline of a Theory of Knowledge.* 1929. Reprint, Toronto: Dover, 1956.

Lindbeck, George. *The Nature of Doctrine: Theology in a Postliberal age.* Louisville, KY: John Knox, 1984.

Lindgaard, Jakob, ed. *John McDowell: Experience, Norm and Nature.* Malden, MA: Blackwell, 2008.

Linsky, Bernard, and Edward Zalta, "Naturalized Platonism vs. Platonized Naturalism." *Journal of Philosophy* 92, no. 10 (October 1995): 525–55.

Locke, John. *An Essay Concerning Human Understanding.* Edited by Peter Nidditch. Oxford: Clarendon Press, 1975. Originally published in 1689.

Lossky, Vladimir. *The Vision of God.* Crestwood, NY: St. Vladimir's Seminary Press, 1983.

Louth, Andrew. *The Origins of the Christian Mystical Tradition: From Plato to Denys.* 2nd ed. Oxford: Oxford University Press, 2007.

Lovibond, Sabina. *Ethical Formation.* Cambridge, MA: Harvard University Press, 2002.

Ludlow, Morwenna. "Divine Infinity and Eschatology: The Limits and Dynamics of Human Knowledge according to Gregory of Nyssa *(CE II 67–170).*" In *Gregory of Nyssa: Contra Eunomium II,* edited by Lenka Karfíková, Scot Douglass, and Johannes Zachhuber, 217–37. Supplements to Vigiliae Christianae 82. Leiden: Brill, 2007.

———. *Gregory of Nyssa: Ancient and (Post)Modern.* New York: Oxford University Press, 2007.

Ludwig, Kirk. "The Mind-Body Problem: An Overview." In *The Blackwell Guide to Philosophy of Mind,* edited by S. Stich, 1–46. Oxford: Wiley-Blackwell, 2003.

MacDonald, Cynthia, and Graham MacDonald. *McDowell and His Critics.* Oxford: Blackwell, 2006.

MacDonald, Paul A., Jr. *Knowledge and the Transcendent: An Inquiry into the Mind's Relationship to God.* Washington, DC: Catholic University of America Press, 2009.

MacIntyre, Alasdair. *After Virtue: A Study in Moral Theory.* 3rd ed. Notre Dame, IN: University of Notre Dame Press, 2007.

———. *Dependent Rational Animals: Why Human Beings Need the Virtues.* New York: Open Court, 2001.

———. *Three Rival Versions of Moral Inquiry: Encyclopedia, Genealogy and Tradition.* Notre Dame, IN: University of Notre Dame Press, 1991.

———"What More Needs to Be Said? A Beginning, Although Only a Beginning, at Saying It." *Analyse & Kritik* 30 (2008): 261–76.

———. *Whose Justice? Which Rationality?* Notre Dame, IN: University of Notre Dame Press, 1988.

Mahmood, Saba. "Can Secularism Be Other-wise?" In *Varieties of Secularism in a Secular Age,* edited by Michael Warner, Jonathan Vanantwerpen, and Craig Calhoun, 282–99. Cambridge, MA: Harvard University Press, 2010.

Maraval, Pierre. "Chronology of Works." In *The Brill Dictionary of Gregory of Nyssa,* ed. Lucas Francisco Mateo-Seco and Giulio Maspero, trans. Seth Cherney, 153–69. Leiden: Brill, 2010.

Marion, Jean-Luc. "The Banality of Saturation." In *Counter-Experiences,* edited by Kevin Hart, 383–418. Notre Dame, IN: University of Notre Dame Press, 2007.

———. *Being Given: Toward a Phenomenology of Givenness.* Translated by Jeffrey L. Kosky. Stanford: Stanford University Press, 2002.

———. *The Erotic Phenomenon,* trans. Stephen Lewis. Chicago: University of Chicago Press, 2008.

———. *In Excess: Studies of Saturated Phenomena.* Translated by Robyn Horner and Vincent Berraud. New York: Fordham University Press, 2004.

———. "Metaphysics and Phenomenology: A Relief for Theology," translated by Thomas Carlson. *Critical Inquiry* 20, no. 4 (Summer 1994): 572–91.

———. "*Mihi magna quaestio factus sum*: The Privilege of Unknowing," translated by Stephen E. Lewis. *Journal of Religion* 85, no. 1 (2005): 1–24.

———. "The Other First Philosophy and the Question of Givenness," translated by Jeffrey Kosky. *Critical Inquiry* 25, no. 5 (Summer 1999): 784–800.

———. *The Reason of the Gift.* Translated with an introduction by Stephen E. Lewis. Charlottesville: University of Virginia Press, 2012.

———. *Reduction and Givenness: Investigations of Husserl, Heidegger and Phenomenology.* Translated by Thomas A. Carlson. Evanston, IL: Northwestern University Press, 1998.

———. "They Recognized Him and He Became Visible to Them." *Modern Theology* 18, no. 2 (April 2002): 145–52.

———. *The Visible and the Revealed.* Translated by Christine Gschwandtner. New York: Fordham University Press, 2008.

Marion, Jean-Luc, and Richard Kearney. "A Dilaogue with Jean-Luc Marion." *Philosophy Today* 48, no. 1 (April 2004): 1–16.

Marmadoro, Anna, ed. *The Metaphysics of Powers: Their Grounding and Their Manifestations.* New York: Routledge, 2010.

Mateo-Seco, Lucas Francisco, and Giulio Maspero, eds. *The Brill Dictionary of Gregory of Nyssa.* Translated by Seth Cherney. Leiden: Brill, 2010.

———. "Creation." In *The Brill Dictionary of Gregory of Nyssa*, edited by Lucas Francisco Mateo-Seco and Giulio Maspero, 183–90. Leiden: Brill, 2010.

McCabe, Herbert. *Law, Love and Language.* New York: Bloomsbury, 2003.

McDowell, John. "Brandom on Representation and Inference." *Philosophy and Phenomenological Research* 57, no. 1 (1997): 157–62.

———. "Criteria, Defeasibility, and Knowledge." *Proceedings of the British Academy* 68 (1982): 455–79.

———. "De Re Senses." *Philosophical Quarterly* 34, no. 136 (1984): 283–94.

———. "The Disjunctive Conception of Experience as Material for a Transcendental Argument." In *Disjunctivism: Perception, Action, Knowledge*, ed. Fiona Macpherson and Adrian Haddock, 376–89. Oxford: Oxford University Press, 2008.

———. *The Engaged Intellect*. Cambridge, MA: Harvard University Press, 2009.

———. *Having the World in View*. Cambridge, MA: Harvard University Press, 2009.

———. "Knowledge and the Internal Revisited." *Philosophy and Phenomenological Research* 65, no. 1 (January 2002): 97–105.

———. *Meaning, Knowledge and Reality*. Cambridge, MA: Harvard University Press, 2002.

———. *Mind and World*. 2nd ed. Cambridge, MA: Harvard University Press, 1996.

———. *Mind, Value and Reality*. Cambridge, MA: Harvard University Press, 2002.

———. "The Myth of the Mind as Detached."In *Mind, Reason and Being-In-The-World: The McDowell-Dreyfus Debate*, ed. Joseph K. Schear, 41–58. London: Routledge, 2012.

———. "Non-Cognitivism and Rule-Following." In *The New Wittgenstein*, edited by Alice Crary and Rupert Read, 38–52. New York: Routledge, 2000.

———. "On the Sense and Reference of a Proper Name." *Mind* 86, no. 342 (April 1977): 159–85.

———. *Perception as a Capacity for Knowledge*. Aquinas Lecture Series. Milwaukee, WI: Marquette University Press, 2011.

———. "Précis of 'Mind and World,'" *Philosophical Issues* 7, Perception (1996): 231–39.

———. "Response to Costas Pagondiotis." *Tiorema* 25, no. 2 (2006): 115–19.

———. "Response to Graham MacDonald." In *McDowell and His Critics*, ed. Cynthia MacDonald and Graham MacDonald, 235–38. Oxford: Blackwell, 2006.

———. "Responses." In *Reading McDowell on Mind and World*, edited by Nicholas H. Smith, 269–305. New York: Routledge, 2002.

———. "Sellars on Perceptual Experience." In *Having the World in View: Essays on Kant, Hegel and Sellars*, 3–22. Cambridge: Harvard University Press, 2009.

———. "Singular Thought and the Extent of Inner Space." In *Subject, Thought and Context*, edited by Philip Pettit and John McDowell, 137–68. Oxford: Clarendon, 1986.

———. "The True Modesty of an Identity Conception of Truth: A Note in Response to Pascal Engel (2001)." *International Journal of Philosophical Studies* 13, no. 1 (2005): 83–88.

———. "Tyler Burge on Disjunctivism." *Philosophical Explorations* 13, no. 3 (September 2010): 243–55.

———. "Virtue and Reason." *Monist* 62, no. 3 (1979): 331–50.

———. "What Is the Content of an Intention in Action?" *Ratio* 23, no. 4 (December 2010): 415–32.

———. "What Myth?" *Inquiry* 50, no. 4 (August 2007): 338–51.

———. "Why Is Sellars's Essay Called '*Empiricism* and the Philosophy of Mind'?" In *Empiricism, Perceptual Knowledge, Normativity and Realism: Essays on Wilfrid Sellars*, ed. Willem A. de Vries, 9–32. Oxford: Oxford University Press, 2009.

———. "Wittgenstein on Following a Rule." *Synthese* 58 (1984): 325–63.

McGinn, Bernard. *The Foundations of Mysticism*. New York: Crossroad, 1991.

———. "The Language of Inner Experience in Christian Mysticism." *Spiritus* 1 (2001): 156–71.

———. Review of *The Darkness of God*, by Denys Turner. *Journal of Religion* 77, no. 2 (April 1997): 309–11.

McGinn, Marie. *Elucidating the Tractatus: Wittgenstein's Early Philosophy of Logic and Language.* New York: Oxford University Press, 2006.

McInroy, Mark. "Origen of Alexandria." In *The Spiritual Senses: Perceiving God in Western Christianity,* edited by Paul L. Gavrilyuk and Sarah Coakley, 20–35. New York: Cambridge University Press, 2012.

McKitrick, Jennifer. "A Case for Extrinsic Dispositions." *Australasian Journal of Philosophy* 81, no. 2 (June 2003): 155–74.

Meredith, Anthony. *Gregory of Nyssa.* New York: Routledge, 1999.

———. "The Language of God and Human Language (*CE II 195–293*)." In *Gregory of Nyssa: Contra Eunomium II,* edited by Lenka Karfíková, Scot Douglass, and Johannes Zachhuber, 247–56. Supplements to Vigiliae Christianae 82. Leiden: Brill, 2007.

Molnar, George. *Powers: A Study in Metaphysics.* Edited by Stephen Mumford. Oxford: Oxford University Press, 2003.

Moore, Andrew. *Realism and Christian Faith: God, Grammar and Meaning.* Cambridge: Cambridge University Press, 2003.

Moran, Dermot. "Analytic Philosophy and Continental Philosophy: Four Confrontations." In *Phenomenology: Responses and Developments,* edited by Leonard Lawlor, 235–66. Volume 4 of *The History of Continental Philosophy,* edited by Alan Schrift. Durham: Acumen, 2010.

Moran, Richard and Martin Stone. "Anscombe on Expression of Intention: An Exegesis." In *Essays on Anscombe's* Intention, ed. Anton Ford, Jennifer Hornsby, and Frederick Stoutland, 33–75. Cambridge, MA: Harvard University Press, 2011.

———. *Edmund Husserl: Founder of Phenomenology.* Cambridge: Polity, 2005.

Moutsoulas, Elias D. *The Incarnation of the Word and the Theosis of Man according to the Teaching of Gregory of Nyssa.* Athens: Eptalophos, 2000.

Mühlenberg, Ekkehard. "Synergism in Gregory of Nsysa," *Zeitschrift fur die Neutestamentliche Wissenschaft* 68 (1977): 93–122.

Mulhall, Stephen. "Theology and Narrative: The Self, the Novel, the Bible." *International Journal for the Philosophy of Religion* 69, no. 1 (2011): 29–43.

Murphy, Francesca. *God Is Not a Story.* Oxford: Oxford University Press, 2007.

Nagel, Thomas. "What Is It Like to Be a Bat?" *Philosophical Review* 83, no. 4 (October 1974): 157–74.

Nelstrop, Louise. *Christian Mysticism: An Introduction to Contemporary Theoretical Approaches.* Burlington, VT: Ashgate, 2009.

Norris, R. A. "The Soul Takes Flight: Gregory of Nyssa and the Song of Songs." *Anglican Theological Review* 80, no. 4 (Fall 1998), 517–32.

O'Shea, James. "Having a Sensible World in View: McDowell and Sellars on Perceptual Experience." *Philosophical Books* 51, no. 2 (April 2010): 63–82.

———. *Wilfrid Sellars: Naturalism with a Normative Turn.* Malden, MA: Polity, 2007.

———. "On the Structure of Sellars' Naturalism with a Normative Turn." In *Empiricism, Perceptual Knowledge, Normativity and Realism: Essays on Wilfrid Sellars,* edited by Willem de Vries, 187–210. New York: Oxford University Press, 2009.

Pasnau, Robert. *Theories of Cognition in the Later Middle Ages.* Cambridge: Cambridge University Press, 1997.

———. *Thomas Aquinas on Human Nature: A Philosophical Study of Summa 1a 75–89.* Cambridge: Cambridge University Press, 2002.

Peacocke, Christopher. "Phenomenology and Non-Conceptual Content." *Philosophy and Phenomenological Research* 62, no. 3 (May 2001): 609–15.

Perler, Dominik, ed. *Ancient and Medieval Theories of Intentionality.* Leiden: Brill, 2001.

Phillips, D. Z. *Wittgenstein and Religion.* New York: Palgrave Macmillan, 1994.

Plantinga, Alvin. *Warranted Christian Belief.* New York: Oxford University Press, 2000.

Pottier, Bernard. *Dieu et le Christ selon Grégoire de Nysse: Etude systématique du "ContreEunome" avec traduction ine'dite des extraits d'Eunome.* Ouvertures 12. Namur: Culture et vérité, 1994.

Preller, Victor. *Divine Science and the Science of God: A Reformulation of Thomas Aquinas.* Princeton, NJ: Princeton University Press, 1967.

Proudfoot, Wayne. *Religious Experience.* Berkeley: University of California Press, 1985.

Putnam, Hilary. "Brains in a Vat." In *Reason, Truth and History,* 1–21. Cambridge: Cambridge University Press, 1981.

———. "The Meaning of 'Meaning.'" In *Mind, Language and Reality,* 215–71. Cambridge: Cambridge University Press, 1975.

Quine, W. V. O. "On What There Is." *Review of Metaphysics* 2 (1948): 21–38.

———. "Two Dogmas of Empiricism." *Philosophical Review* 60, no. 1(1951): 20–43.

Quinn, Philip L. "Towards Thinner Theologies: Hick and Alston on Religious Diversity." *International Journal for Philosophy of Religion* 38 (1995): 145–64.

Rahner, Karl. "Le debut d'une doctrine des cinq sens spirituels chez Origene," *Revue d'ascetique et de mystique* 13 (1932): 112–45. Published later in shortened form in his *Schriften zur Theologie,* Vol. 12: *Theologie aus Erfahrung des Geistes,* edited by K. Neufeld, SJ (Zurich: Benziger Verlag, 1975), 111–36, and translated into English by Dom David Morland in *Theological Investigations* 16 (New York: Seabury, 1979), 81–103.

Rancière, Jacques. *Disagreement.* Translated by Julie Rose. Minneapolis: University of Minnesota Press, 1999.

Rea, Michael. "Hylomorphism Reconditioned." *Philosophical Perspectives* 25, no. 1 (December 2011): 341–58.

Reddy, M. J. "The Conduit Metaphor: A Case of Frame Conflict in our Language about Language." In *Metaphor and Thought*, edited by A. Ortony, 284–310. Cambridge: Cambridge University Press, 1979.

Rescher, Nicholas. *Ignorance: On the Wider Implications of Deficient Knowledge.* Pittsburgh: University of Pittsburgh Press, 2009.

Robbins, Bruce. "Enchantment? No, Thank You!" In *The Joy of Secularism*, edited by George Levine, 74–94. Princeton, NJ: Princeton University Press, 2011.

Robinette, Brian. "A Gift to Theology? Jean-Luc Marion's 'Saturated Phenomenon' in Christological Perspective." *Heythrop Journal* 48, no. 1 (January 2007): 86–108.

Romano, Claude. *Au coeur de la raison, la phénoménology.* Paris: Gallimard/ Folio Essais, 2010.

Rombs, Kathryn. "Gregory of Nyssa's Doctrine of Epektasis: Some Logical Implications." *Studia Patristica* 37, edited by Maurice Wiles and E. J. Yarnold with the assistance of P. M. Parvis, 288–93. Leuven: Peeters, 2001.

Rosenberg, Jay F. "Still Mythic after All Those Years: On Alston's Latest Defense of the Given." *Philosophy and Phenomenological Research* 72, no. 1 (2006): 157–73.

———. *Wilfrid Sellars: Fusing the Images.* New York: Oxford University Press, 2007.

Ross, James F. "Review of Preller's *Divine Science and the Science of* God." *Religious Studies* 5, no. 2 (December 1992): 261–66.

Rudy, Gordon. *The Mystical Language of Sensation in the Later Middle Ages.* New York: Routledge, 2002.

Russell, Matheson. *Husserl: A Guide for the Perplexed.* New York: Continuum, 2006.

Sawicki, Marianne. *Seeing the Lord: Resurrection and Early Christian Practices.* Minneapolis: Fortress Press, 1994.

Schear, Joseph K., ed. *Mind, Reason and Being-in-the-World: The McDowell-Dreyfus Debate.* London: Routledge, 2012.

Schellenberg, Susanna. "The Particularity and Phenomenology of Perceptual Experience." *Philosophical Studies* 149, no. 1 (2010): 19–48.

———. "Perceptual Content Defended." *Noûs* 45, no. 4 (2011): 714–50.

———. "Perceptual Experience and the Capacity to Act." In *Perception, Action, and Consciousness*, edited by N. Gangopadhay, M. Madary, and F. Spicer, 145–60. New York: Oxford University Press, 2010.

———. "Sameness of Fregean Sense." *Synthese* 189, no. 1 (2012): 163–75.

———. "Sellarsian Perspectives on Perception and Non-Conceptual Content." In *The Self-Correcting Enterprise: Essays on Wilfrid Sellars*, edited by Mark Lance and Michael P. Wolf, 173–96. Amsterdam: Rodopi, 2007.

Schiller, Friedrich. *On the Aesthetic Education of Man.* Translated by R. Snell. New York: Frederick Ungar, 1977.

Searle, John. *Expression and Meaning.* Cambridge: Cambridge University Press, 1979.

Sellars, Wilfrid. *Empiricism and the Philosophy of Mind.* Introduction by Richard Rorty and study guide by Robert Brandom. Cambridge, MA: Harvard University Press, 1997. Originally published as "Empiricism and the Philosophy of Mind," in *Science, Perception and Reality* (New York: Routledge, 1963), 127–96.

———. *Kant's Transcendental Metaphysics: Sellars' Cassirer Lecture Notes and Other Essays.* Edited by Jeffrey F. Sicha. Atascadero, CA: Ridgeview, 2002.

———. "Philosophy and the Scientific Image of Man." In *Frontiers of Science and Philosophy*, edited by Robert Colodny, 35–78. Pittsburgh, PA: University of Pittsburgh Press, 1962.

———. *Science and Metaphysics: Variations on Kantian Themes.* New York: Humanities Press, 1968.

———. "A Semantical Solution of the Mind-Body Problem." *Methodos* 5 (1953): 45–82.

Sherry, Patrick. "Disenchantment, Re-Enchantment and Enchantment." *Modern Theology* 25, no. 3 (July 2009): 369–86.

———. "The Sacramentality of Things." *Newblackfriars* 89, no. 1023 (September 2008): 575–90.

Siegel, Susanna. "The Contents of Perception." In *Stanford Encyclopedia of Philosophy*, Spring 2015, edited by Edward N. Zalta. http://plato.stanford.edu/entries/perception-contents/.

———. *The Contents of Visual Experience.* Oxford: Oxford University Press, 2011.

Smith. A. D. *The Problem of Perception.* Cambridge, MA: Harvard University Press, 2002.

Smith, J. Warren. *Passion and Paradise: Human and Divine Emotion in the Thought of Gregory of Nyssa.* New York: Crossroad, 2004.

Sokolowski, Robert. *The God of Faith and Reason.* Washington, DC: Catholic University of America Press, 1995.

———. *Introduction to Phenomenology.* New York: Cambridge University Press, 1999.

Sorabji, Richard. *Time, Creation and the Continuum.* Ithaca, NY: Cornell University Press, 1983.

Speaks, Jeff. "Is There a Problem about Nonconceptual Content?" *Philosophical Review* 114, no. 3 (2005): 359–98.

Stone, Martin. "Wittgenstein on Deconstruction." In *The New Wittgenstein*, ed. Alice Crary and Rupert Read, 83–117. New York: Routledge, 2000.

Stout, Jeffrey. *Democracy and Tradition.* Princeton: Princeton University Press, 2004.

Stout, Jeffrey, and Robert MacSwain, eds. *Grammar and Grace: Reformulations of Aquinas and Wittgenstein.* London: SCM, 2004.

Strandberg, Caj. "In Defence of the Open Question Argument." *Journal of Ethics* 8, no. 2 (2004): 179–96.

Strawson, P. F. "Perception and Its Objects." In *Vision and Mind: Selected Readings in the Philosophy of Perception*, edited by Alva Noë and Evan Thompson, 91–110. Cambridge, MA: MIT Press, 2002. Reprinted from *Perception and Identity: Essays Presented to A. J. Ayer*, edited by G. MacDonald (London: MacMillan, 1979), 41–60.

Tanner, Kathryn. *Christ the Key*. New York: Cambridge University Press, 2010.

Taves, Anne. *Religious Experience Reconsidered*. Princeton, NJ: Princeton University Press, 2009.

Taylor, Charles. "Afterword: Apologia pro Libro suo." In *Varieties of Secularism in a Secular Age*, edited by Michael Warner, Jonathan Vanantwerpen, and Craig Calhoun, 300–324. Cambridge, MA: Harvard University Press, 2010.

———. "Disenchantment-Reenchantment." In *The Joy of Secularism*, edited by George Levine, 57–73. Princeton, NJ: Princeton University Press, 2011.

———. "Foundationalism and the Inner-Outer Distinction." In *Reading McDowell on Mind and World*, edited by Nicholas H. Smith, 106–20. New York: Routledge, 2002.

———. "Modern Social Imaginaries." *Public Culture* 14, no. 1 (Winter 2002): 91–124.

———. "Modernity and the Rise of the Public Sphere." Tanner Lecture on Human Values delivered at Stanford University, February 25, 1992.

———. "Retrieving Realism." In *Mind, Reason and Being-In-The-World: The McDowell-Dreyfus Debate*, ed. Joseph K. Schear, 61–90. London: Routledge, 2012.

———. *A Secular Age*. Cambridge, MA: Belknap, 2007.

———. *Varieties of Religion Today: William James Revisted.* Cambridge, MA: Harvard University Press, 2002.

Terrien, Samuel. *The Elusive Presence: Toward a New Biblical Theology.* New York: Harper and Row, 1978.

Thomasson, Amie L. "Introspection and Phenomenological Method." *Phenomenology and the Cognitive Sciences* 2 (2003): 239–54.

Thornton, Tim. *John McDowell.* Montreal: McGill-Queen's University Press, 2004.

Triplett, Timm, and Willem deVries. "Does Observational Knowledge Require Metaknowledge? A Dialogue on Sellars." *International Journal of Philosophical Studies* 15, no. 1 (2007): 23–51.

Turner, Denys. *The Darkness of God: Negativity in Christian Mysticism.* Cambridge: Cambridge University Press, 1998.

———. "On Denying the Right God: Aquinas on Atheism and Idolatry." *Modern Theology* 20, no. 1 (January 2004): 141–61.

van Beeck, Franz Jozef. "Trinitarian Theology as Participation." In *The Trinity: An Interdisciplinary Symposium on the Trinity*, edited by Stephen T. Davis, Daniel Kendall, and Gerald O'Collins, 295–325. Oxford: Oxford University Press, 1999.

van Fraassen, Bas C. *The Empirical Stance.* New Haven: Yale University Press, 2002.

———. *The Scientific Image.* New York: Oxford University Press, 1980.

Vetlesen, Arne Johan. *Perception, Empathy and Judgment: An Inquiry into the Preconditions of Moral Performance.* University Park: University of Pennsylvania Press, 1994.

van Beeck, Franz Josef, SJ. "Trinitarian Theology as Participation." In *The Trinity*, edited by Stephen T. Davis, Daniel Kendall, SJ, and Gerald O'Collins, SJ, 295–325. Oxford: Oxford University Press, 1999.

Volpe, Medi Ann. *Rethinking Christian Identity: Doctrine and Discipleship.* Oxford: Wiley-Blackwell, 2013.

Wahlberg, Mats. *Seeing Nature as Creation: How Anti-Cartesian Philosophy of Mind and Perception Reshapes Natural Theology.* Umea, Sweden: Umea Universitet, 2009.

Weber, Max. *From Max Weber: Essays in Sociology.* Translated and edited by H. H. Gerth and C. W. Mills. New York: Routledge, 1970.

Wedgewood, Ralph. *The Nature of Normativity.* Oxford: Oxford University Press, 2007.

Wessel, Susan. "The Reception of Greek Science in Gregory of Nyssa's *De hominis opificio.*" *Vigiliae Christianae* 63 (2009): 24–46.

Westbrook, Robert B. "An Uncommon Faith: Pragmatism and Religious Experience." In *Pragmatism and Religion: Classical Sources and Original Essays,* edited by Stuart E. Rosenbaum, 190–205. Urbana: University of Illinois Press, 2003.

Westfall, R. S. *The Construction of Modern Science.* Cambridge: Cambridge University Press, 1977.

Westphal, Merold. "The Importance of Overcoming Metaphysics for the Life of Faith." *Modern Theology* 23, no. 2 (April 2007): 253–78.

———. *Overcoming Ontotheology: Toward a Postmodern Christian Faith.* New York: Fordham University Press, 2001.

———. "Transfiguration as Saturated Phenomenon." *Journal of Philosophy and Scripture* 1, no. 1 (Fall 2003): 26–35.

Willaschek, Marcus, ed. *John McDowell: Reason and Nature.* Münster: LIT-Verlag, 1999.

Williams. A. N. *The Divine Sense: The Intellect in Patrisic Theology.* New York: Cambridge University Press, 2007.

———. *The Ground of Union.* New York: Oxford University Press, 1997.

Williams, Rowan. *Christ On Trial: How the Gospel Unsettles Our Judgment.* Grand Rapids, MI: Eerdmans, 2003.

———. *Christian Spirituality: A Theological History from the New Testament to Luther and St. John of the Cross.* Atlanta: John Knox, 1980.

————. "Macrina's Deathbed Revisited: Gregory of Nyssa on Mind and Passion." In *Christian Faith and Greek Philosophy in Late Antiquity*, edited by L. Wickham and C. Bammel, 227–46. Supplement to Vigiliae Christianae 19. Leiden: Brill, 1993.

————. *Resurrection: Interpreting the Easter Gospel*. Harrisburg, PA: Morehouse, 1982.

————. *Why Study the Past? The Quest for the Historical Church*. London: Darton, Longman and Todd, 2005.

Williams, Timothy. *Knowledge and Its Limits*. New York: Oxford University Press, 2000.

Wittgenstein, Ludwig. *Lectures and Conversations on Aesthetics, Psychology and Religious Belief: Compiled from Notes Taken by Yorick Smythies, Rush Rhees and James Taylor*. Edited by Cyril Barrett. Los Angeles: University of California Press, 1966.

————. *Notebooks 1914–1916*. Edited and translated by G. H. von Wright and G. E. M. Anscombe. Oxford: Basil Blackwell, 1979.

————. *Philosophical Investigations*. 4th edition. Edited and translated by G. E. M. Anscombe, P. M. S. Hacker, and Joachim Schulte. Oxford: Wiley-Blackwell, 2009.

————. *Zettel*. Edited by G. E. M. Anscombe and G. H. von Wright. Translated by G. E. M. Anscombe. Berkeley: University of California Press, 1967.

Wolterstorff, Nicholas. "Entitlement to Believe and Practices of Inquiry." In *Practices of Belief*, vol. 2, edited by Terence Cuneo, 99–100. Cambridge: Cambridge University Press, 2009.

————. "Historicizing the Belief-Forming Self." In *Knowledge and Reality: Essays in Honor of Alvin Plantinga*, edited by Thomas Crisp, Matthew Davidson, and David Vander Laan, 111–35. Dodrecht: Springer, 2006.

Wright, Wayne. "McDowell, Demonstrative Concepts, and Non-Conceptual Representational Content." *Disputatio* 14 (May 2003): 39–53.

Wynn, Mark R. *Emotional Experience and Religious Understanding: Integrating Perception, Conception and Feeling.* New York: Cambridge University Press, 2005.

———. "McDowell, Value Recognition, and Affectively Toned Theistic Experience." *Ars Disputandi* 4 (2004): 20–39.

Yadav, Sameer. "Therapy for the Therapist: A McDowellian Critique of Semantic Externalism in Kevin Hector's *Theology without Metaphysics.*" *Journal of Analytic Theology* 1, no. 1 (May 2013): 120–32.

Young, R. Darling. "On Gregory of Nyssa's Use of Theology and Science in Constructing Theological Anthropology." *Pro Ecclesia* 2 (1993): 345–63.

Zagzebski, Linda. *Divine Motivation Theory.* New York: Cambridge University Press, 2004.

Index

CPSIA information can be obtained at www.ICGtesting.com
Printed in the USA
LVOW12s1955210515

439422LV00003B/5/P